A HISTORY OF THE MODERN WORLD
AN OUTLINE

A History of the Modern World
An Outline

RANJAN CHAKRABARTI
Vice Chancellor
Vidyasagar University

PRIMUS BOOKS
An imprint of Ratna Sagar P. Ltd.
Virat Bhavan
Mukherjee Nagar Commercial Complex
Delhi 110 009

Offices at CHENNAI KOLKATA LUCKNOW
AGRA AHMEDABAD BENGALURU COIMBATORE DEHRADUN GUWAHATI
HYDERABAD JAIPUR KANPUR KOCHI MADURAI MUMBAI PATNA RANCHI

First published 2012

ISBN 978-93-80607-50-4

Published by Primus Books

Laser typeset by Sai Graphic Design
Arakashan Road, Paharganj, New Delhi 110 055

Printed at Sanat Printers, Kundli, Haryana

Contents

Preface

Many of my former students, who are currently engaged in teaching history in schools and colleges frequently lament before me about the dearth of good textbooks in the subject at the pre-degree or degree level. My interaction with the undergraduate (Honours) students at the Department of History, Jadavpur University too, gives me a similar impression. I had the occasion to duscuss the problem with my colleagues in Jadavpur University. Some of them think that this dearth of standard texts is due to the fact that historians in India, who are engaged in fundamental research, rarely write textbooks. While writing the present book, I realized how difficult the work is. You need to sit for hours away from your regular teaching and research assignments and do something which requires wide reading of all the branches of European History including the recent or emerging trends therein.

The present work neither seeks to break new ground nor represent a particular viewpoint. I shall be delighted if the students for whom the book is written find it useful. I eagerly look forward to hear from the teachers and students about their impression of the work. I would like to express gratitude to the Post-Graduate students of my English and American history classes at Jadavpur University, who had been my day to day companions in discussions and debates. My special thanks are due to Dibyendu Satpathy, Mili Ghose, Kaushik Chakraborty and Anirban Banerjee. Without their cooperation I would not have been able to complete the work. Thanks are also due to Aparajita Dhar and Moumie Banerjee.

The responsibility for errors remains mine alone.

Vice Chancellor   RANJAN CHAKRABARTI
Vidyasagar University
West Bengal

CHAPTER 1

The Euro-American World in the Last Quarter of the Eighteenth Century

INTRODUCTION

Europe was going through a political, social, economic, and cultural transformation in the eighteenth century. This century saw far-reaching changes which were to leave behind an enduring legacy. The Treaty of Paris (1763) brought an end to the Seven Years War. Thereafter, the European continent had been free from bloody conflicts for about three decades. However, the Treaty of Paris could not bring peace to Europe forever. Great Britain emerged victorious in the contest for colonial supremacy in Europe and from that moment, Britain concentrated more on her colonial possessions. Her role in European politics appeared to be less prominent. The second half of the eighteenth century was essentially a period which saw fresh political alignments among nation states, the rise of new powers, and breakdown of old political ties. The economic and social changes of the period were even more important. The English Industrial Revolution ushered in a new era of history that had far-reaching social, economic, and cultural impact.

The French Revolution (1789) marked the beginning of the modern era and it infused the spirit of liberty, equality, and fraternity into European society. It was also a period which saw the flowering of nationalism and democracy. The eighteenth century witnessed world's first anti-colonial revolution which occurred in North America. In the realm of intellect the eighteenth century is known as a period of enlightenment. New directions were visible in science, philosophy, and the social sciences and many novel and controversial ideas were prevalent. The main subject matter of this new thought was social, political, and economic inequality. On the whole, it was a period of democratization and emancipation. It is not difficult to trace a common thread among such events as the American Revolution, the French Revolution, and the new developments in the Netherlands, Belgium, and Geneva. Democratic movements however, were not the only trend visible. It was also a period which witnessed the rise and growth of a type of despotism known in history as 'Enlightened Despotism' and what one historian has described as a period of aristocratic reaction.

RESULT OF THE SEVEN YEARS WAR (1756–63)

The Austria-Prussia rivalry, the commercial rivalry between England and France, the military rivalry between France and Prussia, and a host of other factors brought about the Seven Years War. All the major European powers were dragged into this conflict. The battles fought in the Seven Years War did not remain confined to the European continent alone. In fact, the war cast a shadow on Anglo-French relations in India too: the pattern of the war was that of a world war but on a smaller scale. The Seven Years War was concluded by two separate treaties signed in 1763: (1) Peace of Hubertsburg between Austria and Prussia, and (2) The Treaty of Paris between England and France.

One of the most important results of the Seven Years War was the elevation of Prussia to a position of equality with Austria within Germany. Prussia was able to maintain her steady rise to power despite the hostility of the European combination. In Germany, henceforth, a dual leadership was established. Prussia emerged as the chief rival of Austria within Germany. France faced humiliation as a result of the Treaty of Paris. She lost her prestige and colonial possessions: under the terms of the Treaty of Paris, France ceded the whole of Canada, Nova Scotia, and Cape Breton in North America as well as a number of colonies in the West Indies all to Britain. Thus, France temporarily lost her importance among the great powers of Europe. Unlike France, Prussia's position as a great military power was assured by the Peace of Hubertsburg.

Turning to the long-term consequences of the Seven Years War we find the following:

1. It resolved the dispute between England and France for supremacy in India and America. France was ousted from both and thus the war fostered the rise of Britain as the greatest of the commercial powers of the world.
2. Britain now became the mistress of a new colonial empire in two continents. The British occupation of Canada facilitated the coming of the American Revolution.
3. England, in the long run, suffered an economic decline after the War. After 1763 Britain abolished the policy of 'salutary neglect'—coined by Robert Walpole who took for his motto 'let sleeping dogs lie'—and attempted to tighten up its economic control of the American colonies. This policy manifested itself in the imposition of new taxes like the Sugar Act, Stamp Act, etc., which finally made the clash between the two sides inevitable.
4. The defeat of France exposed the weakness of the absolute monarchy and paved the way for the French Revolution.
5. Russian expansion to the East after 1763 triggered of the complex problem of the Eastern Question.
6. The war indirectly created a condition in Germany which proved to be conducive to the growth of German nationalism.

RISE AND FALL OF ENLIGHTENED ABSOLUTISM IN PRUSSIA, AUSTRIA, AND RUSSIA

In the domain of European politics in the eighteenth century, there was no restraining principle or code of conduct to guide the states of Europe in their relations with one another. All moral considerations and obligations to humanity were made subservient to the self-interest of European states. As a result, in the realm of international politics, brute force became the order of the day. However, behind this cruelty and brutality, a strong current of radical thought was rising. It was like a fresh breeze blowing in new ideas, the chief of which was an intellectual development called rationalism. It gave human reason the pre-eminent place in society and considered it to be the only solution to all social, political, and religious problems. These ideas were the two principle features of the eighteenth-century Enlightenment. These new ideas began to influence the activities and policies of many rulers in Europe.

Montesquieu, Voltaire, and Rousseau were the three most influential enlightened thinkers and writers of the age. These enlightened philosophers brought the existing religion, government, and social customs under the scrutiny of human reason. This approach, over the course of time, helped to develop a critical and more liberal outlook which challenged the craze for the supernatural and blind religious bigotry. The emerging frontier of natural science too, was indirectly inspired by the spirit of enlightenment. There was now a new research aptitude in the field of science which found manifestation in the rise of scientific research centres all over Europe. Among the scientists of the period mention may be made of Issac Newton, Benjamin Franklin and Robert Boyle.

The European Enlightenment touched upon various other domains like economics, politics, and social welfare. Under the influence of the Enlightenment there sprouted a new school of economists known as the Physiocrats who questioned the existing mercantile system and advocated a policy of *laissez-faire* (non-intervention of the state in trade and commerce). The most powerful influence on the economic thought of the time was exerted by Adam Smith in his *Wealth of Nations*. The foundations of the existing mercantile system were shattered by the reasoning of this book. It showed that state control diminished the production of wealth. In short, the spirit of reason, as a result of the spread of European Enlightenment, became of great importance. This is precisely why the age of the European Enlightenment is also known as the 'age of reason'.[9]

Enlightened Absolutism (Despotism)

The eighteenth century has been described by scholars as a period of Enlightened Absolutism. Lord Acton called these days the 'repentance of monarchy'. With the concentration of power in the hands of sensible rulers, Europe was poized for great changes of a beneficent kind. Some of the European rulers of this period came to realize that governments should exist for the protection of the people. The monarchs ceased to be selfish and oppressive. The political ideas in the air made the state omnipotent but also reminded it to take account of public interest as distinct from dynastic interests. It was indeed despotism but with a difference. This transformation of the mental outlook of the rulers could be attributed to the influence of rationalism disseminated in the writings of eighteenth-century writers. The Enlightened Absolutes of this period developed interest in the study of philosophy and political science. Frederick II of Prussia, Joseph II of Austria, Catherine II of Russia, and Charles III of Spain were noteworthy among the Enlightened Absolutes of the eighteenth century. They were deeply influenced by the writings of Rousseau, Voltaire, Montesquieu, and Diderot and were sincerely interested in the practical implementation of the enlightened views of the philosophers.

Frederick II of Prussia (1740–86)

Frederick II, or Frederick the Great of Prussia, was undoubtedly the most important figure among the Enlightened Absolutes of Europe during the second half of the eighteenth century. Frederick was well-educated and aware of the responsibilities of a king when he became the ruler of Prussia in 1740. He devoted himself to serving the state, of which he said he was 'the first servant'; a sharp contrast to Louis XIV of France, who is believed to have said, 'I am the State'. Frederick's greatest achievement was to make Prussia a leading European power despite the fact that both her population and resources were much smaller than those of the other front ranking powers.

His military abilities were extraordinary for during the Seven Years War he held his own almost single-handedly against a coalition which included nearly half of the European powers. He almost doubled the area of his kingdom with the acquisition of Silesia and West Prussia. His political philosophy was best expressed when he said: 'Take what you can, you are never wrong unless you are obliged to give back'. In politics, he was indeed an opportunist. The seizure of Silesia and the partition of Poland were acts carried out in defiance of morality and international law. However, it has to be borne in mind that to Frederick, the national interests of Prussia were paramount.

Though Frederick was pre-occupied with military campaigns, he utilized the intervals of peace to improve the economic condition of Prussia. He sought to heal the wounds of war by undertaking various social and economic reforms. He improved agriculture by draining marshes, and boosted the economy of the war-ravaged country by setting up provincial banks and encouraging industries. He restructured the legal code by modifying the harshness of criminal law. He did his best to restore economic strength to the country and to promote intellectual development of his people through opening schools to disseminate learning among his people. His was an absolute monarchy based on the strength of the army and it was indeed despotic. His despotism was enlightenment and thus benevolent, geared solely to promote the welfare and interests of his people. Had he been an ordinary despot he would not have considered himself the 'first servant of the State'. It is this sense of duty to the state and his great care to give comfort to his subjects that prompted his biographer, Thomas Carlyle, to call him the 'last of the Kings'. The office of the king holds a special responsibility and Frederick was fully aware of this. Such kings are rare in history. His diplomatic ability too, was commendable. The alliance which he made with England in 1756, proved to be advantageous to Prussia. He has been aptly given the title 'the Great'.

Henceforth, Prussia and Austria became rivals for the control of Germany. The mutual jealousy of the two powers created a political dualism within Germany and it became the central fact of German history for years to come. The centralized administrative structure left behind by Frederick required a leader of his ability for its successful working. Hence, after his death, decline set in.

Joseph II of Austria (1765–90)

Joseph II ascended the throne of Austria on the death of his mother Maria Theresa in 1780, though he was thwarted by Frederick the Great who brought about Russian intervention to settle the dispute. After cultivating an alliance with Russia he made an attempt to occupy the Balkans while he captured Belgrade from the Ottoman Turks but his plans were frustrated by Frederick the Great who formed a league of German princes known as the *Furstenbund*. The real basis of Austro-Russian Alliance was the project of Catherine II to dismember European Turkey and to distribute the territories between the allies. Joseph II had to call off his aggressive policy towards the Turks due to the threatening attitude of Prussia. The aggressive Balkan policy to Austria were down in the face of the Triple Alliance formed between England, Holland, and Prussia.

Joseph II was an unpractical idealist even though he was inspired by the spirit of enlightenment and his outlook was liberal. His dominions were inhabited by a multicultural population and the unification of different races and elements was one of his chief objectives. However, Joseph II's attempts to impose uniformity were very hasty with the result that he came to be looked upon as an interfering tyrant. His foreign policy too, ended in a failure. Joseph II has been aptly described as the most pathetic figure in history.

Catherine II of Russia (1762–96)

In the eighteenth century, Russia followed an expansionist policy under Peter the Great which brought her to the shores of the Baltic in the north, the borders of Germany in the east, and the Black Sea in the south. However, Peter the Great died in 1725 and Russia was left in deep crisis. Russia was eventually rescued from this crisis by Catherine II who resumed the policies of Peter the Great. Under Catherine, the process of 'Europeanizing' Russia and elevating her position in European politics was resumed with vigour. Catherine was well-educated, a prolific writer of historical articles and dramas, and a great admirer of philosophers like Voltaire and Diderot.

Catherine followed in the footsteps of Peter the Great as far as domestic policy was concerned. As she was herself of Western elected Emperor in the place of his father, Francis of Lorraine, in 1765. His model was Frederick the Great whom he sought to imitate. Joseph, the most enlightened man of his times, was a very competent ruler. As his ideas were much ahead of his own times, they were not appreciated by his subjects.

Joseph II's domestic reforms may be briefly summed up as follows:

1. Joseph II sought to fuse together the various races of his empire into one homogeneous whole. To achieve this goal he undertook fresh administrative reforms and divided his dominions into thirteen administrative units or provinces. The provinces were then subdivided into districts and towns.
2. Joseph made German the official language of his empire.
3. He practically abolished serfdom by allowing the serfs to marry, to sell their land, and to pay a fixed rent instead of labour services.
4. He established equality before law by creating a uniform code of justice.
5. Freedom of expression was encouraged and freedom of the press was ensured. To raise the status of ordinary people, he brushed aside the exclusive privileges of the nobility, the clergy, and the corporations.
6. Joseph II founded schools, encouraged trade and industries, and built a communication infrastructure to foster economic development.
7. Joseph II brought the Church under the State and organized it on a national basis.
8. He promoted a spirit of religious toleration.

To sum up, Joseph's main objective was to unite his dominions under his absolute rule by abolishing all differences of race, language, and religion. His reforms shaved him to be a statesman and were the products of his liberal and Enlightened spirit. However, the reforms were hastily undertaken without considering the fact that they might hit the traditions, prejudices, and age-old customs of the Austrian people.

The same restless activity that characterized the domestic policy of Joseph II can be noticed in his foreign policy. His goal was to establish Hapsburg supremacy in Germany. He sided with Frederick the Great of Prussia temporarily, to prevent Russia from absorbing the whole of that country and he added a large tract of Polish territory to his dominions. He tried to take advantage of the War of Bavarian succession to secure a slice of that territory, but the whole of Europe. In the eighteenth century the tide of aggression began to turn. Turkey now became the victim of aggression and it was the gradual decline of Turkey that gave rise to what is known as the Eastern Question. This problem of the Eastern Question repeatedly posed a threat to the stability of European politics in the nineteenth and twentieth centuries. As to Catherine's Polish policy it may be said that her object was to seize the whole of Poland but circumstances forced her to share it with Austria and Prussia. The First Partition of Poland (1772) did not completely demolish that country and the dismemberment of Poland as a state was finally brought about by two subsequent partitions in 1793 and 1795.

Catherine was one of the leading enlightened despots of eighteenth-century Europe. Her importance in eighteenth-century European history however, lies in the fact that she transformed Russia into a player of great importance in European politics and contributed much to Russia's territorial expansion. She summed up her own achievements regarding foreign policy in the following words: 'I came to Russia as a poor girl; Russia has dowered me richly, but I have paid her back with Azov, the Crimea and the Ukraine.'

Limitations of Enlightened Absolutism

The attempt of the Enlightened Absolutes to introduce Enlightened reforms was indeed laudable and such reforms were successful for the time being. However, they could not bring about lasting solutions. In the long run, enlightened absolutism proved to be a failure. It failed due to certain inherent limitations:

1. The Enlightened Absolutes acknowledged that rulers existed for the good of the people, but they denied that they should be directed by the people. In fact, in the name of enlightenment, they strengthened monarchical absolutism hence enlightened despotism failed to enlist the full support of the people.
2. The success of such a system depended solely upon a single person. When weaker rulers succeeded the efficient rulers, the whole machinery was thrown out of gear.
3. The absolutes very often worked hastily without taking into consideration the age-old traditions and prejudices of the people. The failure of Joseph II of Austria is an example of this.
4. Enlightened Absolutism origin, she went flat out in favour of Westernization of Russia. This policy found manifestation in her patronage of Western education, foundation of schools, and her initiative to develop industry and commerce. Her enthusiasm for a policy of Westernization surpassed even that of her predecessor Peter the Great. She was one of the enlightened absolutes of her times. Catherine offered patronage to higher education and extended assistance to leading scholars like Diderot, the co-editor of the *Encyclopaedia*. Catherine's administration was far more autocratic than liberal for serfdom continued in Russia and the social and economic condition of serfs further deteriorated during her reign. To mobilize popular support she discussed reforms but did not actually undertake reforms. She tightened up the administration by dividing Russia into 44 civil governments and districts. Each of these units was headed by officials appointed by the central government. The clergy was brought under the crown and church property was secularized. Catherine increased the power and control of the Russian monarchy to a very great extent. In this respect her policy was guided by the objectives of Peter the Great.

The principal achievement of Catherine II lies in the realm of foreign affairs. She was fully aware that her position, as a foreigner, would never be strong until she could make common cause with the national aspirations of the Russian people. To rally the Russian people behind her, she adopted an ambitious foreign policy. She laboured hard to implement Peter's idea of expansion into the West into practice. Three European powers—Sweden, Poland, and Turkey were located on Russia's way towards the West. As Sweden had already been conquered by Peter the Great, Catherine concentrated on the other two, Poland and Turkey. She succeeded in destroying Poland, but she could not dismember Turkey entirely. She was however able to conquer a substantial portion of Turkish territory on the north of the Black Sea and to bring Turkey to her knees. Catherine's diplomatic moves were clever and she chose her allies with admirable foresight. When the question of the dismemberment of Turkey occupied her attention, she struck an alliance with Joseph II of Austria, who had equal interest in the Turkish question. It required the shock of the French Revolution in 1789 to overthrow the evils of the *old regime* in Europe.

THE INDUSTRIAL REVOLUTION

In the short span of years between the accession of George III (1760–1820) and that of his son, William IV (1830–7), the face of England changed. Land that for centuries had been cultivated as open fields, or had been left as common pasture, was fenced, villages grew into cities, and the whole of England became dotted with factories. The Industrial Revolution should be viewed both as a movement and as a period of time. Wherever industrial revolutions occurred, be they in England after 1760, in the United States and Germany after 1870, or in Canada, Japan and Russia in the twentieth century, the character and effects were fundamentally the same. Everywhere it was associated with population growth, the application of science to industry, and a more intensive and extensive use of capital. It universally entailed the conversion of many rural areas into urban communities, giving rise to new social classes alongside parallel changes in cultural and intellectual developments. In each case, the course of the movement was affected by circumstances of time and place. In the European example, the Industrial Revolution first occurred in England and shortly thereafter swept over other European countries.

The period branded as the era of Industrial Revolution was essentially a period of transformation. It marked the final phase of the broad transformation from feudalism to capitalism which had begun with the European Renaissance and the Protestant Reformation in early modern Europe. The Industrial Revolution marked the end of old modes of production and it was the final move away from medieval feudalism. Within the feudal-social set-up the economy had been by and large self-sufficient, though the exchange of goods was not totally absent. With industrial revolution, western and central Europe saw the rise of a full-fledged capitalist economy. Such an economy was based on commodity production and market economy. Thus capitalism made its presence felt across the whole world. Under the forceful thrust of capitalism, the Asiatic societies of the east and the feudal societies of eastern Europe were to undergo economic changes too.

Whether or not such a series of changes should be spoken of as the 'Industrial Revolution' can be debated at length. T.S. Ashton (*The Industrial Revolution*) has argued that such changes were not merely 'industrial', but also social and intellectual. The word 'revolution' itself means a suddenness of change so it is not specific to economic processes. The system of human interactions that is known as 'capitalism' had its origins long before 1760, and attained its full development long after 1830. So, it is clear there remains a danger of overlooking the essential fact of continuity within the terminology. The phrase was first used by J.A. Blanqui, a French socialist thinker of the nineteenth century. To Blanqui, the industrialization of the eighteenth and nineteenth centuries was certainly revolutionary and marked the beginning of a new civilization. Arnold Toynbee however, said that the Industrial Revolution was far from revolutionary and was instead a socio-economic transformation. In fact, the Industrial Revolution was more of an evolution than a revolution but despite these nuances, the phrase 'Industrial Revolution' has become firmly embedded in common speech.

Factors Leading to the Industrial Revolution

The Industrial Revolution was multi-causal. A variety of factors over centuries combined to produce this epoch-making event— the Renaissance and the Reformation, geographical discoveries, the rise of colonial empires, the growth of long distance commerce, commodity production, the market economy, and the accumulation of capital—all these led to the birth of new modes of production. One of the major factors which helped to bring about a revolution in the domain of production was the rise of new scientific knowledge. The research of Newton, Galileo and others and their advances into new frontiers of science prepared the ground for later technological inventions.

Equally, with the decline of feudalism, the rise of new monarchies and a new middle class, flow of gold and silver from South America and the African slave trade and many such factors it was clear by the sixteenth century that Industrial Revolution was to take place only in Western Europe. The Industrial Revolution first occurred in England. A question thus arises: why did it occur in England but not in other countries like France or the Netherlands? There are many reasons why England experienced the Industrial Revolution first:

1. No part of the country was far from the sea.
2. Navigable rivers made inland transport easier.
3. The climate was favourable all year round.
4. England had coal and iron and other necessary mineral resources.
5. She was situated beside the North Atlantic Ocean and she had easy access to overseas market.
6. England was greatly advanced in science and technology.
7. She was a protestant country which, according to many writers (for example, R.H. Tawney, *Religion and the Rise of Capitalism*) protestantism fostered the rise of capitalism and made industrialization possible.
8. England was a country where *laissez-faire* prevailed for the English state took a passive role in industrial development,

unlike in France. British economic activities were allowed to develop in the direction that the profit motive would take it, whereas in the continent mercantilist restrictions were maintained.

Cipolla (*Fontana Economic History of Europe*) has rightly remarked that Britain experienced the Industrial Revolution first because the favourable social and political structures, mental attitudes, and scales of value had been developed. Thus, the ascendancy of capitalist practices and bourgeoise attitudes in Britain can partially explain why Britain industrialized first. In contrast, Holland's trade was on the decline and the economic disturbances caused by the French Revolution set France back by 40 years. By 1830, when France had recovered, Britain had turned into the 'workshop of the world'.

The scientific inventions in England in the eighteenth century also paved the way for the Industrial Revolution. The increasing demand for manufactured goods encouraged technological innovations, hence the English textile industry first saw such inventions. In 1738, John Kay invented the flying shuttle, which changed the weaving system and quickened the pace of production. Later, the discovery of the spinning jenny by James Hargreaves in 1764 was a major breakthrough for the textile industry. In 1769, Richard Airkwright invented the water frame and Samuel Crompton invented the spinning mule in 1779. The devices of Hargreaves and Arkwright were further improved by Crompton.

The trend of technological inventions penetrated into other trades as well. John Dudley and Henry Cort invented a new method of melting iron with the help of coal while Humphrey Davy invented the safety lamp thus making the work of the coal miners easier and safer. The most remarkable discovery came in 1765 when James Watt invented steam power. In 1781 steam power was successfully used to run machines. The discovery of steam power laid the foundations of the industrial economy and the application of steam power to machinary for purposes first of production and then of transport revolutionized the economy. Instead of producing things by means of tools and manual labour, it became more and more common to manufacture things using steam-powered machinery.

Consequences of the Industrial Revolution

The Industrial Revolution saw the replacement of handicraft by power-driven machinery. Previously machines were operated mainly by animal, wind or water power. However, animal power was not remarkably greater than human strength, wind was cheap but unreliable, and water was limited by natural constraints. The new technology therefore brought about far-reaching consequences. Large scale production started with the help of machinery in large factories making a vital departure from the old system of domestic manufacturing and cottage industry. This change in the method of production was more significant and far-reaching than that produced by the French Revolution.

Beginning in England in the last quarter of the eighteenth century, and later spreading to other countries in Europe, the Industrial Revolution solved the problem of production. New technology generated new wealth in the society, but this new wealth largely inflated only the purses of the capitalists. Thus while industrialization solved the question of production, it accentuated the problem of distribution. The workers in the factories were starving most of the time and thus, the gulf between the rich and the poor widened. This sparked off disputes between labour and capital and so it is important to note that the new production processes lay at the root of many of important reactions. One of the most important reactions to this huge gap between poverty and plenty was socialism. It is a critique of capitalism and attempts to put an end to the co-existence of extremes of wealth.

Another notable consequence of the Industrial Revolution was imperialism. The industrialized countries of Europe became dependent upon other countries for the supply of raw materials necessary for their industries. It became imperative for the industrializing nations of Europe to control areas which produced these materials. Colonies could then be used as markets for the finished products. Thus, the industrialized European nations turned their eyes to the non-European world and from that moment, began to parcel out the whole world into colonies and spheres of influence amongst the leading European powers. This imperialism later became aggressive and indirectly led to the First World War.

The Industrial Revolution brought about important social changes too. It brought forth two important social classes: the working class and the bourgeoisie. The exploitation of workers, and especially of women and children, led to various movements of social protest. The character of the state also underwent a transformation. The state began to drop the old idea of *laissez-faire* and to extend its reach into economic and social affairs. It assumed new responsibilities including the welfare of women and children with the notable development of an elevation of the status of women.

THE WAR OF AMERICAN INDEPENDENCE (1776)

We hold these truths to be self-evident, that all men are created equal, that they are endowed by their creator with certain unalienable rights, that among these are life, liberty, and the pursuit of happiness.

The Declaration of Independence, 4 July 1776

The American Revolution stands as one of the significant landmarks in the history of the modern world. The main significance of this revolution lies in the fact that it was the world's first anti-colonial struggle. As a result of this revolution a new nation—the United States of America—was born and the Americans were able to escape of the clutches of British imperialism. John Adams, the second president of the United States, declared that the history of the American Revolution began as far back as 1620. 'The Revolution', he said, 'was effected before the war commenced. The Revolution was in the minds and the hearts of the people'. The principles and passions that led the Americans to rebel ought, he added, 'to be traced back for two hundred years and sought in the history of the country from the first plantation in America'. In reality however, the parting of ways between England and America began in 1763, more than a century and a half after the first permanent settlement had been founded at Jamestown, Virginia.

The discovery of the American continent owed its origin to the initiative of Christopher Columbus who was born and raised in Genoa. He nurtured the hope of reaching the East by sailing West and he gained most of his seafaring knowledge and experience in the service of the Portuguese. Denied help from the King of Portugal, he appealed to Queen Isabella of Spain for money, men, and ships to carry out his voyages of exploration. Finally, he undertook his first voyage in 1492 with three ships—*Pinta, Nina* and the *Santamaria*—and discovered the New World. Columbus undertook three subsequent voyages to America in 1493, 1498, and 1502 although he was not aware that he had discovered a new continent and died still thinking that he had been to the fringes of the Far East. Columbus was not even honoured in the naming of the continent. The New World, discovered by Columbus, bears the name of Amerigo Vespucci, a Florentine merchant who claimed to have sighted North America a year (1491) before Columbus' first voyage (1492). Amerigo was the first to publicize that it was a new continent and not the Far East and as proof he wrote a number of fictitious letters describing several imaginary visits to the continent.

Gradually the American colonies grew in size and a number of settlements were established. The thirteen colonies that eventually became the United States were New Hampshire, Massachusetts, Rhode Island, Connecticut, New York, New Jersey, Pennsylvania, Delaware, Maryland, Virginia, North Carolina, South Carolina, and Georgia. The colonies varied in size and were multi-cultural in character. They were under the control of the British Crown and Parliament, though in internal matters they enjoyed considerable autonomy, i.e. the colonial legislature was headed by a Governor who was in charge of colonial affairs. The colonies grew vastly in economic strength and cultural attainment, and virtually all had long years of self-government behind them. Their combined population now exceeded 15,00,000—a sixfold increase since 1700. Though the American colonists enjoyed considerable political autonomy, in economic matters they were subject to various British mercantilist restrictions. Until 1763 however, the British mercantile control over the American colonies was rather loose and the Americans never thought of themselves as subservient. The breach between Great Britain and her colonies became inevitable only after 1763 when English control measures became stringent.

Causes of the Conflict

Throughout the last 50 years of the seventeenth and the first 50 years of the eighteenth centuries, English policies in the American colonies had been based on certain economic assumptions which led to an economic conflict. This conflict rested upon a general economic theory popular in the sixteenth, seventeenth, and eighteenth centuries, known as mercantilism (or Colbertism, after the finance minister of Louis XIV, who pushed the theory to its furthest extent). Mercantile policy was essentially concerned with the welfare of the mother country. The colonies were supposed to produce commodities not obtainable at home, chiefly raw materials, and to use manufactured goods produced in the mother country. Colonies were to offer opportunities for the development of a large merchant marine, wealth to importers and exporters, and opportunities for the investment of capital. Although the roots of British mercantilism can be traced back to the sixteenth century, it was not until the first half of the eighteenth century that the theory came into force. By that time England had become a great maritime power and was on the road to possessing a colonial empire.

The first major mercantile legislation was the Navigation Act, 1651 which sought to curb colonial shipping. It stipulated that no goods manufactured in Asia, Africa, or America could be imported into England or the dominions thereof, except in ships of which the proprietor and a major part of the mariners were English. Though the Americans were capable of developing their independent carrying trade, they were deprived of that right. The provisions of the Navigation Act were further tightened up by subsequent legislations. Apart from shipping, the British mercantilist restrictions operated in the following spheres: (1) import trade, (2) export trade, (3) manufacture, (4) customs, (5) currency and (6) land or westward expansion.

Until 1763, the mercantilist restrictions were poorly enforced, and the colonies had never thought of themselves as subservient. The British mercantilist network was not very rigidly applied and American capitalism grew within the framework of mercantilist control. Americans were able to develop a parallel economy which took advantage of the weaknesses of British controls. But after 1763 however, Grenville and Townshend, backed by George III, made the controls rigid and put an end to the policy of 'salutary neglect': the clash between Great Britain and the American colonies became inevitable. Louis Hacker (*The Triumph of American Capitalism*), an economic historian, has argued that the American Revolution was an economic contest between American capitalism and British mercantilism. To Hacker, the American Revolution was more an economic conflict than a political one.

Due to the laxity of British controls initially, until 1763, Britain had formulated no consistent policy for her colonial possessions. The remoteness of the colonies from the motherland contributed to a growing spirit of liberty among the Americans. Added to this remoteness was the character of life itself in early America. From countries limited in space and dotted with populous towns, the settlers had come to a land of seemingly infinite reach where natural conditions stressed the importance of the individual. The colonists had already developed the habit of considering themselves as a commonwealth, having only a loose association with the British authorities and so to a certain extent, they had adjusted themselves within Britain's soft policy towards America. Therefore, in 1763, when Britain adopted a stricter policy towards America the colonists reacted sharply.

Bernard Bailyn (*The Ideological Origins of the American Revolution*) argues that the American Revolution was above all an ideological, constitutional, and political struggle. The English democratic tradition, as reflected in the writings of English political philosophers like Milton, Harrington and Locke, helped to shape the American mind to some extent. Those ideas were also reconditioned by the environment of the new continent. The colonists had their own democratic tradition: the Americans were also inspired by evangelicalism. The religious groups who arrived in the New World left the Old World in search of more freedom. Bailyn holds that the intellectual developments in the decade before Independence led to a radical idealization and conceptualization of the previous century and a half of American experience. It was the 'age of reason' and the enlightenment that symbolized the prevailing intellectual mood. In the closing years of the seventeenth century, some scholars, philosophers and scientists began to emphasize the power of reason instead of appeal to religion and authority. Thomas Paine, in his revolutionary pamphlet 'Common Sense' (1776) asserted very plainly that it was a matter of common sense for the Americans to sever all ties with the corrupt English monarchy. Like Paine, most of the colonists believed that the doctrine of natural rights incorporated in the British Constitution was guaranteed to Americans by their colonial charters.

The Seven Years War between France and England (1756–63) resulted in a crisis for the British empire. As a result of the war, Britain acquired Canada. The removal of the French threat was significant for the Americans as it cleared the major obstacle on *The Defeat of France* their road to westward expansion. With the conclusion of the Seven Years War Britain accumulated a heavy debt and the British authorities felt that the colonies must bear a part of the cost of imperial defence. However, long accustomed to a large measure of independence, the American colonies were demanding more, not less freedom, particularly now that the French menace had been eliminated. The Americans, at this time were not necessarily looking for complete independence but for an independent relationship between the colonies and the mother country. The British government under George III and his Prime Minister Lord North blundered into creating a situation which resulted in the loss of the colonies altogether.

The Grenville measures, named after the British Prime Minister who came to office in 1763 consisted of the Proclamation of 1763, the Revenue or Sugar Act 1764, the Currency Act 1764, the Mutiny Act 1765, and the Billeting Act 1765. The most momentous of the revenue measures however, was the Stamp Act which was passed by Parliament in March 1765. It provided that revenue stamps be affixed to all newspapers, licences, leases, or other legal documents. The colonists reacted sharply to this Act, trade with the mother country fell in the summer of 1765. Prominent men organized themselves into a group called the Sons of Liberty: political opposition soon flared into rebellion. Inflamed crowds paraded the streets of Boston and spurred on by Patrick Henry, the Virginia Assembly passed a set of resolutions denouncing taxation without representation as a threat to colonial liberties. The Stamp Act Congress consisting of delegates from 9 of the 13 colonies met in New York City in October 1765.

The opportunity to mobilize colonial opinion against parliamentary interference in American affairs was seized by 27 men from 9 colonies. From the point of view of the Americans, it was impossible to consider themselves represented in Parliament unless they had elected members in the House of Commons. Thus, the Americans raised the slogan 'No taxation without representation'. British merchants however, feeling the effect of the boycott of British products, also threw their weight behind a repeal movement, and in 1776, Parliament yielded, repealing the Stamp Act and modifying the Sugar Act. As if to prove the parliamentary right of taxation, the British Parliament in 1767 passed the so-called Townshend Acts, which levied new import duties on glass, lead, paper, and tea. The agitation following the enactment of the Townshend duties was less violent than that stirred by the Stamp Act, but it was nevertheless strong. American merchants again resorted to a boycott of British products.

Equally, the presence of British troops in Boston invited disorder. On 5 March 1770, after 18 months of resentment, conflict between the Americans and British troops flared up. The troops opened fire on a crowd killing three citizens. Dubbed as the

Boston Massacre, the incident was portrayed as British tyranny. This added a spark to an already volatile situation and, faced with such opposition, in 1770, parliament opted for a retreat and repealed all the Townshend duties except for the tea tax. The tax on tea was retained only to demonstrate the British right to tax Americans.

A three-year interval of calm followed. The moderate elements predominant in the colonies welcomed this peaceful interlude. Patriots like Samuel Adams of Massachusetts however, continued to toil for a single aim: independence. In 1773, Britain furnished Adams and his colleagues with an opportunity: the East India Company, hit by a financial crisis, appealed to the British government and was granted a monopoly on all tea exported to America. Due to the tea tax, Americans boycotted British tea and consumed only duty-free smuggled tea. However, armed with the monopoly right, the Company started selling its tea through its agents at such a low price that it even posed a threat to the duty-free smuggled tea on the market. The American merchants now joined the patriots and steps were taken to prevent the East India Company from executing its design. In Boston, the Company's tea agents made preparations to land incoming cargoes regardless of opposition. The answer of the patriots, led by Samuel Adams, was violence. On the night of 16 December 1773, a band of men disguised as Mohawk Indians boarded three British ships lying at anchor and dumped their tea cargo into Boston harbour. This event is known in history as the 'Boston Tea Party'. The Quebec Act 1774, which upheld the right of the French inhabitants to enjoy religious freedom and their own legal custom, praided a further spark. The Quebec Act was classed by Americans as another 'Coercive Acts' and helped to unite the colonists against Britain.

The Major Events of the Revolution

The Boston Tea Party led to the passage of a series of acts known as the Coercive Acts that made reconciliation between Britain and the colonies impossible and further intensified the agitation. On

New Yorkers, contemplating revolution, celebrated their coming liberty
by pulling down King George's statue to be melted for bullets.

the suggestion of the Massachusetts House of Representatives, all the colonies (except Georgia), sent delegates to the first Continental Congress that was held in Philadelphia in September 1774. The Congress took some important decisions:

1. it rejected a plan for a colonial union under the British authority,
2. it drew up a statement of grievances,
3. it agreed upon a scheme to stop trade between the colonies and England,
4. it organized a continental association, and
5. it decided to take military preparation.

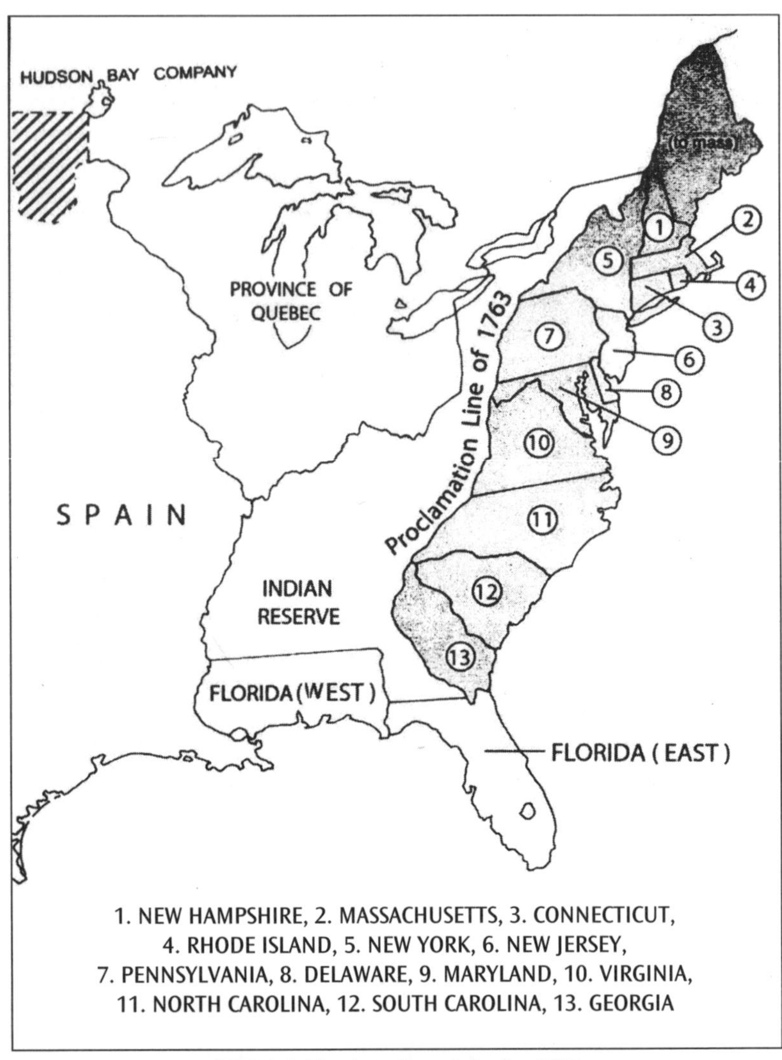

MAP 1.1: The American Colonies 1775

A few months later, General Thomas Gage, the Governor of Massachusetts, tried to destroy the military stores collected at Concord. British troops arrived at Concord on 19 April 1775 after meeting mild resistance at Lexington. On their way back to Boston, the British troops were harrassed by the gunfire of the colonists. In the clashes 273 British soldiers were killed or wounded. Following the events at Lexington and Concord, the Second Continental Congress met in Philadelphia. It chose George Washington as the commander-in-chief of the American forces and drew up a petition to the King which became known as the Olive Branch. However, the fighting continued and in the Battle of Bunker Hill in June 1775, the British troops dislodged the colonists but suffered heavy losses. Britain's decision to continue the War led Continental Congress to adopt the Declaration of Independence on 4 July 1776. At the news of the Declaration of Independence being adopted, thousands of people gathered in the streets of Philadelphia to cheer, welcome, and ring the Church bells. The Declaration of Independence was drafted by Thomas Jefferson

Paul Revere memorializes an early spark to the conflagration in already tense Boston, British responded to snowballs with gunfire, the famous Boston massacre.

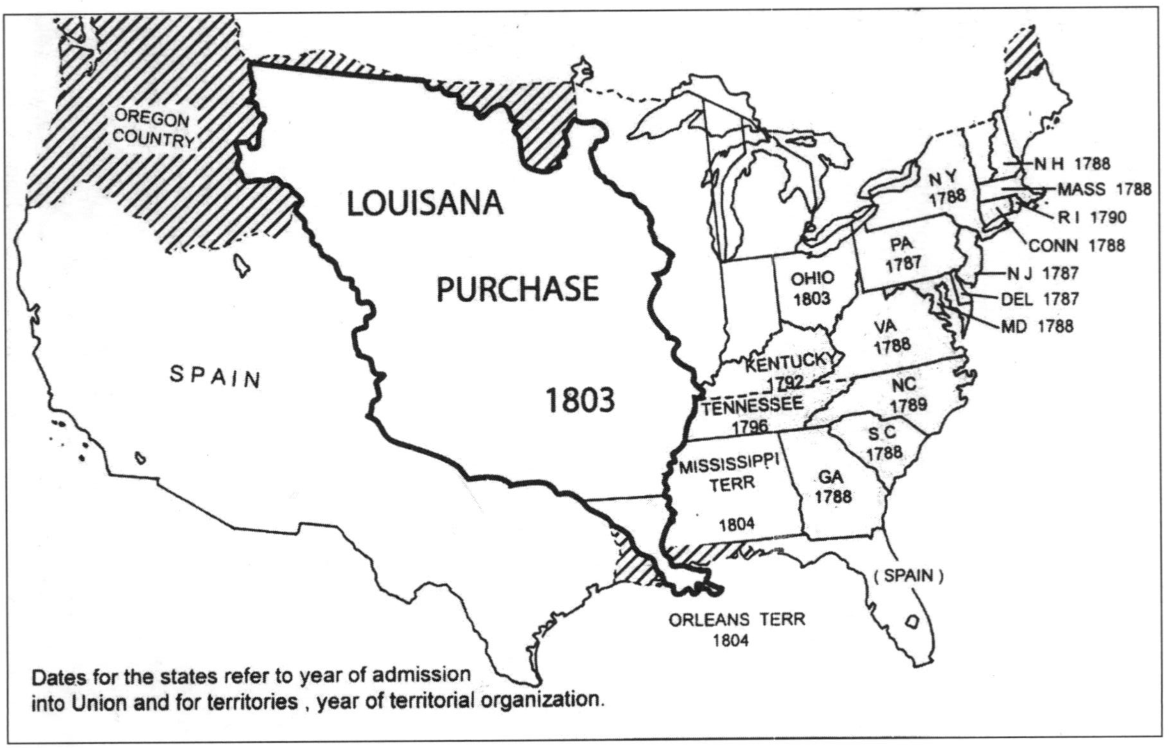

MAP 1.2: USA in 1810

and it remains one of the world's greatest documents on freedom and human rights ever produced. It brought out the reasons why the thirteen American colonies had decided to separate from England, stated a common goal, and helped to politicize the stand taken by the Americans. It marked the formal beginning of the American War of Independence and a revolutionary war that was to last more than six years with fighting in every colony.

The year 1777 saw the greatest American victory in the War in the Battle of Saratoga, the military turning point of the revolution. In this battle the British General Burgoyne surrendered to the Americans. However, the Americans suffered several defeats until France entered the field in 1778. Having concluded a Treaty of Alliance with the new government in 1778, France declared war against England and in 1779 Spain entered the fray as an ally of France.

Finally, with the defeat of Lord Cornwallis at York Town in 1781 the revolutionary war was over and with the Treaty of Paris (1783) Britain recognized American Independence.

Causes of American Success

Though British forces were stronger than the American side led by George Washington, the British were defeated. The American success in the revolutionary war was due to a variety of factors:

1. From the beginning, the British authorities did not attach much importance to the revolutionary effort of the Americans and they mainly relied on mercenary soldiers to suppress them.
2. The remoteness of the American continent and British ignorance of American geography also contributed to the success of the Americans.
3. The British authorities failed to rally the loyalist Americans.
4. The fierce spirit of liberty drove the Americans to success.
5. The military success owed its origin to the extraordinary military leadership of George Washington.
6. The international situation also helped the American revolutionaries.

The active cooperation provided by France and Holland helped to steer the Americans to victory. H.R. Anderson has rightly commented,

that the [fact that the] colonies won their independence against great odds was due mainly to three factors: Nature, Washington and France, Nature was a valuable ally, because the vast extent of the American colonies and the lack of good roads made it impossible to occupy the country effectively without an enormous army.

The Significance of the Revolution

In the history of the modern world the American Revolution stands as a significant landmark. It was world's first anti-colonial revolution. It led to the birth of a new nation which was to become, over the course of time, the greatest workshop of democracy, federalism, and capitalism in the world. The American Revolution also exerted a radical influence on France and many French idealists actively collaborated with the Americans. The American

MAP 1.3: Europe

struggle inspired the French people to rise up against the *ancien régime*. American Independence was also a great blow to the invincible image of Great Britain. It reduced the prestige and the size of the British Empire to a great extent. Richard Hofstadter (*American Political Tradition*) has argued that the American Revolution was conservative in character. Therefore, it may be less significant than the Russian or French Revolutions but there is no doubt that it marked the victory of the spirit of liberty and democracy. Herein lies its importance.

HIGHLIGHTS

- The Seven Years War opened up a new era in the history of Europe. The victory of England established her as a leading colonial and maritime power of the world. On the other hand, the failure of France in the war indirectly hastened the coming of the French Revolution (1789). The Seven Years War also indirectly fostered the American Revolution.
- The second half of the eighteenth century witnessed the start of the Enlightenment period in Europe. The absolute rulers of Europe were influenced by the philosophies of the Enlightenment and began to follow a benevolent policy towards their subjects. Frederick II of Prussia, Joseph II of Austria, and Catherine II of Russia were some of the best examples of Enlightened absolutes.
- The first phase of the Industrial Revolution started in the middle of the eighteenth century. This period saw remarkable technological innovations in the field of cotton textiles. The Industrial Revolution brought about far-reaching changes in the social and economic structure of Britain. The Industrial Revolution occurred in other European nations a little later.
- The American colonists rose up against British domination and high-handedness in 1776. The American Revolution was world's first anti-colonial revolution. It profoundly influenced the French Revolution (1789).

MEMORABLE DATES AND EVENTS

1760   Navigation Act
1733   Invention of flying shuttle by John Kay

1763	Peace of Paris
1764	Sugar Act
1765	Stamp Act
1766	Declaratory Act
1769	Discovery of water frame by Arkwright
	Discovery of steam engine by Watt
1773	Boston Tea Party
1774	Philadephia Congress
1775	The Second Continental Congress at Philadelphia
1776	Declaration of Independence and the Third Continental Congress
1783	Treaty of Versailles
1785	Invention of mule by Cartright
1789	George Washington became the First President of the USA

MEMORABLE PERSONALITIES

Frederick II or Frederick the Great: The King of Prussia, one of the Enlightened Absolutes

Joseph II: King of Austria, one of the Enlightened Absolutes

Catherine II: Empress of Russia, one of the Enlightened Absolutes

George Washington: The First President of the USA

John Adams: The Second President of the USA

Christopher Columbus: He discovered America

George III: King of England at the time of the American Revolution

Townshend: Minister of Great Britain

Samuel Adams: Radical Leader of the American Revolution, organizer of the Boston Tea Party

Thomas Jefferson: The Third President of the USA and the leader of the American Revolution, he drafted the Declaration of Independence

QUOTABLE QUOTES

- 'Especially during the latter part of the eighteenth century did there appear monarchs, known as Enlightened Despots, who under the influence of the teachings of the French philosophy, came to entertain reasonable views of their duties and of their obligations to their subjects.'   —PHILIP VAN NESS MYERS
- 'The middle years of the eighteenth century are marked by a gigantic struggle which alike in its earlier and later phases revolves round

two main international rivalries, the one, that between Prussia and Austria starting from the shock of its novelty, while the other was of all European quarrels the most familiar.'   —H.A.L. FISHER

- 'The quarter of a century which followed 1763 was pre-eminently the era of benevolent or enlightened or philosophical despotism.'
                                                            —REDDAWAY
- 'I am the first servant of the State.'   —FREDERICK II
- 'In an age of enlightenment of despotism the most enlightened was Frederick II.'   —LORD ACTON
- 'The political results of the Seven Years War were considerable. The territorial increase of the possessions and the maritime preponderance of England placed her in the front rank of European nations and at the head of colonizing powers.'   —A. HASSEL
- 'The Industrial Revolution was the transformation in the methods of production and transformation through the general substitution of power driven machinery for hand labour.'   —T.W. RICKER
- 'The remarkable material and cultural progress of the colonies during the middle decades of the eighteenth century were accompanied by the growth of a new kind of self-assurance. Surveying their past achievements and future prospects, many Americans felt that they were fully capable of controlling their own destiny and that they were developing a way of life of their own which made them more than merely transplanted Europeans.'   —H.B. PARKES
- The expulsion of the French from Canada and of the Spanish from Florida by relieving the English colonies of two dangerous neighbours weakened their dependence on the mother country. Having less need of English help, the colonists were the more ready to challenge English pretensions.'   —H.A.L. FISHER

CHAPTER 2

The French Revolution (1789–1815)

INTRODUCTION

In 1789, revolution was the last resort to which the French people could turn if there was to be any chance of wielding a degree of influence within society. Revolutions do not tend to break out due to the will of the people but rather because the people become involved in revolution as victims of circumstance. Throughout the greater part of the eighteenth century, a 'revolutionary spirit' had been growing within Europe. This spirit was one of rationalist criticism and of opposition to powers like the Roman Catholic Church, the absolute monarchy, and the privileged nobility, and it was nursed by a formidable array of French 'men of letters'.

In France the existing social system towards the end of the eighteenth century was called the *ancien régime*. The *ancien régime* was dominated by the aristocracy, its social and economic foundation was feudal, and autocracy was the general political principle. Within the *ancien régime*, the clergy constituted the First Estate, the aristocracy comprised the Second Estate, and the rest of the population formed the Third Estate. Progress in trade and commerce in eighteenth-century Europe gave rise to the emergence of a new social class called the bourgeoisie or the middle class. This bourgeois class was included in the Third Estate and its emergence caused conservation in aristocratic society. The French Revolution can be seen as an example of a bourgeois revolution which sprang from such societal unease 'it was the best of times, it was the worst of times'. As Charles Dickens summed up the revolution in his classic novel, *A Tale of Two Cities*.

THE POLITICAL CRISIS OF 1789: POLITICAL CAUSES

The word 'revolution' generally means a fundamental change in a social system, or structure, and a shift from one type of social system or structure to another. The French Revolution of 1789 can therefore be branded a total revolution. The very thrust of the revolution aimed at the destruction of the feudal social system which had developed in Europe over the last thousand years or so and the establishment in its place of a capitalist or bourgeois social system. However, a revolution is not engineered individually yet when grievances are not redressed in a natural and peaceful way by the monarch and people feel deprived of their basic human needs the path to revolution becomes more clear. In fact, revolution is usually pre-conditioned by growing grievances and discontent within elements of society. The long-standing discontent of the French people found an outlet in this revolution and their revolutionary spirit found expression in the writings of the intelligentsia.

In eighteenth-century Europe, autocratic hereditary monarchies were in power, and France was no exception. Louis XIV, a French king of the Bourbon dynasty, reinforced autocratic monarchy by centralizing his power. The French kings were believers in the divine right of kings and so naturally, there was little scope for popular participation in this form of governance. Much like the British Parliament, the French Estates General assembled irregularly. As the Estates General was not legitimate if it had not been convened by the King, the assembly was not called into session from 1614, with the result that all powers were centralized in the hands of the French King.

The greatest flaw of an autocratic monarchy was that, in this system, the effectiveness of governance and the welfare of the people depended on the efficiency and personality of the king. It meant that if the king was strong, then he could maintain control over his administration and subordinates would execute his instructions. On the other hand, a weak King had little control over his administration. During the reign of Louis XIV officials known as *intendants* ran the administration very efficiently but they became selfish and corrupt during the reigns of Louis XV and Louis XVI.

In France, the king headed the Judiciary so he had the power to sanction a punishment meted out (*lettre de grâce*) and imprison without trial (*lettre de cachet*). The *parlement* was the highest royal court of justice, the most powerful of which was the *parlement* of Paris. The king did not have the power to dismiss the magistrates or judges of *parlement* but the delayed justice, complexities of judicial process, and legal expenses made the judicial system corrupt. Besides, the earlier impartial judicial system as prevalent during the reigns of Louis XV and Louis XVI completely broke down. The prime objective of the *parlements* was to retain the special privileges of the aristocracy to the point that they even began to challenge the king's power to introduce reforms.

The administrative machinery of the former regime had eroded and it was on the verge of complete collapse. Ultimately, the attempt by the autocratic monarchy to centralize power failed. However, despite the decadence and inefficiency of the monarchy, the people of France felt drawn towards it, and they were not in favour of its dissolution. During the early phase of the French Revolution, they had respect for the monarchy. Had Louis XV and Louis XVI been able to fulfil the hopes and aspirations of the people and bring redress to their grievances, the monarchy would potentially not have encountered such a grave crisis and later collapse.

SOCIAL CAUSES OF THE REVOLUTION

In the pre-revolutionary era, French society was divided into three Estates: the First Estate was made up of the clergy, the Second Estate was formed of the aristocracy, and the rest of the population formed the Third Estate. The clergy and the aristocracy constituted the privileged class of society.

The privileged clergy of the First Estate could maintain a separate identity, despite being part of the structures of the state. The King's Law was not applicable to them, and the king had no power to impose tax on them. The clergy, who formed 1 per cent of the French population, were in control of one-tenth of the total land from which they extracted a tithe, erasing them to lead a luxurious life: corruption was rampant in the Church. The clergymen were divided into two classes: the upper clergy, such as bishops, cardinals, archbishops, and abbots who were socially and economically aristocratic, and the lower clergy, which was comprised of the curates, vicars, and other ordinary employees who belonged to the Third Estate. It was the mutual animosity among the members of the different Estates which steered the lower clergy to the path of revolt. The people of the eighteenth century lost respect for the Church and the clergy. They felt repelled by the worldly ways, numerous privileges, and special power of the Church.

The aristocracy of France belonged to the Second Estate. They formed about one-third of the total population of the country and enjoyed various privileges like the clergy. Many owned huge tracts of land and, without paying any taxes, they lived at the expense of the peasants' labour. But the aristocracy was not free from factionalism. However, their power and privileges were curbed in the wake of the revolution.

All the people of France, except those belonging to the First and Second Estates, i.e. clergy and aristocracy, were part of the Third Estate: a total of 96 per cent of the French population. The socio-economic divisions and disparity which characterized the clergy and the aristocracy, were more pronounced among the various communities of the Third Estate. The Third Estate was made up of rich businessmen, industrialists, and intellectuals on the one hand, and the labouring men and peasants on the other. It was this section of the French population who bore the brunt of taxation.

The people of the Third Estate were broadly divided into three groups—the bourgeoisie, the peasants, and the *sans-culottes*. The word bourgeoisie literally means the middle class and though they were a minority in the Third Estate they wielded the greatest influence and considerable financial power. However, they did not all have the same economic or social status. The bourgeoisie included some of the most enlightened, and most intelligent members of French society, yet they were excluded from politics and administration by the privileged estates. It was this incongruence which is part fuelled the bourgeois revolution. As Asa Briggs has commented, 'the middle class is the people'.

The French economy was predominantly agrarian in character. In 1789, out of a total population of 25 million, about 20 million were peasants. Therefore, the significance of the peasantry in the history of the French Revolution is immeasurable, even though they too had divisions among themselves. Unlike in other countries of Europe, most French peasants were landowners. This was, however, not a great advantage for they were overburdened with taxation and were required to pay various taxes to the king, church and clergy to the part that four-fifths of a peasant's income would be spent on paying various dues. As a result of this unbearable load of taxation, peasant hatred of the former system reached extremes.

The people of the urban working class were known as *sans-culottes*. Most of the people of Paris were *sans-culottes* and in 1789, the *sans-culottes* accounted for 6 lakh people in the city. Although it was the workers and skilled labourers who belonged to this class, they were badly paid. Living expenses went up following price rises and foodgrains were particularly costly, yet their wages did not rise correspondingly. This price hike was a major cause of their discontent and led them towards Revolution.

THE ECONOMIC CRISIS OF 1789:
THE ECONOMIC CAUSES

The structural and economic crisis of the *ancien régime* deepened with the coronation of Louis XVI in 1774. With the participation of France in the American War of Independence, the crisis became all the more unbearable. To make matters worse, there was economic backwardness.

The decline in the French economy started in the first half of the eighteenth century. The economic crisis which came in the wake of wars undertaken by Louis XIV, further deepened following the extravagances of Louis XV. The economic reforms undertaken by Louis XVI met with failure because of his weak personality and opposition from the aristocracy. Despite all this, the king and the aristocracy continued to maintain their privileged way of life as before.

There is controversy among historians about the extent to which economic factors were responsible for the French Revolution.

Michelet holds that poverty along with the oppression prevalent in the *ancien régime* was responsible for the Revolution. For Tocqueville, the rise in the economic status of farmers made them stand firm against the existing privileges. Labrousse argues that the French economy, which improved between 1730 and 1770, saw a decline from the 1780s. The destruction of crops and widespread food shortages added to the crisis. The resulting resentment and discontent helped revolution to break out.

The main cause of the economic crisis in France was the disparity in taxation. In the *ancien régime*, the privileged classes was free from the burden of taxation. Only the people belonging to the Third Estate were obliged to pay taxes hence the condition, particularly of farmers, deteriorated most. The pre-revolutionary backwardness of the French economy meant that the exploitation of farmers by feudal lords gained in intensity. The French historian Taine shows that four-fifths of a farmers income would be spent in payment of state tax, religious tax imposed by Church and dues to feudal lords.

Of these, the direct taxes were *taille, capitation, vingtiemes,* etc. and the indirect taxes were *gabelle, aide,* etc. Besides this, they also had to pay tithes or religious tax to the Church. The internal tariff barrier stood in the way of trade, commerce, and industry run by the bourgeoisie. However, it was the social humiliation, more than the economic hardship, of this class which paved the way for their support of revolution. The depression of 1778 and the failure of crops in 1787, on the eve of the French Revolution, was an utter disaster for the French economy. Prices of commodities decreased following the depression and as a result, the profits went down and the labour tell on bad days. Following the failure of crops in 1787–89, food production fell dramatically, leading to an increase in the prices of foodstuff. The hardship of peasants, workers, and the weaker classes therefore intensified.

The only way out of this condition was to cut expenditure and increase income, but French involvement in wars made a considerable dent in the French exchequer. Equally, the extravagance of the French king and the aristocracy worsened the situation. The ministers in the council of Louis XVI—Turgot,

Necker, and Calonne—proposed a restructuring of the tax system to tide them over the economic crisis. Under the prevailing conditions, imposition of a tax on the aristocracy was the only way to solve the problem. However, stiff opposition from the aristocracy made it impossible for Louis XVI to implement the proposal. The empty exchequer inexorably led to the convening of Estates General. This resulted in the 'aristocratic revolt'—the beginning of the French Revolution.

EIGHTEENTH-CENTURY ENLIGHTENMENT AND THE FRENCH REVOLUTION: THE ROLE OF THE PHILOSOPHERS

The growing resentment, discontent, widespread social and economic disparity, and mutual antagonism and enmity among different social classes created an ambience of social unrest and instability. Under extraordinary circumstances, this disquiet took on the shape of a revolution infused with revolutionary spirit. Revolution originates in the human mind and so it is the intelligentsia and philosophers who unwittingly usher in this revolutionary spirit. The radical charges in the field of knowledge and political thought in eighteenth-century Europe is called the Enlightenment.

It was none other than philosophers of this tradition, most of whom were born in France, who brought about the Revolution. France was a country which excelled in philosophy and culture. The notable among the French philosophers were Montesquieu, Voltaire, Rousseau, Diderot, Mably, Lingnet, Quesnay, etc.

Montesquieu (1689–1755)

The most prominent of the exponents of Enlightenment thought was Montesquieu. He was an admirer of the state and social system of England. His first book, *Persian Letters* (*Lettres Persanes*), was published in 1721, followed by *The Greatness and Decadence of the Romans* published in 1731. His greatest work *The Spirit of the Laws* (*De l'esprit des lois*) came out in 1734. In this book he expounded his famous theory of the 'separation of powers'. He held that distinct separation of power among the legislature, judiciary, and administrative wings of government was desirable for without which, it would be impossible to curb an autocracy. Montesquieu was no believer in republicanism or democracy and the constitutional monarchy of England was his ideal. Though his thoughts and ideology were characterized by revolutionary spirit, he was not in favour of revolution. He never spoke about the abolition of privileges of the Church and aristocracy and he also remained silent about the rights of common people.

Voltaire (1694–1778)

In the eighteenth century, Voltaire was famous for his multifaceted genius in the world of political thought. Like Montesquieu he too was an admirer of the English model. The target of his attack was the Roman Catholic Church. For him Church was synonymous with religious bigotry yet far from being an atheist, he was a believer in God. In terms of political belief he was a liberal but like Montesquieu he had faith in the institution of monarchy and his ideal form of government was 'enlightened despotism'. He also neither supported democracy nor cared for the interests of the people.

Rousseau (1712–78)

The greatest thinker among contemporary French philosophers was Jean-Jacques Rousseau. His ideology and thought was more extremist and revolutionary in character than those of all other contemporary philosophers. His well known works were *A Discourse on the Arts and Sciences, A Discourse on the Origins of Inequality, The Social Contract, A Discourse on Political Economy, Emile,* etc. According to Rousseau, man was honest and happy in his natural condition but it was society, which by way of creating division among men, became the source of unhappiness and disquiet. Rousseau set forth this theory in *The Social Contract.* He held that the state and society should evolve out of a social contract between all members of that society and that sovereign power should lie not in the rights of kings, but in the 'general will' of the people.

Rousseau's ideal political form was direct democracy. He believed that in order to ensure social equality and freedom, there was little alternative but to hand over power to the people. Rousseau's thoughts deeply influenced contemporary France and according to Napolean, Rousseau was responsible for the French Revolution more so than anyone else.

The Influence of other Philosophers

Other notable philosophers who, in the age of Enlightenment, disseminated the fruits of scientific knowledge to common people, were Denis Diderot, D'Alembert, Holbach and others. Their initiative and enterprise helped in the publication of an enormous *Encyclopaedia*. Religion and transcendentalism came in for criticism in their writings and they also started writing against feudalism. Francois Quesnay was the founder of the group called the Physiocrats. The Physiocrats comprised, among others, of economists such as Mirabeau, Turgot, Nemours, Gournay, and others. Individualism formed the core of their thought. They fiercely attacked the contemporary economic doctrine of mercantilism, spoke in favour of free-trade, and sharply criticized the internal tariff policy. Their thought is known as a liberal economic theory. They also held that land was the source of all wealth and that wealth increased only through the cultivation of land. For this, everyone should pay tax on land and so all the clergy, the aristocracy, and the bourgeoisie should pay land tax. According to the Physiocrats, the king owned the responsibility for introducing these reforms. This group may therefore be described as supporters of Enlightened monarchy.

Historians differ about the role of French philosophers in the French revolution. According to David Thomson, 'the connection between their [philosophers] ideas and the outbreak of revolution in 1789 is somewhat remote and indirect'. Historians like Mounier and Morse Stephens opined that the propaganda and theory of the philosophers was unsuccessful with the French people.

On the other hand, historians like Taine, Roustan and Dupont firmly believed that the philosophers, by criticizing the *ancien régime*, had in fact weakened the very foundations of the old regime, thereby ushering in the revolution. Needless to say, it is hardly possible to reconcile the two contradictory opinions. However, most of the French philosophers did not live to see the French Revolution and so there was no question of their directly leading the revolution. Judged from this viewpoint, the role of the philosophers could lose some of its significance. However, it is undeniable that the critical and rationalist writings of the philosophers psychologically prepared the French people for the revolution and lent them the mental strength to bear the brunt of the struggle.

THE REVOLUTION:
THE ARISTOCRATIC REVOLT

In pre-revolutionary France, the majority of the people belonging to the Third Estate were of the oppressed sections of society. The first two Estates of the society, viz., the clergy and the aristocracy formed the heavily privileged segment. Naturally, they would always stand on the side of the King for both the aristocracy and the king were dependent on each other. It is therefore of note that it was the aristocracy who initiated the revolutionary process.

The economic crisis overtook the French government a few months preceding the revolution. Louis XVI, after taking over the reins of power, appointed Turgot as the finance minister. Turgot took firm steps towards reforming the administration and laid stress on economizing and reducing expenditure. He proposed the issue of government orders for cuts in the daily expenditure of salaried people, the release of guilds in trade and commerce from government control, and the balanced distribution of expenditure for building roads. However, stiff opposition from the aristocracy made the King back down. Turgot also took exception to the French participation in the American War of Independence. He was ultimately stripped of his charge.

Assuming charge as the finance minister, Necker also adopted the policy of making cuts in expenditure, but France's unwarranted participation in the American war continued to deepen the economic crisis. He took to borrowing to bear the huge expenses of war which added to the burden of debt. This made him order the closure of several state and general departments. However, in pushing through his economic reforms, Necker incurred the displeasure of the aristocracy, and like his predecessor, lost his job. The next finance minister, Calonne, came out with his reform measures. He did not propose equal taxation, for this would have entailed taxing the privileged. However, he suggested enforcing complete state control over salt and tobacco. He also conceived of imposing a tax on every individual, besides uniformly taxing the aristocracy, clergy, and all landowners. To this end he put forward a proposal for removing the internal tariff barrier and a few indirect taxes.

Keeping in mind the ignoble ends of his predecessors, Turgot and Necker, Calonne summoned the Council of Notables, cleverly bypassing *parlement*. Calonne, who had nominated every member of the Council, hoped that they would stand by him. However, the Council, which was made up of members of the aristocracy, opposed his proposal. In April 1787, Calonne resigned. Lefebvre blamed the consequences on Louis XVI arguing that 'the calling of an assembly was an initial surrender: the King was consulting his aristocracy rather than notifying it of its will'.

Brienne, who succeeded Calonne, was compelled by circumstances to adopt the measures proposed by his predecessor for besides reforms, there was no alternative way to save the monarchy. The *parlement* of Paris objected to stamp tax and tax on land and declared that imposition of tax was the responsibility of the Estates General. Louis XVI became annoyed with the magistrates of *parlement* and banished them to Troyes but the provincial *parlements* supported the *Parlement* of Paris. In the long run *parlement* was vindicated and Brienne was forced to give in. It was decided that the Estates General would soon be called into session. Meanwhile, Necker took over from Brienne once more.

The showdown between the King and *parlement* came to a head on 3 May 1788. On this day, *parlement* made a declaration of the fundamental laws of the state. According to the declaration, the right to impose tax was vested with the Estates General, imprisonment under *lettres de cachet* or without trial, as well as the dismissal of magistrates, became illegal, and the traditional rights of the provinces were made inviolable. In retaliation, Louis XVI stripped *parlement* of some of its rights thus the conflict between the king and the aristocracy at last came to the surface. Riots broke out in places like Dauphine, Provence, etc., and even the army was not spared the fury of the mob. On 21 July 1788, the aristocracy and the clergy held a meeting with members of the Third Estate at Vizille and came to an agreement. They demanded that the Estates General and *Parlement* be recovered. It was resolved that represenation of members of the Third Estate would equal the combined strength of the First and Second Estates. The declaration made at Vizille symbolized united protest against the monarchy.

When Necker convened the session of *parlement,* the magistrates demanded that the Estates General of 1789, like one of 1614, be formed of the three Estates. They further demanded equal representation of the three Estates and establishment of the right of each Estate to make decisions for itself. The aggrieved Third Estate reacted sharply to this aristocratic bid to assert political supremacy. They called for doubling the strength of the Third Estate, the combined session of the three Estates and a vote per capita (one man—one vote) system. They were also vocal about national sovereignty and a new constitution. Necker conceded the demands for a two-fold increase in the strength of the Third Estate and voting per capita for he was under the impression that this arrangement would help curb privileges to some extent. As soon as this legislative order was issued the aristocracy resorted to strong protest but Necker assured them of the convening of a session of the Estates General by May 1789.

However, the aristocratic revolt met with initial success, thanks to the support of people shorn of privileges. With the help of popular support, the aristocracy was able to force the government to withdraw the taxes and reconstitute the *parlement.* The common people acted under the impression that a strike against the despotic monarchy and the convening of a session of the Estates General would serve as a panacea for all the national problems. The privileged classes, too, believed that such a course would be beneficial. They thought that this would help add to their power and position but they failed to anticipate the impact of the blow which the ensuing revolution would deal to these privileged classes. The clergy and the aristocracy were forced to part with their privileges in the very first session of the Estates General.

Lefebvre called this capitulation of the king to the aristocracy the 'aristocratic revolution' for Rude, however, this event was no 'revolution' but a 'revolt'. According to him, aristocratic fears only foreshadowed the revolution. He argued that '. . . the revolt of the nobility was, perhaps, a curtain raiser rather than a revolution, for it was the prelude of a revolution. . .'. Rude's view seems justified when one considers the fact that the fundamental changes which characterize revolution did not feature in the revolt of the aristocracy. They wanted neither change nor reform of the old system and their outlook was conservatives not revolutionary.

Death of Louis XVI

However, their revolt undeniably paved the way for the revolution in the future. In fact, it was the summoning of the Estates General, under pressure from the aristocracy, that signalled the collapse of the *ancien régime*. Judged by this yardstick, the event was revolutionary.

The Impact of the Glorious Revolution and the American War of Independence on the French Revolution

The Glorious Revolution of 1688 which saw the assertion of people's power by English Parliamentarians, acted as a great source of inspiration for the French. The most immediate inspiration, however, came from the American War of Independence. The writings of Thomas Palme and Thomas Jefferson added to the democratic aspirations of the French. Many French people like Lafayette, who actively participated in the American Independence struggle, helped to spread the message of popular upsurge back home. The French felt emboldened by the success of the Americans in overthrowing British rule, added to which, the American War depleted French finances and virtually brought France to the brink of bankruptcy. This helped hasten the French Revolution.

The Summoning of the Estates General, 5 May 1789: The Beginning of the Bourgeois Revolution

The Estates General last met in 1614. When it was summoned on 5 May 1789, after a long gap of 175 years, the election of representatives was obviously marked by zeal and excitement. Out of a total 1,214 elected representatives, the clergy, constituting the First Estate, accounted for 308, the aristocrats of the Second Estate numbered 285 and the Third Estate numbered 621. The Estates General met at Versailles on 5 May 1789. Each of the elected members joined the session armed with *cahiers de doléances* which detailed the sufferings of the people in his electoral constituency.

The aristocrats of Estates General wanted little change in its composition and voting pattern. They preferred Estates General of 1789 to be formed in the same way as it had been in 1614 for this alone would help perpetuate their interests. Traditionally, the three Estates, irrespective of their strength in the house, had one vote each. The trouble started when the Third Estate demanded vote per capita system. The fruition of such a demand would have surely ensured the victory of the Third Estate who formed the majority. In the existing system, the aristocracy and clergy, holding two votes as a combined force against the Third Estate, had a clear edge. Besides, the demands of the Third Estate to call a joint session of all three Estates made aristocrats realize that conceding to the demand would strip them of their social status as a privileged class. Naturally, they opted to protect their class interests using royal assistance so as soon as the Estates General met, battle lines were drawn between the Third Estate on the one hand, and the monarchy and aristocracy on the other. The Third Estate ultimately emerged victorious from this clash fought within the constitutional perimeter. Historians termed this particular phase of the French revolution as the 'bourgeois revolution'.

The Third Estate betrayed their revolutionary spirit from the very first session of the Estates General. A deadlock resulted from the demand for a joint session and voting per capita (one man—one vote). As the King remained unrelenting, the opposition made a stand and in a revolutionary move on 17 June the members of the Third Estate declared themselves to be the National Assembly and took the reins of the revolution. This event has three-fold significance: first, it showed that the Third Estate stood united in their demands and goals.

Secondly, the declaration ran counter to established practices and constitutional norms, so obviously was not legally sustainable. Thirdly, the declaration opposed the autocratic power of the king, and in the same breath, gave the impression that the Third Estate alone had sole claim to the sovereign power of the nation.

In no position to concede to the demands made by the Third Estate, the King closed the session. On 20 June members of the Third Estate found the door of the Estates General closed. Led by revolutionary leaders such as Abbé Sieyès and Mirabeau, they immediately gathered at an adjoining tennis court and pledged to not disband until they had framed a new constitution for France. This historic oath is famously known as Tennis Court Oath. Louis XVI was forced to concede to the demand for single casting and the right of the three Estates to sit together. This paved the way for the collapse of the *ancien régime*.

The Fall of the Bastille, 14 July 1789

The people of Paris, is the nerve centre of French politics and administration, exalted over the victory of the bourgeoisie at Versailles. However, the jubilation was short-lived as the King dismissed Necker on 12 July and called in the army. Riots and looting broke out in different parts of France, and assumed nightmarish proportions in the capital of Paris. Revolutionary Parisians seized the Bastille on 14 July which, despite being an empty prison, symbolized the oppression unleashed by the autocratic Bourbon monarchs. About 8,000 people forced their way into the fort and,

People forced their way to the Bastille

Fall of the Bastille

after killing the prison guards and other personnel, took away the arms stored therein. The fall of Bastille is a momentous and unforgettable event in French history. According to Goodwin, 'No other single event in the Revolution had so many sided or far-reaching results as the fall of the Bastille. . . . The fall of the fortress was widely acclaimed as heralding a new birth of liberty, not only in France, but throughout the world.' The fall of the Bastille had a far-reaching effect. First, it put an end to the royal autocracy in France. Second, all press censorship was lifted in its wake. Third, the fall of the Bastille marked the success of armed uprising. The King called off the army within three days and restored Necker to his post, and aristocratic conspiracy had failed for the time being. The permanent committee which had been formed in Paris prior to the upsurge of popular protest came to be known as the Paris Commune and Jean Sylvain Bailly was appointed as mayor. The National Guard was set up to protect peace and property and the King himself visited Paris to appointed Lafayette as the

MAP 2.1: Europe in 1789

commander-in-chief. As a result, the administrative power of Paris passed into the hands of the bourgeoisie. Moreover, the fall of the Bastille added fuel to peasant uprisings all over France.

The Spread of Rural Unrest

The peasant revolt, which erupted in the French provinces in the wake of the fall of the Bastille and the setting up of the Paris Commune, deserves attention. The urban revolution paved the way for the rural upsurge. Trouble had already broken out in the rural areas as early as December 1788 as the rural masses were discontented by feudal oppression. The Parisian revolution simply added fuel to the fire. There was also economic crisis and so, under the circumstances, the peasants of all the provinces of France (except those of Alsace-Lorraine and Brittany) stopped paying tiths. They refused to pay dues to their feudal lords and carry out their feudal duties. The unrest which gripped rural areas of France is called 'Great Fear' in history and such behaviour caused considerable embarrassment for the members of the National Assembly while simultaneously making them aware of their responsibility to remove the grievances of the peasants. In fact, the support of *sans-culottes* or the urban populace, as well as that of farmers, was crucial for the National Assembly. The attack on property unleashed in the wake of this widespread peasant revolt taught the members of the National Assembly a vital lesson. It became evident that in order to ensure the safety of property, some swift concessions would have to be granted to farmers and the feudal burden had to be removed. In a decree on 4 August 1789 as the clergy and aristocracy surrendered their special privileges and feudalism collapsed: the *ancien régime* came to an end.

The Work of the French Constituent Assembly
(1789–91): Successes and Failures

The pledge to frame a new constitution made with the Tennis Court Oath of June 1789 by the representatives of the Third Estate finally materialized on 30 September 1791. When the Estates

General started working on a new constitution, it became a Constituent Assembly and was the new focus of the Revolution. However, Edmund Burke, a British political philosopher and critic of the French Revolution came down heavily on the members of the Constituent Assembly for destroying French society and devaluing the institution of monarchy. For these critics, only the destructive aspect of the Constituent Assembly was apparent. Their views cannot be rejected outright. Indeed, the working of the Constituent Assembly with all its contradictory pulls of creation and destruction showed, for the first time, signs of a constructive enterprise. There is, therefore, no reason to deny the significance of the functioning of the Constituent Assembly.

The declaration of human and civil rights adopted on 26 August 1789, incorporated the key principles of the new constitution which was based on rational thinking. The 'Declaration of the Rights of Man and of the Citizen' produced by the Constituent Assembly and modelled the American and English constitutions, stated that: (1) Every man is free and has equal rights. (2) Everyone is equal before the law. (3) All have equal rights in their choice of profession and royal post. (4) There shall be no discrimination based on birth. (5) The right to property is inalienable. (6) No person shall be arrested and imprisoned illegally. (7) Every person shall have the unfettered right to freedom of speech and expression, activity, and earning.

The new constitution created what can be called a constitutional monarchy. The power of enacting legislation to curb royal authority became vested in the unicameral Legislative Assembly. This Assembly, with a strength of 745 members, was the repository of sovereign power. The king could only exercise a veto right to put on hold any legislation passed by the Assembly, but could not nullify it altogether.

The king had no authority to dissolve the Assembly. The Assembly was invested with the responsibility of regulating foreign policy and it reigned supreme in monetary affairs. Though the king had control over diplomatic affairs, he enjoyed no power to declare war or conclude any treaty without legislative approval.

Document of Tennis Court Oath

According to Lefebvre, this constitutional monarchy was, in reality, a bourgeois republic.

The principle of national sovereignty became applicable in all spheres. The French administration was completly decentralized: France was divided into 83 departments, which were divided into districts, which were split up into cantons and finally, into communes. Even the military organization, like the civil one, underwent change, although to a lesser extent. Under this new direction the king enjoyed little power. The remarkable development was that at every stage of provincial administration, government officials were to be elected henceforth.

The new judicial system introduced by the Constituent Assembly enabled people, irrespective of their social status, to seek justice. The king no longer wielded power over the judiciary and, following the separation of powers; the executive had no control over the judiciary. Judges would be elected by active citizens. Individual freedom was specially protected under the new arrangement. Thus judicial, political, and executive power passed into the hands of the Third Estate.

The immediate cause of the French revolution was the acute financial crisis faced by the government. As a result, the Constituent Assembly had to initiate measures to deal with the crisis. In 1789 the old tax system was virtually abolished and *taille, gabelle,* tithe, etc., were removed. Steps were taken to improve the fiscal condition of the government, i.e. tax was imposed on every landowner and on industry and commerce. Tax was also levied on personal income and movable property.

Efforts were made to increase government revenue by confiscating and nationalizing land and property held by the Church. Paper currency called *assignats* were issued pledging the seized Church property to pay off debts. The policy of free inland trade was adopted and various restrictions were lifted. Uniform weights and measures and the industrial protection policy were introduced throughout the country. The French East India Company's monopoly over external trade was also removed.

Anti-Church feeling ran high during the French Revolution and philosophers also heavily criticized the corruption of the

Church. The reform of the administration rendered church reform inevitable. Catholicism henceforth ceased to be the state religion and protestants were allowed complete freedom of religion. Religious reform laws were codified in France with the Civil Constitution of the Clergy on 12 July 1790. The Church of France was made subservient to the state under the new law and the clergy thereafter became government employees.

The influence of the Constituent Assembly in French history is immeasurable. The Assembly left an indelible mark on all spheres of life—politics, administration, religion, and economy—and was marked by bourgeois traits. Even then, the working of the French Constituent Assembly was not without its flaws.

The constitution, despite incorporating human rights, reflected narrow class interests of the bourgeoisie. Besides, it failed to mention political and social equality, let alone economic liberty. The document was silent on the duties and responsibilities of citizens, and lacked democratic spirit. Under the new constitution, the king and his ministers were still entrusted with the task of executive governance but were given no power to make laws or effect change in the existing ones. On the other hand, members of the legislature could enact legislation and criticize the king and his ministers freely. This disparity led to a growing conflict between the king and the legislature. Regarding economic reforms the Constituent Assembly failed to develop a modern budgetary system. The paper currency *assignats,* which were issued to deal with the economic crisis, became so devalued that at one point the people refused to have anything to do with them. The church reforms created religious differences in France for the clergy and god-fearing people refused to accept the constitution, and thus came to be branded as enemies of the Revolution by the revolutionaries.

Despite all this, the Constituent Assembly can be credited with having established a constitutional monarchy and abolishing the feudal system. Ensuring national unity was undoubtedly the crowning glory of this Assembly. Besides, this constitution was the first to have been written in Europe. The most remarkable development was the unprecedented zeal and excitement discernible in France as well as outside.

The Progress of the Revolution, 1789–93

A newly drafted constitution was implemented in 1791 and the newly formed Legislative Assembly was dominated by a majority of moderates and minority of Jacobins and the Girondins. The first showdown between the legislature and the king took place over the latter's exercise of his suspensive veto against the legislation relating to the clergy who were up in arms over the nationalization of the church. The Parisian mob, led by the infuriated Jacobins, attacked the Tuileries Palace and heckled the King.

On 21 June 1791, the royal family tried to escape to Austria in what has become known as the Flight to Varennes. They were however caught and brought back to the capital under public humiliation. In the meantime, the Duke of Brunswick, a General appointed by the Austro-Prussian government, issued the Brunswick Manifesto warning France of dire consequences should any member of the royal family be treated harshly. This confirmed the suspicions of the Jacobins that the King had clandestine contacts with enemy states like Austria and Prussia.

On 10 August 1792 the Paris commune, encouraged by the Jacobins, attacked the Tuileries Palace and lynched the royal guards. Though the King and the Queen took refuge in the adjacent Assembly, this was also besieged by the mob and the Assembly was forced by the Jacobins to suspend the monarchy and the royal family was incarcerated. Finally, the Constitution of 1791 collapsed. This goes down in history as the 'Second French Revolution'.

With the collapse of the constitution of 1791, electoral law no longer in force and so the Legislative Assembly issued orders for a general election based universal male suffrage. The Assembly formed after the elections in 1792 came to be known as the National Convention. It framed a new constitution, proclaimed France a Republic, and envisaged a legislative body based on universal franchise. The new constitution, however, could not be put into effect because of the emergency situation known as the 'Reign of Terror', which began in 1793.

ACHIEVEMENTS OF REVOLUTIONRY FRANCE:
RESULTS OF THE FRENCH REVOLUTION

The prime concern of the French Revolution was to ensure merit based equal rights for all, doing away with hereditary privileges. Cobban argues that 'Privilege was the enemy, equality the aim'. Some of the worst sufferers in the Revolution were the clergy for the Revolution saw the abolition of separate church courts, its economic freedom, and property ownership. The church, in a word, ceased to have an independent identity and the state now turned secular. No less affected were the aristocracy who also lost their hereditary privileges following the abolition of feudalism. The bourgeoisie—comprising of writers, intellectuals, journalists, professors, artists, etc.—gained social status. The fall of the *ancien régime* led to improvement in the condition of the peasants. For the first time, they became free from the burden of paying taxes to the Church and the agonizing oppression of feudalism.

However, sharecroppers and labourers derived little benefit. Though the revolution ushered in a new era of equality in place of sectarian discrimination, the bourgeoisie were concerned more about their own class interests and less about universal equality.

The French Revolution put an end to divine and autocratic monarchy in France and set up a constitutional one in 1791 based on the English model. That too was ultimately removed to make way for a Republic, which also did not last long and was replaced by the Napoleonic dictatorship. The French Revolution for the first time made it clear that sovereign power rested not with the king or an individual but with the people. It recognized the people's right to governance, though bourgeois supremacy curbed the right of the people who were not given the voting right. France was one of those countries in Europe where a united nation-state came into existence. The sense of unity which initially formed the basis of their existence, suffered from insecurity and a lack of totality but gradually, the French Revolution succeeded in lending cohesion to national consciousness. The bond of national unity was further strengthened by the removal of the internal tariff barrier which led to the expansion of trade and commerce and the creation of a national market but also by equality before the law and a uniform administration throughout the country.

The French Revolution left its mark in the field of education, culture, and thought. Literature and journalism acquired a new tone and temper in the aftermath of the Revolution which also influenced music. All the developments effected changes in the mindset of the French people.

The French Revolution influenced not only France but also different countries in Europe as well. From the French Revolution, Europe learnt nationalism and democratic ideals, besides human rights and individualism. According to Lefebvre, the ideals of 'social democracy' and 'equality' owed their origin to the French Revolution. One can conclude that in some ways it was the French Revolution which gave birth to modern Europe.

The Nature of Foreign Interventions against Revolutionary France

The war waged by the European coalition against revolutionary France can be best explained in ideological terms. During the revolution, France did not adopt an expansionist policy that would engage her in a war with a foreign power. That France became involved in war was due to the anti-revolutionary stance of most European states. Across Europe autocratic kings sensed a threat to their very existence in the revolutionary battle cry of 'liberty, equality and fraternity' in France. This led to desperate military campaigns by European monarchs representing the struggle between the new ideology on the one hand, and the *ancien régime* on the other. The European war began in 1792 with the combined Austro-Prussian invasion of France and was to continued unabated for the next 20 years.

However, more importantly, the European offensive had great effect on the French monarchy. The French king had already lost his autocratic power and had been reduced to a 'titular head'. He could rule only as desired by the elected members of the National Assembly. Developments during different phases of the European war deepened suspicions about the kings loyalties.

Not long before the declaration of war by European powers against France, the royal family had been caught at Varennes while trying to flee Paris in disguise on 21 June 1791. This gave rise to popular suspicions that Louis XVI in trying to escape from the country to make a desperate bid to seek foreign intervention against the Revolution. A section of French people began toying with the idea of overthrowing the monarchy. On 27 August 1791, Austria and Prussia produced the Pillnitz Declaration, appealing to all European monarchs to be united against revolutionary France. The revolutionaries took this declaration to be one of war. Following the death of the Austrian emperor, Leopold II on 1 March 1792, Francis II who was a staunch anti-revolutionary, ascended the throne. He turned down French pleas for the expulsion of counter-revolutionary refugees from France out of Austria. Moreover, he did not agree to pull back troops stationed on the French border during Leopold's tenure. Consequently, the Assembly formally declared war against Austria on 20 April 1792. Francis II, in league with the Prussian king, Frederick William II, advanced towards France with approximately 80,000 soldiers. Foreign states were under the impression that the leaderless revolutionary France would soon be defeated in war. The reality was very different. The Duke of Brunswick, the commander-in-chief of the combined army of Austria and Prussia, made a declaration under pressure from the counter-revolutionary refugees of France, which is known as the 'Brunswick Manifesto'. It warned that revolutionaries is valued in the war would be severely dealt with after victory and that there would be repurcussions if the royal family were harmed. Needless to say, the warning had the reverse effect. The French, fired by patriotic zeal, vehemently supported the war effort. Shrugging off the early defeats, the National Army of France ultimately repulsed the invaders and saved the Revolution.

The French Revolution enriched political vocabulary unlike anything before. Terms like 'moderate', 'radical', 'progressive' or 'reactionary', commonly tossed about in modern day political language, owe their origin to the Revolution. In fact, the French Revolution was unique in terms of socio-economic and political fall-out. Varying strands of thought developed around the Revolution which shook the existing social order to its foundations. The developments at different stages of the revolution produced varied reactions among the people. For example, the way the new constitution drafted by the Constituent Assembly (1789–91) curbed the royal power left many people dissatisfied, as they were strong believers in the authoritarian power of the king. These people were called 'reactionary'. Those who were happy with the direction of the Constituent Assembly were termed 'Centrist', 'Radicals', or 'Extremists' and had faith in neither. Extremists believed that the fruits of the revolution needed to be exposed to the grass roots.. In the post-1791 phase this group achieved political ascendancy.

Paris was the hub of political extremism in France. The most important medium of transmission for extremist thought was the Parisian 'club' or 'associations'. Each club played host to politicians of a single shade of thought. Jacobins and Cordeliers were the most influential of them all.

Of all the radical clubs of Paris, Jacobins stood out for shaping the public opinion of France in the most revolutionary ways. Under the able leadership of Danton, Mairaft, and Robespierre, they organized a popular uprising against the constitutional monarchy thus inaugurating the 'second phase' of the French Revolution. This led many to regard the establishment of 'Republican France' in 1792 as the 'Second French Revolution'.

As was said earlier, the *sans-culottes,* in league with the extremists, exerted pressure on the National Assembly resulting in the abolition of the monarchy. Dethroned on 10 August 1792, Louis XVI was imprisoned at Temple. A decision was taken simultaneously that the newly elected National Assembly would frame a Republican Constitution.

The newly elected National Assembly, renamed National Convention, first met in a session on 22 September 1792. The dismissal of the king, however, failed to make France a true Republic because supporters of the monarchy engineered troubles in different parts of France to help external enemy. As the news of advancing coalition army reached Paris, the rampaging mob ruthlessly killed 'the enemies of the revolution' which comprised of the aristocracy, clergy, and government employees. This mass killing goes down in history as the 'September Massacre'.

National Convention (1792–95)

Though the establishment of the First Republic after the collapse of monarchy in 1792 had been called the 'Second French Revolution', it failed to match the scale of the First French Revolution in terms of popular response. The new government under the National Convention was faced with monumental problems, both domestic and foreign. The newly elected members of the National Convention first met on 22 September 1792. On the inaugural day the members unanimously declared France to be a republic (1792), i.e. the First French Republic. The members, despite their unanimous declaration, were sharply divided in their opinions. However the retreat of the Prussian army in 1792 helped to strengthen the revolutionary spirit. This was the first military success of Revolutionary France.

The lack of cohesion among the members of the National Convention seriously affected the working of the house. The Girondist-Jacobin conflict basically centred around the leadership of the Convention. The Girondists, ideologically speaking, held that under the Republic it was necessary to consolidate the successes of the revolution. For the Jacobins, on the other hand, the fruits of the revolution could not reach the people with mere declaration of the Republic.

This accounted for sharp differences between the Girondists and the Jacobins over the future of the deposed King Louis XVI. The Girondists opposed the execution of Louis XVI. The Girondists, however, did not have the same level of unity as the Jacobins. Moreover, the support enjoyed by the Jacobins from *sans-culottes* and Paris Commune made them a force to reckon with, despite being a relatively small faction. It was at their insistence that the National Convention pronounced Louis XVI guilty, and passed his death sentence by the margin of a single vote. He was guillotined on 21 January 1793.

The Reign of Terror

The conflict between the Girondists and Jacobins came to a head in the wake of the execution of Louis XVI in 1793 and with the result that the Jacobins expelled the Girondists from the National Convention. Following the fall of the Girondists and with the support of the *sans-culottes* of Paris, the Jacobins set up an autocratic revolutionary government to deal with the emergency which was growing out of war and internal revolt. The rule of this revolutionary government is known as the 'Reign of Terror'.

French historian Aulard opined that war inevitably begets a reign of terror, as autocracy is key to national security. Mathiez however, held that the Jacobins were prepared to sacrifice their class interests not only for victory in war but also to bring about a social revolution and spread its benefits to the *sans-culottes*. According to Soboul, all of the emergency measures adopted by the Jacobins for the resolution of the revolutionary crisis were due to mounting pressure from the *sans-culottes* of Paris. Despite their differences over various aspects of the revolution, most of these historians hold the same opinion about the fundamentals of terror and believe that it was created by prevailing circumstances.

Execution of Robespierre

Terror was indeed a reaction to the invasion of foreign autocratic monarchies and to conspiracy within the country by the autocratic collaborators.

The terrorism introduced by the National Convention was primarily intended to restore law and order by strengthening the central authority and meting out punishment to the opponents of the revolution. It also organized the military in preparation for war. The Committee of Public Safety was formed to supervise all these activities and the Girondists had to reluctantly accept this. However, the elected head of the Committee of Public Safety, Maximilien Robespierre introduced an individual dictatorship in France for about a hundred days. To quote Robespierre, 'The government of the Revolution is the despotism of liberty against tyranny.' The Committee of Public Safety made the Reign of Terror effective through the use of the twin organs of (a) The Committee of General Security and (b) The Revolutionary Tribunal. The Committee of General Security looked after law and order while the Revolutionary Tribunal was a criminal court to judge anti-revolutionaries. Besides, under the Law of Suspects, passed on 17 September 1793, anyone could be arrested for anti-revolutionary activities and tried by the Revolutionary Tribunal. Robespierre derived his inspiration from Rousseau for Rousseau's thought baptized him in the doctrine of sovereignty of the people and embodied the ideology of the Jacobins. For Robespierre to oppose the Revolution was treason and so he held that when it came to taming rebellion and thwarting foreign aggression, there was little alternative but for a rigid and ruthless system of terror.

During the Terror, thousands of people were imprisoned on the mere suspicion of being a revolutionary. Eventually, pressure on overflowing prisons had to be eased through administering the death sentence. During this period, about 20,000 people were executed by the guillotine.

In reality, the Reign of Terror was an emergency arrangement which could not be anything but short-lived. The authoritarianism unleashed by Robespierre and his followers in the name of upholding the revolutionary ideology was too much for many. It evoked discontent in different circles and this opposition eventually made a broad united front against Robespierre. In fact, it was the *sans-culottes* who played a crucial role in bringing about Robespierre downfall. The Reign of Terror came to an end with the execution of Robespierre by guillotine on 28 July 1794. The post-Robespierre phase of the Convention later came to be regarded as the Thermidorian Reaction, so-called because the event took place in thermidor of the revolutionary calender.

After this, the Convention undertook the task of drafting a new constitution which purported to defend France against the twin dangers of democracy and dictatorship. Neither the constitution of 1791 nor that of 1793 was acceptable to the new rulers. The new constitution envisaged a bicameral legislature in place of the unicameral one. In the meantime, the ideology of the French revolution had undergone fundamental changes which were reflected in the functioning of the National Convention. Concerned over the form of extremism that manifested during the Reign of Terror, many of the members were very restrained and so extremism gave way to political moderation.

France under the Directory (1795–99)

The system of governance ushered in by the new constitution in 1795 (following the Thermidorian Reaction), is known as the Directory. As the new constitution provided for franchise based on wealth, the rule of the Directory was called a bourgeois Republic. Far from being a document of human and civil rights as incorporated in the Constitution of 1789, this constitution was a declaration of the rights and duties of citizens, of which the right to property was foremost. The power of legislation was vested in *Les Anciens,* or the Council of Elders, and *Les cinq-cents,* or the Council of Five Hundred. Responsibility for administration generally rested with the five members of the Directory.

Faulted on many counts, the Constitution of 1795 lacked effectiveness. The power of the common people and the aristocracy had not been recognized under the rule of the Directory which was in fact characterized by political uncertainty due to: (1) constitutional weaknesses and limitation, (2) the incompetence and inefficiency of the Directors. According to David Thomson, 'they [the directors] presided over the final liquidation of the Revolution'. Equally, the Directory was preceded by a steep rise in prices of commodities and the Directors could neither contain the price spiral nor restore internal order. This led to growing popular discontent against the Directory and the Directors owed their continued existence to the army.

France had already been engaged in war with Sardinia, Austria and England when the Directory came to power. During this time, Napoleon Bonaparte was the commander-in-chief of the French army and was fighting Austria and Sardinia. He came out victorious in the war due to his spectacular military tactics and besides spreading French influence from 1796, he defeated the Austrian army. Under the Treaty of Campo Formio in 1797, Napoleon forced Belgium and Austria not to intervene in Italy and despite his abortive expedition to Egypt people gave him to hero's welcome. The failure of the Directory to deal with internal disorder encouraged the people to find a saviour in Napoleon. Taking full advantage of his new position, Bonaparte forcibly engineered the fall of the Directory and captured power in France in 1799.

Rise of Napoleon to Power

Napoleon Bonaparte was born into an aristocratic family of Corsica on 15 August 1769. His lineage helped him study at the *Ecole Militaire*. He joined the French artillery as a Second Lieutenant at the age of 16. A product of the revolution, Napoleon returned to Corsica to engage in politics, only to be banished with his family in 1793. His belated return to the volatile French political scene was marked by utmost caution.

Returning to the army, Napoleon seized control of Toulon from the English and Spanish invaders in 1793 and re-established French supremacy there. This development was a watershed in his growing ascendancy for the military expertise he displayed in the battle earned him a promotion to Brigadier general. The fall of Robespierre led to Napoleon's dismissal and arrest but Barras, the leader of Thermidorian Reaction, released him. In 1795, he saved the National Convention from the rampaging supporters of monarchy and he was thus elevated to the rank of General.

The rule of the Directory failed to deal with the internal problems adequately, but its success in foreign affairs was due to the military genius of Napoleon. He took on the might of the European coalition, defeated Sardinia, then, forcing Austria to sign the Treaty of Campo Formio in 1797, Napolean annexed a large part of Italy. He took on the English army in Egypt in order to isolate England from the anti-French coalition but his victory in the Battle of the Pyramis could not spare him defeat in the Battle of the Nile and so his Egyptian expedition did not succeed. Still, on his return home, Napoleon was idolized.

Meanwhile, the misrule of the Directory caused popular resentment. Abbé Sieyès took the initiative of introducing a new form of government in place of the Directory. As a constitutional expert, Sieyès took it upon himself to draft a new constitution based on the principle of 'Authority from above and confidence from below'. Napoleon staged a *coup d'état* in collusion with Directors Abbé Sieyès and Barras to end the rule of the Directory and form the Consulate.

This is known in history as 18th Brumaire. Under the Consulate, power was invested in three Consuls but Napoleon, as the First Consul, was all-powerful. He was appointed Consul for life following a national plebiscite. In 1804, Napoleon declared himself to be the Emperor of France.

CAUSES FOR THE SUCCESS OF NAPOLEON

Napoleon had a meteoric rise in post-revolutionary France. His rapid rise to the pinnacle of his power and glory was due to his individual talent and conducive circumstances. The Revolution completed the breakdown of old values initiated by the enlightened philosophers of the eighteenth century, but it stopped short of building social organization. Napoleon however was capable of building a stable social polity by virtue of his practical sense, administrative ability, and sheer will-power. The people of France also wanted their country to emerge out of the ravages of war and regain peace and so this national mindset helped Napoleon in his mission.

The persistent bid of the European coalition to thwart the Revolution evoked an unprecedented jingoism in France. Napoleon catered to this by crushing the foremost states of Europe in a whirlwind fashion. People of the vanquished nations found in him a saviour of liberation.

The key to Napoleon's success, besides his military genius, was his uncommon personality and soaring ambition. That is why he could take over the reins of power in France, despite his humble beginnings as an ordinary soldier.

His able administrations which he started fashioning along with his war effort as the First Consul, complemented his military success. Napoleon consolidated the gains of the Revolution, besides ensuring the peace and security of the nation against foreign aggression. All this helped him to become a national icon virtually overnight.

The Napoleonic Reforms

Assuming power in 1799, Napoleon realized that the French had become thoroughly disgusted with powerless governments and internal disorder. Taking over as Consuls he devoted himself to the internal reconstruction of France. He aimed at fashioning a cohesive administration that would preserve 'equality', and remain in keeping with this revolutionary ideal. He was, however, against the concept of 'liberty', another revolutionary ideal, for he equated it with disorder.

The Council of States was the highest forum of the administration and Napoleon, who chaired the house, also nominated its members. The Council played a significant role as the source of legislation as well as being an administrative and judicial body. Every department would be monitored by a Prefect who was appointed by the First Consul.

The Judiciary, too, underwent some fundamental changes. Judges were elected even in the early phase of the Revolution but Napoleon did away with this. Judges would, henceforth, be appointed by the government and once appointed, they could not be removed from their posts. This ensured the independence of the Judiciary. The police organization was also strengthened.

The responsibility for initiating economic reforms rested with Gaudin who was very able in this regard. In 1800, the Bank of France was set up to try to restore economic order and in 1803, this Bank was granted the sole power of issuing bank notes, albeit under state control. His sympathy with the bourgeoisie, as well as his popularity among them, meant that far from toeing *laissez-faire* line, Napoleon followed a mercantile policy. He laid stress more on agriculture than on trade and commerce. He introduced a new tax structure which was in keeping with the economic means of citizens and new employees were recruited to collect direct tax. Napoleon also ensured the stability of the franc. Between 1799 and 1814, 75 million francs were in circulation. Thus reinforcing the economic foundations of the country.

The educational system under Napoleon was aimed at producing able administrators and skilled technicians for the benefit of the state. He showed indifference to the education of women, and primary education failed to get much of his attention. More than a hundred reconstituted government schools were entrusted to the Director of Public Instruction. His primary focus was on military education, technical education, and scientific research. Though education ranked high on the list of his priorities, people were denied the right to freedom of speech and periodicals with anti-government views were not allowed to circulate.

From the outset, the army attracted the careful attention of the First Consul and Napoleon kept intact the military organization shaped by the Revolution. As regards religion, Napoleon was liberal and tolerant and under his stewardship, religious alienation, which was a legacy of the Revolution, gave way to a realistic solution. The Concordat of 1801 struck between the Pope and Napoleon, settled the dispute involving Church and the Revolution. The French Catholics, aggrieved by the anti-clerical policies pursued during the Revolution, came out in support of Napoleon. Under the Concordat, highly-powered clergymen were included on the govemment pay-roll as state appointees. The Pope, in turn, needed assent to the nationalization of church property during the Revolution.

One of Napoleon's crowning achievements were his legal reforms for he completed the challenge of codifying the French laws. Code Napoleon, containing 2,287 articles, was written in 1800 following a long laborious process. The Code, comprising of civil, criminal, and trade sections, lent legal recognition to feudal aristocrats. This legal document incorporated ideas of individual liberty, equality before the law, the secular character of the state, freedom of thought, and freedom of profession. Code Napoleon, however, curbed women's rights to a large extent for it did not approve of equality between men and women. That Napoleon could not fully break with the past was evident from his individual effort—in the face of strong resistance—to build a new aristocratic class called the Legion of Honour, based not on birth but on merit.

Napoleon and the Revolution

Napoleon who said, 'I am the Revolution', asserted in the same breath 'I destroyed the Revolution'. Contradictions not withstanding, the utterances were present in his policy. His work seemed to be in one way an extension of the revolution. From another stand-point it might suggest a return to the earlier social order. He not only organized the *ancien régime* but consolidated the revolution as well.

Napoleon showed himself to be at once the heir of the Revolution and the product of the reaction against it. Of the foundational principles of the Revolution, he was opposed to 'liberty', but he adopted the principle of 'equality' in social and fiscal matters and his famous civil code enshrined this. Thus, the social basis of France remained revolutionary even though Napoleon did not respect political liberty, which was the grand idea of the Revolution. He considered liberty as a disturbing factor that prevented the efficiency of the state so by centralizing the administration, he did much to revive the *ancien régime*. In this sense, he may be regarded as the 'destroyer' of the revolution.

Expansion of the Napoleonic Empire until the Treaty of Tilsit, 1807

In 1793, the European monarchs banded together in a power bloc against France in 1793. The death sentence of Louis XVI fostered the emergence of this power bloc. This alliance was formed of Austria, Prussia, Spain, Portugal, and England. During the Reign of Terror, the alliance failed to make much headway and was ultimately routed. France regained Belgium from Austria and Toulon from England in 1795 and only Austria and England continued in their efforts against France.

As First Consul, Napoleon urgently proceeded to deal with the second coalition of European monarchs in order to ensure the security and freedom of the French state. Under the Directory, Napoleon defeated Austria and imposed the Treaty of Campo Formio in 1797. The French border ran along the Rhine up to the Batavian Republic (Holland) but following the annexation of Savoy from Sardinia, in the south-east it stretched to the Alps. Two Republican states in Italy and the Batavian Republic came up surrounding France. Their over-dependence on France rendered the latter invulnerable to foreign invasion. France was temporarily left with no enemy except England after the Treaty of Campo Formio Napoleon started military operations against England in Egypt to curb the former's influence in the East.

In the meantime Austria, England and the Second Coalition

Battle of Waterloo

formed in Europe. Turning Napoleon's absence to their advantage, the Coalition completely drove The French out of Italy and Germany. As a result, the Directory lost military prestige in popular perception and so it is little wonder that the abolition of Directory by Napoleon evoked little resentment among the French, who were itching for a fitting reply to the Second Coalition.

At first Napoleon adequately prepared his army for war by ensuring a good supply line and selecting able commanders. Then, through diplomacy and terror tactics, he isolated Russia from the coalition and formed an armed neutral coalition comprising Prussia, Sweden, and Denmark against Britain in northern Europe. In 1801, he defeated Austria in two successive battles in the Italian and German theatres of war and forced the signing of the Peace Treaty of Luneville. It led to Austrian acceptance of the Treaty of Campo Formio in 1797. On the other hand, England, who was still invincible in naval battles, defeated France in the Battle of the Nile in 1798. Despite this victory, England had to accept French supremacy in Europe and signed the Treaty of Amiens in 1802. It was, however, a short-lived armistice, for both England and France sought to establish hegemony in Europe.

In the meantime, Napoleon had been elected Consul for life in a national plebiscite in 1802. His internal reform measures as Consul further enhanced his popularity. Taking advantage of his growing popularity Napoleon declared himself Emperor of France in 1804.

Prior to this declaration, war broke out once more between Napoleonic France and England, under provocation from the latter. Conservative England considered Napoleon to be the embodiment of destructive revolution and moreover, France's growing ascendancy strongly challenged British economic interests in the lower parts of Europe and the Mediterranean. In 1805, Lord Nelson routed the combined fleet of France and Spain at Trafalgar, at the expense of his life thereby reasserting the naval might of England.

On the eve of the Battle of Trafalgar, Napoleon marched troops along the English channel (1803–4) to invade England. But, diverted by the Austrian crisis, he had to put off his plan.

The defeat at Trafalgar made it impossible for Napoleon to make much headway.

On the other hand, the victory at Trafalgar emboldened England to form the Third Coalition against Napoleon comprising of Austria, Sweden, and Russia, and later Prussia. Napoleon, using his military genius, routed this coalition as well by taking on the might of each state of the coalition in turn and handing out defeat. For example, he captured Vienna after defeating Austria at the Battle of Ulm in 1805.

Following the defeat of the combined forces of Austria and Russia in the Battle of Austerlitz in 1805, Austria was compelled to sign the Treaty of Pressburg. Under the terms of the treaty, Austria had to vacate all the occupied Italian territories. Napoleon also defeated Prussia and Russia in two separate battles in 1806 and 1807 respectively. This completed the humiliation of the Third Coalition. The defeat at the Battle of Friedland is 1807 forced the defeated states to conclude the Treaty of Tilsit with Napoleon in 1807. Under the treaty, the Prussian empire was dismembered, the size of its army reduced, and large compensation for war demanded. In the meantime, Napoleon had put up an economic blockade against England known as the Continental System, in which Russia consented to help.

The Treaty of Tilsit catapulted Napoleon to the pinnacle of his glory. For a brief moment, he became the ruler of most of Europe. Napoleon, however, knew for certain that the supremacy of France in Europe would never be unchallenged until the defeat of England and so, after the conclusion of this treaty, he renewed his efforts to destroy England.

COLLAPSE OF THE NAPOLEONIC EMPIRE:
THE CONTINENTAL SYSTEM

From the invasion of Egypt to the Battle of Trafalgar (1805) Napoleon suffered defeats against England. He realized that he would never defeat Britain in direct battle and so he devised a new method known as the Continental System.

Soon after his ascent to power in 1799 Napoleon pursued a tariff

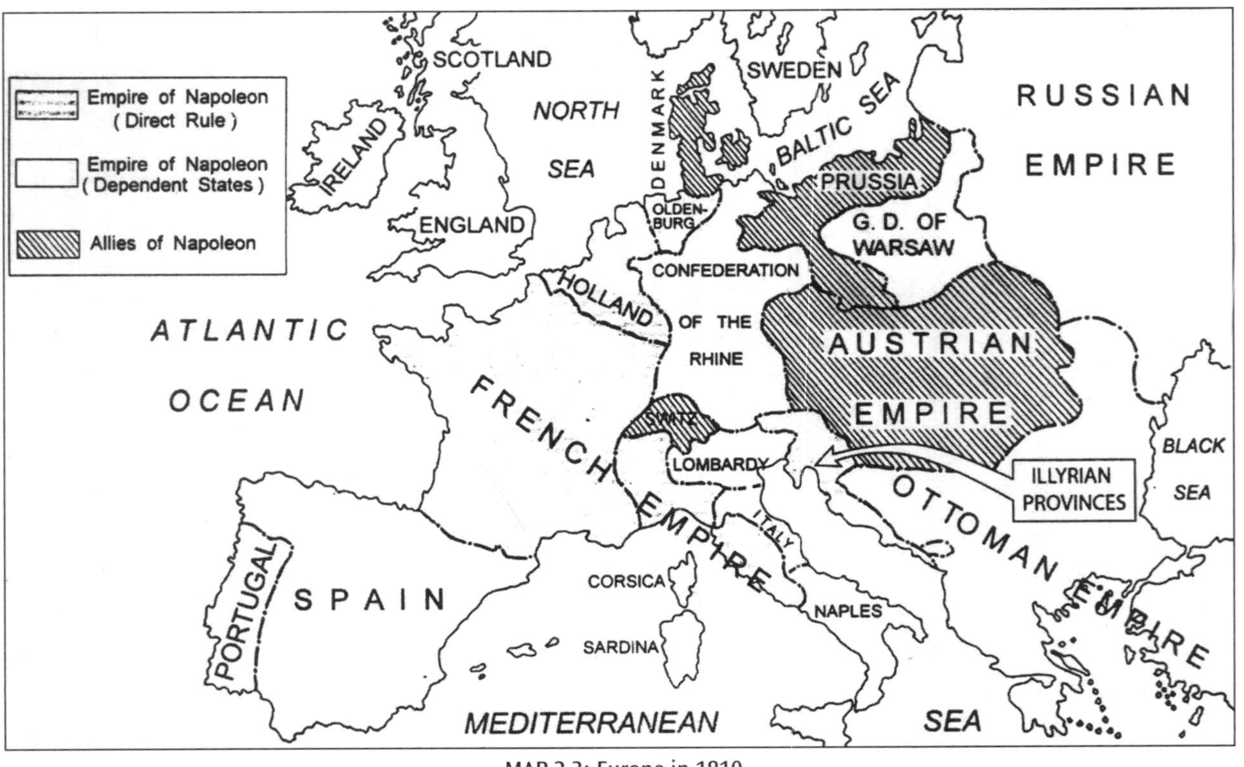

MAP 2.3: Europe in 1810

protectionist policy in trade. Under this policy, the entry of British goods into the area lying between France and its 'natural boundary' was prohibited. The tarrif protection helped the French textile industry survice the competition from its British counterpart. The policy of tariff protection, however, was not applied to cripple the British trade for the ultimate surrender of England.

However, the Napoleonic victories of 1806–7 completely changed the contours of European politics. Following the cooperation of Spain, Portugal, Russia, and Austria circumstances became conducive to the prohibition of the entry of British ships and goods into the European territory as a whole. As an initial measure, Napoleon issued the Berlin Decree in 1806 which declared a 'blockade' of the British Isles. The decree which banned trade with Britain and its colonies, primarily aimed to cripple British trade and force their surrender to France. Britain responded to the Berlin Decree with Orders-in-Council in 1807 which declared a counter-blockade in the areas of Europe under Napoleonic influence. Under the new measure, if anyone was barred from buying British goods he could not buy the same from other countries. By further widening the scope of the Continental System, Napoleon replied to the British Orders-in-Council with the Warsaw Decree (1807), Milan Decree (1807), and Fontainebleau Decree (1810), in which he declared that any ship complying with the British order would be confiscated at European ports as British property. However, while British maritime supremacy continued, it was impossible for the Napoleonic measures to be effective. Still, the Continental System did not prove inimical to Britain. One third of British goods and three-fourths of colonial products were previously exported to Europe and so Britain did face some economic difficulties following the embargo on trade. Her maritime supremacy did not allow the Continental System to prove disastrous however, for she had other markets to fall back on.

In the meantime, Napoleon's allies began to slip out of his control, as they faced a stalemate in the sphere of trade. Turkey, Protugal, Spain along with its colonies, and even Russia opened up their markets. Moreover, the Dutch port, under the rule of Joseph

Bonaparte, a brother of Napoleon, opened itself to British goods. Not only the states under Napoleon and the allied countries, but also the French themselves turned against the Continental System. The French navy was not powerful enough to make the Continental System effective and England found it easy to make counter-resistance more effective. Lastly, the reverses suffered by the French army on different war fronts by 1808 nullified the Continental System.

In attempting to assert his supremacy over the whole of Europe, Napoleon went too far. He invaded Spain, which resulted in the Peninsular War and he himself admitted that the 'Spanish ulcer' which had caused him pain. It was again the Continental System which accounted for the deterioration of his relationship with Tsar Alexander I and the abortive Moscow expedition. As the Pope refused to accept the Continental System, Napoleon committed the mistake of imprisoning him after occupying his Kingdom. The Continental System, was undeniably, responsible, to a very great extent, for all these blunders.

Reaction to Continental System in Europe and Napoleon Expansion

The effectiveness of the economic blockade which Napoleon imposed on England through the Continental System, depended on the cooperation of other European countries. In other words, it required a total embargo on the entry of British goods into all European ports. After the issue of Berlin Decree, Napoleon took a few measures in this direction. He ensured the success of the Continental System in Italy, Naples, Westphalia, and Tuscany by appointing rulers of his choice in these areas. Tsar Alexander I of Russia also assured France of all help under the Treaty of Tilsit. Napoleon found it difficult to control recalcitrant Portugal which refused to accept the Continental System because of its intimate trade ties with England and so Napoleon subdued Portugal by marching his army through Spain. However, this intervention in Spanish affairs led to the Peninsular War.

In 1807 the French army captured Lisbon facing little resistance, and prohibited entry of British goods into Portuguese ports. In this way the Continental System was enforced in Portugal. Napoleon then looked to occupy Spain when the opportunity arose after internal trouble there. Napoleon forced the Spanish king, Charles IV, to step down and proclaimed his brother Joseph Bonaparte as the King of Spain (1804).

The aftermath was not pleasant for Napoleon for the Spaniards, setting aside all their differences, organized themselves in a united national struggle against foreign occupation in the same way the French had during the French Revolution. An identical strain of thought was running throughout Portugal about this time. The Peninsular War formally started with the arrival of the English Commander, Arthus Wellesley in December 1808. The Peninsular War which Napoleon called the 'Spanish ulcer' continued from 1808 to 1814. Napoleon could not lead his men from the front and this long, drawn out war claimed more than 3,00,000 French soldiers. Besides, the hitherto invincible French army in land battles had its glory and reputation shattered.

Napoleon brought about his own disaster while trying to enforce the Continental System. The Franco-Austrian War of 1809 was a case in point. Inspired by the anti-French stance of Spain and Portugal, Austria took the initiative to get rid of French influence. Austria formally declared war against France in 1809. In the fierce Battle of Wagram Austria was ultimately defeated by France and forced to sign the Treaty of Schonbrunn in 1809 but though Austria suffered heavy losses following the defeat, the Battle of Wagram convincingly exposed Napoleon's military weakness.

Despite all the discontent and wars of the Napoleonic empire, no one could foresee its inevitable doom. However, in the next couple of years, Napoleon looked ready to fall. His differences with Alexander I of Russia was a major contributory factor in this regard. The relationship between Napoleon and Alexander I deteriorated after the Treaty of Tilsit in 1807 and culminated in the Napoleonic invasion of Russia in 1812. The Treaty of Tilsit had simply effected a settlement but no meeting of minds and neither side. None cared to redeem the pledges made to each other. For example, Napoleon lent little help in Russian expansion towards Turkey, while Alexander I hardly insisted on England coming to a settlement with France. Napoleon, however, had pinned his hopes on the support of Alexander I for the success of the Continental System but Russia failed to keep her promise due to domestic pressure. Industrialization at that time was still a long way off and Russia had to depend on England for the supply of necessary goods. Therefore, initial support for the Continental System had a rapid and telling effect on the Russian economy. Businessmen and the middle class of Russia, let alone common people, became vocal in their protests against Alexander I for the support he had extended to the Continental System. Under the circustances, he had to open Russian ports to the unrestricted entry of British goods into Russian market. The rift between Napoleon and Alexander I following this finally resulted in the French expedition to Russia in 1812 after a year of preparation.

Napoleon strengthened his *Grande Armée*, or 'Grand Army', to 6,00,000 soldiers for the Russian expedition. This army entered Russia on 5 June 1812. Napoleon had to face adversity from the outset. His victory in the Battle of Borodino led Russian historians to regard it as their moral victory. The *Grande Armée* encountered a graver reality on reaching Moscow where the bitter cold and acute shortage of food took a heavy toll. Pushed to the edge of defeat, Napoleon offered an armistice to Alexander I which was refused. The dropping temperatures forced Napoleon to abandon the expedition. Only 95,000 soldiers out of 6,00,000 eventually made it back to France.

There, despite the military reverses, Napoleon rapidly built his army afresh. The significance of the failure of France in the Russian expedition lay elsewhere. The abortive mission helped break the myth of the invincibility of Napoleon in Europe, and brought back European states into a coalition against France. Thus started the Battle of the Nations or Battle of Leipzig in 1813. Their joint struggle gained in intensity when England joined the War of Liberation which was initiated by Frederick William III of Prussia (1797–1846) along with Russian help. As Austria, Holland, and Italy joined the coalition, the fight against Napoleon turned into the Battle of the Nations and the Napoleonic Empire fell with the defeat at the Battle of Leipzig. Unable to withstand the combined offensive of the Allied powers comprised of Austria, Russia, Prussia, and England, Napoleon ultimately abdicated the French throne and went into temporary exile to Elba in 1814. In the meantime, European statesmen had been engaged in redrawing the map of Europe at a conference in Vienna.

In February 1815, Napoleon returned to southern France from Elba. The rousing welcome he received there encouraged him to attempt to seize power once more, using the assistance of ex-soldiers. However, the ultimate downfall of Napoleon came at the Battle of Waterloo in 1815 in which he was defeated by the British general Wellington. The period of 100 days during which Napoleon ruled France after his return from Elba to the route at Waterloo is also known as the Hundred Days. Napoleon lived in exile on the island of St. Helena in the South Atlantic until his death in 1821. Thus, the first revolutionary autocrat in the world met with his end.

The Causes of the Downfall of Napoleon Bonaparte

The process of the fall of Napoleon set in even before the completion of his empire building project. His political life came to an end with his defeat at Waterloo in 1815 yet Napoleon became a legend within his lifetime. He left a permanent imprint on every department of the French administration due to his original thinking. Ironically, his failures had been predetermined by precisely those very qualities which helped in his spectacular rise.

According to David Thomson, the fall of Napoleon started with the breach of the Treaty of Amiens in 1802. For Grant and Temperley, the process set in after the Treaty of Tilsit in 1807: the causes of Napoleon's downfall can be examined against several yardsticks.

The foundations of the Napoleonic empire were unstable from the very beginning. The early responses of the French to the Napoleonic measures for securing peace and stability in the country did not last long to the point that the dividing line between Napoleon and autocratic monarchy soon got blurred in popular preceptions. The disillusionment turned at one point of time into the liberation war against the one-time deliverer from bondage.

Limitless ambition was another reason for Napoleon's fall. Had he confined his war operations to the extent that they would help consolidate revolutionary gains and protect the frontiers of the country, he would not have met with such opposition. Napoleon undoubtedly brought back a semblance of peace and order to France and his successive victories in war also restored national pride. However, the relentless pursuit of military adventures eventually left people weary.

They stopped extending their moral support and military might turned out to be a source of disloyalty. The failure of the Continental System hastened Napoleon's fall. He did not have sufficient naval power to enforce the blockade successfully or to rival British naval supremacy. The Continental System badly affected the economic interests of European countries dependent on British goods and soon they articulated their resentment in public. Napoleon, in trying to force the blockade of British merchant ships sailing into European harbours, brought about a long and unnecessary war.

Napoleon injured the national pride of the Spaniards by putting his brother Joseph Bonaparte on the Spanish throne. The French army met with near defeat in the Peninsular war against the combined forces of Spain and Portugal, suffered heavy casualties, and the Spanish resistance turned into a national liberation war. The Spaniards exerted a strong influence on other European countries. Realizing his mistake, Napoleon remarked that it was the 'Spanish ulcer' which had proved to be disastrous for him.

Napoleon's downfall was further facilitated by his invasion of Moscow in utter disregard of the Russian climate and topography. Far away from Central Europe, hard winters made Moscow inaccessible for any military campaigns. When Napoleon realized this bitter truth and finally decided to return home, it was too late and the Moscow expedition cost him dearly in terms of loss of soldiers pride, and prestige.

The Pope's refusal to accept the Continental Blockade led Napoleon to annex the Papal kingdom. This caused an adverse response from European catholics while the earlier Concordat of 1801 signed with the Pope had turned the protestants against Napoleon. Thus, he alienated the entire Christian world, which did not prove beneficial for his empire.

Napoleon's success in war hinged mainly on his use of military *blitzkrieg* tactics. His personal marshalling of forces was the key to French success in this form of offensive hence the army commanders of other European countries now began to focus on those theatres of war where Napoleon was not present to command his men.

The French army under Napoleon had been initially inspired by patriotic zeal and a revolutionary spirit to sacrifice their lives for the motherland. As the empire spread in the later phase, people of different nationalities like Poles, Danes, Germans, Italians, and the Dutch joined the army not for revolutionary ideals but to serve their own narrow self-interests.

The bourgeoisie who had backed Napoleon's rise to power, felt their interests threatened when he got involved in unnecessary warfare to satisfy his growing ambition. Extended war efforts called for larger mobilizations of resources which put added pressure on the state finances. The bourgeoisie, who had to bear the added burden, felt utterly disillusioned with Napoleon to the extent that they ultimately parted ways with him.

Men of uncommon genius often tend to forget their limitations and find themselves under the spell of mounting ambition. Napoleon was no exception. He gained and clung to power largely through the use of military power, and he tended to impose his wish on his countrymen, people of defeated states, and even on his advisors. Had Napoleon taken lessons from Trafalgar it is possible that he would not have met his Waterloo.

HIGHLIGHTS

- The French Revolution was multi-causal in character. There were political, social, economic, and intellectual causes behind the Revolution. A combination of factors brought about the downfall of the *ancien régime*, or the old order, and paved the way for the Revolution.

- The Revolution began as soon as the Estates General was summoned. The Estates General was converted into a Constituent Assembly and embarked upon the job of framing a new constitution. The new constitution was ready by 1791. In accordance with the new constitution, autocratic monarchy was abolished and a constitutional monarchy was created.

- The royal family was arrested. At this time a few European countries threatened to attack France to display their support of the French monarchy. The King was executed by the revolutionaries which led to utter chaos within France. Amid this restlessness, France was attacked by a coalition European powers.

- The political chaos and the external threat triggered off the Reign of Terror in France. Peace was restored by this Reign of Terror.

- Between 1795 and 1799, France was under the Directory. It was during the rule of the Directory that Napoleon rose to power. Napoleon eventually became the Emperor of France and took to reforming the French government and administration. His reforms were inspired by the message of French Revolution.

- The Treaty of Tilsit marked the highest point of Napoleon's career. The Treaty of Tilsit (1807) was signed between Napoleon and Tsar Alexander I of Russia.

- Napoleon's chief enemy in Europe was England. He envisaged an economic blockade of Europe, known as the Continental System, to ruin England, but this ended in failure and marked the beginning of the end for Napoleon.

- The failure of Napoleon could be ascribed to the Continental System, the Peninsular War, and the Moscow invasion. The Battle of Waterloo (1815) finally sealed the fate of Napoleon forever.

MEMORABLE DATES AND EVENTS

1769	Birth of Napoleon
1789	The Estates General met for the first time since 1614
1789	June 20—Tennis Court Oath
	July 14—Fall of Bastille
	August 26—Declaration of the Rights of Man and the Citizen
1791	The New Constitution of France
	August 10—The 'Second' French Revolution

1792	National Convention
1793	June 2—Beginning of the Reign of Terror
1794	July 27—Assassination of Robespierre
1804	Code Napoleon
1805	October 21—Battle of Trafalgar
1807	Napoleon's conquest of Portugal
1813	Battle of Leipzig
1815	June 18—Battle of Waterloo
1821	May 5—Death of Napoleon

MEMORABLE PERSONALITIES

Louis XV: French King of the Bourbon Dynasty
Louis XVI: French King of the Bourbon Dynasty
Montesquieu: French Philosopher and author of the *Spirit of the Laws*
Voltaire: French Philosopher and Writer
Rousseau: French Philosopher and Writer
Robespierre: A French leader of the Revolution and one of the chief exponents of the Reign of Terror
Napoleon Bonaparte: The Emperor of France
Tsar Alexander I: The Emperor of Russia

QUOTABLE QUOTES

- 'Actual social and political conditions in the eighteenth century did not square, anywhere in Europe, with newer philosophy and science. Despite the attitude of a growing number of intellectuals the masses all over Europe continued to live within a framework of social, political and ecclesiastical usages which derived from earlier times and which were not essentially different in the eighteenth century from what they had been in the sixteenth century.'   —C.J.H. HAYES
- 'The Revolution was an outcome of a struggle between classes, of a movement for social equality by the bourgeoisie.'   —RICKER
- 'The causes of the French Revolution were economic and political, not philosophical and social.'   —MORSE STEPHENS
- 'The connection between their [Philosophers] ideas and the outbreak of revolution of 1789 is somewhat remote and indirect.'

                —THOMSON

- 'In France the faults of the system were not more glaring than elsewhere, but, it was there . . . that they came under closest scrutiny, and it was there that the Old Regime was first to go to pieces. In general it may be said that the government was not deliberately oppressive, but that the system in operation was so full of faults and anomalies that it worked undue hardship on the people while from the practical standpoint it failed to solve the problem of meeting its needs.

  —RICKER

- 'Chief among the causes of the French Revolution were the abuses and extravagances of the Bourbon monarchy; the unjust privileges enjoyed by the nobility and the higher clergy; the wretched conditions of the poorer classes of the people and the revolutionary character and spirit of French philosophy and literature.'   —MYERS

- 'The revolution came because the monarchy was unable to solve the question of privilege, was not strong enough, in a word, to overthrow the remains of feudalism which, in France as in most other continental countries, cumbered the ground.'   —H.A.L. FISHER

- 'The tenor was an emergency despotism—a dictatorship of distress as one of its champions put it. It was founded on the theory that only by establishing a despotism could civil war be ended, unity restored and the country helped in a condition to defend itself against the enemy at its doors. . . .'   —RICKER

- 'The immediate causes of the French Revolution of 1789 must be sought, not in the economic grievances of the peasants, nor in the political discontent of the middle class, but in the reactionary inspirations of the French aristocracy.'   —GOODWIN

- 'No other single event of the Revolution had so many sided and far-reaching results as the fall of the Bastille.'   —GOODWIN

- 'Tilsit, was, in a sense the turning point of his [Napoleon's] fortunes.'

  —RICKER

- 'The *sans-culottes* were the immediate producers. Peasants or artisans, in order to have their own lives at their disposal, it was first of all necessary for them to cease to be attached to the land or under allegiance to someone else. Without them and their inherent hostility to the aristocracy, there would not have been a bourgeois revolution.'   —ALBERT SOBUL

- 'The victory over feudalism and the *ancien régime* did not signify, however, the simultaneous appearance of new social relations and new economic structures. It is patently obvious that after ten years of revolution, society would not yet be essentially bourgeois not the economy specifically capitalist.'   —ALBERT SOBUL

CHAPTER 3

Revolution and Reaction in Europe (1815–1848)

THE CONGRESS OF VIENNA (1815)

The fall of Napoleon brought Europe face to face with various problems. The state frontiers had been repeatedly changed and several old dynasties had been dashed out in the preceding two decades. In several parts of Europe, a new social and political system based on the French model had been imposed. With the removal of Napoleon in 1814, the reconstruction of Europe by the victors became imperative. The first steps in this direction were taken with the Treaty of Paris (1814), when the status and frontiers of France were settled. It was decided that the Bourbons would be restored and that the boundaries of France were to be those that had been in place in 1792. Thus was enunciated the doctrine of legitimacy.

The treaty further indicated that the victors aimed to restore the boundaries of the European countries to those that had existed prior to the outbreak of the revolutionary wars. The Congress of Vienna was convened to decide the redistribution of land, although the principles by which the distribution was to be carried out, had already been fixed by the Treaty of Paris. Belgium was to be united to Holland to form the Kingdom of the Netherlands, Switzerland was to be independent, Germany was to form a federation of independent states, and Italy was to consist of independent states.

The Congress of Vienna was an assembly in which most of the European powers were represented. However, the four greatest powers who had played the major role in defeating Napoleon had by far the strongest voice in the decisions reached. This 'Big Four' comprised of England, Russia, Prussia, and Austria. Metternich, the chief minister of Austria, was the most outstanding personality among the assembled diplomats. He presided over the Congress

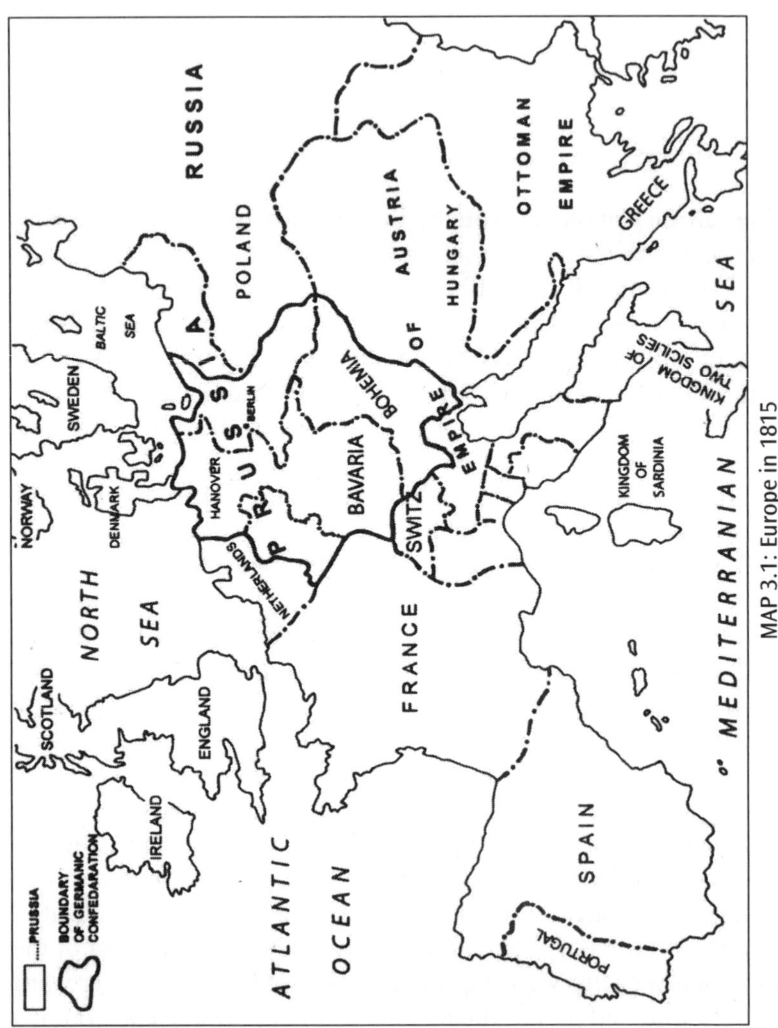

MAP 3.1: Europe in 1815

and became its guiding spirit. Apart from Metternich, other leading diplomats present at the Vienna Congress included Tsar Alexander I of Russia, Frederick William III of Prussia, and Lord Castlereagh of England. France was represented by Talleyrand, a former Bishop and former supporter of Napoleon.

The chief task was to restructure the states system of Europe which had been dislocated by Napoleon. The diplomats of the Vienna Congress represented the *ancien régime*. They sought to brush aside the ideas generated by the French Revolution and so the territorial arrangements they envisaged were calculated to make Europe safe against any future French aggression. The work of the Congress was therefore guided by three principles: (1) balance of power, (2) legitimacy, and (3) compensation.

A critical task before the Congress was therefore that of territorial resettlement. The Congress exposed such selfish interests and led to such a scramble for concessions that it was cynically described by its Secretary as 'a meeting of the victors to divide the spoils of the conquered'. This selfishness was reflected in the fierce quarrels that broke out over the allocation of Saxony and Poland between Russia and Prussia on the one side and Great Britain and Austria on the other. Russia wanted the whole of Poland and Prussia the whole of Saxony. These differences became so serious that the negotiations almost collapsed. Frictions also arose over the question of the dismemberment of France as proposed by Prussia.

It was decided that the boundaries of France were to be pushed back to the borders which she had held at the time of the outbreak of the Revolution in 1789. Steps were taken to encircle her with a girdle of powerful states to act as bulwarks against any future aggression. France was still regarded as the source of all disturbances in Europe. Holland and Belgium were united into one kingdom, Switzerland was restored to her previous position of independence, and the Germanic Confederation under the presidency of Austria was created to take the place of what was the former Holy Roman Empire. Spain was again placed under the rule of her despotic Bourbon King. Italy was partitioned into numerous small states and placed under the controlling influence of Austria and the Kingdom of Piedmont Sardinia was strengthened. The peacemakers were anxious to provide guarantees for the future peace of Europe and so they entered into two alliances—the Holy Alliance and the Quadruple Alliance—with this end in view. By these means, the diplomats at the Vienna Congress sought to maintain the European balance of power.

The principle of legitimacy was implemented by asserting that legitimate sovereignty belonged only to the old ruling dynasties. Therefore, these ruling dynasties should be restored and so the great powers turned their attention to the task of restoring the monarchies wherever possible. France was allowed to retain her monarchical frontiers, and she was also guaranteed some of her revolutionary constitutional gains. The old Bourbon monarchy was restored in the person of Louis XVIII.

Thus, the validity of the changes made by Napoleon was denied and the pre-revolutionary conditions were restored as far as possible. It was in accordance with the principle of legitimacy that the rule of the Bourbons was restored in France, Spain, Naples, and elsewhere. All the states which had contributed to the destruction of the Napoleonic power were rewarded in various ways. Russia received Central Poland, Turkish territories and Finland. Prussia received Western Pomerania, part of Saxony and some Rhenish provinces, Austria lost Belgium but received Lambardy and Venetia in Italy and the Illyrian provinces on the Adriatic Sea. Sweden received Norway. England received Malta, Heligoland and protectorate over the Ionian Islands, Ceylon, the Cape of Good Hope and other colonial territories and certain commercial advantages. However, the principle of legitimacy was in many cases compromised by the necessity of providing compensations largely in the form of land to the victors at the cost of the defeated party.

The diplomats who met at Vienna sought to set the clock back to 1789 and to restore the old orders that had been destroyed by Napoleon. However, the principles of the French Revolution were too firmly entrenched to be overthrown and a quarter of a century of hopes and aspirations could not be obliterated by a stroke of a pen. The forces of nationalism were making themselves felt in many directions and this seriously undermined the settlement made in 1815.

The chief criticism of the Vienna Congress is that the forces of nationalism, which had so greatly helped the Kings of Europe to defeat Napoleon, were entirely ignored by keeping Germany and Italy divided, Poland dismembered, and by uniting Belgium and Holland. Some historians have gone so far as to say that the supreme task of the nineteenth century was to undo the work of the Vienna Congress. Most of the important territorial arrangements made in 1815 could not survive the shocks of the next half a century.

The real charge that may be brought against the diplomats of the Vienna Congress is that they ignored the challenge of the French Revolution. They failed to see that the new forces of democracy and nationalism could not be suppressed by autocratic control. The diplomats have been denounced as reactionary and devoid of statesmanship for they wilfully shut their eyes to these new forces in order to secure the balance of power and dynastic interests. True to the traditions of the *ancien régimes*, they treated the peoples of Europe as pawns in the game of dynastic aggrandisement. Another serious criticism of the settlement was the disrespect shown to the views of the smaller states. The principle of legitimacy was not extended to benefit the smaller states like Venice and Genoa.

The work of the Congress of Vienna had been often criticized with undue harshness. Although the work of the Congress was retrograde and reactionary, it 'mark[ed] not only the close of an old epoch but the beginning of a new'. Some of the measures adopted by the Congress were pregnant with immense possibilities. In defence of the peacemakers of the Vienna Congress, it can be argued that no once in 1815 could foresee how deep seated the new feeling of nationalism would turn out. At that time nationalism and democracy were still innovations so the vast majority of the population was not in a position to profit from them. The Congress, consisting of practical statesmen anxious to secure as much as possible for their states, could not be expected to prescribe solutions to principles which were as yet in an experimental stage.

One of the positive contributions of the Vienna Congress was that there was no major war for 40 years. It has to be borne in mind that the hands of the Vienna diplomats were tied by the agreements and treaties made between the allies themselves before the Congress met. As the First Treaty of Paris had laid down the general plan according to which the settlement was to be made, the doctrine of legitimacy was merely a recognition of the fact that any stable settlement must be founded as far as possible upon pre-existing rights.

Another charge often made against the Vienna Congress, is that in redefining the boundaries of states, too much emphasis was laid on the 'heartless system of statistics' which specified the number of people every state was to contain. However this method did establish a balance of power that has remained the main plank of international relations ever since. In giving the control of Europe largely to the great powers, the Vienna Congress inaugurated what has been called the Concert of Europe, which was a precursor to the League of Nations.

So in many ways, the Congress of Vienna provided the foundations on which the Europe of the nineteenth century were to be built. In the final analysis however, the fact remains that in the name of international peace, the Congress inaugurated an era of repression and reaction. They thought in terms of traditional diplomacy, dynasties, and states, not in terms of popular sympathy and national expression. They lacked the sort of statesmanship which would take note of the forces of the age and create an enduring structure based on the reconciliation of the past and present.

THE METTERNICH SYSTEM

Metternich guided the policies of the Austrian empire from 1809 to 1848 and for about three decades he was the most important figure in Europe. Among the host of figures who crowded the stage from 1815 to 1830, he stands out as a not able personality in the history of Europe. His character and policies have been met with almost universal condemnation. His love of intrigue and espionage was enshrined by Napoleon: 'He mistook intrigue for statesmanship.' Alexander I of Russia regarded him as a liar. To his contemporaries he was the arch-conspirator against the causes of nationalism and liberalism. Modern historians have represented him as the embodiment of the narrow policy of reaction which held sway in Europe from the fall of Napoleon to the revolutions of 1848.

Metternich dominated his age just as Napoleon Bonaparte had done albeit it using a different method of diplomacy. He claimed to exercise a moral dictatorship of Europe and was fully aware of his importance within the new order. The political system he envisaged was guided by three main principles: (1) a return to pre-revolutionary political order, (2) the suppression of nationalism and the democratic ideas triggered off by the French Revolution, and (3) protection of Austrian interest in European politics.

The historical importance of Metternich lies in his continual opposition to everything encompassed within the term 'French Revolution', which to him was a gangrene that had to be cut out of European politics. He regarded absolute aristocratic monarchy as the best political regime. He was a conservative minister, called himself a man of the *status quo,* and his doctrine was the doctrine of immobility. The repressive mechanism which he created to implement his ideas is commonly called the Metternich System. To preserve autocracy, he advocated armed intervention to suppress any people who rose against their ruler.

That Metternich was an opportunist and a reactionary may be admitted, but two important points must be kept in mind when we try to explain his character and policy. In the first place, he lived in an age during which an almost irrepressible process of disintegration had set in all over Europe. Two decades of incessant war had been followed by the war cries of the newborn nationalists and liberals who, at that early stage, had little to offer other than vague ideas. Under the circumstances, the supreme need of Europe was peace. For Matternich, to maintain the *status quo* required the maintenance of peace, and the best way to ensure peace was to destroy that which destroyed the peace. Secondly, Metternich was primarily concerned with the interests of Austria. He was quick to understand that the development of national

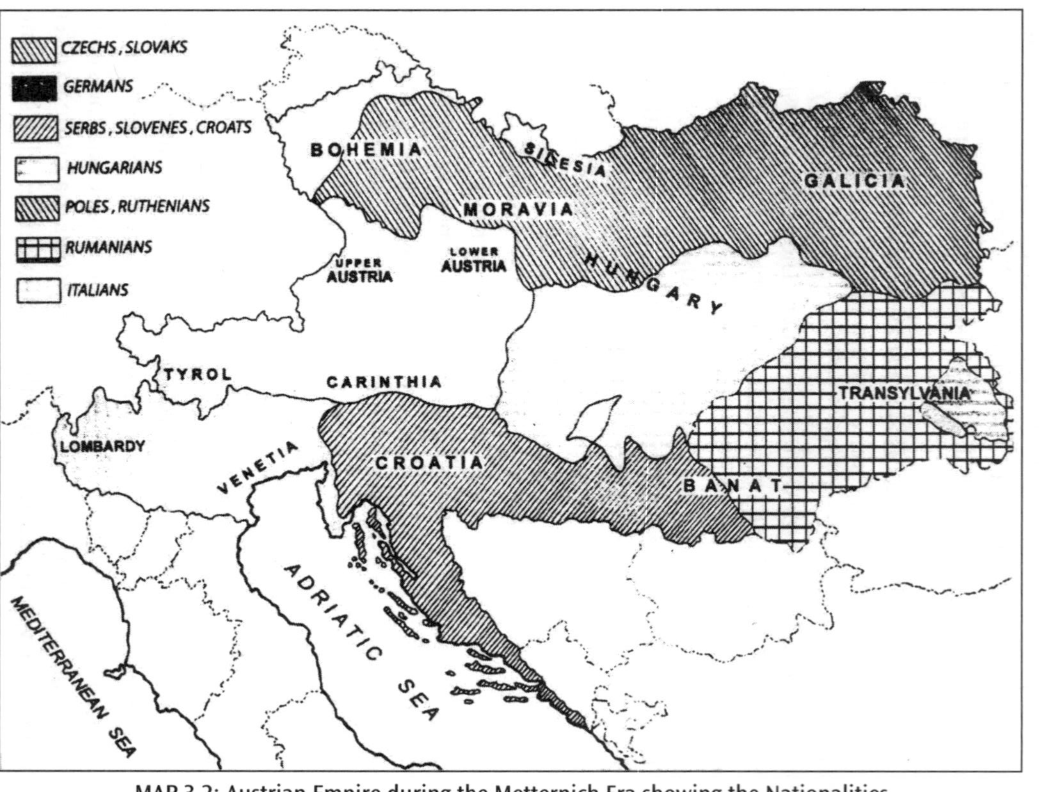

MAP 3.2: Austrian Empire during the Metternich Era showing the Nationalities

feeling would only lead to the disruption of the empire. He felt the popular opinion, if allowed to express itself freely, would let loose racial antagonisms, hence he was opposed to democracy and nationalism. Thus, to keep the Austrian empire intact, he had to appeal to the old principles of legitimacy and authority and to suppress the newborn revolutionary movements in Germany and Italy. He performed his duty well and for many years, he succeeded in maintaining the integrity and prestige of Austria. For example, he was against the Russian expansionist policy for the sake of the security of the Austrian empire. The Metternich system therefore found manifestation both in his internal and external policies.

To Metternich, the most dangerous thing was revolution. It was a malady that was not confined to any single country in Europe, therefore all signs of liberalism in any country had to be crushed. This implied the right of the great powers to interfere in the affairs of other states and thus was developed the right of intervention as elaborated by Metternich. The Quadruple Alliance Treaty (1815) was used by Metternich to suppress revolutionary movements in Italy, Spain, and Portugal. The Austrian Chancellor became the Chief Commissioner of Police of Central Europe to root out revolution from all over the continent. According to the terms of the Quadruple Alliance, the first reunion of the European statesmen was held in 1818 at Aix-la-Chapelle to consider what was to be done with France. Metternich's supremacy over European affairs dates from the Congress of Aix-la-Chapelle. If Metternich ultimately failed to dictate to Europe and America, he certainly succeeded in imposing his authority over Germany. Austria was the President of the German Confederation, but treated the Diet of the Confederation (in which representatives of all the German states were sealed) as a mere department of Austria's foreign office. He also prevented other German states from granting liberal constitutions to their subjects. The notorious Carlsbad Decrees, passed at his instance, laid Germany under the heel of reaction. Student societies were dissolved, spies were appointed, and heavy censorship of the Press was established. When the idealist Tsar Alexander I formulated the Holy Alliance, Metternich found it necessary to placate that powerful sovereign by recognizing it formally, although unofficially he described it as a 'loud sounding nothing'.

There was however plenty of flammable material all over Europe and in 1848, the second wave of revolution in France provided the spark which set it alight. Movements of revolt broke out in the Austrian dominions. Metternich was compelled to leave the country which he had ruled for 40 years and to take refuge in England. With him collapsed the *ancien régime* in Europe.

REACTION AND REVOLUTION (1820)

The real object of the Vienna Settlement was to restore, wherever possible, the pre-revolutionary conditions of Europe. Metternich presided over the Congress system and became its guiding spirit. The Concert of Europe was devised by the 'Big Four'—Austria, Russia, Prussia, and England and was engineered by these powers to preserve the political arrangements made in the Congress of Vienna. The Concert of Europe had its origin in the Quadruple Alliance which was geared to maintain the future peace of Europe. The peacemakers were actually divided into two alliances: (1) the Holy Alliance and (2) the Quadruple Alliance (1815). The Holy Alliance was based on a declaration by Alexander I of Russia, but it was a failure. The European system between 1815 and 1825 was therefore guided by the Quadruple Alliance which was controlled by Prince Metternich of Austria. It soon degenerated into a dictatorship of the 'Big Four' in the interest of absolutism and reaction.

The Holy Alliance was never a reality and the Quadruple Alliance failed due to the lack of union among the allies. From a wider point of view, it may be said that the years 1815–30 witnessed the rise and fall of international alliances against revolutionary tendencies. The long war against France was partly 'a war for eradicating the international revolutionary movement'. It was a crusade that was continued even after Napoleon's downfall and one which failed in the case of the Spanish American colonies and Greece and succeeded in Italy and Spain. However, the fall of the Bourbons in France (1830), the independence of Belgium (1830), and the fall of the Tory Party in England (1830–2), were noteworthy breaches in the conservative system initiated by the victors in 1815. Europe could not be ruled indefinitely by a policy of negative conservatism but until Europe recovered from the exhaustion of the French wars, Metternich's power was unchallenged. However after 1830 when Europe was renewing its youth, his power became feebler and feebler, until in 1848 it completely disappeared.

REVOLUTION IN THE SPANISH COLONIES OF SOUTH AMERICA (1820)

One of the most important challenges facing the major European powers, who met under the leadership of Metternich at Troppau (1820), was the Spanish question. Ferdinand VII, the King of Spain had already been compelled to grant a constitution to Spain and accept a liberal ministry. For two years the King submitted to the constitutional restrictions, but secretly he appealed to the Concert of Europe to rescue him. However, the restoration of Ferdinand's authority was not merely a European question for it had non-European ramifications too. Spain had an extensive empire in the west, including South America, Mexico, and a part of the present-day United States. Ever since the French conquest of Spain (1808), these colonies had become practically independent of their mother country and an extensive trade had grown up between them and England, which was profitable to both the parties. In the Spanish colonies of Latin America, a freedom struggle had started in the last quarter of the eighteenth century. This struggle for emancipation from the clutches of Spanish imperialism could be attributed to the following factors: (1) The brutalities of the Spanish rulers made the colonial subjects determined to fight for independence. (2) The success of the Americans in their revolutionary war greatly inspired the colonial subjects of South America. (3) The ideas of democracy and liberalism which emanated from the French Revolution had been a constant source of encouragement to the colonized.

The colonial subjects revived their revolutionary war under the leadership of Simon Bolivar in 1816. Bolivar had an unusual leadership quality in that he was able to organize a combined army which comprised men from different South American states. Bolivar defeated the Spanish army, created the Republic of Great Columbia in 1819, and became the First President of the Republic. Subseqently, New Granade, Panama, and Ecuador were liberated and brought under the Republic followed by almost the whole of Latin America. The combined revolutionary forces, under the leadership of Bolivar, captured Peru and to acknowledge the contribution of Bolivar to the freedom movement of South America, Peru was named Bolivia (1825).

To decide the policy of the Concert with regard to the Spanish question, both in its European and American manifestations, a Congress was summoned at Verona (1822). Canning, the English Foreign Secretary, made England's policy quite clear to the Concert: England was quick to grasp that if Ferdinand was restored to absolute authority on the Spanish throne, he might be tempted to re-establish his power over the Spanish colonies. Canning made it quite plain that though England had remained neutral during the European phase of the conflict, she would consult only her own interests if the American phase of the conflict developed. Canning found a powerful ally in the United States who found that the break away of the colonies was to her advantage. In 1823, President Monroe proclaimed to the Congress that the American continent was closed to further European colonization, and that the United States would consider it a manifestation of an unfriendly disposition if the allies made any effort to extend their political system into the New World. This attitude became known as the Monroe Doctrine (1823) and it was based on the principle that the American continent was meant only for Americans. Shortly thereafter, the independence of the colonies was recognized both by the United States and England. Thus, Metternich's attempts to dash out nationalist uprisings in the Spanish Colonies were countermanded by England and the United States. The liberation of the South American people and the birth of the Republican states indicated the triumph of nationalism and liberalism over conservatism and reaction.

THE GREEK WAR OF INDEPENDENCE

The Greek War of Independence, which began in 1820, brought the Eastern Question or more accurately the near Eastern Question to the surface. The problem was one of finding a successor to the Turkish power in the Balkans. In 1453, the Ottoman Turks had captured Constantinople. Towards the end of the seventeenth century, the Turkish power began to decline. In 1789, the Turks ruled over the whole of the Balkans Penninsula, south of the Danube, and the principalities of Moldavia and WalacMa. The Turkish Empire was huge in extent but it was fast decaying. The Ottoman Empire was very multicultural and contained many different religions and languages. The Turks never really attempted to incorporate their subject races into a compact empire. In the south were the Greeks, who boasted of their descent from the ancient Greeks. The Christians within the empire mostly belonged to the orthodox Greek faith which had separated itself as early as the tenth century from the Latin Christianity prevalent in western Europe. The Christians were sharply divided among themselves both racially and economically. As the Ottoman rule was declining, a serious power vacuum came to the surface marking the beginning of the problem of the Eastern Question.

Russia became interested in Turkish affairs due to geographical, racial, and religious factors. From the time of Peter the Great (1689–1725), Russia began to look westward and so there was a natural enmity between Russia and Turkey. Until the end of the eighteenth century, the European states believed that ultimately, European Turkey would be partitioned between Russia and Austria. However, in the nineteenth century, there arose new claimants in the form of the Christian nations in the Balkans—the Serbians, the Greeks, the Bulgarians, etc. The barrier of religion prevented the Turks from amalgamating with their Christian subjects. The most important nationalist revolt against the Sultanate of Turkey was that of the Greeks.

There were various causes behind the Greek War of Independence: first, as the Greeks had always been well-treated by the

Ottoman Government—several occupied superior administrative posts, and the Ottoman navy was controlled by them—there grew an educated middle class among the Greeks and it was they who started the Greek national revival. Second, towards the end of the eighteenth century, there began a literary renaissance which made the Greeks aware of their classical heritage. Third, though remote and backward, the Balkans were not completely unaware of Western influences. Their contact with French revolutionary ideas infused into them a new political consciousness. Fourth, although the Greeks were well-treated by the Turkish Government, they were not entirely free from racial discrimination particularly in matters relating to taxation or recruitment.

Thus, dissatisfaction with the existing state of things led the Greeks to form secret societies. The goal of such secret societies was to liberate the Greeks. The most powerful of these secret societies was the Hetairia Philike (the Association of Friends) which brought thousands of Greeks together and conducted a powerful propaganda for Greek independence. In 1821, the Greeks rose against the Sultan and the War of Independence began. During the early phase of their struggle they fought alone against the Turks but in the last two years they were helped officially by the European powers. The Greeks expected support from the Tsar, as he was the protector of the orthodox Christians living in the empire. The leader of the Greeks—Ypsilanti—was a General in the Russian army but the Tsar was persuaded by Metternich not to offer any help to the Greeks on the grounds that it was part of the 'universal organized spirit of insurrection'. The Western powers were not in favour of Greek ambition. Only the educated Europeans in different countries believed that it was a clash of civilizations.

As the Sultan felt he could not suppress the Greek rebellion alone, he appealed for help to Mehmet Ali in 1824, his viceroy in Egypt, who possessed a disciplined army and a powerful navy. Meanwhile, Russian public opinion took a radical turn in favour of the Greeks. Nicholas I and the British government signed the Protocol of St. Petersburg in 1826, agreeing that Greece should become an autonomous state tributary to Turkey. France also joined this accord. England, France and Russia now demanded, as per the Treaty of London, an armistice from the Sultan. They wanted to compel the Sultan to accept the terms of the Protocol or if he refused, to conclude the armistice.

In the naval battle at Navarin in 1827, the allied fleet destroyed the Turkish navy. England was embarassed by the destruction of the Turkish navy as it had been always her policy to support Turkey against Russia. England's primary aim was that Russia should not get the sole credit for liberating Greece while Russia took the opportunity to declare war against Turkey in collaboration with France. England, fearing that the new principality would become Russia's vassal, insisted upon Greece being created as an independent Kingdom. European power politics resulted in the creation of a small autonomous state for the Greeks. The boundaries of the new kingdom stopped at a line drawn from the Gulf of Volo to the Gulf of Arta and did not include Greek speaking districts in the north.

The European diplomats did not know that the newly created Balkan state would want to get rid of all control—whether Turkish or Russian. The spirit of nationalism, which was to influence Europe so profoundly in the nineteenth century, asserted itself for the first time in the Balkans. It was the Eastern Question that finally dissolved the Concert, for it could hardly offer any solution to the problem. The principalities of Moldavia and Wallachia became practically independent of Turkey in the Treaty of Adrianople and so they now became more exposed to Russian influence than ever before. Russian domination in the Near East became so prominent that Wellington announced that Turkish power in Europe no longer existed. The Greek War of Liberation brushed aside the three principles of the Congress of Vienna—Balance of Power, Legitimacy, and Compensation. It also demolished Metternich's ambition to return to the pre-revolutionary situation and negate the forces generated by the French Revolution of 1789. Herein lies the importance of the Greek War of Independence.

THE JULY REVOLUTION OF 1830 AND ITS IMPACT

The spirit of revolution took such deep root in France that a number of revolutions took place in that country subsequent to the great Revolution of 1789. In 1830, France witnessed a revolution popularly known as the July Revolution, which constitutes an important landmark in the history of modern Europe. In this context, a review of post-Napoleonic France in all her socio-economic implications is necessary. The Revolution of 1789 demolished the feudal structure of landholding and land passed into the hands of the peasants and peasant proprietors. Church property also met with a similar fate. Napoleon accepted this Revolutionary Settlement and left no scope for the recovery of land already distributed to the peasantry. This arrangement ushered in a great change in the social pattern of France.

As an outcome of the elimination of feudalism, an affluent and neo-peasantry emerged in the social spectrum. This group acquired considerable influence in their rural setup and became too strong to be ousted from their holdings. However, these neo-peasants who profited from the Revolution were apprehensive of dispossession in the event of a return to power by the Bourbons in France. So, when Louis XVIII was restored to the French throne in 1814, after the fall of Napoleon Bonaparte, these peasants viewed him with great suspicion even though he had recognized their individual rights. As the peasants had no franchise, they apprehended that the franchised section in the Assembly might injure their interests with new laws enacted in the Assembly. Hence, Louis XVIII began his reign at a disadvantage due to the distrust of the neo-peasant group which was growing into a considerable force.

It has to be admitted that the Industrial Revolution in France was a delayed process and came only after the Fall of Napoleon (1815). France lacked conditions necessary for such industrialization:

1.　In France, capital could not be properly exploited. Constant war expenses and lavish court luxuries forced capital to be loaned out to the state whereas in Britain, advancement in agriculture and expansion of trade multiplied British capital which was utilized in industrialization.

2. The forced enclosure system in Britain for sheep breeding precluded open field agriculture and dislodged many peasants from the land who then formed the core of the industrial labour force. France was basically an agricultural country and the peasants were attached to their land and so the labour force was not so strong.

3. England had its market in the colonies whereas France had lost many of her colonies by the eighteenth century. Though Britain had lost her thirteen colonies which formed the United States, she retained a wide empire yet France lacked a wider market.

4. The policy of protection followed by France was not conducive to industrial development.

5. France did not have a sizeable merchant navy like England.

6. Raw materials were abundant in Britain, especially coal, whereas France was not rich in coal which was essential for industrialization.

7. British entrepreneurs had an advantage as they could work or function spontaneously and free from state control. In France, state control was rigid and entrepreneurs had to work under constraints.

8. Scientific inventions in Britain created newer fields for industrialization but in the eighteenth century France was more engrossed in the Revolution. In spite of all these disadvantages, industrialization did take place in France after the Fall of Napoleon. Though the process was not so rapid and was comparatively narrow in scope, it gave rise to far-reaching social changes.

Industrialization in France enormously enhanced the economic prosperity of the bourgeois class. In pre-revolutionary France, the nobility enjoyed a superior position in society because of their aristocratic backgrounds and landed wealth. The Revolution snatched away their power and privileges. The bourgeoisie became the most prominent social grap and the post-Napoleonic period witnessed their phenomenal rise due to concentration of wealth in their hands. The upper bourgeoisie consisted of bankers, industrialists, and shipping magnates who were social climbers, preferring to establish matrimonial connections with the aristocrats in order to exalt their family background. The middle group consisted of the mercantile community while the petty bourgeois group was composed of people engaged in small trade or who were salaried people such as teachers, lawyers, professional men, and bureaucrats. This class was numerically superior.

Below this level were the urban labour force and the rural peasantry. Industrialization gave birth to a class of industrial labourers. The *sans-culottes* of the revolutionary days now came to be known as the *proletariat.*

The condition of the labourers in France was far from satisfactory for they had no trade union rights and strike was forbidden and so labour discontent was widespread. The rural peasantry was in a similar state and they were under the heels of the rural moneylenders and there was no law for their protection.

The period witnessed growth of new cities besides Paris and Versailles like Lyons, Avignon, and Orleans, and the concentration of population in these cities brought accompanying problems like shortage of accommodation, water scarcity, and health hazards. Simultaneously however, communication improved and distance posed no problem. It brought the French people of different places closer.

The Vienna Settlement of 1815, in its attempt to reject the French Revolution and the Napoleonic era as a mere interregnum in the monarchical establishment of France, confirmed the Restoration of Louis XVIII (1814–24), brother of ill-fated Louis XVI of the Bourbon dynasty, as the king of France. The restoration of the monarchical order and crowning of a Bourbon ruler however, did not signify, as was expected by the Vienna stalwarts, the restoration of the old regime. In fact, very little was restored except the Bourbon dynasty.

Like other Bourbon monarchs, he was a believer in the divine right theory, but his long exile had made him realize that the days of traditional rule and ignoring the people were over. This softened his attitude and made him relatively liberal, hence the new monarchy had a promising start. With an attitude of compromise and accommodation, he granted a Charter on 4 June 1814 to his people which promised a constitutional parliamentary regime.

According to this Charter:

1. The executive power was vested in the king and foreign policy, the signing of treaties, declaration of wars, and the appointment of ministers and officials were his prerogative.
2. The Legislative Assembly had the right to pass laws which were to be ratified by the king.
3. France was to have a bicameral legislature made up of: (a) the Council of Peers and (b) The Chamber of Deputies, which could enact or amend laws subject to royal assent.
4. Voting power was confined to a property qualification by which any person who paid a direct tax of 300 francs on property was eligible to vote.
5. The Code Napoleon and the principle of equality before law was recognized.
6. The revolutionary settlement was recognized.
7. Personal liberty and freedom of worship of the French people were also recognized.

Supposedly, the Charter limited the despotic power of the Bourbons but it was not without limitations: (1) Louis XVIII sought to fuse together the traditional concept of the divine right of kings and the new spirit of liberalism. It proved to be an uncomfortable blend. (2) According to the Charter, the ministers of the king were not responsible to the Legislative Assembly, so the Assembly had no control over the executive. (3) In the fresh elections the Moderates came to power led by Decazes and Guizot and their motto was to make royal of the nation and nationalization of the Crown. Under these Moderates, France entered into a new phase and their rule won the confidence of people. State finances were organized and annual budgets were prepared so. France was able to pay off her war indemnity. As a result, the Congress of Aix-la-Chapelle (1815) voted for the withdrawal of the allied army from

France and she was admitted to the Concert of Europe. France was at peace but this peace was to be a mere interval.

In 1820, a fanatic Republican named Louis Pierre Louvel murdered the Duke de Berry who was a nephew of Louis XVIII (son of Count of Artois, the younger brother of Louis XVIII), and therefore the future successor of the Bourbon monarchy. Aiming to eliminate monarchy this gave a severe blow to three years of progress. There was a great reaction against the moderates for their inefficiency to prevent such an incident in which the Ultra-Royalists were favoured by the people.

In 1821, therefore, a reactionary Ultra-Royalist ministry under Villele was formed. It undid the work of the Moderates. Taking advantage of Louis XVIII's illicit relation with Madame du Cyla, Villele was able to profoundly influence the King through this lady and started his policy of repression.

In order to restore the old Regime the following measures were adopted: (1) civil liberties were curtailed, (2) press censorship reimposed, (3) universities were brought under church control, and (4) franchise was restricted by a further increase in the property qualification so nearly three-fourths of the voters lost their franchise. In foreign policy, France moulded to the reactionary policies of the Concert of Europe and helped to crush the liberal movement in Spain (1823) and to suppress its Constitution. In 1824, Louis XVIII died and his policy of compromise fell into disuse since he was under the spell of the ultras and his death closed a chapter in the history of France.

On Louis XVIII's death in 1824, his brother the Duke of Artois ascended the throne with the title of Charles X (1824–30). The reactionary phase now attained new heights through his ruthless efforts to revive the *ancien régime*. Charles X's coronation contained elaborate rituals of the pre-Revolutionary era and signified early on his determination to revert France to the *ancien régime*. His reign witnessed a hardening of reactionary attitudes.

The Villele ministry formed during Louis XVIII's reign retained power until 1827. With the help of Villele Charles X adopted some reactionary steps:

1. Indemnity law, or the law of compensation, was passed in order to pacify the émigré nobles who had been dispossessed of their estates by the Revolution. To meet this colossal expenditure, he reduced the interest on government loans from 5 per cent to 3 per cent. This affected the income and profit of the upper bourgoisie and bankers hence they were infuriated. Political parties also resented this policy of compensation for the émigrés for they were considered traitors.
2. The importance of the clergy was highlighted and a bishop was brought in to head the educational department. Penalties for blasphemy (abusing religion) and sacrilege (non-reverence to religion) became more stringent. These measures hurt the anti-clerical sentiments of the bourgeoisie.
3. In 1827, the National Guard (the citizens militia organized in Paris after the Fall of Bastille, 14 July 1789 was disbanded.
4. New laws were passed on the succession question which emphasized the rule of primogeniture (property inheritance by the first born), thus making a mockery of the Revolutionary principle of equality.

Under tremendous pressure, this law had to be abandoned and Villele had to resign in 1828. The ministry of Jean Baptiste Gay, vicomte de Martignac lasted only for 2 years (1828–9) but he was a liberal among the moderates and it was his initiative that was responsible for the abandonment of the law of primogeniture. However, his liberalism was frowned upon by Charles X and he lost his power.

In 1829, Charles X brought Polignac, an ex-émigré, to power. He was very reactionary and was hated by Moderates and Liberals alike. A petition demanding his dismissal was submitted to the King and tension prevailed so the King dissolved the Chamber of Deputies. French elections were held in March 1830 and the Liberals won the majority. As the new chamber was more hostile, the King refused to summon the Chamber. Instead he issued four ordinances on 26 July 1830 known as July Ordinances. The July Ordinances contained moves: (1) to dissolve the Chamber of Deputies before it could meet, (2) to silence the press, (3) to revise the electoral law by which a large number of the bourgeoisie were defranchised, and (4) to annual the Charter of 1814. Such a reactionary move was furiously disapproved of by all the deputies and different political parties registered their protest.

Journalists such as Thiers, Mignet, and Carrel who were associated with *Le National* instigated the people to resist these ordinances which violated the fundamental rights granted by the Charter. Liberals joined with the journalists and the Parisian students played a significant role in this protest movement. Barricades were constructed and street fighting and near civil war ensued. When the situation was almost out of control, Charles X proposed to repeal the July Ordinances, but the decision came too late. Revolution broke out, the royal army was overpowered, and Charles fled on 30 July 1830, leaving the throne of France vacant. The self exile of Charles X during the Revolution, meant that a sort of revolutionary arrangement was needed and so the liberal deputies of the Chamber proclaimed Louis Philippe (1830–48), the Bank of Orleans as the new king. Louis Philippe I (1830–48) was a member of the secondary branch of the Bourbon family. His father, Philippe Égalité, was a cousin of Louis XVI, Louis XVIII, and Charles X but he was a Liberal and supported the execution of Louis XVI. His son Louis Philippe took an active part in the Revolution of 1789 and the capture of Bastille. He had no sympathy for the Bourbons and so the peoples' choice fell on him to be the head of state. Significantly, he was titled not the King of France but the King of the French by the will of the people. The white lily flag of the House of Bourbons was discarded in favour of the tricolour (the revolutionary flag bearing revolutionary nostalgia).

The dynasty also changed to an Orleanist dynasty instead of that of the Bourbons. In the new constitution some restraints were imposed on the royal power:

1. In the new constitution, reference to the divine right of kings was deleted.
2. The Charter no longer remained a voluntary gift of the king to the people but the king himself was bound by it.
3. Article 14 of the previous Charter (4 June 1814) which authorized the promulgation of the July Ordinances (26 July

1830) was discarded, signifying that no royal ordinances could override or flout the laws of the realm.

4. Catholicism, which had been described as the religion of France (or the state religion), became officially known as the religion of the majority of the people. This change paid homage to the secular ideals of the French Revolution.

5. The electoral laws were revised by relaxing property qualifications, even though a large majority were still deprived of voting rights.

6. The new constitution restored civil liberties and the freedom of the press.

7. Finally, it also reduced the personal expenses of the monarch.

Significance

The whole process that is known as the July Revolution of 1830 was fought and won not for the establishment of an extreme democracy or a republican government but to get rid of the aristocratic and clericalist attitude of the restored Bourbons. It aimed at creating a subtle balance between authoritarian and parliamentary systems, and in this respect, the Revolution bore close semblance to the Glorious Revolution of 1688 in England. The greatest significance of this revolutionary upsurge was that it proved the futility of both the Vienna Settlement of 1815 and the Concert of Europe, and it nullified the stagnant and artificial status which they tried to maintain in the name of the preservation of peace. Though the revolutionaries had not yet succedeed in dislodging the reactionary edifice created by Metternich, they gave an effective forewarning of the serious cataclysm that would ultimately topple the entire Metternich structure of repression.

The July Revolution and the Orleans monarchy which followed in its wake did not bring any radical change. Many scholars including Robinson and Beard, are reluctant to call it a real Revolution for the Revolution of 1830 made only a few innovations. Cobbani suggests that the July Revolution was essentially a conservative revolution. Though the Revolution was condemned and Louis Philippe was ridiculed as the 'King of the barricades', the great powers made no attempt to restore Charles X to the throne or to dislodge the revolutionaries. By implication, it proved the inherent strength of the Revolution. A great significance of the Revolution was its abruptness and speed for as there was no real civil war, the powers of Europe could not directly intervene. Equally, the entire episode caught them unaware and gave them no time to deliberate on a plan of action. From this angle it was a spectacular performance: the July Revolution destroyed the king-clergy-nobility axis; established the supremacy of the wealthy bourgeoisie, and gave Europe no time to intervene.

The Revolution created a reawakening of the masses. Political activities and discussions increased in societies and clubs and the labour force began to stir. The socialist doctrines of St. Simon were widely circulated during this time. The July Revolution was not confined to the geographical limits of France. H.A.L. Fisher has observed that: 'sparks from the Paris furnace flew fast and far and fell among the unsound timbers of the Congress of Europe'. It triggered repercussions in Belgium, Poland, Germany, and Italy. The independence of Belgium from Holland in 1831 was the first nationalist triumph to be effected by the influence of the July Revolution. Though reactionary forces triumphed in Poland, Germany, and Italy, the Revolution did shake conservative Europe with its new message of national and political awakening. Britain recognized the July monarchy and other powers could not venture to repudiate it. This Revolution profoundly influenced Britain and led to the Parliamentary reforms of 1832 which liberalized the franchise. This stir affecting other European countries was a revolution by itself.

Controversy Over the Issue of the Inevitability of the Revolution of 1830

On the issue of the inevitability of the July Revolution historians hold diverse views. The group led by David Thomson believes that the Revolution could have been averted. First, if Louis XVIII had had a successor of his calibre and temperament to hold the balance between the concept of the divine right of kings and constitutionalism, the situation would have been different. Louis

XVIII was flexible and capable of making compromises and so, in spite of difficulties he could keep the situation under control. However, he was succeeded by Charles X who was not elastic and who did not accommodate liberalism. His policies of stern repression naturally evoked antagonism among his subjects. The Revolution may be looked upon as the outcome of the failure of Charles X who wanted to set the clock of history back to pre-revolutionary France. Second, critics hold the opinion that the two oppositional or leftist parties, the Liberals and Radicals, were not yet so militant as to revolt against the monarch. They virtually accepted the restored Bourbon monarchy and the changes they desired were fairly modest. Had Charles X honoured the concessions granted by the Charter of 1814 and implemented the constitutional experiment formulated in the Charter, the question of a revolt would not have arisen. Instead, Charles X invited only trouble by his adament promulgation of the July Ordinances which revoked the fundamental rights granted by the Charter. So, the revolt, by implication, was forced on the people. Third, Charles X did not have the wisdom to foresee that the parliamentary government needed continuity and practice to allow healthy conventions to grow. By dissolving the elected Chamber by an ordinance he only aggravated the discontent of the people.

The other group of scholars, led by Cobban and Lipson, held that the July Revolution was inevitable and that nothing could have stopped it. Indeed it was a continuation of a historical process. First, they point out that the spirit of revolution kindled in 1789 could not have been suppressed by offering minor concessions here and there. Louis XVIII tried to patch up a compromise, but the concepts of divine right and constitutionalism were not compatible and there was too wide a gap between the monarch and the people. Second, the Charter which posed a restraint to royal absolutism and its inherent drawbacks still contained Article 14 of the Charter, which gave enormous power to the king to promulgate ordinances. The July Ordinances represent a misuse of Article 14 and so the potential for a revolution was already intrinsic to the political system. Third, France at that time had various shades of political opinion. The Ultra-Royalists were more royalist than the king and so an ultimate clash over the principles of power was inevitable. The July Ordinances only hastened the process. Fourth, the view that the Liberals were not a vibrant force does not bear scrutiny. In fact, they became a force to be reckoned with and they enlisted the support of the powerful student community of Paris and were aided by the journalists, who propagated ideas about the freedom of the press and speech, and greater curtailment of monarchical power. The Charter of 1814 was not acceptable to them and they were vocal in their protest. So in many ways, it was a clash of ideals which pushed France to the path of Revolution.

FEBRUARY REVOLUTION OF FRANCE (1848) AND ITS IMPACT

France at that time was divided into four major political parties:

1. The Ultra-Royalists, or extreme royalists composed of émigré nobles and resentful clergy who wanted the King to rule without the Charter and favoured absolute royal power.
2. The Radicals or Extreme liberals, comprising Republicans, Democrats, and Bonapartists who considered the Charter insignificant. They were in favour of a Republic in France and felt the need for labour welfare laws.
3. The Constitutionalists or Moderates, who were in favour of a policy of compromise within the framework of the Charter. The upper bourgeoisie and liberal nobles were the majority in this group.
4. The Liberals denounced the Charter as they considered it to be insufficiently liberal and wanted some modifications. The middle bourgeoisie were the members of this party. There were different phases when different parties came to power in the post-Napoleonic era.

From Monarchy to Republic

The July Revolution of 1830 was not an end but the beginning of a process in France which culminated in the February Revolutions of 1848. Louis Philippe made a dramatic start from the outset of his reign in the aftermath of the July Revolution of 1830. He displayed a liberal attitude but eventually he failed to keep tempo with the changing time and his conservative inclinations and dynastic ambitions were exposed.

The July monarchy was basically a partnership of the king and the middle class (which Karl Marx called 'the Joint Stock Company for the exploitation of France's national wealth'). This alienated other groups:

1.	The legitimists composed of old the clergy and nobility who were attached to the old institutions, and who considered Louis Philippe to be an usurper and representative of the bourgeoisie. They demanded the restoration of the Bourbons as the legitimate rulers.
2.	The Republicans who glorified the Republic of 1792 and criticized Louis Philippe for his alliance with the moneyed class at the cost of the common people. This period witnessed a spectacular rise in the support of the Republic. This perhaps was a contribution from the contemporary historical works of Jules Michelet and Lamartine (*History of Girondins*) which were strongly pro-Republic.
3.	The Catholics were excluded from all affairs.
4.	The Bonapartists wanted to revive the days of Napoleonic glory. Cultivation of Napoleonic legend was Louis Philippe's brainwave to gain popularity and this eventually went against his own interest.
5.	The Socialists emerged as a left-wing branch of the Republicans for industrialization took place in France after the fall of Napoleon and this gave impetus to socialist ideas. The Industrial Revolution in France was first mentioned by Adolphe Blanqui in 1837.

Due to industrialization in France, the factory system was coming into vogue. While wealth was flowing, the working class was suffering from low wages, and poor living and working conditions. The employers subjected them to strenuous labour in order to attain maximum profit at minimum cost. This creating the problem of capital and labour. Exploitation of women and child labourers pushed them below the subsistence level. These disparities led to strong criticisms of capitalism by theorists like St. Simon (1760–1825), Fourier (1772–1837), Proudhon (1809–65) and Louis Blanc. Proudhon and Louis Blanc exercised tremendous influence on the working class. Louis Blanc, the popular agitator emphasized in his book *The Organization of Labour*, that the state should foster co-operative factories and guarantee a modest wage to all workers. The State should provide work for all able-bodied citizens and protection and aid to the infirm and the disabled. The Socialists felt that their cause had no chance unless the July monarchy was overthrown as Louis Philippe and his bourgeois partners had no interest in the welfare of the working class.

Meanwhile consciousness grew among the workers through a variety of publications on the problems of the working community. Various societies like the Society of the Famines, the Society of Seasons, the Society of the Rights of Man, and others emerged. The working class gradually formed opinions and ideas and began to view the government with suspicion.

All these anti-monarchy groups were known as Parties of Movement while the Pro-monarchy group was called the Party of Resistance. The result was discontent and distrust between the groups and a series of sporadic uprisings. These may be classified into three distinct phases: (1) 1830 to 1836, (2) 1836 to 1840, and (3) 1840 to 1848.

During the first phase (1830–6), a revolt broke out in 1831 in the city of Lyon. It was a revolt of the silk-weavers against economic injustice as they were underpaid. Louis Philippe suppressed this revolt with the support of the bourgeoisie and their demand for a wage rise was turned down. Initially the Revolt of Lyon was not political, but the way in which it was suppressed brought unity among the labourers. Their resentment was directed not only against their employers but also against the government. These craftsmen gradually became involved in political agitations.

The city of Paris witnessed the next revolt in 1831 which was anti-clerical in nature. A violent mob attacked the cathedral of Notre Dame for the mood of the people of Paris was against the Church. This was also suppressed. In 1832 the Legitimists organized a revolt to depose Louis and place Charles X's grandson on the throne as the legitimate heir. It was however, a failure. In 1832 a republican revolt broke out but it was a miscalculated move and in 1835, an attempt was made to assassinate the king. That too was unsuccessful.

These revolts failed because they were sporadic in nature and there was no coordination among the opposition groups. They did however mirror the unpopularity of the Orleans monarchy. Consequently, the government became more repressive, censorship of press became more stringent, and publication of many leading papers was stopped. This only intensified popular indignation and began to pave the way for the collapse of the July monarchy.

During the second phase (1836–40), some sort of stability was restored to France. In 1836, Louis Napoleon, the nephew of Napoleon Bonaparte, made a futile attempt to seize the throne. In 1840 the Bonapartists again revolted but were suppressed even though it was clear that the Napoleonic legend had influenced a large section of people who then became active opponents of the Orlean monarchy. Even in his foreign policy Louis Philippe faced a crisis for the July Revolution of France had affected many European countries. He could not totally ignore the liberal movements out of fear of being labelled as a reactionary, nor could he annoy the monarchs of Europe whose recognition was necessary for stabilizing his position. Initially he gave support to the movement for the independence of Belgium but when the Belgians offered the crown to his son, the Duke of Nemours, he had to decline the offer due to British opposition. He also supported the liberal movements in Spain and Italy but from 1835, he geared French foreign policy to please Britain. The dull and tame foreign policy of Louis Philippe deprived France of the Napoleonic glory which still inspired the French. They were tired of the vacillating attitude of the government under British pressure.

The Anglo-French understanding broke down over the Spanish marriage. Louis Philippe, in order to enhance his prestige in the international field, wanted to establish matrimonial connections with Spain. Queen Isabella of Spain and her sister Louisa were both of marriageable age and so Louis Philippe wanted his son (the Duke of Montpensier) to be married to Louisa, sister of the Spanish ruler. Britain objected to this proposal for fear of a Franco-Spanish alliance and offered two conditions for the Franco-Spanish marriage. Marriage of Louisa to the French Prince could take place provided: (1) Isabella, the Spanish ruler was married first (preferably to a Spanish Bourbon prince), and (2) She had an heir to the throne. Louis Philippe agreed to this but later violated the agreement and Isabella and Louisa were married on the same day. Louis became unpopular among his people because of repeated failure in his foreign policy and the Anglo-French understanding broke down, leaving Louis Philippe isolated.

During the third phase (1840–8) Louis found in François Guizot a person to his liking. He was a reactionary and opposed all reformers. He ran the government by manipulating elections, bribing legislators, offering them posts and advantages, and turning down the demands for extension of the franchise. This narrow and corrupt government ran through an alliance between the King and the upper bourgeoisie for their mutual benefits irritated both the upper and working classes. The younger generation, acquainted as it was with the new forces, could not tolerate this reactionary regime that opposed all change. Discontent over repression at home and negative policy abroad intensified due to economic distress. The crop failures of 1846 and 1847 led to a rise in food prices and associated hardships. Demand for reforms thus gathered momentum.

In the words of Tocqueville, France 'at this moment was sleeping on a volcano'. It was the question of franchise that precipitated the crisis. Under the leadership of liberal leaders like Lamartine and Odilon Barrot, a campaign for parliamentary reforms was launched. Adolphe Thiers, who was the leading minister from 1832 to 1836 (and Prime Minister in 1840), organized a reform party within the Chamber, which demanded extension of the franchise and the elimination of office-holders from the Chamber of Deputies. Guizot turned down these demands. The reformists thus reacted by stirring public opinion through the press and organizing a series of 'large banquets' as forums for political discussion. Alarmed, Guizot prohibited political 'banquets'. A large 'banquet' was scheduled for 22 February 1848. The prohibition order complicated the situation and people took to the streets with the slogan 'down with Guizot'. Initially, the agitation was constitutional and demanded the dismissal of Guizot. Louis Philippe dismissed Guizot, but his soldiers shot at the agitators and this infuriated the mob to the point that violent riots broke out. Constitutional agitation against an unpopular minister now transformed into a movement for the abolition of the monarchy in favour of a Republic. Louis Philippe tried to pacify the people but failing, he left for England on 24 February 1848, abdicating in favour of his grandson.

The Republicans and Socialists proclaimed France a Republic on 24 February 1848 and ordered fresh elections to the Assembly which was to frame a new constitution. Within a span of just 18 years, France was transformed into the Second Republic (1848–52) with great rapidity and in the context of many precipitating circumstances. However, it did not last long and became a transient phase before the formation of the Second Empire (1852–70).

Course of the 1848 Revolution

The February Revolution of 1848 made France a republic. The government was dominated by La Martine, the Republican leader, and Louis Blane the Socialist. Very soon dissensions arose between the two political groups. The Republicans were satisfied with the abolition of the monarchy but the socialists and the turbulent elements in the Parsian mob wanted to reorganize the society on a socialist model.

Under pressure from Louis Blanc, national workshops were established where the unemployed were guaranteed work by the state. However, they were not managed properly and the government engaged the workmen in unproductive tasks. The scheme did not succeed and it was not favoured by the republicans. They became objects of ridicule. The rift further widened over the election of the Constituent Assembly in April 1848. It had an overwhelming Republican majority and the socialists were thrown into the background. The Republican-dominated Assembly refused to create a Minister of Labour which infuriated the labour force so in May, they attacked the Assembly and had to be suppressed by the National Guards. The government closed the national workshops and the workmen were given the alternative either to join the army or the projects of public work: they declined both.

The anti-socialist bloc was further strengthened as the peasantry joined the republicans. On 22 June 1848, Paris again became a centre of mob violence and fierce fighting took place for three movement was the Frankfurt Parliament, the first National Parliament of the German speaking people of Central Europe. It was the result of the revolutionary democratic nationalism of 1848. Eventually, however, the old Federal Constitution was restored and Germany made a humiliating surrender to Austria.

In 1848 revolution broke out in all parts of the Austrian dominions. The Hapsburgs had to deal with nationalist and democratic revolutions in Vienna, Italy, and Hungary. Metternich fled to England and the Emperor abdicated. However, one by one the revolutionary movements collapsed and were suppressed. The Hungarian revolt was suppressed with the help of Russia. Nevertheless, the 1848 Revolutions were a step forward in the direction of democracy and freedom in Europe.

THE SECOND EMPIRE IN FRANCE: LOUIS NAPOLEON

Napoleon III or Louis Napoleon Bonaparte, was the son of Louis Bonaparte who was a brother of Napoleon Bonaparte. Exiled from France in 1816, he lived in Switzerland, Italy, and Germany. He joined the Italian Revolutionary Society of the Carbonari in 1831 and participated in the insurrection against the Pope. Then, he turned his attention to formulate his political theories and started writing articles. He made two premature attempts—in 1836 and in 1840—to seize the French throne. He was also imprisoned for six years but finally managed to escape in 1846. Then came the Revolution of 1848 when Louis Philippe was overthrown and the Republic was established in France. Louis Napoleon was elected to the Assembly and shortly thereafter, he became the President of the Republic. Within a period of four years he became Emperor of France and he continued to hold this position until 1870. Napoleon III rose to power by taking advantage of the Bonapartist sentiments of the French people. The autocratic reaction during the reigns of Louis XVIII and Charles X served to remind the French people of the good brought by revolutionary age, when Napoleon had offered them equality. The low profile and inglorious foreign policy of Louis Philippe stood in sharp contrast to that of Napoleon Bonaparte. Napoleon III was therefore able to capitalize on the legend of the previous Emperor to rule the French people.

Napoleon III cautiously enlisted the support of all political and social groups in the state during the four years of his presidency of the French Republic (1848–52). In 1852, he assumed autocratic power by a *coup d'état* and then a national plebiscite which confirmed him as the Emperor. His internal policy, though autocratic, was generous and enlightened. He was proud to declare that his empire rested on the vote of all French men and that liberalism was the main pillar of his governmental system. He always encouraged the labour force to believe that he was one of them. He initiated social legislation for the first time in France. He also patronized the capitalists and businessmen by introducing a policy of free trade and by stimulating both industry and commerce. After 1860, the autocratic character of his regime gradually made way for liberalism and an attempt was made to introduce a parliamentary form of government.

His foreign policy however, was a failure and it contributed to the fall of the Empire. During 25 years of his reign, he participated in four great wars. He made a good beginning with the Crimean War which gave him victory as well as prestige but his Italian policy was timid and ungenerous. He tried in vain to establish a subservient Roman Catholic empire in Mexico. Finally, in his dealings with Bismarck, he betrayed his own inability to cope with that great diplomat and the result was defeat in the Franco-

German war and the fall of the Second Empire. His neutrality at the Battle of Sadowa proved to be suicidal in the long run and finally, his defeat at the Battle of Sedan (1870) against Prussia brought about the end of the Second Empire.

The reasons that led to the failure of Napoleon II are obvious:

1. His character was not strong enough to bear the great pressures of rule for he was by nature cautious.
2. His policy was only piecemeal to stave off immediate problems.
3. During the last leg of his reign, these character defects were intensified by sickness.
4. In spite of his effort to conciliate all segments of the French people, he never succeeded in gaining the full support of any strong party in the state.
5. It was a misfortune that he had to deal with a man of Bismarck's stature, for he was a statesman able to bring the whole of Europe to its knees.

HIGHLIGHTS

- After the fall of Napoleon Bonaparte, the leaders of Europe met at the Congress of Vienna (1815) and sought to reorganize Europe. The diplomats embarked upon a project to suppress nationalism and liberalism. They followed three major principles: (1) Legitimacy, (2) Balance of Power, and (3) Compensation.
- Metternich, the Austrian Minister, presided over the Congress and became its guiding spirit. His policy was conservative and reactionary and his sole aim was to revive peace in Europe.
- The ideas of the Vienna Settlement were challenged by the Spanish colonists of Latin America. The second important threat to the ideas preached by Metternich came in the form of the Greek struggle.
- France became the power house of revolution in Europe. The July Revolution of 1830 sealed the fate of the Bourbon monarchy forever. After the February Revolution of 1848, France became a republic for the second time.
- Louis Napoleon became the President of the Second French Republic. Later he became an Emperor and assumed the title of Napoleon III. His reign came to an end in 1870.

MEMORABLE DATES AND EVENTS

1814	Foundation of Hetairia Philike
1815	Congress of Vienna
1819	Carisbad Decree
1824	Formation of Great Republic of Columbia
1827	Accession of Charles X to the throne
1829	Naval Battle of Navarino
1830	Treaty of Adrianople
1848	July Revolution
1852	February Revolution
1870	Foundation of the Second Republic of France
	The Foundation of the Second Empire in France
	Battle of Sedan
	Fall of Louis Napoleon

MEMORABLE PERSONALITIES

Metternich: Chancellor or Prime Minister of Austria, leader of the European Union which emerged in the Congress of Vienna

Alexander I: Tsar of Russia. He represented Russia in the Vienna Congress

Talleyrand: He represented France in the Congress of Vienna

Castlereagh: Foreign Minister of Britain, the English diplomat at the Vienna Congress

Ypsilanti: Leader of the Greek War of Independence

Louis XVIII: King of France

Charles X: King of France

Louis Philippe: King of France at the time of February Revolution of 1848

Louis Napoleon: He became Emperor of France and assumed the title of Napoleon III

QUOTABLE QUOTES

- 'The Congress of Vienna was one of the most important diplomatic gatherings in the history of Europe, by reason of number, variety and gravity of the questions presented and settled.' —HAZEM
- 'It would be wrong to blame the makers of the settlement for failing to appreciate the power of nationalism and liberalism which few understood in 1815.' —THOMPSON

- 'He [Metternich] could swim like a fish in the sparkling whirlpool of Vienna.'   —KETELBEY
- 'The fundamental weakness of Metternich's famous system was that it only retarded, it could not avert the day of reckoning .'

  —GRANT AND TEMPERLY
- 'The foundation of the European states system of the nineteenth century was laid at Vienna by the monarchs and plenipotentiaries who assembled there by agreement after the defeat of Napoleon to dispose of the lands which had been surrendered and to resettle a disturbed continent.'   —D.M. KETELBEY
- 'In making the adjustments, it can be said that the diplomats troubled themselves much with principles. They deluded themselves with the idea that the French Revolution had been nothing but a passing storm, and if the fabric of Europe were re-built a little stronger, on the old foundation, it could resist such storm in future'.   —T.W. RICKER
- 'The Concert of Europe had gone to pieces on many rocks chiefly [but] on Great Britain's withdrawal and in the mutual jealousies of the powers.'   —D.M. KETELBEY
- 'The Revolution of July (1830) is notable as the act of a single city. Paris decided the fate of France. Before the royalists in the provinces had time to open their eyes, the issue was decided against the White Flag at the Paris barricades.'   —H.A.L. FISHER
- 'The revolution which most people seemed to want but no one seemed to expect, finally occurred. In February 1848, economic stress, combined with political agitation, easily overthrew a regime that in the end proved singularly hollow and the King, like his unlamented predecessor, took the road to exile. A few seemed to want his infant grandson, a republic was proclaimed.'   —T.W. RICKER

CHAPTER 4

The Second Phase of the Industrial Revolution

INTRODUCTION

Historians disagree as to the chronology of the Industrial Revolution in Britain. Some scholars think that the second phase of the Industrial Revolution began in 1815. Eric Hobsbawm (*Industry and Empire*) however, has identified the period between 1840 and 1895 as the second phase of the English Industrial Revolution. During the first phase, the main pillar of industrialization was cotton textiles and the Industrial Revolution primarily centred round this particular industry. The age of cotton textiles lasted until the first half of the nineteenth century and thereafter, the focus shifted to capital goods industries like coal, iron, steel, etc. With the arrival of the 'iron age', England entered into a fresh era of industrialization. The first phase of the Industrial Revolution was, by and large, labour intensive, whereas, the second phase saw a more capital intensive system of production. The pace of industrialization was faster in the second phase and its impact could now be felt all over Europe.

THE SWITCH OVER TO THE SECOND PHASE OF INDUSTRIALIZATION

In the words of Eric Hobsbawm, 'Whoever says Industrial Revolution says cotton.' Of course Hobsbawm admits that the British Industrial Revolution was by no means only based on cotton and indeed cotton lost its primacy after a couple of generations. Yet, cotton was the initial pacemaker of industrial change. It expressed a new form of society-industrial capitalism, based on a new form of production: the factory. W.W. Rostow has acknowledged that the cotton industry was 'the original leading sector' in the 'first take off'. The three major inventions which revolutionized and mechanized the cotton industry were: (1) James Hargreave's spinning jenny invented in 1764 and patented in 1770, (2) Richard Arkwright's waterframe, patented in 1769, and (3) Samuel Crompton's spinning mule, patented in 1779. The three inventions removed the serious limitations of traditional cotton production in England and fostered a new system of production. They laid the foundations of a large scale factory industry and the way was opened to the development of new products suitable for a mass market. Spinning began to be concentrated hereafter in factories and weavers could now rely on constant supplies of yarn. Within a quarter of a century, cotton manufacturing became one of the most significant industries in England. By 1802, it probably accounted for between 4 and 5 per cent of the national income and by 1812 this had risen to between 7 and 8 per cent. Many explanations have been offered by economic historians for this remarkable breakthrough in the cotton industry. The progress of the cotton industry was spectacularly rapid. By the end of the eighteenth century, it had added over $5 million to national income and a similar amount to the declared value of exports. However, the cotton textiles industry was more labour intensive unlike the heavy capital goods industries which flowered in the second phase.

P. Deane suggests that the most important reason for the ability of the cotton industry to maintain its profit was that it enjoyed an almost continuous flow of cheap labour. One explanation for the early success of the cotton industry was that the final product was not so new that it had to create its own demand through changing tastes. Indian calicoes and muslins had long been in active demand in the markets served by British merchants.

The textiles industry was transformed with organization and technology and domestic handicraft manufacturing gradually changed into capitalist factory industry. The British iron industry also underwent a technological transformation in the last quarter of the eighteenth century. It began to be able to satisfy a long established need with the production of commodity so different in quality and price from what had previously been produced in

Britain, that, it was virtually a new industry. Iron was primarily a producer's good rather than a consumer item and in the last quarter of the eighteenth century, iron began to be used widely in construction work. However, it was not until the middle of the nineteenth century, when the demand for iron and steel to construct railroads, locomotives, machinery and gas and sanitation systems greatly expanded, that the demand for iron and steel could escalate the industry to a revolutionary extent. Until the arrival of the railways and until machinery came to be applied on a large scale, all over Europe, iron could not form the core of industrialization. The switch-over from cotton to iron took place most distinctly from the 1840s. This period also marked the beginning of various other capital goods industries including coal, transport, and railroad. The growing demand for capital goods prepared the ground for the second phase of the Industrial Revolution.

The iron industry created waves of progress in various other industrial sectors through 'backward and forward linkages' (Rostow). By 'backward linkages' Rostow meant the demand for raw materials, including mining and the processing of iron ore. Regarding the 'forward linkages', the iron industry, which supplied a cheap and useful industrial material, gave birth to new possibilities in iron manufacturing. In the engineering industry, it was used for the production of railways, armaments, telegraph poles, and various precision tools for example.

The First Industrial Revolution had enabled the British capitalists to accumulate a huge amount of capital. This capital was now in search of new avenues for investment. No more investment in the cotton industry was possible as it had already reached its optimum level. Moreover, the textile industry was incapable of absorbing much capital as it was basically labour intensive in nature rather than capital intensive. The growth of the iron and steel industries and the heavy capital goods industries now enabled the capitalists to freely invest the accumulated capital, which was ready for deployment: a further explanation for the beginning of the second phase of the Industrial Revolution in the mid-nineteenth century (apart from the technological breakthroughs in the iron industry).

Between 1830 and 1850, it has been estimated that approximately 6,000 miles of railways were opened in Britain. This was mostly the consequence of two extraordinary bursts of concentrated investment followed by construction: (1) the 'little railways mania' of 1835–7 and (2) the 'gigantic railway mania' of 1845-70. Railway construction at home was followed by the construction of railways abroad using British capital, materials, and equipment. Coal was indispensable for railway locomotion and so the railway brought about a quick expansion in the coal mining industry. The construction of railway systems up until the 1870s led to worldwide economic activity. Railways helped to shape a new world economy in which Britain for many years lay at the centre. The manufacture of precision tools in various capital goods industries also brought about a high rate of standardization in production.

Nineteenth century industrialization may have been started by the late eighteenth century textile innovations, but continuous industrialization would have been inconceivable without the steam engine and the tenhnological progress in the iron, steel, and other capital goods industries. Even today, as P. Deane (*The First Industrial Revolution*) says, underdeveloped countries are inclined to see the establishment of the steel industry as an initial step out of economic stagnation.

Results of the Second Phase in Britain

The results of the second phase of the Industrial Revolution may be briefly summed up as follows:

1. The production of heavy goods industries like coal, iron, and steel increased to a very great extent.
2. The expansion of those industries created new employment opportunities in Britain. Coal mining in particular, generated employment.
3. With the development of heavy goods industries, a new class of skilled workers and mechanics was born.
4. The transport network between the different countries of Europe was strengthened by the coming of railways and

steamships. International trade reached new heights and England became the 'workshop of the world'.

5. British capital found its way to other countries of the world and British capitalists began to invest their capital and technical knowledge in different corners of the globe.

6. The heavy goods industries were capital intensive in character and this led to the tendency to form joint stock companies to avoid individual risk.

7. There was a great exodus of rural labourers to the cities in search of employment. As agriculture was unable to absorb the unemployed population, they looked to the growing industrial cities for employment, thus multiplying the population of the cities. New industrial cities like Manchester, Liverpool, and Leeds were born.

8. Rapid urbanization brought various problems to the surface like public health, housing, sanitation, water supply, etc.

9. The advanced technology of the Industrial Revolution solved the problem of production.

It generated new wealth in society but, this new wealth went chiefly in one direction: to the purses of an elite minority. Thus, the problem of distribution remained and the gulf between the rich and the poor widened during this final phase of the Industrial Revolution. The increasing inequality led to a chain of reactions in society. One such reaction manifested in the growth of socialism.

INDUSTRIALIZATION IN THE CONTINENT

England was the country which experienced the Industrial Revolution first. She became the 'workshop of the world', the whole of England became dotted with factories and new industrial cities came into existence. Industrialization however, did not remain confined to England alone. Other European countries like France, Germany, and Russia went through a similar process. Europe reached the climax of its material development with world supremacy in industrial production. The basic spark was the Industrial Revolution which had began in the seventeenth century in England which later spread to Western and Central Europe, but the process of industrialization varied from one country to another. The differences between the different nations in the degree of industrialization, gradually fostered a spirit of national rivalry among them. Every European nation tried to surpass the others in developing its machine industries, exploiting its natural resources, stimulating its trade, both domestic and foreign, and increasing the social security and purchasing power of its citizens. Economic nationalism thus became the order of the day everywhere in Europe and it brought with it tariff wars, colonial rivalry, and exploitation of the underdeveloped countries of the world. This economic nationalism appeared in its most aggressive form in Germany during the decades following 1870.

France

Industrialization in France was delayed by the political disorder which stemmed from the Revolution. The earliest industrialization effort in France can however be traced back to the time of Napoleon Bonaparte although Napoleon's attempt to deprive England of her world market by imposing the Continental System met with limited success. There is a debate as to the exact dating of the French Industrial Revolution. According to a well known American economist, the process of industrialization in France took off between the Vienna Congress (1815) and the February Revolution (1848), but the French Industrial Revolution was not in its full blast until 1860. The Industrial Revolution proper started during the reign of Louis Philippe (1830–48), for he patronized the French capitalists, brushing aside the interest of the working classes. To protect the nascent French industries he restructured the tariff system to keep foreign manufactured products away from the French market. It was during the reign of Louis Philippe that the railroad first made an appearance in France. In 1837, the first steps in this direction were made when Paris was connected with a nearby city. Apart from the railroad, the communication network as a whole was strengthened by constructing new roads and bridges. It helped to facilitate the movement of commodities and to create a national market.

The pace of industrialization in France was quickened with the arrival of Napoleon III. The railroad network was enlarged and between 1850 and 1870, 10,000 miles of railroad were constructed. Napoleon III also inspired the private business initiative of many leading French families. The Bank of France, too, owed its origin to the efforts of this ruler. As a result of the growth of the railroad, other capital goods industries like coal, iron, and steel, received new encouragement, while French textiles, silks, and perfume became world-famous. The reign of Napoleon III also saw the beginning of various programmes for the welfare of the working class.

By 1870, France held second place in the global export trade. However, French industrialization had suffered from three major limitation from the beginning:

1. France had been predominantly agrarian in temperament. This attachment to agriculture made the pace of French industrialization very slow.
2. France had a scarcity to coal which limited the scope of internal expansion.
3. The political unrest of the revolutionary period had also delayed the coming of the Industrial Revolution in France.

Germany

The period between 1871 and 1914 is particularly important in the history of Germany. Germany made great progress in the industrial field during these years. It has been rightly pointed out that during the 30 years following the unification of Germany in 1871, Germany achieved what England had previously done in the course of a century. The Industrial Revolution in Germany was helped by British, French, and American influences, but by 1913 Germany had outstripped all other European nations and emerged as the most powerful rival of England and the United

States in terms of world trade, banking, insurance, and shipping. This industrial progress of Germany was fostered by several factors:

1. The political unification of the country under Bismarck gave a great impetus to German industry and trade.
2. The acquisition of Alsace-Lorraine from France in 1871 also helped the industrial growth of Germany because the region was very rich in iron ore and had a developed textiles industry.
3. The patronage of German banks, which directly participated in the management of industries.
4. The excellent quality of German human resources also contributed to the Industrial Revolution.
5. The extension of railways, waterways, and postal and telegraphic communications also aided industrial growth.

The coal and iron industry of Germany made a phenomenal progress after 1871. The British economist, Keynes, has observed that the German empire was built more truly on coal and iron than by blood and iron. There were enormous coal deposits in the Rhineland, Westphalia and Silesia. Iron ore was abundant in Silesia and Alsace-Lorraine. The annual output of coal in Germany increased from 29 million metric tons in 1871 to 191 million metric tons in 1913. Similarly, the output of pig iron increased from 1.5 million metric tons in 1871 to 19 million metric tons in 1913. Germany thus outstripped England in the production of pig iron, and stood second only to the United States. This tremendous increase in the output of coal and iron was reflected in the expansion of industry in general, and it increased specialization in iron and steel products. This helped to build up the German railroad system and to create one of the finest merchant fleets in the world. It also helped to expand the arms and ammunition industry. Among other industries which developed during this period, the automobile industry, chemical and electrical industry, and the textile industry are also noteworthy. This process of industrialization in Germany was accompanied by a rapid population growth increasing urbanization and a great expansion of Germany's world trade.

Russia

It was not until the mid-nineteenth century that the Industrial Revolution in Russia could make headway. Industrialization in Russia started properly after the accession of Tsar Alexander II to the throne in 1855. In 1861, he abolished serfdom in Russia which helped industrialization as the freed serfs could offer their services to the capitalists. Many took up employment as industrial workers in the factories. The coming of the railroad in Russia quickened the base of industrial development and coal mining and the iron industry developed, centring round the construction of the railroad. Russian industrialization continued during the reign of Tsar Nicholas II. From the 1890s, the Russian authorities concentrated on the problem of capital shortage and encouraged the industrialists to look for foreign loans.

The golden age of Russian industrialization was the period between 1890 and 1913. By 1914, more than 2,000 million roubles had been invested in industries. Russian banking too, flowered between 1890 and 1914. This period also witnessed a tremendous growth in the heavy capital goods industries, including iron and steel. Therefore, much before the Bolshevik Revolution of 1917, Russia had become industrially quite advanced.

Other Countries

Among other nations of Europe which experienced considerable industrial growth in the nineteenth century, mention may be made of the Netherlands, Belgium, and Italy. Industrial progress in Belgium owed its origin to the patronage of the English capitalists. Both the Netherlands and Italy also became industrially advanced. The nineteenth century saw the development of heavy capital goods industries including iron, steel, coal and the railroad in these countries. Spain, Sweden, Austria, and Poland also underwent, a similar process at about the same time but all were to a lesser extent than the countries mentioned above.

THE WORKING CLASS MOVEMENT

The period branded as the era of the Industrial Revolution was essentially a period of transformation. It marked the beginning of the final phase of the broader transformation from feudalism to capitalism and capitalism made its presence felt all over Europe. In the capitalist mode of production the factories and heavy machineries were owned and controlled by the capitalist class. A definite polarization of industrial society between two main classes—capitalists and workers—was visible. Actual production in the factories was done by the workers but the workers had very little and so for survival, they were required to continuously sell this labour power for wages. This wage was however, not enough to keep the worker properly clothed or fed and thus, the Industrial Revolution could not solve the problem of distribution. The new wealth produced by advanced technology chiefly went to inflate the economic power and wealth of the capitalists and so the gulf between the rich and the poor widened. Out of this disparity between the rich and the poor sprang disputes between labour and capital, and many socio-economic problems came to the fore. Thus, the Industrial Revolution evoked a chain of reactions at various layers of the society. One such reaction was the growth of socialism as a direct challenge to capitalism, which sought to put an end to an economic structure which permitted the coexistence of extremes of poverty and plenty.

According to Engels (*The Condition of the Working Class in England*) the new factories like 'pyramids', which conveyed the story of mans' 'enslavement'. At the beginning of the Industrial Revolution in England, factory life was very tough. Women and children were made to work 12 to 16 hours a day in poor working conditions and with severe disciplinary measures. Employers preferred to employ women and children as their wages were less than men but wages generally paid to the labourers were very low. Advocates of *laissez-faire* economics maintained that it was not the duty of the government to intervene between the employers and employees. In 1799, the Combination Act was passed prohibiting the formation of trade unions in England. It forbade the establishment of any union of workers which might try to decrease working hours or increase wages. As England was the first country in the world to experience the Industrial Revolution, the English working class were the first to experience the hardships of industrialization.

In the early phase of the English Industrial Revolution, life was made particularly difficult for those workers, who for economic reasons, were completely at the mercy of their employers. In unskilled work and in trades where skilled artisans were threatened by the introduction of machinery, workers would frequently resort to violence. For those working in the declining handicraft trades, the violence culminated in organized machine-breakings in 1812–14 of mechanized looms when the demand for manufactures was restricted by Napoleon's Continental System. This is known in history as the Luddite Movement. It is derived from the name of Ned Ludd above whose signature a declaration was issued announcing the intention of the Nottingham framework knitters to break and destroy the new machinery of the lace trade although various acts of machine-breaking both preceded and followed this declaration. The Luddite Movement was an essential stage on the road towards a working class consciousness. Although the Luddite Movement was crushed by the authorities, it paved the way for the next stage of the working class agitation in England.

The Luddite Movement raised new questions in the minds of the radical intellectuals of the time. A need was felt to reform the existing combination laws against trade laws. The Combination Act of 1824 finally repealed all previous statutes concerning trade unions and declared that trade unions would no longer be treated as illegal. The legality of the working class unions was further enhanced by the Combination Act of 1825.

These legislations brought trade unions into existence for the trade unionists were no longer considered to be 'outlaws'. Until the passing of the Acts of 1824 and 1825, trade unions had been operating secretly but hereafter, they were allowed to negotiate openly with the employers regarding the wages, service conditions, etc., of the workers. The early phase of trade unionism in England did not bring much relief for the workers. During this period the individual unions were too preoccupied with their own regional conflicts to spare much thought for building up a wider national organization. The trade union movement declined by the 1830s and the working class became temporarily disinterested in the movement.

The working class, disenchanted with trade unionism, now sought to bring about political reforms through the Chartist Movement. Chartism was the campaign for democratic rights which swept over Britain between 1838 and 1848. The movement stands as one of the significant landmarks in the history of radicalism and marked a period during which working class radicals took over leadership from the middle class reformers. William Lovett, the founder of the London Working Men's Association, and Francis Place drew up the 'People's Charter' as the political programme of this movement. This Charter included a radical programme of six demands for political reform. The demands taken together aimed at the democratization of the franchise and major voting reforms. The Charter became the general rallying point for the discontents of the working class. Coming during a period of grave economic crisis and mass unemployment, the call for the Charter fired the imagination of the English working class. Engels declared that the Charter was 'sufficient to overthrow the whole English constitution, Queen and Lords included'.

The Chartist Movement took on greater dimensions in 1848, the year of revolutions in Europe and also of trade depression. The Chartists however, could not cope with the coercion of the state power and in 1848, when the movement flared up for the last time, the demonstrators were ruthlessly suppressed by soldiers under the command of Duke of Wellington. The full strength of Chartism lay in the North, among the handloom weavers and stockingers, who were suffering as a result of industrialization and whose only hope lay in the passionate denial of industrialism. The Chartist Movement was also the first working class attempt to build a broad national party with their own well-formulated demands. V.I. Lenin commented: 'England was giving the world the first broad, truly mass and politically clear-cut proletarian revolutionary movement'. Chartism left a permanent mark on the democratic tradition of England. It generated a new national consciousness and social awareness about the evils of industrialization. After Chartism had petered out, there was again a resurgence of the trade union movement in the 1850s. There began a long period of industrial expansion and economic growth during which trade unionism entered a phase of steady expansion and consolidation. The unions formed during the 1850s are often referred to as the New Model Unions and such unions were meant for the more skilled sections of the working classes.

With the rapid progress of industrialization in Europe, working class agitation became fairly regular in other countries of Europe too. Both in France and Germany, an organized working class movement came to the surface by the mid-nineteenth century. However, such movements were underground for the right to organize working class societies was not acknowledged in France or Germany until the last quarter of the nineteenth century. The working class movement reached a new height in Europe with the growth of socialist ideas.

SOCIALISM

One of the most important forces in the modern world, socialism was a direct result of the Industrial Revolution. The Industrial Revolution solved the question of production. It generated new wealth but as this new wealth only went to a minority, it could not solve the question of distribution. The gulf between the 'haves' and 'have-nots' continued to increase and out of this gap between the rich and the poor sprang disputes. Socialism was a direct challenge to capitalism and sought to put an end to an economic structure such as exploitative.

The development of the factory system produced certain evils such as bad housing, very limited education, excessive labour, among many other poor living and working conditions. On the other hand, the development of the factory system meant the simultaneous development of the capitalist system, upon which it rested. The presence of capitalists and labourers represents an unequal division in the world of industry. While the condition of the capitalists gradually improved, that of the workers deteriorated. So instead of being complementary, capitalism and labour became two antagonistic forces. It is this struggle between capitalism and labour which is known as socialism.

There are various stages in the growth of socialism. First came the intellectual phase, of which the utilitarians—Jeremy Bentham, James Mill, and John Stuart Mill—were the prophets. It was followed by the Utopian phase of which Robert Owen in England and St. Simon and Charles Fourier in France were the greatest upholders. The Utopian socialists however, could not suggest any convincing method for eradicating capitalism. The idea advocated by Robert Owen for example, was essentially non-violent and cooperative socialism but such ideas evaded the realities of political power, and bypassed the question of property rights. Utopian Socialism aimed simply to dislodge capitalism without any encounter. The Utopian Socialists however, anticipated many of the ideas later preached by Karl Marx and so Marxism did not develop in a void: Marx has his forerunners among the Utopian Socialists.

Marxian Socialism

Karl Marx was born in 1818 in Prussia and was educated in Germany. Marx was the founder of modern scientific socialism. He put forward his theory of scientific socialism in his *Communist Manifesto* (1848). Marxian Socialism has four important features:

1. It rests upon the economic interpretation of history. In other words, according to the theory, economic conditions have determined the entire course of history, and history is but the record of economic conditions and the institutions and ideas to which they have given birth.
2. According to Marxists, the conflict between capitalists and wage-earners is but a phase of the age-long economic struggle between social classes. History is but the progressive record of this desperate and destructive struggle of classes and primarily between employers and labourers.

3. Socialist belief in the inevitability of a social revolution is the third feature of Marxian Socialism. This is the idea that when there is a society divided not into several classes but only into two, and those two are sharply differentiated by increasing disparities in the distribution of wealth, then there can be only one outcome—a social revolution. This polarization of the society, Marx held, would occur only in a capitalist society where extreme forms of poverty and plenty co-exist. The working class, or proletariat, would unite against the bourgeoisie and seize power.

4. One of the most important characteristics of Marxian Socialism is its international character: 'Proletariats of all countries, unite' (Marx). The idea that all socialists are brothers or comrades rings through the Communist Manifesto and it clearly reflects the international character of the socialist movement.

In the revolutionary theory of Karl Marx, another important aspect is the concept of the state. In traditional bourgeois political thinking, the state is regarded as a natural and necessary institution because it is necessary for men's moral and material development. Marx however holds that state has never been, and can never be a corporate community aiming at the common good. Instead, he argues, that it has always been, and shall always remain an organization by which the dominant economic class rules over and exploits the non-ruling class. The *Communist Manifesto* describes the state to be the 'executive committee' of the bourgeoisie. Engels defines it as nothing more than a machine of oppression of one class by another. Marx's main interest lay in the sphere of political economy. His work, *Das Capital*, delineated these ideas in three volumes: volume I, published in 1867; volume II, published by Engels in 1885; and volume III, published in 1894. The creation of Marxist political economy laid the scientific basis for communism and so the philosophical impact of *Capital* is beyond doubt. In these works, Marx comprehensively developed the major aspects and principles of Marxist philosophy and applied them to the study of the capitalist system of economic relations. Lenin and his disciples and followers developed Marxism further under new historical conditions in Russia and it was embodied in the victory of socialist revolutions in a number of countries. It now furnishes the scientific foundations for the activities of communist and workers' parties.

HIGHLIGHTS

- The English Industrial Revolution took place in two phases. The first phase brought about a revolution in the field of cotton textile production. The second phase of industrialization centred around the capital goods industries like iron, steel, and coal. The pace of the Industrial Revolution quickened during the second phase. It gave a boost to various engineering industries and brought about far-reaching changes.
- The Industrial Revolution did not remain confined to England alone. A few years later, other European countries also experienced the Industrial Revolution and so the Netherlands, Germany, France, and Russia became industrialized.
- The Industrial Revolution stands as one of the significant landmarks in the history of the world. Everywhere it evoked a chain of various political, social, and economic reactions leaving a permanent imprint on the course of future European history.
- The Industrial Revolution brought forth a new class in the society: the working class. The workers were poorly paid as the bulk of the profit was monopolized by the capitalists. This brought about a conflict between labour and capital.
- This conflict between labour and capital led to the rise of socialism in Europe. Socialist ideas made considerable headway in Europe for a time. Karl Marx put forward the theory of Scientific Socialism.

MEMORABLE DATES AND EVENTS

1811	The beginning of Luddite Movement or machine-breaking movement
1818	Birth of Karl Marx
1833	First Factory Act
1838	The beginning of railroad in Belgium
1839	The beginning of railroad in Germany

1847	The foundation of the Communist League
1848	The Chartist Movement
	The Publication of the Communist Manifesto
1855	Accession of Tsar Alexander II
1861	Abolition of Serfdom in Russia

MEMORABLE PERSONALITIES

Ned Ludd: Leader of the Luddite Movement
Louis Philippe: King of France
Louis Napoleon: The French Emperor
Bismarck: Chancellor of Germany
Tsar Alexander II: Tsar of Russia
Nicholas II: Tsar of Russia
Karl Marx: Author of the Communist and a great socialist thinker

QUOTABLE QUOTES

- 'The Industrial Revolution was the transformation in the methods of production and transformation through the general substitution of power driven machinery for hand labour.'   —T.W. MILKER
- 'What was distinctive of the new capitalism was that it was not, as in previous ages, mainly agricultural or mainly commercial, but to a predominant degree, industrial. It involved a divorce between capital and labour over a wide sphere of economic work in which capital and labour had been generally combined. The employing class bought labour, the working class sold it. For the old relations based on custom and sweetened by human sentiment there was now substituted the cash nexus between master and man.'   —A. FISHER
- 'The rise and fall of Chartism were a barometer of industrial and agricultural distress in England.'   —DAVID THOMPSON
- 'England was giving the world the first broad, truly mass, and politically clear cut proletarian revolutionary movement.'   —LENIN
- 'By these channels [The Chartist Movement], a new and healthier wind blew through the community, a new national consciousness and social conscience about the ills of industrial England were begun....'
    —DAVID THOMPSON

CHAPTER 5

The Rising Tide of Nationalism

INTRODUCTION

Nationalism was 'the one great and novel features of the international difficulties of the nineteenth century'. It was felt that men united by a common tradition, a common language, and common economic interests should not be politically separated. This feeling appeared most strongly not among those nations which had already won a large measure of national independence and unity (France, Britain, and Spain for example), but among those who were still without a nation state. The period between 1815 and 1850 was one of struggle between the antagonistic forces of liberalism and conservatism. The Congress of Vienna (1815) sought to bridle the new forces released by the French Revolution but the forces of revolution were too firmly entrenched to be overthrown. The July Revolution (1830) and the February Revolution (1848) in France sparked widespread popular movements all over Europe which were to demolish the whole structure created by the Vienna Congress. The success of liberalism as reflected in the Revolution of 1830, which established a constitutional government, was a triumph of liberalism. Henceforth, people rose on behalf of freedom and self-government, for example, in Belgium, Germany, Italy, Poland and England.

Towards the beginning of 1848, Germany, Austria and Italy were already in a restless state. The news of the February Revolution in Paris found them all in a receptive mood. It was the first uprising on a large scale against an unpopular government and its rapid success inspired the peoples of central Europe them to try to get rid of the repressive regimes. The February Revolution acted as a model which ignited the flames of revolution in Central Europe. However, the nationalist movements in Italy and Germany were due to strictly local causes and they would have occurred sooner or later.

UNIFICATION OF ITALY

Ever since the fall of the Roman Empire, Italy had been a mere 'geographical expression'. She was divided into numerous petty states, some of which were under the rule of foreigners. For centuries, Italy had been the battleground of contending nations. The Napoleonic conquests had temporarily resolved this political chaos. The centralized system of Napoleon dashed out the petty states who were hostile to each other. In this sense the Napoleonic conquests paved the way for the flowering of a sense of national unity. The Congress of Vienna however, sought to turn the wind in a different direction. It made an attempt to bring back the pre-revolutionary condition in Europe. The Napoleonic creations were swept away and Italy passed again under the control of Austria. Austria directly ruled in the Provinces of Venetia and Lombardy, and the petty rulers who ruled in Tuscany, Parma, Lucca, Modena, Naples, and Sicily were completely under Austrian influence. The Pope ruled in Central Italy. Only the king of Piedmont-Sardinia belonged to a national dynasty and was immune to the reactionary influence of Austria.

The restoration of the old order in 1815 was unpopular, and the democratic and nationalist ideas began to work among the people like a wild-fire. The impulse towards unity and liberalism which the Italians had received from Napoleon, could not, however, be wiped out by tyrannical repression. It drove the discontents of the people underground.

The Carbonari Movement

The Carbonari Movement played a cardinal role in the early phase of the Italian nationalist movement. Underground societies, notably that of the Carbonari, were formed everywhere. They helped to spread the ideas of liberalism and nationalism in Italy.

To him and to his followers, the claim of Italian nationality was not a matter of analysis and reason, but of passionate and almost religious belief. Carbonaries were revolutionaries engaged in organizing armed uprisings to liberate Italy from Austrian control. The Carbonaries had a mass base and they drew their supporters from all segments in the society including workers and middle classes. Uprisings broke out in the 1820s in Naples, Piedmont, and Lombardy. However, the authorities suppressed those uprisings with a firm hand. The July Revolution in France encouraged the Carbonaries of Italy to rise up in rebellion in the 1830s. The Austrian army however, ruthlessly crushed the Carbonari terrorists. The revolutionary outbreak in 1830 and 1848 in favour of the freedom movement ended in a failure. But such failures did not weaken the cause of nationality, it rather quickened it.

Mazzini and Young Italy Movement

After the failure of the revolutionary movement of the 1830s the Italian Unification movement was guided by Mazzini (1805–72) and his Young Italy Movement (1831). Mazzini and his Young Italy constituted a quickening influence in the world of ideas and gradually the whole peninsula began to stir with the feeling of patriotism for a united Italy, which as yet existed only in imagination. Hazen has aptly commented, 'Mazzini was the spiritual force of the Italian resurrection, the prophet of a state that was not yet'. He was one of the great Italian patriots of his times and freedom of the motherland to him, was the most important issue. He was sentenced to imprisonment for his association with the revolutionary activities of the 1830s. While in exile he realized that freedom could not be achieved with sporadic terrorist uprisings. He realized the necessity of a political awakening of Italy on a mass scale. From this realization ensued the society of Young Italy, which, with its more definite aims and more inspired direction, soon superseded the Carbonari as the nucleus of nationalist revolution.

As Mazzini said, 'place youth at the head of the insurgent

multitude, you know not the secret of the power hidden in those youthful hearts'. From Piedmont there spread all over Italy, societies of young men, dedicated to the achievement of a national republic. Most of Mazzini's life was spent in exile, but he guided the movement effectively from outside Italy. He encouraged the younger generation to sacrifice their lives for the cause of their motherland. Under the leadership of Mazzini quite a number of mass uprisings took place in 1848 as part of the revolutionary wave sweeping across Europe. The movement however, petered out due to lack of coordination among the activists of the Young Italy movement and the brutal policy of repression followed by the Austrian authorities.

Many Italians felt that Mazzini's ideas of a republican and united Italy were too sweeping and therefore impractical. They did not like the way in which the Young Italy movement wasted precious Italian lives in small and weak insurrections. So, some moderates advocated the Union of Italy under Charles Albert, King of Piedmont, while others—the Neo-Guelfs (the Catholics)—wanted a federation under a regenerated papacy. In spite of differences of opinion as to how it was to be done, these three schools of thought—republican, Savoyard, and Papal—agreed on a similarity of aim: Austria must be driven out. They all contributed to the great national awakening known as 'Risorgimento' (resurrection) which now began to stir all Italy. The result of this fermentation of ideas was increasing dissatisfaction and unrest. Everybody felt, as Charles Albert put it, 'Italy will do it herself'.

Cavour (1810–61) and the Unification of Italy

Within Italy there were three sharply distinct schools of thought. Mazzini and his followers wanted to establish an Italian Republic. The Neo-Guelf party led by some eminent Catholic thinkers discovered in the reforming zeal of Pope Pius IX, a national hero, and centred their scheme around the idea of a federation under a Papal presidency. The monarchists, led by Cavour, the Prime Minister of Piedmont, wanted to bring about unity on a liberal monarchical basis under the ruling dynasty of Piedmont. As a result of the failure of the revolution of 1848, the Republicans and the Neo-Guelfs were discredited and the hopes of the nationalists now centred around Piedmont.

Cavour himself said that 'Piedmont, gathering to itself all the living forces of Italy, will soon be in a position to lead out mother country to the high destinies to which she is called'. The issue had been simplified and the solution that appealed to the bulk of the people was the leadership of the king of Piedmont. Considering the risk which Charles Albert had taken and the sacrifices he had made, his dynasty had been marked out as the standard bearer of Italian liberty and unity. When Victor Emmanuel II succeeded his father Charles Albert, great efforts were made by Austria to induce him to withdraw the constitution granted by his father. But he firmly refused. Thus Piedmont, the only state in Italy that had a constitution, became a liberal oasis in the desert of authoritarianism.

Cavour wanted to emancipate Italy from Austria and to unite her under Piedmont, or the House of Savoy. He knew that only with European support and foreign alliance could his great end be achieved. The multiple problems of Austrian rule, princely interests, and Papal power, could not be solved by popular revolts, nor by the unsupported efforts of a comparatively minor state, the Kingdom of Sardinia, but only by internal cooperation, by European diplomacy, and by war. Cavour devoted his efforts to the task of securing international cooperation. The programme and objectives followed by Cavour may be divided under four principle heads:

1. to free Italy from Austrian control,
2. to establish Piedmont-Sardinia as the powerhouse of Italian unification,
3. to prepare Piedmont as the centre of the Italian national movement through economic and constitutional reforms, and
4. to internationalize the Italian problem and thereby gain foreign support.

To achieve these goals Cavour introduced a number of political, economic, and social reforms in Piedmont-Sardinia meaning that Piedmont-Sardinia emerged as a powerful state under Cavour.

David Thomson has aptly remarked, 'Cavour's economic reforms were the basis of his political success'. Cavour was the real 'brain' behind the Italian unification while Mazzini was the 'heart' and Garibaldi the 'sword'. According to his programme Cavour participated in the Crimean War, entered into an alliance with Napoleon III, and fought against Austria in the Austro-Sardinian War. Cavour's immediate aim was to make Italian unity an European question so with this end in view, he began judicious literary propaganda, so that he might win 'the battle of Italian freedom in the field of journalism'.

The Crimean War provided Cavour with the opportunity for one of his skilful diplomatic strokes. Piedmont had no interest in the issue between Russia and the Anglo-French Alliance, but the latter wanted help and support. Cavour joined the Anglo-French Alliance, not as a subsidiary power, but as an equal, with a view to making Piedmont an important factor in international politics. The success of Italy in the Crimean War indirectly facilitated the Italian unification. Cavour received a seat at the Peace Conference in Paris where he got the opportunity to internationalize the Italian issue. Cavour was sure that in acting alone, unity would not be reached and so it was his mission to win France over to his side. The really decisive step was taken in the Pact of Plombières (1858). Napoleon III and Cavour met at Plombières and 'having met on no other ostensible purpose than to drink the waters, planned between them a war with Austria and a reorganized Italy'. Napoleon III promised to support Cavour in a war with Austria on condition that Cavour provided a pretext which would justify the former's action in the eyes of Europe.

After returning home, Cavour started preparations for war with Austria and in 1859, Austria declared war against Piedmont. France also joined the war with Piedmont. The Austro-Sardinian War was followed with interest by nearly every power in Europe. The Austrians were defeated in the Battle of Solferino on

24 June 1859. This victory allowed Piedmont to annex Lombardy and Milan. In the Central Italian States the people drove away their rulers and invited the King of Piedmont to rule over them. However, Napoleon III suddenly realized that a united Italy would not be conducive to the interests of France and so he decided to strike an alliance with Austria and signed the Treaty off Villafranca (without consulting Cavour) in 1859. Cavour requested King Victor Immanuel to ignore the Treaty of Villafranca, but the king was reluctant to engage in a confrontation with France. He came to an agreement with Austria in the Treaty of Zurich (1859) which concluded the Austro-Sardinian War. Cavour felt dejected and he decided to resign from the government of Piedmont-Sardinia. The Treaty of Villafranca however, could not stop the process of the Italian unification. The people of Italy were determined to drive out the foreigners and unite under Piedmont-Sardinia. Cavour reconsidered his earlier decision and joined the government again as Prime Minister. Before Cavour died in 1861, he had succeeded in bringing the whole of Italy except the province of Venice and the city of Rome under the rule of the King of Piedmont with the help of the soldier Garibaldi.

It is interesting to compare the gifts and achievements of Cavour with those of Bismarck. Both of them were creators of great national states. Both of them were great diplomats. Both of them were great administrators. Cavour's task was more difficult than that of Bismarck, for the resources at his disposal were small, and the international complications which he had to confront were serious. Cavour gave to Italy that parliamentary form of government which strengthened her and lasted for more than half a century, Bismarck was a reactionary and established an autocratic government which ultimately destroyed his work and defeated its own purpose.

Garibaldi and the Italian Unification

Apart from Cavour another major architect of the budding Italian nation was Guiseppe Garibaldi (1807–82). He was a great patriot, soldier, and a republican. The chief mission of his life was to

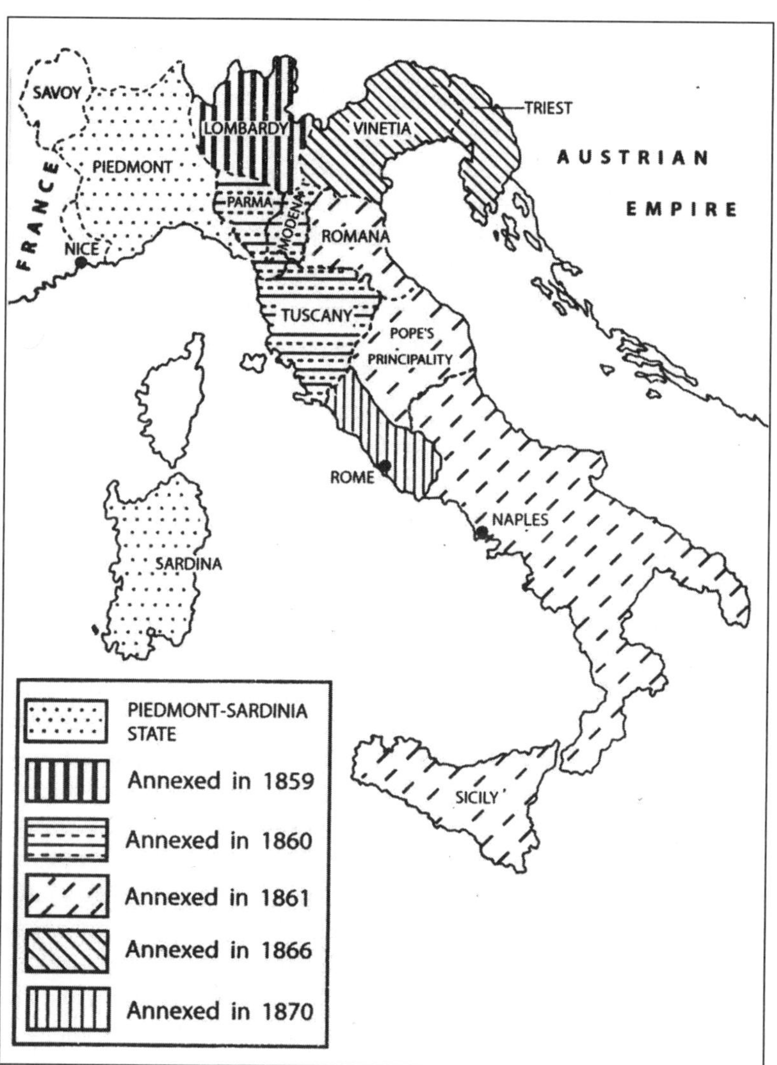

MAP 5.1: The Unification of Italy

make Italy independent. Earlier in his life he was a member of the 'Young Italy'. In 1860 a mass popular upsurge broke out in Naples and Sicily against the reactionary policy of the Bourbon monarchs. At this hour of crisis the rebels appealed to Garibaldi who promised them to help provided the intended revolt took place in the name of Italy and Victor Emmanuel. Garibaldi collected at Genoa, his volunteer army the famous 'Red Shirts' in preparation for an expedition to support the rebels. Cavour fully sympathized with the objectives of the expedition but found his position a very difficult one. As the Piedmontese Government was theoretically on good terms with the Government of Naples, it was the duty of Cavour, to prevent the port of Genoa from being used as a base of attack against the latter. Cavour decided to treat Garibaldi as an unauthorized and independent adventurer and outwardly maintained a neutral stand. Garibaldi led his army towards southern Italy. He conquered the whole of southern Italy and decided to set up a republic which would include Rome. Garibaldi's success brought forth a complex problem. Flushed with success, Garibaldi thought of pushing on to Rome, but Cavour realized that such an action would drag Italy into a war with France. Moreover, Cavour did not want to give Garibaldi, who was a republican, the upper hand. Unwilling to risk civil war, Cavour decided to take a bold step. He despatched Victor Immanuel II, at the head of the royal troops, to take over from Garibaldi. People from places like Sicily, Naples, and Umbria voted for union with the Kingdom of Sardinia-Piedmont and so to avoid civil war, Garibaldi voluntarily surrendered all his power to Victor Immanuel II in November 1860, refused all honours and rewards, and left for his island home of Caprera. In 1861, Victor Immanuel was declared the King of Italy. Thus, before Cavour died in 1861, he had succeeded in bringing the whole of Italy, except the province of Venice (which remained under Austria) and the city of Rome (which remained under the Pope), under the rule of the King of Piedmont.

With the Austrian army guarding Venice and the French army stationed in Rome, it seemed that the Italian unification would remain incomplete. However, the international political situation fostered the unification of Venice and Rome within a short period. Bismarck declared war against Austria in 1866 and Italy sided with Bismarck. Austria was defeated in the Battle of Sadowa in 1866 and forced to leave Venice. When France was defeated at the Battle of Sedan (1870) by Prussia, Rome was integrated into Italy. Thus, by 1870 the Italian unification was completed and a new nation was born.

THE UNIFICATION OF GERMANY

For centuries, Germany had been politically speaking, little more than a geographical expression divided into numerous principalities, dominated by the spirit of provincialism, and under the control of many petty princes, despite some efforts by the Holy Roman Emperors to create a central authority.

The focal point of the history of nineteenth-century Germany was the struggle for unification. It was not an abrupt phenomenon but a continuous process through a good deal of hardship and upheaval, and over a long period of time. Germany emerged as a conglomeration of 300 independent states, both large and small after the Peace of Westphalia in 1648. Of these states, Prussia, under the Hohenzollen family, emerged as a prominent rival of Austria. However, both Prussia under Frederick Wilhelm II (1786–97) and Austria under Franz Joseph I (1792–1833) had to suffer the humiliations of Napoleonic attacks. In the reconstruction of Germany, Napoleon's basic plan was to enhance the power of the lesser German states in order to neutralize Austria and Prussia. Napoleon formed a political union called the Confederation of the Rhine in 1806 with Bavaria, Wurtemberg, Baden and 13 other minor states from south-eastern region. These states renounced their allegiance to the Holy Roman Emperor and accepted Napoleon as their protector. Therefore the Holy Roman Emperor Francis II, also renounced his title and assumed the new title of Francis I, Emperor of Austria in 1806. The new organization aimed at countering Austria and Prussia. Since the crushing defeat at the Battle of Jena (1806) which resulted in the loss of Berlin, Prussia remained subjugated to Napoleon.

A process of regeneration began as a result of the patriotic writings of great intellectuals, as well as the efforts of a group of patriots of whom the most important was Baron von Stein. It was under his influence that a thorough programme of social reorganization took place. Serfdom was abolished, careers were thrown open to talent, and class distinction was removed. Stein's colleague Scharmhorst also made extensive changes to the structure of the army. Humboldt reformed the system of education.

These reforms invigorated Prussian national spirit and Napoleon's defeat in Russia (1812) therefore stimulated Prussia to resist Napoleon. The regenerated Prussia, along with Britain, Russia, and Austria crushed Napoleon at the Battle of Leipzig in 1813.

There were various problems regarding the unification of the Germanic states into a united Germany:

1. The Vienna Settlement of 1815. Under the leadership of Metternich, the region was organized into a loose confederation of 39 states whose affairs were to be controlled by a Federal Diet under the Presidentship of Austria. Austria did not want a united Germany as Metternich apprehended that the spread of nationalism in as heterogeneous empire would lead to disintegration of the Hapsburg Empire. Metternich's policy, thus, was to maintain status quo and to suppress liberal activities.

2. The spirit of separatism among the states was very strong. None were ready to surrender their individual identity for a greater cause.

3. Though there were many emotional, racial, and linguistic similarities among the Germanic people, they had strong feelings of regionalism which precluded a unification.

4. Religious difference was another important obstacle: North Germany (Hesse, Cassel, Nasau) was predominantly protestant and the south was mostly Catholic. Thus there was a marked religious divide.

5. Ideological differences between the liberals and Radicals also prevented any common approach. Reactionary forces

were against unification but equally, liberals of all shades of opinion, who had vision for a united Germany, also could not create a common platform. Liberals were grouped under different categories—liberals, radicals, progressive, right, left and centre—so various group interests overshadowed the greater objective of unification. Radicals were anti-monarchy and advocated a republican form of government, while most others were in favour of a united federal Germany. Liberals emphasized voting rights on property qualifications while the radicals insisted on universal franchise. The groups were not unanimous about the territorial extent of Germany: the idea of a Greater Germany (the inclusion of Austria along with non-German elements), or a Little Germany (the inclusion of German-Austria minus non-German elements) became a subject of controversy.

6. It was also difficult to reach unanimous decision over the issue of which state should assume leadership of the programme of unification; strong regionalist sentiments ceased them to drift away from the main agenda.

Another formidable obstacle was the structure of the Austrian Empire. Though in Austria the Germans dominated numerically, there were also other ethnic groups. Without Austria, German unification in its initial stage was unthinkable, while a unified Germany did not envisage the inclusion of non-German elements of Austria because of the racial and linguistic differences. Hence, there was a dilemma which gave rise to the problem of Greater Germany (including Austria) and Little Germany (or Austria minus non-German elements). In fact, Austria posed the greatest obstacle to the unification of Germany as it intended to dominate German affairs.

Development of the spirit of liberalism was a significant feature in the process of unification. The Napoleonic wars and the subsequent reforms that he introduced in reorganized Germany made a deep impression on the German mind. The political triumph and later overthrow of Napoleon had created a liberal attitude among a section of the intellectuals. Inspite of political disunity, a kind of emotional integration among the German people began to crystallize.

From the eighteenth century, as a reaction to the scientific nature of the Enlightenment, the counter-trend of Romanticism, which emphasized the role of sentiment and emotion as a guide in the search for truth spread across Europe. This wave of Romanticism steered Germany along a different line. As the French Revolution in 1789 was closely linked up with rationalism and intellect, German Romanticism originated as a counter to the French approach. Enslavement of Germany by Napoleonic France transformed German Romanticism into an anti-foreigner proposition. As a result, a spirit of patriotism entered into the Germanic mentality. Emotion became the driving force in place of rationalism, and this was reflected in the creative field and in philosophy. There was also an intellectual awakening and the professors of universities began to propagate liberal ideas among the youths who then began to carry these messages to all the German states. This awakening alarmed Metternich for it threatened the ideas of the Concert of Europe, and so a period of repression followed with the proclamation of the Carlsbad Decree (1819) which suppressed all liberal inclinations among the students and intellectuals. The spirit of nationalism thus took the shape of an undercurrent.

The Prussian king, Frederick William III (1797–1840) could not counter the towering influence of Metternich in Austria. Though Prussia was as yet unable to provide political leadership, it sponsored a tariff union of German states called Zollverein in 1818. Under this union, all custom duties were abolished and free trade among German states was established. All states joined this body except Austria. The significance of the Zollverein was enormous:

1. Numerically small, commercial, and industrial groups improved their socio-economic status due to free trade among the states.
2. With the improvement of their economic position, a political awareness began to surface and the bourgeoisie began to feel

that they should have political rights. This strengthened the liberal movement in Germany.
3. Its psychological impact was great. By breaking traditional barrier it brought the Germans closer.

The liberal movement in Germany was in an embryonic stage in the 1820s. The July Revolution of 1830 however, rocked the German liberals and the rulers of Saxony, Hanover, and Hesse were compelled to grant Charters similar to the French Charter of 1814 even though Metternich made them ineffective. However, by 1840, liberalism was gathering momentum. In 1840 Frederick William IV (1840–61) ascended the Prussian throne. He was not a liberal but he was an impulsive Romantic and the liberals felt inspired to exploit Frederick William IV's relaxed press censorship laws: demands for a constitutional government became louder. The February Revolution of 1848 inspired the German liberals and in Baden, Saxony, Baveria, and Wurttemberg, rulers were forced to concede to demands for a constitutional government.

In February 1847, it was announced that a United Diet or united Landtag, consolidating various local and provincial assemblies for all the States, would be called and be invested to convert the Prussian ruler to the cause of unity. There was however a temporary setback: the Berlin crowd that had assembled to congratulate the King at the royal palace made some seditious remarks that infuriated the King. To disperse the crowd a few shots were fired on them and riots broke out. Frederick however, changed his attitude later and a temporary compromise followed.

In March 1848, the German nationalists (51 in number) met at Heidelberg and decided to convene a German National Diet elected by universal adult suffrage to draft a federal constitution for a united Germany. Responding to popular demands, the Diet of the German Confederation at Frankfurt authorized popular elections which were duly held. The elected Assembly, which was dominated entirely by the liberals met in May 1848. This was not known as the Frankfurt Parliament and though it was not summoned by any ruling authority, it had nearly 600 elected members. Its suddenness took the rulers by surprise and they could not mobilize opposition quickly enough to oppose it. It was comprised of intellectuals, lawyers, journalists, teachers, and members of the petty bourgeoisie. Neither the nobility nor the peasants nor the working class had any representation. Its aims were three fold: (1) to achieve German unification constitutionally, (2) to draft a constitution for united Germany, (3) to adopt fundamental rights for the German nation. Soon however, friction started over three issues: (1) the problem of the territorial extent of Germany, i.e. Greater Germany which included Austria along with her non-German elements, or Little Germany which included Austria minus her non-German elements, (2) problems over the nature of the constitution: United German Republic or United Federal Germany, (3) the problem of leadership. After prolonged debate it was decided that they would adopt Little Germany as a federation under a hereditary emperor, with a parliament of two chambers, one representing the states and the other, the people.

The Parliament offered the crown to Frederick William IV of Prussia (1840–61) in February 1849 but he refused to accept due to the prevalent Austro-phobia and jeolousy of other states. This refusal frustrated the liberals and they rose up in revolts. The Prussian troops suppressed them and dissolved the Parliament. There were many causes of the failure of the liberals:

1. They lacked political experience.
2. There was no organization and no effective leadership.
3. They lacked military backing to push forward their demands.
4. There were ideological differences.
5. The liberal movement was bourgeois in nature and lacked the support of the peasantry and labourers so they had no mass contact or rural base.
6. They faced universal opposition from the rulers and conservative bloc (nobility, clergy).
7. Confusion over nationalism encouraged Bismarck to flout liberalism with the bait of nationalism and that by means of an aggressive policy.
8. Bismarck's war-cry changed the mood of the people. He created a split in the liberal camp and changed their passion

into reality. The liberals failed but the infrastructure necessary for the unification was their creation.

With the accession of William I (1861–88), a new chapter opened in the history of Prussia. He believed that German unity must come through military action and so he reorganized the military machine and invited Bismarck to head his ministry. In a memorable speech Bismarck announced that the German problem could not be solved by parliamentary decrees but only by 'blood and iron'. To implement his policy, two things were required: (a) rennovation of the Prussian fighting machine, (b) prevention of international intervention to eliminate Austria from German leadership. He was aware that German unity could only be achieved through military action against Austria, and France, and also Denmark regarding the question of the practices of Schleswig-Holstein. Hence he made preparations and pretexts for war which dragged Prussia towards military action.

The Role of Bismarck (1862–90)

Bismarck, who was Minister-President of Prussia from 1862 to 1890 and Chancellor of the German Empire from 1871 to 1890, has been described as 'the greatest man the age produced, greatest in the political manifestations of his powers and in the influence which his achievements have exercised in the history of the world'. To him Germany owed her unity. To him the Prussians owed their greatness and their Empire. Through the creation of the German Empire, he gave new direction to the history of Europe, and to the history of the world. He has been recognized to be one of the greatest diplomats of the nineteenth century, and for more than twenty years he was a great arbiter of all international problems.

Bismarck's long career may be conveniently divided into two periods. During the first period (1862–71), his aim was to unite Germany under the leadership of Prussia. During the second period (1871–90), his aim was to maintain the position won by Germany and to make her the arbiter of the destiny of the European nations. Bismarck did not believe in democracy or democratic procedure. He openly declared that 'the great question of the day will not be decided by speeches or majority resolutions, but by blood and iron'.

Thus, a new era in German history began when William I succeeded Frederick William IV, first as regent in 1858, and then as king in 1861. He was practical, direct, and clear-sighted but he was politically conservative. He had some sympathy with German aspirations for national unity but he was convinced that Prussia required a stronger army, so that she might seize the sovereignty of a united Germany. In 1859, new bills for national expenditure were laid before the Prussian Parliament, but the liberal majority objected to the army estimates and thus created a sharp conflict between the crown and the Legislature. William ignored the constitution and tried to carry out the intended reforms but the situation became critical and seemed to be developing towards the abdication of William I. Bismarck stood with the King against Parliament and in 1862 the king appointed Bismarck the Minister-President of Prussia. Bismarck and the King won the struggle and put the bills into effect, in spite of the opposition of the Diet: parliamentary ideals were defeated.

King Frederick William IV had described Bismarck as 'a red reactionary, smacking of blood, only to be used when the bayonet governs unrestricted'. This can be seen as a comment on Bismarck's internal policy for he had no faith in parliamentary and democratic government and was a staunch monarchist. He believed that Prussia owed her greatness to the character and statesmanship of rulers like Frederick the Great, and was convinced that a strong monarchical system of government was essential for the expansion of Prussia into a great German Empire. He also had a marked contempt for the sincerity of public opinion.

In the sphere of foreign policy his aim during the period 1862–71 was to unite the Germanic states under the leadership of Prussia. There are several obstacles to be the idea of German unity, the first of which was the fact that his outlook on European politics was always Prussian rather than Germanic: 'Prussians we are, and Prussians we will remain'. German Unity was for him nothing more than an extension of Prussian power. He clearly

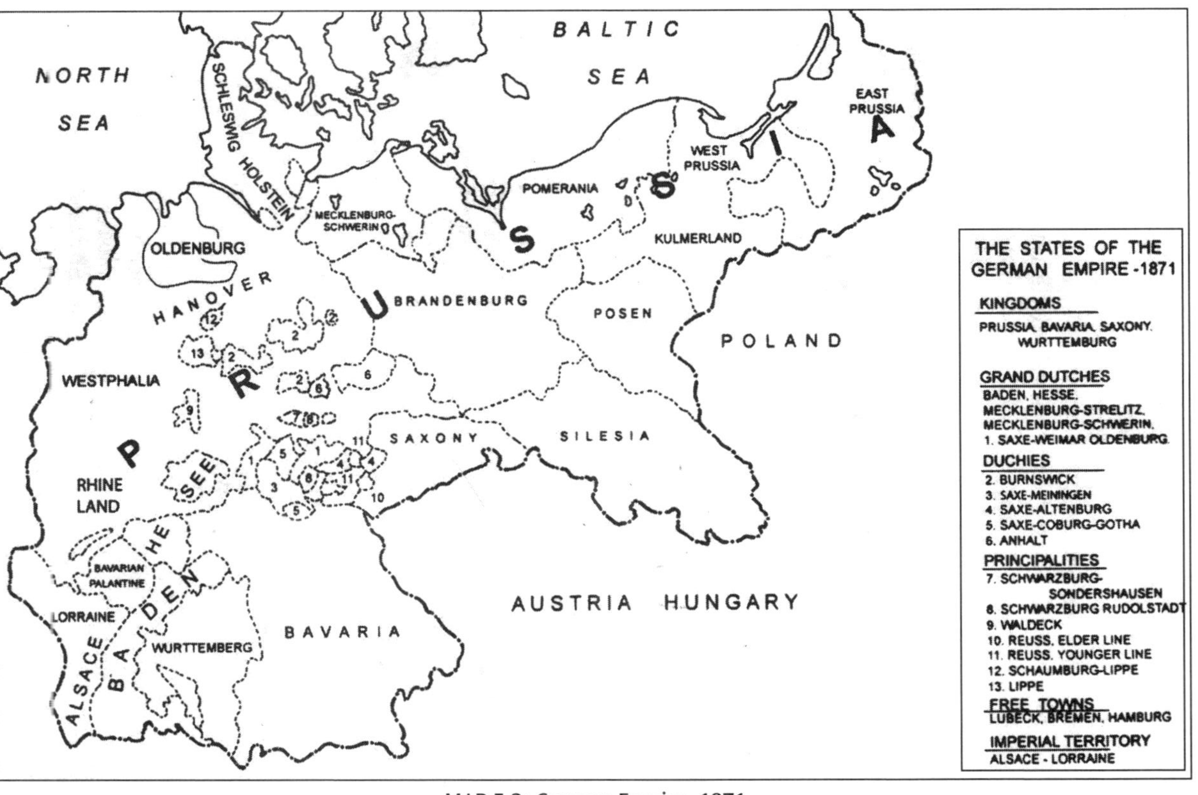

MAP 5.2: German Empire, 1871

understood that Austria and Prussia were natural and historical rivals, and that 'the union of Germany under Prussian leadership could only be achieved at the price of war with Austria'.

The second obstacle to German unity was the innate antagonism which existed between Prussia and the smaller German states. 'Bent upon preserving their particular individualities, they (i.e. the smaller German States) leaned naturally upon the power (i.e. Austria) whose policy was the defence of status quo, and looked apprehensively and suspiciously toward the Kingdom (i.e. Prussia) which had already once declared itself the champion of German nationality, and which might adopt under vigorous direction a progressive policy of union in which they might be submerged.' The third obstacle was the anticipated attitude of France. Prussia was her rival, and it was easy to see that France could not allow Prussia to destroy the Balance of Power in Central Europe by creating the nucleus of a mighty Empire. Between 1864 and 1870, Bismarck brought about the Unification of Germany through three wars: (1) war with Denmark, (2) the Austro-Prussian war and (3) the Franco-Prussian war.

Bismarck had to wage these three wars before these obstacles were removed and Germany could be united. The first of these wars arose in connection with the Schleswig-Holstein Question. This question had become a byword for obscurity, in as much as it was 'loaded with a mass of historical and legal detail' with which very few men were fully acquainted. Within the southern frontier of Denmark there lay the two provinces of Schleswig and Holstein, which were admittedly no part of Denmark, but, which had been for long claimed by the ruling dynasty of Denmark. These two provinces however retained their own representative assemblies and laws of succession. The King of Denmark only became Duke of Schleswig and Holstein after he had been accepted as such by their own assemblies and statutes passed by the Danish Parliament became operative in these provinces only after they had been approved by their assemblies. Schleswig was predominantly Danish in character, but Holstein was largely German. Holstein had formed part of the Holy Roman Empire (which ceased to exist in 1806), and it had been reorganized as a member of the

Germanic Confederation by the Congress of Vienna in 1815. The King of Denmark sat in the German Federal Diet at Frankfurt in his capacity as Duke of Holstein.

This 'ancient, irregular, and incomplete' relationship between Denmark and the two provinces had endured for centuries, but troubles began during the early years of the nineteenth century. As the sentiment of German nationality developed in Germany, there grew a feeling that some means might be found to incorporate both the provinces within Germany. But the Danes, inspired by the same sentiment desired the closer incorporation of the provinces within the Kingdom of Denmark: 'claimant Teutonism raised the banner of unredeemed Germany; claimant Danism that of unredeemed Denmark'. In 1848, the claim of the King of Denmark, Frederick VII (1848–63), to the two provinces was challenged by the Duke of Augustenburg. Revolutionary risings convulsed the provinces during the years 1848–51, but were put to an end by the Treaty of London in 1852, which temporarily restored the status quo.

Henceforth, the Danes began to pursue a deliberate policy of forcible 'Danizing' which was supported by King Frederick VII, who made a new constitutional arrangement which was inconsistent with the terms of the Treaty of London. This arrangement was ratified by his successor, Christian IX (1863–1906). Schleswig and Holstein protested and with the support of Germany, renounced their allegiance to Christian IX and accepted Frederick, the Duke of Augustenburg, as their legitimate ruler. Bismarck however wanted to annex Schleswig and Holstein to Prussia. The fact that Prussia had no right to the provinces did not trouble him in the least, for he knew that the strength of the Prussian army constituted her greatest claim. He made a hasty alliance with Austria, and the combined forces of Prussia and Austria defeated Denmark and occupied the two provinces. A conference of the great powers sat in London, but, it broke up without a decision on how to respond, and so the victors agreed to divide the spoils. The Convention of Gastein 'plastered over the cracks' between Austria and Prussia, providing that the former was to occupy and administer Holstein and the latter was to occupy and administer Schleswig.

The handling of the Schleswig-Holstein Question was a great diplomatic triumph for Bismarck. 'He had driven Austria, a generation ago the leader of Europe, where he would have her go; the force of his will he had impressed upon Europe. . . .' He had extended the Prussian state, and he had revealed something of the vast potentialities of a united Germany.

Bismarck's second war was then directed against Austria. He had to drive Austria out of Germany so that Prussia might capture the leadership. His plan was to utilize the many germs of discord which were contained in the Convention of Gastein in such a way that Austria might be forced to appeal to arms. It was the French Emperor Napoleon III, who seemed to hold the balance in his hands, for if he opposed the Prussian scheme of humiliating Austria, Bismarck would be helpless. In a famous interview, Bismarck induced him to promise the neutrality of France in the event of an Austro-Prussian war. Bismarck then concluded a secret treaty with Italy by which Italy promised to help Prussia in a war against Austria.

The ground being prepared for war, Bismarck began to invent pretexts. He made the idea federal reform the chief ground of dispute, for he knew that Austria would not accept the radical proposals of democratic reform which he had advanced. Bismarck's calculations were correct, and war began.

The Austro-Prussian War (or the Seven Weeks War) lasted only for seven weeks, of which the decisive fighting only lasted ten days. Prussia fully utilized her military advantages in terms of command, equipment, and general efficiency. The central battle of the campaign took place in Sadowa when Austrian forces were shattered. Peace was concluded in the Treaty of Prague (1866). Bismarck resolved neither to humiliate nor to injure Austria beyond reconciliation, for he knew that her friendship would be necessary for his purposes in the future. As per the terms of the treaty, Austria surrendered Venetia to Italy. She renounced her claim in the organization of the Germanic states. A North German Confederation was formed under the presidency of Prussia. Schleswig and Holstein were to go to Prussia. Thus, Prussia advanced a considerable way towards the unification of Germany under her own leadership.

Bismarck's third war was directed against France. 'Fundamentally the cause of the Franco-Prussian conflict was the deep rivalry between the two countries.... The startling growth of Prussian power and the unexpected demonstration of her strength had given to Europe, and more especially to France, and unmistakable challenge. Prussia's victory was a menace to French international prestige, and possibly to her national security.' 'It is France that was beaten at Sadowa,' said a great French General. The Germanic peoples, on the other hand, resented the undue interference of France in their affairs.

Bismarck knew that France had to be humiliated before Prussia could secure a legitimate position in Central Europe. The inconsistent policy of Napoleon III gave him the excuses which he wanted and conflict between France and Germany became inevitable due to French designs on Bavaria, Belgium, and Luxembourg. The immediate excuse for war was supplied by the Hohenzollern candidature for the throne of Spain. The Spanish throne, vacated by the expulsion of Queen Isabella, was offered by the Spanish government to Prince Leopold of Hohenzollern, who was a relative of the King of Prussia. His accession to the Spanish throne would have been a great gain to Prussia both politically and commercially and so it was naturally opposed by France. French protest compelled Leopold to withdraw his candidature. Bismarck was convinced that war was necessary for the interests of Prussia and so he released the now-famous Ems Telegram in which he represented an interview between the Prussian king and the French ambassador where the French had insulted the king. The war began. The victory of Prussia in the Battle of Sedan in 1870 was decisive. In the famous palace of Versailles, King William of Prussia was crowned Emperor of Germany. By the Peace of Frankfurt (1871) France surrendered Alsace-Lorraine. 'The Franco-German War made Germany mistress of Europe and Bismarck master of Germany. The political unification under Prussian leadership, for which Bismarck had waged three wars, and for which revolutionaries of 1848, thinkers, poets, philosophers, and historians, had all in their different ways, prayed or worked for, was at last completed.

THE POLISH REVOLTS

'The future of Europe', said Napoleon, depends 'upon the ultimate destiny of Poland'. Poland was dismembered in three stages in 1772, 1793, and 1795 according to the greed of neighbouring powers. The Congress of Vienna helped to establish Russian domination over most of Poland but the conquests of Poland by Napoleon had already unleashed some of the principles of the French Revolution in Poland. So, when Poland was next parcelled out to Prussia and Russia, the spirit of Polish nationalism was beginning to emerge. The July Revolution of 1830 in France inspired the Polish nationalists to free themselves from Russian domination. But this outburst of Polish nationalism in 1830 ended in a failure due to lack of popular support. The Russian authorities had no problem in putting down the movement. Hundreds of Polish nationalists were imprisoned and thousands fled particularly to France. The spirit of nationalism among the Poles thus thrived outside Poland.

In 1846, a nationalist uprising broke out in Galicia, master-minded by the feudal aristocracy of Galicia against Austria. The Polish peasants, who were much repressed by these feudal magnates, made common cause with the reactionary Austrian authorities headed by the Chancellor Metternich and thus with the help of the peasantry, the Austrians were able to suppress this feudal insurrection.

After the failure of the revolts of 1830 and 1846, the Poles remained silent for some time. However, from the 1860s, a number of secret societies became active in Poland. The secret societies became powerful enough that in 1863, they were able to organize a popular rebellion in Poland. Tsar Alexander II had adopted a very conciliatory policy towards Poland and had relaxed the repressive system of Nicholas I. Despite this and the fact that he had given Poland a great deal of autonomy within the Empire, patriotic Poles raised the banner of revolt in 1863. They wanted to set up Poland as an independent republic. England and France sympathized with the national aspirations of the Poles and protested against the Russian policy towards Poland. Bismarck however, sided with the Tsar and ultimately, the Polish movement was supressed. After this revolt Poland was brought under the Russian Empire entirely by Tsar Alexander II.

HIGHLIGHTS

- The post-Vienna Congress period saw outbursts of nationalism all over Europe. During this phase, the Italian Unification and the German Unification were completed.

- In Italy secret societies or Carbonaries were formed with the aim of liberating Italy through revolutionary terrorism. Mazzini, who founded the Young Italy Movement, led the second phase of the Italian Unification movement. However, the uprising organized by Mazzini ended in a failure.

- After the failure of the Young Italy Movement, the leadership of the Italian Unification passed into the hands of Cavour. Piedmont-Sardinia became the powerhouse of Italian Unification and Cavour united a substantial portion of Italy through his diplomatic moves.

- Mazzini's disciple Garibaldi quickened the process of Italian Unification by conquering Sicily and Naples. The battles of Sadowa and Sedan finally completed the Unification of Italy.

- Like Italy, Germany too, remained fragmented for a long time. During the Napoleonic era the Germans for the first time had the opportunity to experience some sort of political unity. The real architect of the German Unification was Bismarck who unified Germany with three major wars.

- Poland was partitioned in the eighteenth century. The Partition of Poland gave a great blow to the political aspirations of the Poles and their nationalist aspirations were frustrated. The Poles united and revolted in 1830, 1846 and 1863 but their attempts ended in a failure.

MEMORABLE DATES AND EVENTS

1832   Foundation of Young Italy
1848   Frankfurt Parliament
1852   Cavour became the Prime Minister of Piedmont-Sardinia
1854   Crimean War

1856	Peace of Paris
1858	Treaty of Plombières
1859	Treaty of Villafranca
1862	Bismarck became the Prime Minister of Prussia
1866	Battle of Sadowa
	Treaty of Prague
1870	Battle of Sedan
1871	Treaty of Frankfurt

MEMORABLE PERSONALITIES

Napoleon Bonaparte: Emperor of France
Mazzini: The leader of Italian Unification, the founder of Young Italy
Count Cavour: The Prime Minister of Piedmont-Sardinia
Victor Immanuel II: King of Piedmont-Sardinia
Napoleon III: Emperor of France
Garibaldi: Leader of Italian unification movement, Disciple of Mazzini
Bismarck: Prime Minister of Prussia
Frederick William IV: Emperor of Russia
William I: Emperor of Prussia
Nicholas I: Czar of Russia
Alexander II: Czar of Russia

QUOTABLE QUOTES

- 'Italy is nothing more than a geographical expression.'

  —METTERNICH

- 'Mazzini was the spiritual force of the Italian resurrection, the prophet of a state that was not yet.'   —HAZEM

- 'Among the makers of modern Italy he [Mazzini] holds an imperishable place.'   —LIPSOM

- 'The great questions of the day will not be decided by speeches, or majority resolutions but by "blood and iron".'   —BISMARCK

- 'The year 1866 is a turning point in the history of Prussia, Austria, France and Europe.'   —HAZEN

- 'The Franco-German made Germany mistress of Europe and Bismarck master of Germany.'   —KETELBEY

- 'It [the Zollverein] was a direct preparation for the Empire of 1870.'

  —KETELBEY

CHAPTER 6

The American Civil War
(1861–1865)

A house divided against itself cannot stand. I believe this government cannot endure permanently half-slave and half-free.
— ABRAHAM LINCOLN SPRINGFIELD
Illionis, 17 June 1858

INTRODUCTION

The American Civil War is an historical irony. The founders of the new nation had believed that their country would stand as a model for other societies to emulate, yet in just a few decades, American citizens failed to resolve internal difference via any other solution than civil war. Despite the conflicting social, cultural, and economic interests of the people of the thirteen colonies, the founding fathers were able to create unity for the new nation. In the middle of the nineteenth century no country in the world was more interesting to other nations than the United States, and few attracted more distinguished visitors. Yet, visitors quickly found that there were really two Americas—a North and a South—and the speed of progress itself held latent dangers for the maintenance of sectional harmony.

New England (Rhode Island, Massachusetts, New Hampshire, Connecticut, etc.) and the middle Atlantic states were the main centres of manufacturing, commerce, and finance. At the same time, shipping had reached the height of its prosperity, and vessels flying the American flag plied the seven seas, selling and buying in all the countries of the world. In the South, the chief source of wealth was the cotton crop, although there was rice culture along the coast, and sugar and tobacco in the bordering states. The plantation economy of the South was labour intensive in nature and for its survival, slavery proved indispensable. The institution of slavery and the fate of the African-Americans became a big issue in the conflict between North and South.

The Civil War was the first major interruption in the processes of material and social construction with which the Americans had been occupied since the founding of the first colonies. The main cause of the Civil War was that the North and the South had developed deeply divergent social ideals. This divergency was too basic to be settled by the usual Anglo-Saxon methods of argument, compromise, and peaceful adjustment. Massachusetts and Virginia, for example, had always represented different social and economic principles, and different modes of living. The North was more dynamic, more progressive, and more interested in commercial development. In contrast, the South was more static, and more leisurely in commercial development and more 'feudal'. These conflicts of ideals were in themselves not unduly problematic, but the issue of slavery caused sharp divisions that open warfare ensued. It was an institution which the North was learning to ridicule and which the South regarded as the very foundation of its society and economy. The results of this war, in the victorious North as well as the defeated South, were cynicism, corruption, and frustration. In one sense, American society never fully recovered from it.

CAUSES OF THE AMERICAN CIVIL WAR

The American Civil War stands as a significant landmark in the history of the world and it is a period that has caused many historiographical debates. Historians like J.F. Rhodes saw it as a moral conflict which not only destroyed slavery but also preserved the Union, thus, making possible the nation's rise to greatness. Recent scholarship on the subject too, focuses on slavery as the chief cause of the war. A. Nevins has characterized the Civil War as 'a war over slavery and the future position of the Negro race in North America'.

During the first half of the nineteenth century slavery was an institution recognized by land and custom in fifteen out of the sixteen states within the United States. The institution was intimately linked up with the plantation economy of the southern states and with the interests of the planter class, i.e. the ruling class. In the eyes of the law the slave was a chattel: he could be sold, exchanged for other kinds of property, or given away. For centuries, slave-holders believed that to hold slaves in bondage was not inconsistent with morality. However, at the end of the eighteenth century slavery began to be condemned by moralists both in England and America.

Conflicting interests in the North and the South became increasingly apparent. Resenting the large profits amassed by northern businessmen from marketing the cotton crop, southerners attributed the backwardness of their own section to northern aggrandizement. Northerners, on the other hand, declared that slavery was wholly responsible for the backwardness of the South. Early in the nineteenth century, a strong and vocal Abolitionist Party began to rise in the North, and slavery began to be attacked in moral and religious terms. The Abolitionists declared that no slave-holder was 'innocent' and that slave-holding was a 'crime'. The most powerful of all North America abolitionist propaganda was a work of fiction, H.B. Stowe's novel *Uncle Tom's Cabin*. Abolitionists arguments were received with increasing favour in the North, but Southern planters continued to believe that slavery had a moral justification. They tried to point out that even the Bible recognized but never condemned human bondage.

Slavery was an economic necessity for the South. The planters of the South knew that their prosperity depended upon slave labour. Cotton culture and its labour system came to represent a vast investment of capital in the South. By 1850, seven-eighths of the world's supply of cotton was grown in the American South. Slavery increased concomitantly and in national politics, Southerners chiefly sought protection and enlargement of the interests represented by the cotton-slavery system. Anti-slavery Northerners saw in the southern view a conspiracy for pro-slavery aggrandizement, and in the 1830s their opposition became militant.

The issue of slavery is one of the most important factors which dragged the Americans into the Civil War. It was closely connected with the westward expansion. That is, the history of

Slave Cabin

the United States in the nineteenth century is essentially a story of continuous westward movement. New areas were cleared and brought under human habitation and so as settlement moved to the west, new states were created and brought under the American federation. Whenever a new state was created, the Northerners tried to make it a free state without slaves, while the Southerners tried to turn it into a slave state. Finally, the recognition of slavery alienated the United States from the sympathies of the more liberal governments of Europe.

Such a vital national issue could not be pushed aside. From time to time, various attempts were made to arrive at a compromise acceptable to both the groups. For example, in 1787, an ordinance prohibited slavery north of the Ohio River. The 1820s saw a new phase of agitation which owed much to the dynamic democratic idealism of the times and to the new interest in social justice for all classes. In its more extreme form, the Abolitionist movement in America intended to put an immediate end to slavery. This extremist approach found a leader in William Lloyd Garrison, a young man of Massachusetts, who combined the heroism of a martyr with the crusading zeal of a demagogue. On 1 January 1831 Garrison produced the first issue of his newspaper, *The Liberator*, bearing the annoucement: 'I shall strenuously contend for the immediate enfranchisement of our slave population.' However, despite the ongoing Abolitionist movement, the ordinance of 1787 was modified by the Missouri Compromise (1820) in which Missouri was admitted as a slave state, and the parallel of the latitude of her southern boundary was fixed as the northern limit of slavery in lands west of Missouri. This arrangement lasted until 1850.

In 1845, the acquisition of Texas—and soon after, the territorial gains in the south-west resulting from the Mexican War—converted the moral question of slavery into a burning political issue. Up until then, it had seemed likely that slavery would be confined to the areas where it already existed, but then new questions were raised: Was slavery to be allowed in New Mexico, Texas, and Columbia? Were the Abolitionists to be allowed to defy the Fugitive Slave Act of 1793 and to assist in the escape of runaway slave? On every one of these questions the North disagreed with the South. At last, two statesmen named Henry Clay and Daniel Webster brought about the Compromise of 1850: 'that makeshift of despairing statesmanship'. California was admitted as a free state, but slavery in the other territories was to be regulated by their own inhabitants. A new Fugitive Slave Law was passed, empowering the Federal Government to hunt and restore runaway slaves.

For those who witnessed the achievements of the Compromise of 1850, the Civil War must have appeared to be a great irony. They had looked upon the Compromise as the final word and not even the worst estimates could have predicted that it would last hardly a decade. The problem lay in the fact that the Compromise resolved only material differences. It had no answer to the demand for the abolition of slavery which the Abolitionists justified on moral and emotional grounds. By the Kansas-Nebraska Act of 1856, the Missouri Compromise was repealed and the people of Kansas and Nebraska were allowed to determine for themselves whether they would own slaves or not. This Act declared that the people of each territory would vote on the question of slavery and only if the majority were favourable to slavery would it be a slave state. In 1857, the judgement of the Supreme Court in the Dred

Scott case gave a new dimension to the slavery question. Dred Scott was a Missouri slave, once the property of an army surgeon who took him to Illinois, a free state, and to Minnesota, where slavery was forbidden by the Missouri Compromise. On his return to Missouri, Scott was persuaded by some Abolitionists to bring a suit to the Missouri Court for his freedom on the ground that residence.in a free territory had made him a freeman. However, the court declared that Scott was of African descent and therefore was not a citizen of Missouri and so Scott's residence in Minnesota had not affected his status as a slave. The Missouri Compromise therefore was unconstitutional and seemed null and void. The effect of the court ruling was to declare that the Federal Legislature had no right or power in regard to the extension or restriction of slavery. The new Republican Party had been hoping that it would be able to prevent the extension of slavery if they were in power at the centre but this hope was shattered by the Dred Scott Case.

Charles and Mary Beard (*The Rise of American Civilization*) see the Civil War as a struggle between two economic groups—the Northern industrial business interest and the Southern planter aristocracy—for the possession of the government of the United States. Before the Civil War, Northern and the Southern interests had clashed on issues like tariffs and banks but on those occasions, the conflict was avoided through compromises. However, in the 1860s, a bloody conflict became increasingly inevitable, and the final choice had to be made between a backward agricultural slave economy and an advanced democratic and industrial economy. Thus, apart from the institutional conflict over the issue of slavery, the Southerners also believed that their economic troubles were due to Northern exploitation and Northern domination over the fiscal and tariff policies and therefore that their problems could be solved only by political independence.

Scholars like C.W. Ramsdell and Kenneth M. Stampp also think that slavery was unimportant and that it was neither a moral issue nor the single important cause of the Civil War. Faulkner (*American Economic History*) argues that, 'Slavery was the surface issue, the real conflict went deeper'. But the slavery question should not be diluted into a bigger framework of causes. It was slavery, and slavery alone, that finally made it impossible for the two sections to remain at peace within the same federal union.

Immediate Causes

The victory of Lincoln was one of the immediate causes of the Civil War. In the Presidential election of 1860 the Republican Party nominated Abraham Lincoln as its candidate. Party spirit soared as leaders declared that slavery could spread no further for Abraham Lincoln had long regarded slavery as an evil in society. The disunity of the opposing Democrats, led by Stephen A. Douglas, helped the Republican Party to win the election of 1860. Secondly, the secession of the Southern states served as another immediate cause of the war. The secession from the Union, if Lincoln were elected, was a foregone conclusion. Once the election returns were certain, a specially summoned South Carolina convention declared 'that the Union now subsisting between South Carolina and other states under the name of the "United States of America" is hereby dissolved'. Other southern states promptly followed South Carolina's example, and on 8 February 1861, they formed the Confederate States of America under the leadership of Jefferson Davis.

The Civil War Begins

Less than a month later, on 4 March 1861, Abraham Lincoln was sworn in as President of the United States. In his inaugural address, he refused to recognize the secession, considering it 'legally void'. His speech closed with a plea for restoration of the bonds of union. The South ignored the plea and on 12 April confederate guns opened fire on the Union soldiers stationed at Fort Sumter in South Carolina. All hesitation was now swept away from the minds of the Northerners. In the seven states that had seceded, the people responded promptly to the appeal of their leaders, Jefferson Davis. The action of the slave states that had thus far had remained loyal was now tensely awaited by both sides. The people of each side of the conflict entered the war with high hopes of an

MAP 6.1: 1861 – Outbreak of the Civil War

early victory. In terms of material resources the North enjoyed a clear advantage: 23 states with a population of 22 million were arrayed against 11 states inhabited by 9 million. The industrial superiority of the north exceeded even its advantage in manpower, providing it with abundant facilities for manufacturing arms and ammunition, clothing, and other supplies. Similarly, the rail network in the North contributed to federal military prospects.

Thus, the question of slavery was merged into the problem of secession: 'Whether the Civil War was fought for slavery or for the right of secession, it is not necessary to distinguish. The two were inseparably intertwined'. In the Mississippi Valley, the Union forces won an almost uninterrupted series of victories. Union troops could advance some 320 km. into the heart of the Confederacy. Under the command of General Ulysses S. Grant, Union forces made a sudden attack a Siloh, on the bluffs overlooking the Tennessee River, and held at until reinforcements helped repulse the Confederates.

On 1 January 1863, President Lincoln issued an Emancipation Proclamation, freeing the slaves in the rebelling states and inviting them to join the armed forces of the North. The Proclamation thus declared the abolition of slavery to be an objective of the War in addition to the declared objective of saving the Union. The Confederate States were finally defeated in April 1865. On 9 April 1865, General Robert E. Lee of the Confederate States surrendered to General Ulysses S. Grant of the United States of America. Within a few days of their surrender however, President Lincoln was assassinated at Ford's theatre by John Wilkes Booth.

EFFECTS OF THE CIVIL WAR

The victory of the North in the Civil War finally decided that slavery was to be abolished and that the 'compact theory of the Union' was to be given up. The United States was to be an 'indestructible Union of indestructible states'. The Southern Americans gradually regained control of their government by intimidating the former African slaves in order to prevent them from voting, and the Northern politicians gradually lost interest in the question. The

Civil War

African was no longer a slave, but he still had few 'rights which the white man was bound to respect'. Although the North no longer attempted to change the Southern pattern of racial relationships, the other results of the Civil War were more enduring. Henceforth, the South was unable to protect herself from the exploitation by Northern banking and business corporations or to maintain her agrarian way of life. More than twelve million American citizens were exposed to continuous insult and discrimination solely because of the colour of their skins. As the civil rights movement gained momentum in the 1950s and 1960s, historians of the Civil War gave more and more attention to slavery and race relations as central issues in the sectional conflict of the 1850s and 1860s. Eugene Genovese, for one, saw the War as growing out of the Southern planters' efforts to protect and expand the slave system.

ABRAHAM LINCOLN AND THE CIVIL WAR

The Americans see the Japanese attack on Pearl Harbour during the Second World War and the 11 September 2001 terrorist attack on the World Trade Center, New York and Pentagon as serious threats to American democracy, yet, the Civil War was perhaps the greatest crisis they have ever faced. It was Lincoln who guided the nation to a resolution of this crisis. Nathaniel Stephenson has aptly remarked that the history of America during these darkest days, is largely the history of Lincoln. The Lincoln legend has come to have a hold on the American imagination that defies comparison with anything else in political mythology. If the Lincoln legend gathers strength from its similarity to the Christian theme of vicarious atonement and redemption, there is yet another strain in American experience that it represents equally well. Lincoln was a pre-eminent example of that 'self-help' attitude which Americans have always admired. He was born in 1809 in a log cabin and spent the early years of his life as a labourer or soldiering among the American Indians. He then studied law and became a lawyer. His political career began in the Illinois legislature, where however, he failed to make his presence felt. Lincoln was not, of course, the first eminent American politician who could claim humble origins, but few have been able to demonstrate such a sudden ascent from relative obscurity to high eminence and none has maintained such simplicity while scaling such heights.

Abraham Lincoln first came to prominence during a great political debate which he had with Stephen Douglas. The senatorship of Illinois having fallen vacant, Douglas and Lincoln appeared as rivals, the latter being the nominee of the Republican Party. Slavery was the central theme of the debate. Douglas was superior in education, oratorial skill, and personal magnetism, but when it came to the ability to debate the moral aspects of the problem, the advantage lay with Lincoln. Although the election went in favour of Douglas, the debate brought Lincoln to the attention of the country.

In 1860, Lincoln was elected the President of the United States. This victory of the Republican Party seriously alarmed the South. The South found itself in a very difficult position. As Lincoln was opposed to slavery it was felt that the South's only hope lay in secession. Thereafter, the Southern states seceded and Lincoln's efforts to maintain the Union by peaceful means failed. The Civil War began in 1861.

Abraham Lincoln is still an enigma and a subject of great controversy. Writers like Richard Hofstadter (*American Political Tradition*) have portrayed him as a skilful politician whose cleverness turned every situation to his and the Party's advantage. Hofstadter argues that Lincoln criticized slavery only after the Kansas-Nebraska Act which breathed political life into the slavery issue. He suggests that he was an opportunist who by his 'House Divided' speech, on 16 June 1858, united the Abolitionists and racists to get enable him to get into the White House. However, Hofstader's argument is not very sound: as a member of a committee which was to report on slavery, appointed by the Illinois State Legislature in 1837, Lincoln clearly stated that slavery was 'bad' and 'unjust'. Again, in his speech delivered at Peoria in 1854, Lincoln declared that he hated the 'current zeal' for the spread of slavery. Like a true humanist he argued that 'the great mass to mankind consider slavery as a great moral wrong' and that slavery was 'a crime against humanity' and a 'burning shame to the nation.'

It is true that it was not until 1854 that Lincoln publicly denounced slavery on moral grounds, condemning it as a 'monstrous injustice'. Even then he did not want to abolish it, but to limit its expansion. In his position as a politician, Lincoln had to be careful not to attack slavery too radically as it could be construed as an attack on the Union itself. That is, he took pains to say that he was not an Abolitionist. Although he was anti-slavery. He tried to reconcile two irreconciliables: (1) preservation of the Union and (2) the Emancipation of the slaves. At heart he was a convinced Abolitionist, 'If Slavery is not wrong, then nothing is wrong', he said. When the Southern states seceded, Lincoln's efforts to maintain the Union by peaceful means failed.

The Civil War began in 1861. Military necessity now forced his hands. On 1 January 1863, Lincoln issued the Emancipation Proclamation, freeing the slaves in the rebelling states and inviting them to join the armed forces of the North. When the South seceded, Lincoln realized that to preserve the Union war was necessary. He carefully manipulated the circumstances which forced the rebels to put themselves on the wrong side by attacking Fort Sumter. He appealed to the American conscience by saying that the revolt was against American heritage—it was against Democracy, Union and Humanity. He said, 'The government will not assail you, you can have no conflict without being yourselves the aggressors. Thus, he placed the Federal government within a defensive framework and shifted the responsibility for secession to the Confederacy, leaving the South no alternative but to remain in the Union or make war. When the war was on, the radicals thought that Lincoln was half-hearted because he held in his speech regarding the rights of the slave states so long as there seemed to be a chance of saving the Union in that way. Lincoln's primary aim was to save the Union: 'If I could save the Union without freeing any slave, I would do it, and if I could do it by freeing all the slaves, I would do it.' He gave popular voice to the fundamental issues of his day, and defended the principles of the Union itself, he was a leader whose abilities brought the nation through crisis to the preservation of the Union and the elimination of slavery.

Lincoln's greatest gift to the nation and to humanity was his Emancipation Proclamation (1863) by which 4 million slaves were freed. On 13 April 1863, Washington was illuminated to celebrate Lee's surrender, and joyous crowds paraded in the streets. The next evening Lincoln went to attend a performance at Ford's Theatre and there he was assassinated by a confederate supporter and actor, John Wilkes Booth.

Maintenance of the Union was the central fact of Lincoln's political life. Without the Union there could be no democracy, and without democracy there could be no Union. Slavery stood in contravention of democracy, and the threat of secession threatened the Union. Lincoln's previous speeches, although marked by a definite conviction that slavery was wrong, had been often fumbling and confused and not always candid. But once in office, he gradually rose to a great moral stature and determined to oppose slavery and secession for the sake of the Union. Today Lincoln continues to be admired and respected in the USA for these acts. There stands in Washington DC, a statue of Lincoln with hands outstretched towards life and light.

HIGHLIGHTS

- New England (Rhode Island, Massachusetts, New Hampshite, Connecticut, etc.) and the middle Atlantic States became the centres of commerce and finance. While the North became the centre of manufacturing, the South concentrated on a plantation economy chiefly based on slave labour.
- The differences between the North and the South, over the course of time, bred a sense of antagonism and sectionalism. The two sides clashed with each other over the issue of slavery.
- The situation took a turn for the worse with the election of Lincoln as the President of the United States. The Southerners needed slave labour to sustain their economy but Lincoln's attitude to the problem convinced them that the North would make an attempt to abolish slavery.
- The Southern states seceded from the Union. The attack on Fort Sumter in April 1861 led to the beginning of the Civil War.
- The Confederate troops were finally defeated by the Union forces. In 1863 Lincoln issued an Emancipation Proclamation by which four million slaves were freed.
- Lincoln was assassinated in the Ford Theatre by I.W. Booth on 14 April 1865.
- The Civil War stands as one of the significant landmarks in the history of the United States.

MEMORABLE DATES AND EVENTS

1809   Birth of the Lincoln
1820   Missouri Compromise
1831   Publication of *Liberator*
1850   Compromise of 1850
        Publication of *Uncle Tom's Cabin*
1854   Kansas Nebraska Act
        The birth of the Republican Party
1861   Lincoln became President of the United States
        The beginning of the Civil War
1863   1 January, Emancipation Proclamation
1865   Surrender of General Lee
        Assassination of Lincoln

MEMORABLE PERSONALTIES

Abraham Lincoln: President of the United States at the time of the Civil
   War
Stephen Douglas: Senator from Illionois
General Ulysses S. Grant: General of the US Army
Robert E. Lee: General of the Confederate States of America
I. W. Booth: Lincoln's assassin

QUOTABLE QUOTES

* 'A house divided against itself cannot stand. I believe this government
  can not endure permanently half-slave and half-free.'   —LINCOLN
* 'If slavery is not wrong, then nothing is wrong.'   —LINCOLN
* 'If I could save the Union without freeing any slave, I would do it; and
  if I could do it by freeing all the slaves, I would do it.'   —LINCOLN
* 'It was slavery, and slavery alone, that finally made it impossible for
  the two sections to remain peaceably within the same federal union.'
  —M.M. PAKES
* 'Whether or not secession was legally permissible—a question on
  which there were legitimate difference of opinion—it was certainly
  true that the democratic and peaceful American way of life could not
  have been preserved if the Union had been split into two mutually
  hostile sections.'   —H.B. PARKES
* 'Instead of glory, he [Lincoln] once said, he had found only "ashes
  and blood". This was, for him, the end product of that success myth
  by which he had lived and for which he had been so persuasive a
  spokesman. He had had his ambitions and fulfilled them, and met
  heartache in his triumph.'   —R. HOFSTADTER

CHAPTER 7

The Eastern Question

INTRODUCTION

The 'Eastern Question' or the 'Near Eastern Question' is considered to be one of the most difficult and complex problems in the history of modern Europe. The problems which centred round the Eastern region of Europe are known as the Eastern Question. This geographic region is also known as the Balkans. The Balkan Peninsula comprises the mountainous country between the Danube and the Aegean Sea. This part of Europe has a multi-racial population and includes the Greeks, the Serbs, the Bulgars, and the Albanians. The nationalities of Greece, Bulgaria, Albania, etc. had stemmed from the multicultural and multi-ethnic composition of the population of this region. For centuries, the Ottoman Empire had ruled the Balkan people who were predominantly Greek Orthodox Christians headed by the Russian Orthodox Church. Primarily, they constituted a distinct class of military overlords although served as a source of political restlessness in the region.

The Ottoman Empire, which grew up gradually, included the diverse people of the Balkans. As the Ottoman empire began to show some semblances of decay in the eighteenth century, a political vacuum began to unfold in this part of Europe. This political restlessness of the region came to be known as the Eastern Question and could be ascribed to the following factors: (1) elements of decline in the Ottoman Empire, (2) the political aspirations of the Christian people of the Balkan Peninsula, (3) the increasing Russian aggression in the region, and (4) the response of England, France, and Austria to Russian expansionist policy in the Balkans.

THE ORIGINS OF EASTERN QUESTION

The 'Eastern Question' unfolded due to a number of factors. To begin with, the rapid decline of the great Ottoman Empire was one of one factors behind one rise of one problem. The Ottoman Empire had dominated a substantial portion of Europe in the sixteenth and seventeenth centuries but by the eighteenth century it was in some ways overstretched. The fundamental weakness of the empire lay in its administrative system. The Ottomans had a great army and were adept soldiers but they never displayed much aptitude for civil government. The administration of the empire was in some areas paralysed by widespread corruption and the continuous intrigues of the nobility left the central authority weak. As a result, the provincial governors or Pashas became largely autonomous and often disloyal to the central government. The misgovernment in the distant provinces often triggered off rebellions by the Christian subjects. Such rebellions were often severely crashed by the authorities. Thus, armed conflicts and social restlessness became a chronic feature of the Ottoman political economy which adversely affected the vitality of the empire in the long run.

Second, the Turkish Empire included a diverse, multicultural, and multi-ethnic population which included the Greeks, the Bulgarians, the Albanians, and others. Linguistically, culturally, and religiously, there was hardly any common binding force. The Ottomans for example largely followed the Islamic faith. However, even the various European races were not united, despite the fact that the majority of them practiced Christianity. Taking advantage of any weakness in the Ottoman Empire, the various subject races, which symbolized various nationalities, attempted to assert their independence from their Ottoman rulers. They were inspired by the ideas of nationalism which had been spreading across Europe after the French Revolution. For example, Greece attained independence in 1829 after their independence wars. Egypt emerged as a nation in 1841. The nationalist ideology made considerable headway in Romania, Bulgaria, Bosnia, Sarajevo, and other places. The Balkans thus turned into a laboratory for nationalist experimentation, giving birth to the Eastern Question.

Third, the perceived instabilities of the Ottoman Empire aroused both the apprehension and ambitions of the Great Powers of Europe. As a result, there ensued a series of international crises over the solution of the question. The problem was multi-faceted. In one sense, it was the problem of the rise of Christian nationalities in the Balkans, but in another sense it was the problem of the growing weakness of the Ottoman Empire. Both these developments exerted some influence on the policy of the powers who had interests in the Near East. The complex character of the problem was aptly described by Lord Morley who described the Eastern Question as a 'Shifting, interactable, and interwoven tangle of conflicting interests, rival peoples, and antagonistic faiths'.

One of the constant factors behind the rise of the Eastern Question was the ambition of Russia. Russia wanted to take advantage of Ottoman weaknesses to expel her from Europe and to occupy her position. The aim of Russian foreign policy during the eighteenth century had been to enrich herself at the cost of Turkey. The Treaty of Kuchuk-Kainarji (1774) was an important landmark in the history of Russian aggrandizement at the expense of the Ottoman Empire, for it gave Russia a firm grip on the northern shores of the Black Sea and offered the Black Sea to Russian navigation. Thus remaining a key barrier to Russia's expansion towards the Black Sea and the Mediterranean. The Peace of Jassey (1792) recognized the Russian annexation of Crimea. Thus, for Russian economic interests to continue to expand, Russian expansion towards Turkey and its ultimate dismemberment became key facets of Russian foreign policy. Two factors delayed the dismemberment of Turkey, the one military, the other geographical. The Ottoman Empire was not as weak as Poland from the military point of view and she was somewhat remote from the centre of political gravity until the mid-nineteenth century.

Fourth, the steady growth of Russian power in the Near East endangered the position of Austria, France, and England. These powers were not prepared to accept the steady growth of Russian influence in the area as they feared it might disturb the balance of power in Europe. Russia claimed herself to be the champion of pan-Slavic nationalism, cutting across national boundaries. As Austria had a Slav population, this idea was disturbing from their point of view hence, Austria was opposed to Russian expansion in the East. France disapproved of Russian aggression in the East so it might pose a serious challenge to French economic and commercial interests in Syria and Egypt. Again, the catholics of Balkans looked to France for guidance. France had also secured the guardianship of the Holy Places in the East. This concession caused constant quarrel with the Greek monks whose cause was supported by Russia. To England, Russian expansion in the Near East was particularly alarming for it threatened the security of the Indian Empire. England also feared that Russian control over the Black Sea and the Mediterranean might eventually endanger her international naval supremacy.

Thus, the Eastern Question did not remain a local question but became a matter of international concern. It involved the interests of all the leading powers of Europe who did not want to see Turkey as the 'Sickman of Europe'. From the points of view of England, France, and Austria it became imperative to prevent the dismemberment of Turkey by containing Russian expansionism in the region.

THE CRIMEAN WAR

The Crimean War was one of the most important episodes in the history of the Eastern Question during the nineteenth century. It began as an apparently insignificant conflict between Russia on the one side, and England, France, and Turkey on the other, but its effects were so far-reaching that they 'disturbed the states system established at Vienna' in 1815. The Crimean War reopened the Eastern Question and helped to internationalize the issue further.

Causes

The Crimean War has been called the most perfectly useless war that has been waged in modern times. 'On a London monument erected in memory of soldiers who had fallen at Balaclava and

Inkerman is chiselled the word Crimea. Place the East letter first and you have the verdict of history on this war.' Though this opinion represents an extreme view, that the war broke out on a very trivial issue. The war broke out as a result of the contest between the Latin Christian priests and the Greek Christian priests over the control of the Church in Jerusalem. France supported the Latin priests and Russia sided with the Greek priests. The catholics of Turkey looked up to France for guidance. France had secured the right over the Holy Places in the East in 1774 by the Treaty of Kuchuk-Kainarji. This brought France into constant quarrel with the Greek monks whose cause was backed by Russia. The issue came to the surface when Napoleon III revived the French right over Jerusalem in 1852.

Russia too, put forward her counter claim on the Greek Church and on the orthodox Christians of Turkey. Turkey readily accepted the French claim but she turned the Russian demand down. In response, Russia captured without any provocation, Wallachia and Moldavia, the Danubian Principalities. This was done to exert pressure upon Turkey to concede Russian demands. In retaliation, the Sultan of Turkey declared war against Russia in October 1853. As a Russo-Turkish War involved interests which vitally affected all the great powers, they could not afford to remain as spectators. England, France, and Piedmont-Sardinia joined the war in support of Turkey in March 1854 and this marked the formal beginning of the Crimean War. The religious conflict between France and Russia served as the immediate cause of the war but the conflict soon escalated.

Kinglake, the contemporary English historian has remarked that it was Napoleon III of France who provoked this 'perfectly useless war', but recent research suggests that Napoleon III's responsibility for the outbreak of the war was not as great as Kinglake would have us believe. The Greek monks found their patron in Tsar Nicholas I of Russia, who had already been trying to partition the Ottoman Empire with a view to increasing Russian influence and territory in south-eastern Europe. In 1853, in the course of his conversation with the British ambassador to St. Peterburg, Tsar Nicholas I spoke of Turkey as a country that 'seemed to be falling to pieces'. He described Turkey as the 'sickman of Europe', who was dying. The Tsar therefore felt that it was very important to come to an arrangement with regard to the 'sick man's' territories before his death. He proposed a joint Anglo-Russian partition of Turkey, but England did not want to see the dismemberment of Turkey for England knew that Russian expansion into Turkey would lead to increasing Russian influence in the Mediterranean and the Black Sea. She was aware that in such case, her own naval and commercial supremacy might face a serious challenge. England also feared that Russian control over Turkey might threaten the security of her Indian empire.

France and Austria too, wanted to control Russian advances into Turkey. Napoleon III also wanted to signalize his accession to the French throne with a dazzling foreign policy, which he hoped would reconcile the French people to his rule. The desire to avenge the failure of Napoleon Bonaparte's Moscow invasion in 1812 was also in his mind. France joined the war as a victory over Russia would maintain the prestige of France in the East, which had sunk low owing to the timid policy of Louis Philippe. Thus, the interests of the great powers can be seen as prime causes of the war. Piedmont-Sardinia supported France in the hope that Napoleon III would help her against Austria in uniting Italy. Austria remained neutral although she regarded Russian expansion in the Balkans as a menace to her interests. Prussia adopted the same policy. Tsar Nicholas I had wrongly anticipated that England would not go to war and that Austria would assist him. By the time he had realized his mistake, it was too late.

As Russian forces occupied Wallachia and Moldavia in 1853, a war became inevitable between Turkey and Russia. European diplomats, however made a last minute move to prevent the outbreak of a conflict. England, France, Prussia, and Austria met at Vienna and drew up a document known as the Vienna Note. The Vienna Note emphasized the need to protect the Christian subjects of Turkey and it was also an appeal to Russia to withdraw troops from Wallachia and Moldavia. This diplomatic initiative however, could not prevent the outbreak of the war and the Crimean War broke out in March 1854.

Course of the War

The Allies (England, France, Turkey, and Piedmont) concentrated their operations in Crimea and marched upon Sebastopol, defeating the Russians in a battle on the river Alma in 1854. The allied troops then besieged Sebastopol, and the rest of the war centred on this seige and on the Russian efforts to raise it. Russia was forced to yield from exhaustion, for she could not solve the problem of supplies and the difficulties of transport in a vast country without railways and with few roads. Defeated in the battles of Balaclava on 25 October 1854 and Inkesman on 5 November 1854 crushed by winter, and disorganized and unnerved by the death of Nicholas I in 1855, the Russians were forced to sue for peace. The Crimean War was brought to an end with the Peace of Paris in 1856. Alexander II, Nicholas I's successor to the Russian throne, concluded the Peace of Paris in 1856. The terms of the Peace were as follows: (1) The Black Sea was neutralized and opened to the merchant ships of all nations. Both Russia and Turkey were prevented from creating arsenals on their shores. (2) The river Danube was thrown open to all nations. (3) Russia gave up her protectorate claims over the Christian subjects of the Sultan. She also surrendered southern Bessarabia. (4) Finally, the Great Powers collectively guaranteed the independence and territorial integrity of the Ottoman Empire, and the Sultan was formally admitted to participate in public law and the Concert of Europe.

Results

The Crimean War began as an apparently insignificant conflict between Russia on the one side and England, France, and Turkey on the other, but its effects were far more far-reaching. Historians however disagree as to the importance of the war. Some scholars think that it was the most unnecessary war and that it could not solve any problem. Those who try to play down the importance of the war think that it could not, in any way, contribute to the solution of the Eastern Question. There is yet another group of scholars who think that the Crimean War was an important episode in European history, particularly in terms of the results it produced. As David Thomson has remarked, 'It was a fumbling war, probably unnecessary, largely futile, certainly extravagant, but rich with unintended consequence.' On balance however, the Crimean War can be seen as an important chapter in the Eastern Question and a prelude to some of the most important political developments of the nineteenth century. A.J.P. Taylor has observed that 'mutual fear, not mutual aggression caused the Crimean War, nevertheless it was not a war without a purpose'.

Though the Crimean War could not provide an enduring solution to the Eastern Question, it produced far-reaching direct and indirect consequences. The direct consequences were as follows: (1) Russian advances towards the Black Sea were checked. The Russian influence over Turkey was considerably tailored and Russia was forced to evacuate those areas which she had occupied earlier. (2) For the first time, Turkey was recognized as a member of the European 'family of nations' and invited to a European congress. She was now declared to be an integral part of the European system and so the European powers took up the responsibility of maintaining the territorial integrity of Turkey. (3) Napoleon III of France had gained ample glory from the Crimean War and so his authority in France was greatly strengthened. Paris had become the seat of a great international conference (the Peace of Paris) presided over by a French sovereign.

The indirect results of the war were even more important:

1. 'It was out of the mud of Crimea that a new Italy was made and less obviously, a new Germany'—Cavour. Piedmont-Sardinia participated in this war with a view to win the sympathies of England and France. By sending 17,000 men on the side of the Allies, Cavour won the goodwill of Napoleon III which proved to be of immense value in his future work for the Unification of Italy. France reciprocated by offering help against Austria. Without this foreign aid, Cavour could never have driven Austria out of Italy.

2. The Russian advance had been checked on the Danube, but

Russian energy was now steered in the direction of Asia. She began to expand in Central Asia which threatened the safety of the British Indian Empire.

3.   Russia suffered heavily from the war. She lost about half a million men and her resources were drained. The corruption of the Tsarist regime now became public knowledge in Europe and so the Tsar was widely discredited and in the long run the dissatisfaction of the people flared into popular discontent.

4.   The war fostered the rise of nationalist forces in the Balkans which in turn had a variety of repercussions in European politics.

5.   An unexpected but positive outcome of the Crimean War were the improvements in camp sanitation and the health of soldiers that were effected by Florence Nightingale. She organized a nursing team to take care for the sick and wounded soldiers. This also marked the nascent beginning of the movement which later came to be known as the Red Cross.

EASTERN QUESTION FROM THE TREATY OF PARIS (1856) TO THE TREATY OF BERLIN (1878)

The Peace of Paris failed to provide an enduring solution to the Eastern Question. By the Treaty of Paris (1856), the [Porte] had been admitted as a member of the European system from which she had previously been excluded. It was expected that Turkey would take steps to become modern and democratic, but no such transformation took place. The Balkans remained under the Sultanate of the Ottoman Empire.

Just as the Greeks had been inspired to revolt by the French Revolution, the examples of Italian and Germanic national movements inspired the Serbians, the Bulgarians, and the Romanians and a wave of intense nationalism swept over the Balkans after 1870. This restlessness in the region reopened the issue of Eastern Question. In Russia, the official and military circles wanted to erase the humiliations of the Crimean War. Russia was looked upon as the leader of the Slavs and so sympathy was aroused

MAP 7.1: The Balkans in 1878

among all the slavic nationalities when Russia was defeated in the Crimean War. Russia wanted to use this Pan-Slavism in her own advantage. Russia hoped that by championing the cause of the Slav people against the Ottoman Sultan, she could transform them into Russian satellites. The envoys of this movement were sent to the Balkans to stimulate and agitate racial consciousness among the Slavs of Serbia, Bosnia, and Bulgaria. It was from these districts that the next episode of the Eastern Question arose.

Explosive forces were at work across the Balkan peninsula. The peasants of Bosnia and Herzegovina felt their position all the more acutely when compared with their Serbian counterparts just across the border, who were free from all these grievances. As Turkey was becoming bankrupt, the government imposed a heavy burden of taxation. In 1874, following a bad harvest, the peasants of Herzegovina rose in revolt. The Sultan failed to suppress the rebellion as the rebels were solidly backed by Russia and Serbia. Austria, Serbia, and Russia proposed to exert pressure on the Sultan to implement reforms but this could not be implemented due to the opposition of England.

Meanwhile events in Constantinople took a turn for the worse, Abdul Hamid II (1876–1909), a very resolute and shrewd ruler came to power through a palace revolution in 1876. The threat of European intervention triggered off a corresponding religious and racial fanaticism among the Turks. Under the umbrella of Slavic nationalism, the Bulgarians rose in revolt at this time, but troops were deployed to crush the insurgents. About 12,000 Bulgarians were slaughtered in cold blood. The Bulgarian atrocities shocked the whole of Europe. Disraeli's famous pamphlet 'Bulgarian Horrors and the Eastern Question' concluded with the words, 'Let the Turks now carry away their abuses in the only possible manner, namely, by carrying off themselves . . . one and all, bag and baggage . . . from the provinces they have desolated and profaned'. Diplomatic moves were made to persuade the Sultan to adopt a democratic constitution but to no avail. A general conference of European powers met at Constantinople and drew up a programme of reform for Turkey. However, after the conference, the Sultan of Turkey forgot to implement the reforms.

The Turkish government dared to defy the united voice of Europe because they knew that Britain would surely come to their rescue if the situation became too critical for Turkey. This attitude of Turkey was further reinforced by a speech which Disraeli delivered in London in which he threatened Russia that Britain would not hesitate to enter into a war with Russia if it was a righteous war.

The last attempt at a compromise failed in March 1877 when Turkey refused to accept the Protocol of London which was a compromise formula evolved by the great powers. After the failure of the compromise, Russia decided to act alone and took to the field against Turkey. Before declaring war on Turkey however, Russia entered into a secret agreement with Austria by which it was agreed that Austria would maintain an attitude of benevolent neutrality in the event of a Russo-Turkish War and that as a reward, she would gain certain territories from the Ottoman Empire in future. Having arrived at this agreement with Austria, Russia declared war on the Ottoman Empire in April 1877. The Russian troops marched very quickly and within a year they appeared before the gates of Constantinople.

Turkey was now compelled to sue for peace and the Treaty of San Stefano was concluded in March 1878. The treaty had the following important clauses:

1. It was decided that Serbia, Montenegro, and Romania were to be independent of Turkey. These principalities which once belonged to Turkey had already become autonomous, but from now on, they were to be regarded as fully independent.
2. It was decided that Bosnia and Herzegovina would be autonomous, but that they would still remain within the Ottoman Empire.
3. Reforms were to be introduced for the Armenian subjects living in Asia Minor.
4. It was decided that a kingdom of Greater Bulgaria would be set up under the nominal control of the Ottoman Empire but with a Christian government and a national militia.
5. It was settled that Russia would get a large chunk of territory

in Asia and also the territory of Bessarabia in Europe from Romania. In return for Bessarabia, Russia would grant Rumania a strip of territory called Dobruja.

The Treaty of San Stefano, which practically decreed the dissolution of the Ottoman Empire in Europe, was a great diplomatic triumph for Russia but the treaty left many parties disgruntled and had to be revised. For example, the Treaty of San Stefano satisfied only one of the Balkan nationalities, namely the Bulgarians, and so all other Balkan peoples were dissatisfied. Romania was dissatisfied because though she became independent, she had to surrender the whole of Bessarabia to Russia, a territory which was almost completely inhabited by Romanian people in lieu of the much poorer district of Dobruja. The Greeks were dissatisfied because all their hopes of pushing towards the north were shattered when the much coveted Macedonia was given to Greater Bulgaria.

So far as the great powers were concerned, England and Austria had reasons enough to be dissatisfied with the treaty of San Stefano: (1) England was afraid that the creation of Greater Bulgaria would establish Russian supremacy over the Balkan peninsula and transform the Black Sea into a 'Russian Lake'. Bulgaria, it was feared, would become a mere Russian satellite and a springboard from which Russia could launch an attack on Constantinople at any time in future. (2) Austria was dissatisfied because she had not obtained any compensation for remaining neutral during the Russo-Turkish War and she wanted to enrich herself at the cost of the Ottoman Empire. England and Austria, therefore, insisted that the treaty of San Stefano must be submitted to a conference of European powers for revision and reconsideration. Russia was at first most unwilling to allow this. She felt that she alone had shed her blood and spent her money to save the Christian subjects of Turkey and the slight compensation which she had received was not out of proportion of her efforts. However, the defiant attitude of Disraeli and his melodramatic gestures of war compelled Russia to concede and so the Treaty of San Stefano was submitted to a conference of the great powers of Europe which met in Berlin under the chairmanship of Bismarck in June 1878.

Disraeli and Salisbury represented England at the Berlin Conference and the former practically dominated the entire show. The diplomats altered the terms of the Treaty of San Stefano and signed a new treaty called the Treaty of Berlin in which it was decided:

1. To split up the kingdom of Greater Bulgaria into three smaller kingdoms. Macedonia was returned to the Ottoman Empire, Bulgaria proper became an autonomous kingdom under Ottoman authority, and Eastern Rumelia was placed under a Christian governor appointed by the Ottoman Sultan. The return of Macedonia was prompted by the fear that through this part of the kingdom of Greater Bulgaria, Russian influence could reach the Mediterranean.

2. The Treaty of Berlin conferred upon Russia certain districts in Armenia taking from Turkey but from Russia.

3. The Treaty of Berlin permitted Austria to indefinitely administer the principalities of Bosnia and Herzegovina where the revolt had originally started in 1875. Though Austria was asked to administer these two principalities, they were still formally under Ottoman suzerainty.

4. England received the island of Cyprus in the Mediterranean and in return, she undertook to guarantee the integrity of the remaining Ottoman dominions in Asia. This English occupation of Cyprus was to continue so long as Russia occupied the Armenian districts.

5. The independence of Serbia, Montenegro, and Rumelia, all of which had once belonged to the Ottoman Empire was now formally recognized.

Disraeli's return from the Congress of Berlin was considered to be a veritable triumph in which he had achieved 'peace with honour'. However, the Treaty of Berlin also failed to remove the grievances of the Balkan nationalities. Though it is likely that there could have been no solution which would equally please all the Balkan nationalities because their claims were often in violent conflict with one another, the main defect of the Berlin settlement was that it completely sacrificed the interests of the Balkan Christians in order to satisfy the great powers. Thus, we find that Greece remained discontented because Macedonia was handed back to the Ottoman Empire. Romania was dissatisfied because she had to surrender Bessarabia to Russia in exchange for a much larger, yet poorer territoty—Dobruja. Serbia was extremely unhappy because Bosnia and Herzegovina, which were Serb districts, were handed over to Austria. It became a bone of contention between Austria and Serbia and ultimately became an indirect cause of the First World War.

Britain was unable to change the character of the Treaty of San Stefano so far as the advantages which Russia had obtained from this treaty were concerned. That is, the Treaty of Berlin modified the Treaty of San Stefano but did not nullify it. However, within Russia there was strong criticism of the Treaty of Berlin. There was a general feeling that the fruits of Russia's victory over the Ottoman Empire in the war of 1877 had been snatched away by Britain and Austria. Coming to the question of peace, though there was no major war in Europe for nearly three decades after the Treaty of Berlin, the treaty contained the seeds of many future wars. It was over the question of Macedonia that the Balkan War started in 1912 and the Austro-Serbian rivalry played a fundamental role in triggering the First World War.

THE EASTERN QUESTION FROM THE TREATY OF BERLIN (1878) TO THE FIRST WORLD WAR (1914–18)

The Berlin Congress failed to unlock the Eastern Question. Instead of preventing the dissolution of the Ottoman Empire, the Berlin settlement merely delayed the extinction of Turkey. In the history of European diplomacy however, the Congress of Berlin marked a turning point for Bismarck, who presided over this Congress. He made no attempt to help the Tsar, nor did he try to defend those clauses of the Treaty of San Stefano to which England and Austria objected. Bismarck had perhaps no positive desire to alienate Russia, but in effect, this was the revolt of his actions. He soon realized that the time had come when he must choose between his two eastern neighbours, Austria and Russia, and ultimately he chose Austria. Though the Reinsurance Treaty (1881) re-established friendly contacts between Germany and Russia, the Dual Alliance became the sheet anchor of German foreign policy from 1879 onwards.

The Balkan Wars (1912–13)

The First Balkan War started in 1912 and it arose chiefly out of Turkish misrule in Macedonia. The Berlin Settlement had restored Macedonia to the Ottoman Empire but it did not prevent Turkish misrule there. In September 1911, taking advantage of Ottoman weakness, Italy declared war and sought to seize the territory of Tripoli in North Africa. The Italian invasion of the Ottoman Empire stimulated risings in Macedonia and Albania where the local people were unhappy with Ottoman rule. Bulgaria, Serbia, Greece, and Montenegro formed a League to oust the Ottoman Empire from Europe. King Ferdinand of Bulgaria was the prime mover behind this alliance of the Balkan states. He took the initiative in uniting the four Balkan states for a common cause and he also entered into a secret treaty with Serbia which outlined the division of spoils among these two powers in the event of victory. Turkey attempted to overcome the Balkan League and she also obtained an assurance from the Great Powers that they would not permit any change in the territorial status quo of the Ottoman Empire in Europe. However, despite this assurance, the Ottoman government failed to rise to the occasion and the Balkan League was soon victorious.

The Great Powers now intervened and imposed an armistice upon the fighting states and summoned a peace conference in London. However, the peace conference failed to produce the desired results and war was soon resumed. Turkey was again defeated. The First Balkan War was finally brought to an end by the Treaty of London (1913) in which Turkey gave up all her possessions in Europe except Constantinople and a strip of territory along the Straits of Dardanelles. The division of the spoils of war however, proved to be a very difficult task on account of the demands of the Balkan allies, and the conflicting ambitions and interests of the great powers.

The victory of the Balkan League in the First Balkan War was generally interpreted as a gain for the prestige of Russia and correspondingly as a loss to Austria and Germany. Serbia, who had been an active member of the Balkan League, tried to expand her territories at the cost of the defeated power for she wanted to seize Albania. This was strongly opposed by Austria because Serbia was an ally of Russia and there were also fears that if Serbia became powerful, the integrity of the Austrian Empire itself might be threatened. That is, there was a large number of Serb or Yugoslav people within the Austrian Empire and so it was felt that if Serbia became powerful, these people could demand a merger with Serbia. Austria therefore protested against Serbia's attempt to grab Albania and ultimately the conflict was averted only by setting up Albania as an independent state under the rule of a German prince. Serbia thus failed to gain access to the Adriatic Sea and became a source of even greater discontent towards Austria. An international conflict was averted by the creation of a new kingdom of Alliance, but, this again precipitated a war among the Balkan allies which is known as the Second Balkan War.

The creation of an independent Albania prevented a war between Austria and Serbia but another international conflict was precipitated. Serbia, being deprived of Albania, demanded as compensation a part of Macedonia which had been previously allotted to Bulgaria. Encouraged by Austria-Hungary, King Ferdinand of Bulgaria, refused to comply with this demand and so Serbia was thus alienated from Bulgaria. A bitter quarrel also developed between Bulgaria and Greece over the disposition of Thrace which was claimed by both powers. Serbia and Greece then declared war on Bulgaria, and was shortly joined by Romania and Turkey. Romania was afraid of being overshadowed by Greater Bulgaria and Turkey wanted to take revenge on Bulgaria but also to recover part of the territories which she had to surrender at the end of the First Balkan War. The Second Balkan War was of a very short duration. Attacked on all sides by four different powers and unable to secure any assistance from the Great Powers, Bulgaria was quickly defeated and compelled to sue for peace. By the Treaty of Bucharest in August 1913, Bulgaria was compelled to make territorial concessions to all of her opponents. Serbia was assigned the greater part of Macedonia while Greece was offered the island of Crete, Southern Macedonia, and Western Thrace. Romania got a small piece of territory from Bulgaria, and Adrianople was restored to the Ottomans.

The net result of the two Balkan Wars was the virtual dissolution of the European Ottoman Empire. In the end, this empire lost nearly 90 per cent of her former European territory and was confined to the south-eastern corner of the Balkan Peninsula. The greatest benefactors were Serbia and Greece while the worst sufferer was Bulgaria. However, the two Balkan Wars could still not solve all the problems facing the Balkan peoples. Rather they merely served to intensify the nationalism and stimulate the spirit of self-aggrandizement in the Balkan states. Bulgaria knew that she had contributed most to the decline of the Ottoman Empire and yet had not got much in return. Therefore, Bulgaria was now extremely eager to avail herself of any opportunity to humiliate Serbia and to take back Macedonia. The spirit of rivalry between Austria and Serbia was also intensified by the two Balkan Wars. This was mainly due to the creation of Albania. Russia again appeared in the role of the protector of the Balkan states. Finally, Turkey undertook military reforms, became more nationalist in spirit, and concluded a diplomatic and economic alliance with Germany. All these developments prepared the ground for the outbreak of the First World War.

HIGHLIGHTS

- The Ottoman Empire gradually collapsed in the nineteenth century. The declining Ottoman Empire, the nationalist aspirations of the people in this region, Russian expansionism, and the responses of the European powers gave birth to a unique problem of modern history.

This problem is known as the Eastern Question. In short, the Eastern Question grew out of the restlessness of the Balkan Peninsula.

- The Crimean War (1854–6) constitutes one of the important chapters in the history of the Eastern Question. Although the Crimean War was primarily a Russo-Turkish War, the Great Powers of Europe also became involved. The war finally came to an end with the Peace of Paris in 1856.

- The Peace of Paris could not solve the problems in the Balkans. It only delayed the fragmentation of the Ottoman Empire. The Eastern Question became even more complicated due to the rise of Balkan nationalities, Russian aggression, and the weakening of the Ottoman Empire. The Russo-Turkish War that followed in 1877, was brought to an end by the Treaty of San Stefano. This treaty symbolized the victory of Russia over the Ottoman Empire.

- The European Powers had reservations about the terms and conditions of the Treaty of San Stefano. The Berlin Conference met in 1878 to review the previous treaty and frame a fresh treaty called the Berlin Treaty. This too, failed to resolve the Balkan problem.

- Taking advantage of the weakness of the Ottoman Empire all the European Powers pushed to expand their power.

- The Balkans remained a source of disorder in European politics. Balkan nationalist aspirations continued unresolved and there were two major wars in the Balkans—the First Balkan War and the Second Balkan War. The dismemberment of the Ottoman Empire was complete after the First World War in 1919.

MEMORABLE DATES AND EVENTS

1774	Treaty of Kuchuk-Kainarji
1854	The Crimean War
1856	Treaty of Paris
1878	Treaty of San Stefano
	The Berlin Congress
1912	The Balkan League
	The First Balkan War
1913	Treaty of London
	The Second Balkan War
	Treaty of Bucharest

MEMORABLE PERSONALITIES

Tsar Nicholas I (1825–55): Tsar of Russia when the Crimean War was fought
Napoleon III: Head of the French Republic
Cavour: The Prime Minister of Piedmont-Sardinia
Bismarck: Chancellor of Germany
Disraeli: Prime Minister of Britain
Abdul Hamid II: Sultan of Turkey

QUOTABLE QUOTES

- 'The Crimean War occupies a peculiar place in the history of Europe in the nineteenth century.' —DAVID THOMSON
- 'It was a fumbling war, probably unnecessary, largely futile, certainly extravagant, but rich with unintended consequences.' —A.J.P. TAYLOR
- 'The settlement reached at the Congress of Berlin had the remarkable outcome that it left each power dissatisfied and more anxious than ever.' —DAVID THOMPSON
- 'Incidentally we may assume that the Treaty of Berlin was breaking down as had the Treaty of Paris. A repetition of the demand that Turkey should reform was treated with the same indifference as of old. The Sultan knew that he could profit by the usual rivalries and do nothing.' —T.W. RICKER
- 'Let the Turks now carry away their abuses in the only possible manner, namely, by carrying off themselves . . . one and all, bag and baggage . . . from the provinces they have desolated and profaned.' —DISRAELI

CHAPTER 8

First World War (1914–1918)

INTRODUCTION

The First World War is one of the most significant events in the history of the world. The typology of this war was of a qualitatively different kind and of a greater magnitude than any war which preceded it. More important than the military significance of the war were its social, political, economic, and diplomatic consequences. Historians disagree as to the causes of this war and the debates on the subject continue. David Thomson (*Europe Since Napoleon*) has remarked that, 'The most important thing about the First World War is that it was unsought, un-intended and the product of a long sequence of events which began in 1871'. The international situation in Europe for a little over two decades before the war was one of 'armed peace'. The powers of Europe had become aligned into two hostile camps through a number of alliances. Bismarck's diplomatic efforts culminated in the formation of the Triple Alliance between Germany, Austria, and Italy in 1882. At the same time, he attracted Russia to his side by making separate agreements with her in the *Dreikaiserbund* treaties and the Reinsurance Treaty of 1887. In time a counter system of alliance grew up in Europe to meet the threat of the new alliances.

CAUSES

The First World War that began in 1914 marked the advent of a new era in European and world history. It was essentially a war between the European nations who at that time controlled most of the world. James Joll argues that any single explanation for the outbreak of the war is likely to be too simple. An amalgam of factors including intellectual, socio-economic, political, and diplomatic, contributed to this horrifying conflict of unprecedented proportions.

The developments that had the most profound historical effect by the closing decades of the nineteenth century, involved the expansion of Europe overseas. The countries of Africa and Asia were opened to European influence on a far greater scale than ever before. This led to imperialist rivalry among the great powers to ensure greater political influence in Europe as well as in Asia and Africa. The industrial developments of Europe led to the concentration of capital in fewer and fewer hands. Financiers were finding it difficult to invest their money profitably. The European market became saturated and consequently it became essential to search for new fields or avenues of investment overseas. This need forced the European powers to divide the world between themselves in a 'scramble' for new colonial markets and new areas in which to invest their capital. This struggle, in its turn, led to direct annexation of territories overseas. The European powers had almost entered into a competition for establishing colonies in Africa and Asia in the middle of the nineteenth century. Britain established the largest number of colonies in Africa. She was followed by Belgium, France, Portugal, Spain, and Holland. The result was that rivalry between these powers escalated and imperialism necessarily culminated into war.

The insurgent nationalism of the late nineteenth century provided the background for the First World War. The European nations were all out to establish their racial superiority at the cost of other countries. This trend found its greatest manifestation in Germany for the Germans considered themselves to be the 'master race' who were destined to rule the entire world.

System of Alliances:
Triple Alliance/Triple Entente

The enduring hostility between France and Germany was one of the most constant factors in international diplomacy between 1871 and 1914. In many ways Germany was regarded as a dominant state of Europe during this period. In the immediate aftermath of German Unification under Prussian leadership, the primary object of Bismarck's diplomacy was to place the new German Empire on safe foundations. To achieve this, Bismarck needed to ensure that France, the greatest potential enemy of Germany, remained isolated. Only thus could he prevent France from seeking revenge for their defeat at German hands in the Franco-German war of 1870 (especially the Battle of Sedan) and also the recovery of Alsace-Lorraine, which she had to hand over to Germany. Bismarck knew that if Germany was involved in hostilities with another European power, there was a danger that France would side with Germany's opponents. He therefore set out to isolate France diplomatically and to deprive her of potential allies and supporters: (1) He adopted a conciliatory attitude towards Austria-Hungary. (2) He took pains to cultivate the friendship of Italy. (3) He attempted to avoid giving offence to England and sought to secure her goodwill. (4) He succeeded in coming to a friendly understanding with Russia.

In 1872, Bismarck persuaded the emperors of Germany, Austria, and Russia to form a League of Three Emperors which came to be known as *Dreikaiserbund*. This alliance did not endure long primarily because Austria and Russia had conflicting interests in south-eastern Europe. In 1875, there was also a war scare between France and Germany in which Russia showed herself to be an uncertain ally. It is probable that from that date onwards, Bismarck was determined to cultivate more definitely the friendship of Austria.

In 1878, in consequence of the Russo-Turkish War, Russian ambitions came into conflict with the interests of Austria and Britain. At the Congress of Berlin (1878) Bismarck therefore exerted his influence against Russia. The result was that the Russo-German relation became strained. In compensation however, Bismarck secured a firm alliance with Austria. In 1879, a secret treaty was concluded between Germany and Austria known as the Dual Alliance. It provided that if either party, Germany or Austria, was attacked by Russia, then the other party would be bound to render military assistance.

After placing Germany's friendship with Austria on a secure

foundation, Bismarck tried to ensure the stability of Europe by turning towards Italy. France and Italy were then aspiring for colonial expansion in Africa. Using Franco-Italian rivalry over Tunis as an excuse, Bismarck persuaded Italy to forget her hereditary enmity towards Austria and in 1882 concluded a secret military pact between Italy, Austria-Hungary, and Germany. This was known as the Triple Alliance, a defensive alliance in part against France and in part against Russia.

However, for Bismarck the friendship of Austria and Italy was not enough and he tried to reconcile Russia so that the eastern frontier of Germany might remain secure. In 1884, he concluded the famous Reinsurance Treaty which guaranteed Russian neutrality in the event that Germany came under attack. It may be said, therefore, that during the years 1878–90, 'Germany, under Bismarck's guidance, was the pivot of European politics, that Bismarck's policy was directed, by a balancing of alliances, toward the status quo, the isolation of France, and the comprehensive protection of Germany, in short, that the peace of Europe rested on the Bismarckian system.'

Britain, another great European power, kept equidistant from both the alliances until Kaiser William II's new naval policy from the 1890s set Britain against Germany as well. After the fall of Bismarck in 1890, Kaiser William II took upon himself to direct German policy in Europe. He did not accept Bismarck's view that Germany was a 'satiated' country; he believed that the Germans were a nation capable of 'infinite expansion' and were destined to dominate not only Europe but the whole world. He tried to secure colonies which would offer an outlet for surplus population and expanding commerce. German colonial ambition called for the construction of a large and powerful naval fleet. This was looked upon as a challenge to England's age-long naval supremacy. The result was the alienation of England and Russia. Britain was driven into forming a league with her own traditional enemy, France and so in 1904, an Anglo-French agreement was concluded. In 1907 an agreement between Russia and England, that is, the Anglo-Russian Convention, settled the outstanding disputes between the two countries relating to Afghanistan, Tibet, and Persia and thus the three great powers came together and formed the Triple Entente.

By the beginning of the twentieth century Europe became divided into two armed camps. On one side stood Germany, Austria, and Italy, united by the Triple Alliance, and on the other stood, France, England, and Russia banded together in the Triple Entente. Constant friction and growing hostility between these two systems of power made Europe advance steadily towards the First World War.

The Morocco Crisis (1905–6)

The Moroccan crisis was the first of a series of incidents that culminated in the outbreak of war. France could never forget the loss and humiliation inflicted on her by the Germans at the battle of Sedan in 1870 and so she was on the lookout for an opportunity to recover the provinces of Alsace and Lorraine which had been annexed by Germany. Moreover, the French people resented Bismarck's persistent efforts to isolate them and encircle France with potential enemies. The problem of Morocco in North Africa provided the justification for an open rupture between Germany and France.

Morocco was an independent Mohammedan province and one of the few remaining areas of Africa not controlled by any European power. Partly because of its rich iron deposits, and partly because of its strategic position, it had aroused the interest of many European powers like Spain, Britain, France, Germany, and Italy. In the Anglo-French Treaty of 1904, Britain had promised to render diplomatic support to French interests in the province, on the understanding that France would recognize Britain's position in Egypt. The French claim over Morocco was opposed by the German Emperor Kaiser William II, who appeared personally at Tangiers. Loudly proclaiming indifference of Morocco and the sovereignty of her Sultan, the Emperor insisted that all foreign powers were entitled to enjoy equal commercial and economic interests in that country. The German Emperor also demanded an international conference to be held to discuss the Moroccan problem. In 1906 a conference duly met at Algeciras in southern Spain. Although, Germany thus won a diplomatic victory, this action only served to strengthen the Anglo-French entente. It also brought Britain into more cordial relations with Russia. The Algeciras Conference (1907) decided that France could not annex Morocco entirely, but she was authorized, subject to a certain amount of international control, to regulate the affairs of the country. The diplomatic victory remained with Germany, but the substantial profits went to France.

The Bosnia Crisis (1908)

The Bosnia Crisis of 1908 aggravated the tensions. Bosnia-Herzegovina had been brought under the administration of Austria by the decision of the Berlin Congress (1878). Taking advantage of the Young Turk Revolution in Turkey, Austria absorbed these two provinces within her empire in 1908. This naturally inflamed Serbian nationalist sentiment against Austria, since these provinces included a million Serbs among their population. The Serbs appealed to their fellow Slavs, the Russians, for help in the expectation of French and British support. Britain and France were however only lukewarm in their response. Austria-Hungary backed by Germany, was opposed to any such conference and no help for Serbia was forthcoming. Germany on the other hand put pressure upon Russia to recognize Austria's annexation of Bosnia and Herzegovina. Although, it proved to be a triumph of for the Austro-German Alliance, it had unfortunate results. Serbia became violently hostile to Austria and this quarrel culminated in the outbreak of the war. Thus, the dispute between Austria and Russia over the Balkans was one of the cardinal causes of the First World War.

The Agadir Crisis (1911)

The Agadir Crisis was a further development of the Moroccan crisis. France was bent upon the annexation of the Moroccan province. On the plea of serious internal disorder she marched her troops into the Moroccan capital of and refused to withdraw them. Germany sent a warship, the *Panther* to the Moroccan port of Agadir. The ostensible reason was to defend German interests, but in reality, it was in the hope of blackmailing France into giving up some of France's colonial possessions elsewhere in Africa, preferably the French Congo in return for recognizing French interests in Morocco. The British were worried, that if the Germans acquired Agadir, they could construct a naval base which could threaten British trade interests and so Britain stood out firmly on the side of France. Germany, on the other hand, decided not to force the question to the point of war and Germany and France were able to reconcile their differences passively in the Treaty of Fez, July 1911. Germany agreed to recognize the establishment of a French protectorate over Morocco and in return, France ceded to her two strips of territory in the French Congo. In 1912, France formally declared Morocco as a protectorate. The Agadir incident was a further defeat for Germany and instead of breaking up the Triple Entente, it strengthened it.

The Balkan Wars

The growing demand for national self-determination in the Balkans had two targets, Austria-Hungary and Turkey. Many thousands of Serbs and Bulgarians, as well as Greeks, were still living under Turkish rule. The experience of Young Turk rule caused Greeks, Serbs, Montenegrians and Bulgarians to unite into the common front of the Balkan League. On 8 October 1912, Montenegro declared war on Turkey, and within a week Bulgaria, Greece, and Serbia did the same. By the end of the month, they had defeated every Turkish army in Europe capturing most of the Turkish territories in Europe. A conference of ambassadors of European countries met in London under the chairmanship of the British Foreign Secretary Sir Edward Grey. The resulting settlement apportioned the former Turkish lands among the Balkan states. However, the Serbs were not happy with their gains as they wanted Albania so as to have an outlet to the sea. However,

Austria, Britain and Germany insisted that Albania should became an independent state to a deliberately limit Serbian expansion southwards.

By May 1913, with the conclusion of the Treaty of London between the Balkan states and the Turks, the Turkish rule in Europe had virtually ended with the notable exception of Constantinople itself, and the eastern part of Thrace. However, within a month the victorious allies became enmeshed in a quarrel over the spoils. The Bulgarians were dissatisfied since they were hoping to gain Macedonia most of which was occupied and retained by Serbia. Bulgaria therefore attacked Serbia, starting the world war. The Bulgarian plan did not succeed, because the Greeks, the Romanians, and the Turks rallied to support Serbia. The Bulgarians were defeated and by the Treaty of Bucharest in 1913, they forfeited most of their gains from the first war: they lost part of Macedonia to Serbia and much of Thrace to Greece.

Militarism

Another important cause of the First World War was militarism. The word 'militarism' includes at least two different concepts: (1) it implies the existence of the dangerous and burdensome mechanisms of large standing armies and powerful navies with their attendant evils of suspicion, espionage, fear, and hatred, and (2) it implies the existence of a body of influential military and naval officers who tended to dominate over the civil authorities in times of political emergency. The system of maintaining large standing armies was initiated by France during the Revolutionary and Napoleonic periods. It was later used by Prussia under Bismarck. Finally, after 1871 the system came to be respected and widely adopted across Europe. It meant that every powerful nation would go on expanding its military and naval forces indefinitely. The psychological attitude of the military officials was dominated by a belief in the inevitability of war and since they regarded war as inevitable, they wanted to draw up plans of military action and mobilization of troops years in advance. They always wanted to be ready with their technical plans of action. Sometimes the details of these plans were not known even to the foreign ministers of the nations concerned.

Immediate Cause

The incident that was the immediate spark of the war was the assassination of the Archduke Franz Ferdinand, heir to the throne of Austria. The Archduke was paying an official visit to the Bosnian capital of Sarajevo when he, along with his wife, were fired at and killed by a group of terrorists on 28 June 1914. Austria suspected that the hand of the Serbian Government lay behind the murder and that behind the entire plot lay a great conspiracy to cause the disintegration of the Hapsburg Empire.

On 23 July 1914, the Austrian ministerial council sent an ultimatum to Belgrade, Serbia demanding the apprehension of the criminals who were hiding there and their handover to the Austrian authorities. Serbia rejected the ultimatum. Using this incident as an excuse, Austria declared war on Serbia exactly one month after the assassination on 28 July 1914. The anti-Serbian move of Austria was fully backed by Germany under the terms of the Triple Alliance.

COURSE OF THE WAR

The machines of war were set in motion. The Central Powers, viz., Germany, Austria, Hungry, and Turkey were confronted by the Allied Powers of Russia, France, Britain, Serbia, and Belgium. At first Germany and Austria thought that the war was likely to be a localized one and that Austria was sure to come out victorious. However, any crisis in south-eastern Europe was bound to attract the attention of the big European powers. When Austria attacked Serbia, Russia took the Serbian side and made ready for war. Germany asked Russia to withdraw her forces and on Russia's refusal, Germany declared war against Russia on 1 August 1914. Since France had formed an alliance with Russia, which was aimed against their common rival Germany, she sent her troops in support of Russia and as a consequence, Germany declared war on France on 3 August 1914.

Initially Britain remained neutral. When the war began between Germany and France, England demanded from both of them, a guarantee to respect Belgian neutrality. Germany violated this agreement and marched her troops into Belgium using that country as a corridor from which to invade France. This German attack on Belgium and also Luxembourg alarmed Britain, and she was left with no other alternative but to resist German attack on Belgium as a German occupation of Belgium was likely to have endangered her security. The escalation of tension reached its culminating point when Austro-Hungary also declared war on Russia on 6 August 1914.

The War spread to Asia when Turkey joined the Austro-German Alliance. Japan declared war against Germany in August 1914 to prevent the spread of German influence on the Chinese coast and Italy entered the war in 1915. The entry of the United States of America in April 1917 brightened the prospects of victory for the Allies.

GERMAN RESPONSIBILITY FOR THE WAR

The simple explanation that the First World War was the direct result of German policies and German ambitions has been the centre of controversies about the origins of the war ever since. It has led to a detailed examination of the diplomatic archives to support or refute the view that Germany was solely responsible for the war. It has also made the question of German 'war guilt' the main theme of innumerable political and historial discussions.

English historians hold that the provocative speeches and activities of the German Emperor Kaiser William II were responsible for preparing an ambience of war. Modern historians however, are not inclined to assign unilateral responsibility of the war on Germany. They point out that although it was German militarism which ignited the spark, all the combatants should share the responsibility for creating a war-like tension. Imanuel Geiss (*Origins of the First World War*) has argued that imperialism, specifically in its German manifestation, provided the general framework, while the basic tensions and principles of national self-determination constituted, with its revolutionary potential, a permanent but latent threat to the old dynastic empires and built up tensions in south-east Europe. The determination of the German Empire—then the most powerful conservative force in the world after Tsarist Russia—to uphold conservative and monarchic principles by any means, against the rising tide of democracy, made the war inevitable. It was the violation of Belgiam neutrality by Germany which brought Britain into the First World War. The danger of the military authorities prevailing over the civil ones proved to be much greater in the European autocracies like Germany, Austria, and Russia than in England and France.

THE VERSAILLES SETTLEMENT

The war came to an end on 11 November 1918 with the surrender of Germany. At the end of the First World War the victorious Allied Powers met in Paris in 1919 to arrange the terms of peace. The Paris Peace Conference, was inaugurated on the 18 January 1919, the exact date on which, 48 years ago the Hohenzollern King of Prussia was proclaimed as the Emperor of Germany. The venue of the Conference was also the same Hall of Mirrors to the royal palace of Versailles, where King William I of Prussia was proclaimed as the German Emperor. This clearly indicated that the Allied Powers were at last going to undo the achievements of Bismarck and the Hohenzollerns. The choice of the date and place of the Paris Peace Conference clearly illustrates the popular psychology in the Allied countries, particularly England and France.

Owing to persistent war propaganda and personal experience of the horrors of the war, the great majority of the people of the Allied countries came to believe that it was Germany and Austria who were mainly responsible for the war, and that these two powers must therefore be punished severely. Even the experienced statesmen representing the four big powers: Clemenceau of

France, Orlando of Italy, Lloyd George of England, and Theodore Roosevelt of the United States voiced the popular demand for punishing Germany and Austria. The assurance given by Woodrow Wilson, the President of the United States, in his famous Fourteen Points (1918), to the effect that the punishment would be directed not against the defeated peoples but against their autocratic governments, was bound to evoke displeasure in the midst of this general clamour for revenge.

Though the Paris Peace Conference was attended by the representatives of the Allied Powers and their associated nations, the important decisions were taken by the representatives of the four big powers—England, France, Italy, and the United States. The actual work of the Conference was done by small committees in complete privacy and the representatives of the defeated nations were not allowed ever to enter the Conference Hall. It was only on the 7 May 1919, that the German representatives were allowed to attend the Conference because on that day they were presented with the terms of Versailles Treaty, which had already been settled by the big powers and formally endorsed by the Peace Conference. The German representatives were critical about the terms of the treaty and found it contradictory to the assurances given by Wilson in his Fourteen Points, on the basis of which Germany had agreed to lay down arms and to make peace in November 1918. The criticisms of the German emissaries were not taken serious note of and the German Constituent Assembly, known as the Weimer Government, had to accept finally the terms of the treaty as presented by the Allied Powers on 23 June 1919.

Five days later, the Treaty of Versailles was formally signed by Germany, followed by four other treaties with the remaining combatants. These were the Treaty of Saint-Germain with Austria (September 1919), the Treaty of Neuilly with Bulgaria (November 1919), the Treaty of Trianon with Hungary (June 1920) and finally, the Treaty of Lausanne with Turkey (1923). These five treaties were supplemented by numerous conventions and mutual agreements among the Allied Powers themselves. All these treaties and conventions are collectively known as the Versailles Settlement.

Versailles Treaty (1919)

The First World War that broke out on 28 July 1914 came to an end on 11 November 1918 when defeated Germany unconditionally surrendered to the victorious Allied Powers. Representatives of the 'allied or associated belligerent powers' met in Paris in January 1919 to lay down the conditions of peace, after the end of hostilities. This Conference of the representatives of the European powers, which assembled at the Hall of Mirrors in Versailles, was a more widely representative body than even the Congress of Vienna had seen.

The composition of the Conference was significant. To it came representatives of not only the Allies but also of the Associated Powers. Thirty-two nations were represented in the Paris Peace Conference: of these there were ten representatives from the five countries of England, France, Italy, the United States, and Japan who formed the Council of Ten. The conduct and the main terms of the peace settlement were determined by the 'Big Four'— President Woodrow Wilson of the United States, Clemenceau of France, Lloyd George, the Prime Minister of Britain, and Orlando, the Italian Premier. The actual settlement was consequently, a series of bargains and compromises between these four powers.

On 28 June 1919, the Allied and Associated powers concluded the Treaty of Versailles with Germany. With the Treaty of Versailles, peace was formally restored throughout the world. The following territorial, economic and military provisions were stipulated by the Treaty of Versailles:

A. Territorial Provisions

  (i)   Germany restored the province of Alsace-Lorraine to France.

  (ii) She had to surrender the small frontier areas around Eupen, Malmedy, and Moresnet to Belgium.

  (iii) She also renounced her former customs union with Luxembourg.

  (iv) After a plebiscite, Denmark received northern Schleswig, which had been seized by Prussia and Austria in 1864. Southern Schleswig voted to remain with Germany.

(v) Germany ceded the port of Memel and its hinterland to the principal Allied and Associated powers for eventual transfer to Lithuania.

(vi) Germany was to cede the greater part of the provinces west of Prussia and the province of Posen to Poland. Danzig, the main port of west Prussia, was to be a free city under the League of Nation's administration, because its population was wholly German.

(vii) Germany renounced, in favour of the principal Allied and Associated powers, all her rights and titles over her overseas possessions. The German occupied territories of China were given over to Japan. The other German occupied territories were placed under the mandate of the League of Nations.

B. Military and Naval Provisions

Some military and naval provisions were imposed upon Germany so as to reduce her armaments and prevent her from assuming any aggressive role that might disrupt international peace and security. These may be briefly summed up as follows:

(i) German armaments were strictly limited to a maximum of 1,00,000 troops and only six battleships.

(ii) The production of tanks, armoured cars, military aircraft, and submarines was banned.

(iii) A committee was set up to monitor German war-production.

(iv) Conscription or voluntary military service was done away with.

(v) The Rhineland was to be permanently demilitarized, that is, German troops were not allowed in the area.

(vi) German naval fortifications at Heligoland were to be destroyed or dismantled.

(vii) The Kiel Canal areas was to be demilitarized.

(viii) The German warships were ordered to be surrendered to England.

(ix) A contingent of the Allied Army was posted in Germany to ensure that Germany abided by the terms of the Treaty.

(x) Germany's army was to be used only for the maintenance of her internal peace and the defence of her frontiers.

C. Economic Provisions

Harsh economic terms against Germany were included in the treaty:

(i) The war guilt clause fixed the blame for the outbreak of the war on Germany and her allies alone.

(ii) In addition, she was to pay 'reparations' for the damage inflicted upon the civilian population. The Allied Powers failed to reach an agreement on the volume of reparation to be paid, and so the matter was left to an international body called the Reparation Commission, which recommended the payment of £660 million as war compensation by Germany to the Allies.

(iii) France was granted the coal mines of the Saar region in Germany for a period of 15 years. After 15 years, the local inhabitants would decide by a plebiscite as to which country they would prefer to join.

(iv) Germany was also to surrender most of her Merchant Navy.

(v) She was required to deliver large quantities of coal to France, Belgium, and Italy and iron and rubber to the other Allied Powers.

(vi) The Allied Powers were to occupy the left bank of the river Rhine for 15 years. This was to be done as a guarantee for the fulfilment of the treaty.

D. Political Provisions

During the First World War, proposals for the establishment of a peaceful international organization were formulated and discussed in different countries. The most important advocate of this new point of view was the American President Woodrow Wilson. The delegates to the Paris Peace Conference set up a commission to consider the formation of the proposed international organization. The commission recommended the setting up of an international leader under the name of the League of Nations. Its aims and objectives were set out in the League Covenant which was later incorporated into the Treaty of Versailles.

Evaluation

The Treaty of Versailles was one of the most controversial settlements ever signed in history. An examination of the terms of the Treaty of Versailles reveals that the Allies were motivated by two principles while concluding a peace settlement with Germany, these were: (1) to take penal measures against Germany for her war crimes, (2) to prevent her from doing anything that could prove detrimental to the peace and security of Europe in the future. However, the Treaty of Versailles was viewed with suspicion by the Germans for the treaty was regarded by the Germans as a dictated peace which had been imposed upon them. The Germans were not allowed to participate in the discussion at Versailles and were escorted in and out of the Hall of Mirrors under military guard: they were simply presented with the terms and told to sign. These unnecessary humiliations evoked hatred and bitterness in the minds and hearts of the Germans.

Second, the amount of reparations was so high that the Germans protested it would be impossible to pay. Her large colonies and areas rich in mineral resources had been snatched away from her thus reigning in her national economy. The Germans, therefore, soon began to default on the payment of their reparation instalments. Third, the disarmament clauses of the treaty were deeply resented by the Germans because although the Allied Powers made guarantees of a universal reduction of armaments, and while efforts were made to disarm Germany by reducing her military power to a minimum level, the victorious Allied Powers, did nothing to disarm themselves. For example, Britain continued to harbour a powerful navy, France kept an army posted along the river Rhine, and Poland raised an army twice as large as that of Germany.

Fourth, the Versailles peace settlement included certain principles, which could not be carried to their logical conclusion in practice. The theoretically admirable principle of national self-determination stood at the centre of Wilson's fourteen points. This principle was applied to justify the rights of the Poles and others, but it was assured while deciding whether German-Austria would be a part of the German republic.

The injuries thus inflicted on German interests and prestige by the harsh terms of the Treaty of Versailles, were a cause of the Second World War. Hitler aimed to make Germany peerless in Europe by repudiating the humiliating clauses of the treaty and so it could be argued that the Versailles Treaty contained some of the seeds of the Second World War.

TREATIES WITH OTHER DEFEATED POWERS

Treaty of Saint-Germain, 10 September 1919

The Treaty of Saint-Germain was signed with Austria on 10 September 1919. By this treaty, the Austro-Hungarian Empire was broken into pieces. It restricted the frontiers of Austria to Vienna and a small area surrounding it which contained a German speaking population. A new state, Czechoslovakia, consisting of the Austrian provinces of Bohemia and Moravia, was created. Austria also lost Slav-dominated Bosnia-Herzegovina to Serbia which along with the Dalmatian coast made up the newly formed kingdom of Yugoslavia. Similarly, Austria had to cede Bukovina to Romania, Galicia to the reconstituted state of Poland; and the south Tyrol Trentino, Istria, and Trieste to Italy. The Hapsburg empire thus disintegrated as various nationalities declared themselves independent. As Austrian boundaries were redrawn, she, like Germany, had to pay reparations for war losses and reduce her military strength.

Treaty of Neuilly, 27 November 1919

By this treaty, Bulgaria lost territories to Greece, Yugoslavia, and Romania. The Treaty also entailed a curtailing of strength in the Bulgarian armed forces.

Treaty to Trianon, 4 June 1920

This treaty dealt with Hungary removing Hungary from Austria and making it into a separate state. Some Hungarian territories were taken over and distributed among Romania, Yugoslavia, and Czechoslovakia. The territories of Slovakia and Ruthenia were given over to Czechoslovakia, Croatia and Slavonia to Yugoslavia, and Transylvania and part of Temonvre to Romania. Thus, nearly one-fourth of the Hungarian nationals were assigned to neighbouring hostile states. Critics have pointed out that Hungary was the most poignant case, in which the principle of national self-determination was violated.

Treaty of Sèvres, 10 August 1920

This Treaty was signed by the Allies with Turkey on 10 August 1920. According to the terms of this treaty: (i) Turkey was to lose Eastern Thrace and some islands in the Aegean to Greece, (ii) she was compelled to surrender her suzerainty over Egypt, Sudan, Cyprus, Morocco, Tunis, Tripolitania, etc., (iii) Syria became a mandated territory under France, whereas Palestine, Iraq, and Transjordan became British mandated territories, (iv) The Dardanelles Strait and the river Bosphorus were to be permanently open so that they could be used by ships of all countries in times of war or peace.

Treaty of Lausanne, 24 July 1923

The loss of so much territory to Greece outraged Turkish national feeling. Led by Mustafa Kemal, they rejected the treaty and so a new settlement was reached between the Allies and the republican government of Turkey. This treaty came to be known as the Treaty of Lausanne and was signed in July 1923. This treaty provided for the complete separation of Syria, Palestine, and Mesopotamia from the Ottoman Empire and abolished the formal suzerainty of Turkey over Egypt. Only Eastern Thrace including Constantinople was allowed to remain in Turkish possession.

THE LEAGUE OF NATIONS

A great deal of idealism had been roused by the First World War in different European countries. After the conclusion of the

War, there was a strong demand for some sort of international machinery to be set up for preserving world peace. It was this cause which President Wilson of USA, took up in his famous Fourteen Points, drafted in 1918. Though the establishment of a League of Nations was the last item in the Fourteen Points, Wilson repeatedly declared that it was the most essential part of the peace settlement. Later on, at the Versailles Peace Conference, Wilson made several concessions to his fellow negotiators in order to enlist their support for this idea. In fact, the Versailles settlement is studied under three different heads: (1) territorial arrangements, (2) measures to punish the defeated powers, and (3) establishment of the League of Nations.

The League of Nations formally came into existence with its headquarters at Geneva on 10 January 1920. Before the close of the war in January 1918, Wilson circulated the 'Fourteen Points' as conditions for the restoration of peace. One of these conditions was that: 'A general association of nations should be formed under a specific covenants for the purpose of affording mutual guarantees of political independence and territorial integrity to great and small states alike.' After detailed discussion at the Versailles Peace Conference the constitution of the proposed international organization was incorporated in the Treaty of Versailles.

The document in which the objectives and constitution of the League were laid down was known as the Covenant. The Covenant of the League of Nations included 26 Articles, specifying its objectives, structure, etc. The primary aims of the League were as follows:

1. To generate international cooperation and to achieve international peace and security by avoiding armed conflict.
2. It was also agreed that all nations must refrain from armed conflicts until every effort had been made to settle all disputes by peaceful means.
3. To have open, just, and honourable relations between nations.
4. To honour international laws as rules of conduct among governments.

5. To have respect for treaty obligations in the dealings of organized peoples with one another.
6. If any nation violated these principles, others were to bring economic sanctions against it, and in the last resort, apply military pressure.

The League of Nations functioned through the following organs:

1. The General Assembly, which consisted of the representatives of all the members of the League. Every member state could send a maximum of three representatives or delegates, but was entitled to only one vote. The Assembly met every year in September, but special sessions might be held in times of emergency. The Assembly discussed various matters effecting international peace. It elected the temporary members of the council, controlled the budget, admitted new members to the League, and elected with the Council the Judges of the International Court of Justice.
2. The Council of Judges was the executive organ of the League of Nations. It was comprised of four permanent members and four non-permanent members. The permanent members included Britain, France, Italy, and Japan. The non-permanent members were elected by the Assembly for a term of three years. The Council sat at least three times a year. Like the Assembly, the Council might consider any question that effected world peace or threatened the harmony of international relations. It was to enquire into any international dispute submitted to it, and it could then refer these disputes to the Assembly. The Council's important resolutions had to be unanimously approved by all its members in order to become effective. Whenever any member state committed an act of aggression, the Council could recommend economic sanctions against it.
3. The third important agency of the League of Nations was the Secretariat at Geneva. It consisted of a Secretary General with a large number of bureaucrats serving under him. The Secretary General was appointed by the Council with the

approval of the General Assembly. The task of the Secretariat was the collection of data and information to be discussed in the Assembly and Council meetings. It also prepared the agenda and resolutions for meetings in the Assembly and in the Council.

4. The League also had a permanent Court of International Justice, with headquarters in The Hague. The Court was set up to interpret international treaties and other legal complexities among nations and to give its verdict on cases of international disputes. The decisions of the court were binding to both the parties involved in the dispute.

Apart from these four principal agencies, the League of Nations functioned through other bodies as well. These included the Permanent Mandates Commission, Minorities Committees, and several other committees to deal with economic and cultural relations among nations. There were also committees like the International Labour Organization.

'Like the Holy Alliance,' Ketelbey argues, 'the League was an expression of desire of a war-weary world to preserve international peace and stability.' According to Lipson, the League sought 'to transform the war mentality of man into a peace mentality'. The membership of the League rose to 51 in 1921, to 57 in 1932, and 60 in 1934. Though Wilson was instrumental in securing the general acceptance of the Covenant by other countries, the US did not become a member of the League as the US Senate refused to approve the Treaty of Versailles. Germany joined the League in 1926 and Soviet Russia in 1934.

The League of Nations was initially a success. It secured the withdrawal of Serbian troops from Albania, it resolved a quarrel between Italy and Greece over Corfu, and bridged a frontier dispute between Greece and Bulgaria. It settled the Swedish-Finnish quarrel over the Aaland islands. In the economic sphere it assumed responsibility for the financial solvency of Austria and Hungary, and it supervised the settlement of over a million Greek refugees from Asia Minor and Eastern Thrace in Greece. The first decade of the League closed with the Kellog-Briard Pact (1928), by which, the parties to the Pact bound themselves to avoid war while reserving the right of self defence.

Failure

In the 1930s, the League suffered a series of reverses in the face of the conflicting interests of the Great Powers which culminated eventually in its complete collapse. It failed to contain the aggression of Japan in Manchuria (1931) and Italy in Abyssinia (1935) and Albania (1939). It failed to properly handle the problem of the Spanish Civil War (1936–9) and was helpless in the face of Hitler's aggression in Austria, Czechoslovakia, Mlemel and Poland (1938–9). It failed to check the Russian invasion of Finland (1939). One by one, the Great Powers of Europe defied the League and gave up their membership. Japan and Germany left the League in 1933, Italy in 1937 and Russia was expelled. By 1940, England and France alone of the Great Powers were left in the League.

The League of Nations failed due to a multiplicity of factors:

1. It was limited by the fact that it was not universal in its membership.
2. Whenever the need for the application of economic or military sanctions arose, not all the members of the League were prepared to shoulder the obligations imposed by the Covenant. The League itself had no military or administrative power to enforce its will upon recalcitrant states.
3. According to Lipson, the 'lukewarm and negative' attitude of France, particularly her anxiety to maintain her 'traditional friendship' with Italy during the Abyssinian crisis, was a great blow to the League.
4. The autocratic states like Germany and Italy were unversed in the habits of parliamentary compromise, and unaccustomed to the authority of the majority vote-principles according to which the League supervised its business under the Anglo-French influence.

Though the League failed to preserve international peace, it strengthened the spirit of international cooperation and in a long term sense, provided a model for the United Nations. The International Court of Justice, in particular, convinced the world of the need for such a body. The League made some important contributions to the solution of many socio-economic problems. The League served as a dress-rehearsal for the United Nations and so herein lies its importance.

HIGHLIGHTS

- The rising tide of nationalism in Europe provided the background of the First World War. A variety of causes combined together to produce the first global war in the history of human civilization. Aggressive nationalism, the commercial and colonial rivalries among different European powers, and the polarization of Europe into two hostile camps through a series of alliances and military competition between the powers brought about this war.
- The Moroccan crisis, the Agadir crisis, and finally the Serajevo assassination of Archduke Ferdinand in Bosnia helped to quicken the conflict. Some scholars think that the rise of Germany was the major cause of the war, but England, France, Russia, and Austria were equally responsible for the war.
- The First World War came to an end with the surrender of Germany in 1918. The Paris Peace Conference met in 1919 to conclude a peace treaty.
- The Treaty of Versailles was imposed upon Germany by the victors. The germs of the Second World War were present in the conditions of the Treaty of Versailles for it was a 'dictated peace'.
- The post-war peace efforts led to the creation of the international organization known as The League of Nations. In the long run however, the League of Nations was unable to meet the demands of the European political context.

MEMORABLE DATES AND EVENTS

1870   The Battle of Sedan
1878   Berlin Treaty
1879   Dual Alliance

1882	Triple Alliance
1911	Agadir Crisis
1914	28 June—Assassination of Archduke Ferdinand at Sarajevo
	28 July—Austria attacked Belgium
1918	Wilson's Fourteen Points
	11 November—Surrender of Germany
1919	28 April—Foundation of the League of Nations
	28 June—Treaty of Versailles
1925	Locarno Pact
1931	Japan captured Manchuria
1933	Japan resigns from the League of Nations
1946	Fall of the League of Nations

MEMORABLE PERSONALITIES

Bismarck: The Chancellor of Germany
Kaiser William II: Emperor of Germany
Francis Ferdinand: Archduke of Austria
Woodrow Wilson: President of the United States of America
Lloyd George: Prime Minister of Britain
Clemenceau: Prime Minister of France
Orlando: Prime Minister of Britain

QUOTABLE QUOTES

- 'The most important thing about the First World War is that it was unsought, un-intended and the product of a long sequence of events which began in 1871.' —DAVID THOMSON
- 'This was the first general conflict between the highly organized states of the twentieth century, able to command the energies of all their citizens, to mobilize the productive capacity of modern industries, and to call upon the resources of modern technology to find new methods of destruction and of defence.' —DAVID THOMSON
- 'Political association in the Balkans especially, need not be the cause of very far-reaching repercussions. But this one set in motion a train of events whose ultimate effect was the collapse of the house of Europe as it had functioned in peace for nearly half a century.'
  —RENE ALBRECHTE CURIE

- 'The often-heard cry "Italia Irrendents" (unredeemed Italy), therefore, was one of the causes of war.'   —LANGSAIM
- 'By 1914 the sickman of Europe was no longer just Turkey, it was Europe itself, feverish and turbulent, and with strong suicidal tendencies.'   —DAVID THOMSON
- 'Russia, seeing in the Austrian demands another attempt to extend the power of the Dual Monarchy in the Balkans, and consequently a menace to her own ambitions there, declared the cause of Serbia her own. "In no circumstances will Russia be indifferent to Serbia's fate", telegraphed the Tsar to Serbia on 27 July, Austria-Hungary was warned that on the movement of Austrian troops against Serbia Russia would mobilize.'   —KETELBEY
- 'A more serious demonstration of the national rivalry was seen in the military competition which turned Europe into a congress of vast armed camps. At the beginning of the new century nations stood, face to face, armed, as never before, to the extent of all the resources of a scientific age and of a democratic treasury, for only a democracy can afford such preparations.'   —KETELBEY

CHAPTER 9

Arab Nationalism

INTRODUCTION

When the Ottoman Empire reached its pinnacle of glory, countries like Syria, Palestine, Arabia, Trans-Jordan, Lebanon, Iraq, etc., fell within its orbit. However, the prolonged rule of the Ottomans could not completely impede the growth of cultural awareness and the heightening of the spirit of individualism in the subjected countries. It is true that the people of the vanquished territories bowed to the Ottoman Sultan for his superior military might, but they did not owe any common allegiance to their Turkish overlord.

Moreover, when the Ottoman emperor started to portray himself as the Caliph, the Muslims of those countries became all the more indignant. This was quite natural because the Muslims of these countries considered Hussein of Mecca as their Caliph. Hence, political and religious factors together contributed to the growth of disloyal sentiments among the Arabs. In the process, this enhanced their unfriendly and hostile attitude towards the Sultan. The Reis Efendi Atif, while reporting on the seeds of revolutions sewn in different parts of the Empire, had diagnosed that nationalism and liberalism were the two forces in the nineteenth century that would shatter the Empire. At the opening of the twentieth century, the twin questions of an Arab nationalism separate and distinct from Ottomanism, and the formation of an independent Arab national state, were in the minds of only a very few. However, the nationalist movement and feelings surrounding it were already reaching a degree of development that could explode at any moment onto the international scene.

It was amid this situation that in October 1914, the Turks stumbled into a major European war, as allies of the Triple Alliance. Turkey had already been at war from 1911 to 1913, but, her involvement in the clash of great powers was a new and shattering experience.

In the war, as Turkey sided with the Germans, the Sultan recognized the need for active Arab co-operation. This call fell upon unreceptive ears and the outright hatred of the Arabs for the Turks more than counter-balanced any Islamic coalition. However, the immediate Arab reaction was twofold. One group looked upon the outbreak of a war involving Turkey and the European states as an opportunity to obtain a united and independent Arab national state. The other group, consisting of princely Arab families and their clients regarded the war as a time to rebel against the Ottoman Sultan and to try to establish independent Arab kingdoms.

The British Government seized this opportunity and encouraged the latent Arab national sentiment against the Ottoman Sultan. The British roughly calculated that any effort to awaken the nationalist sentiments of the Arabs and to encourage their rebellion against the Sultan, would obviously weaken the foundations of the Ottoman Empire. This would make it weaker and therefore would enable the Allied troops to crush her with less difficulty. While the First World War was unfolding in the Middle East and shattering the Ottoman Empire, it was under the encouragement of such British liaison officers as Colonel T.E. Lawrence, Colonel C.C. Wilson, and Sir Reginald Wingate, that the Arabs began to express themselves as a nationally conscious people. Colonel Lawrence, in particular, became friendly with Emir Faisal, a son of Hussein of Mecca and with the Arabs, in general. He was very popular in Turkey and came to be known as Lawrence of Arabia. On receiving British equipment and funding, the Arabs under Hussein, the Sharif of Mecca, broke out in revolt and Faisal captured Aaaba and Mean. He entered Damascus in October 1918, at the same time as the British.

The Paris Peace Conference, 1919

Indeed, all this greatly boosted up the newly rising Arab nationalism. However, just as the nascent Arab national sentiment was emerging German failures on the Western front in the summer of 1918 and the collapse of Germany, spelled the end of warfare in the Middle East. With the conclusion of the Peace of Paris in 1919, in the Hall of Mirrors at Versailles in France, the First World War formally came to an end. Although under the initiative of Colonel Lawrence, Arab nationalism had reached great heights, on paper not much space was available to give proper shape to the Arab nationalist sentiments. In fact, much to their disappointment, the Arabian states were categorized as 'mandated' territories and placed under the supervision of the League of Nations.

At the Paris Peace Conference, the representatives were persuaded by the British Government to recognize Hussein as the ruler of Hedjaz, his third son Faisal as the ruler of Iraq, and his other son Abdullah as the ruler of Transjordan. A result of the utter dissatisfaction of Arab aspirations was the direct control of Britain over Iraq and Transjordan. Although the independence of Hedjaz was recognized, Palestine was put under a British mandate and Syria under the supervision of France. All these came as a shock to the Arabs and their national aspirations were injured by the inclusion of Syria and Palestine as mandated territories under the European states. The rearrangement of the Arabian states by the European powers after the First World War was to a great extent responsible for the continuing discontent of the Arabs.

The rule of Faisal, who was selected by the British to be the King of Iraq, introduced a spirit of confidence among the Iraqis and made them stronger. To free their country from the clutches of foreign interference, the Arabs started an agitation against the British, which, after continuous agitation, meant that Iraq became independent in 1932.

This enabled King Abdullah of Transjordan to exert greater efficiency in administrative matters. In this regard, he was mostly assisted by British officials. Abdullah, in a similar way to Hussein of Hedjaz, was immensely indebted to the British. Hussein became extremely dependent on the British and such dependency on the British made the Arabs all the more resentful and hostile towards him. This boiling situation helped Ibn Saud to capture Hedjaz which was newly named as Saudi Arabia. A born leader, Ibn Saud restored confidence. He provided able guidance and a just and honourable administration, all of which brought the economic prosperity to Saudi Arabia. He also did away with many of the commercial privileges that foreigners had so long been enjoying in Arabia. This gave a fillip to the local merchants and to their mercantile and commercial operations. He also initiated the modernization of transport for the economic upliftment of his country.

The British under General Allenby captured Palestine and the Ottoman province of Jerusalem in 1917 and so until 1 July 1920, it was occupied and administered by the British army. The Balfour Declaration, made by the British foreign minister Balfour, stated that Britain 'viewed with favour the establishment in Palestine of a national home for the Jewish people'. This intended to establish a link between the British military and the Jewish population of Palestine, through which the latter would join the Allied forces during the First World War. As a natural result of this declaration, a great majority of Jews started to flock of Palestine and to settle there once it was given the status of a 'mandated' territory under the British. The influx of the Jews in large numbers in Palestine was much to the disliking of the Arabs and they resisted the coming of the Jews into 'their' territory. In reality, zionist aspirations went beyond the Balfour Declaration and sought 'Palestine as the national home of the Jewish people and the right of the Jewish people to build up its national life in Palestine'. They worked toward that goal and purchasing land, supporting new immigrants, building schools and hospitals, setting up industries, and financing projects, were made possible by the extensive financial resources of the Jewish community. The Arabs could not parallel the activities of the Jews and many could not resist selling property to the Jews for inflated prices. This tended to reduce their status to that of 'foreigners' within their original homeland. Since the Arabs were the majority population, they hoped to become an integral part of the eventual Arab national state. The influx of Jews into Palestine inspired a multitude of fears and thus there started open clashes between the Jews and the Arabs.

A commission was appointed by the British Government to resolve the matter. The British wanted to incorporate Palestine into their empire because of its proximity to the Suez Canal, its suitability as an outlet for oil and its strategic position with respect to Arabia. The commission proposed dissection of the country into two parts, for the Arabs and Jews respectively. The project was however rejected by both parties.

Meanwhile hostilities between the two communities increased and assumed a serious overtone. Moreover, anti-British activities started and Palestine was in open revolt and on the verge of civil war. This coincided with the pressure of Hitler upon Czechoslovakia, the Munich Accord and the nadir of British prestige. After the Second World War, the Palestine Commission was appointed by the United Nations to provide a solution to the Palestine issue. In accordance with its recommendations the country was partitioned into two halves, whereby Israeli was given to the Jews.

Syria was a hub of Arab nationalist aspiration, but after the First World War, the Allied Supreme Council answered Syrian demands for independence by imposing a French 'mandate' over Syria. Although full legal title to the mandate did not materialize until the Treaty of Lausanne (1923), the actions of 1920 confirmed the French possessions. Detailed French administration began at once and along the lines of 'divide and rule': for example, under the new arrangement, the minorities residing within Syria were dealt with separately. This deliberate policy of dividing the people produced further resentment among the Arabs and so there was severe opposition to the French Government. French military forces failed to keep the political agitation of the Syrians under control and finally, facing the problem of war in Europe and in the face of stiff opposition, the French government had to give in by concluding a special treaty with Syria in 1936, thereby acknowledging her independence.

Lebanon, also became a victim of French diplomacy. She was also made a 'mandated' territory under France and though the Arabs had desired independence, the Allies had refused to grant it. This incited the Lebanese uprisings. At this time British concessions to nationalism elsewhere in Iraq and Egypt persuaded France to initiate treaty arrangements with Lebanon (along with Syria) and the independence of Lebanon was recognized by a separate treaty in 1936. However, the outbreak of the Second World War put such plans on hold.

During the Second World War, the German occupation of France led to the creation of the Vichy Government, in France, supervised by the Nazi regime. Accordingly, Syria and Lebanon also fell within the purview of the Vichy Government. Parallel to this, the French General Charles de Gaulle independently organized the Free French Forces with the support of the French troops stationed in Africa. Before the war ended, the army of de Gaulle, in alliance with British armed forces, captured Syria and Lebanon and agreed to recognize the unconditional independence of these two countries in 1941. Hence, after a prolonged period of resistance and shifting fortune, Syria and Lebanon gained independence in 1941.

Equally, the small state of Yemen, situated in the south-western corner of the Arabian peninsula, contained politically minded individuals who also held nationalist aspirations. Though small, the state of Yemen also felt the nationalist pull to assert its independence against the controls of the Ottomans. An opportunity to materialize her dream for independence was fully availed of by Syed Mohammed Ibn-al-Rashid, when in 1911, Italy clashed with the Ottoman Empire. During the course of the First World War, Yemen emerged as a fully independent country and her sovereignty was directly acknowledged after the war was over.

Towards the end of the Second World War, many Arabs devoted much time and energy to the promotion of Arab national unity. Thus, in 1945 the Arab League was formed. The Arab League fostered unity among its member states which included Saudi Arabia, Egypt, Transjordan, Lebanon, Yemen, Syria, and others. This organization operated on the principles of equality, fraternity, and mutual understanding of the idea of the Arab nation. Above all, the creation of the League was intended to ward off any kind of foreign aggression against the Arabs and to protect their liberty and sovereignty.

The entry of Turkey in the First World War on the side of the Germans, induced Great Britain to unilaterally declare the establishment of a protectorate over Egypt. The reason for the British intervention was to guarantee freedom of passage through the Suez Canal and to use Egypt as a military base for British

MAP 9.1: Arabian States

forces. Two days after the end of the war in Europe, Jaglul Pasha, an ardent Egyptian nationalist who led the Wafdist Party showed his willingness to go to Paris to put forward the independence programme of Egypt at the Paris Peace Conference. At this juncture, the British restricted Jaglul Pasha's movements within Egypt and even arrested him and his followers. The Egyptian reaction was spontaneous and it stimulated vigorous nationalist feelings against the British. Although the British were out of touch with the prevalent sentiments in Egypt and became ready for a compromise, the latter would not concede to anything other than complete independence. Eventually the British government unilaterally declared the end of the protectorate over Egypt. Her status was elevated to that of an independent sovereign state. Sultan Faud became the King of Egypt, although Britain retained security of communications and defence. Although the presence of British military forces in Egypt meant that Egyptian independence was not yet complete, the Egyptians were firmly determined to remove the British presence from Egypt. In 1936, the dispossession of her forces in Egypt was accepted by Britain except for a wider area in the Suez Canal Zone, although the implementation of the treaty awaited the end of the Second World War. After the war when Egypt entered the UN as a chartered member, she confronted Great Britain with the allegation that the provisions of the Anglo-Egyptian Treaty of 1936 had infringed upon Egyptian sovereign rights beyond a point tolerable to an independent state. In retrun, Britain confirmed that she was willing to withdraw her forces from Egypt in two phases, the first by March 1947, followed by the second in 1949. However, British forces still remained in the Canal Zone on the plea of protecting the Suez Canal.

At this time the internal strife started. It came to an end when General Naguib and Lieutenant Colonel Nasser forced King Faruq to abdicate. Egypt was declared a republic in 1953 and under the presidential regime of Naguib, Britain was compelled to evacuate her forces from the Canal Zone. In the meantime, Nasser replaced Naguib as President and under his efficient administration, the Egyptians and the neighbouring Arab nationalists rejoiced is the knowledge that they had become independent of the Western imperialist powers. The development of the Arab countries and the forging of Arab unity were the twin goals that Nasser had set for himself as the leader of the United Arab Republic.

THE EMERGENCE OF MODERN TURKEY

In 1908, a new chapter opened in the Eastern Question, which was not closed until the whole of Europe was in flames. In the July of that year, a revolution occurred within the Ottoman Empire which was organized by a group called the 'Young Turks' who were mostly educated in the West. They were desirous of rejuvenating the decaying state, and of reorganizing it along Western lines. They wanted to see a great nation free from the tutelage of foreign powers emerge out of the Ottoman Empire. The Young Turks overthrew Abdul Hamid II (1909–18) sent him into closely guarded seclusion, and proclaimed his brother Mahmed V, the Sultan of Turkey for he was more amiable to the idea of constitutional monarchy.

Until 1918 the Young Turks held the reins of governmental control in Turkey. While remaining in power, they attempted to establish homogeneity among all the diverse components of the Turkish Empire. However, the hopes roused by the Young Turks, soon proved to be illusory. Their main efforts were devoted to the policy of 'Turkification' of all the non-Turks and to the arduous task of instilling a nationalist feeling among all the Turks within the Ottoman Empire. The non-Turkish communities were therefore bitterly opposed the Young Turks' 'Turkification' drives. The most violent storm broke out in Albania but it was quelled in 1911 after a diplomatic grant of considerable local autonomy. Finally, the Balkan states declared war on the Turks. When the Balkan Wars were over, the Young Turks found themselves deprived of almost all their possessions in Europe, except Thrace and Constantinople. However, the final dismemberment of European Turkey took place only after she had suffered serious setbacks in the two world wars.

In the First World War, Turkey allied with Germany marking a significant turn in the history of the Ottoman Empire. German failures on the Western Front and the imminent collapse of Germany by the summer of 1918, spelled the end of warfare in the Middle East. The war brought many changes to Turkish society, which disintegrated so fully under the terrible impact of the war, that, Asquith declared 'the sick man had really died this time'. The end of the Turkish state such that Asquith could declare that 'his resurrection was impossible'.

At the same time however, the war generated many new and positive forces in the Turkish society. As Lipson has opined, 'one of the unexpected effects of the war of 1914–18 was the rebirth of Turkey'. With the gradual waning of the power of the Young

Turks the man who stormed into the political scene was Mustafa Kemal Pasha. Under his able leadership a new age in Turkey began. While the Turks flocked to Kemal for guidance, he set to work at once on the double task of organizing a movement and building a powerful army. The humiliating articles of the Treaty of Sèvres (1920) were strongly repudiated and rejected by the Nationalist Party under the leadership of Mustafa who was finally able to extort far more favourable terms from the Allies in the Treaty of Lausanne in 1923.

Sidney Nettleton Fisher observes that modern Turkish nationalism first saw the light of day in central Anatolia and its birth pangs were a series of wars of independence against the several enemies of Turkey. Mustafa Kemal, Turkey's military and political midwife, was born in Salonika in 1811 into a modest home. He attended military schools in Monastir and Istanbul where he distinguished himself particularly in mathematics and oratory. An early teacher had given him the sobriquet 'Kemal', meaning perfect, a name he eventually came to use almost exclusively. It was here that he was deeply influenced by the ideas of the French Revolution.

He began his military career under the Sultan but was opposed to autocratic rule and so he was soon transferred to Damascus as punishment for pertaining in anti-Sultanate activities. There he took active part in the various revolutionary societies that honeycombed the army prior to the Young Turk Revolution of 1908. He founded a secret opposition group called 'Watan' or 'Fatherland' with the aim to liberate Turkey from the autocratic rule of the Sultanate.

In 1908 Mustafa Kemal contacted the Young Turks and took part in their work. With their support he led the army to Istanbul and forced Sultan Abdul Hamid II to initiate administrative reforms. However, soon after, he became disenchanted with the Young Turk Movement and abandoned politics for a while. In 1910, he attended the great French military academy and here he developed further admiration for the socio-political life of the French. In 1915, he was recalled to Turkey to take part in the Turko-Italian War and the First World War and in these wars, his major military victories brought Mustafa both promotion and fame.

Kemal assumed the leadership of Turkey at a time when its very existence was threatened by the reverses of the First World War. After having declared Turkey a republic, Kemal set up a rival government in the Anatolian city of Ankara in Asia Minor in 1920. He became the head of the state and the commander-in-chief of the army there while, meanwhile, Sultan Mehmud VI (1918–22) ran a parallel government at Constantinople. In the late 1920s, however, events turned in Kemal's favour. The signing of the Treaty of Sèvres caused an immense reaction in Turkey against the regime that had accepted it. The Turks now found themselves completely stripped of the whole of Thrace and the historic city of Constantinople too, was temporarily placed under international control. The terms were therefore accepted by the Turkish government but rejected by the Nationalist Party under the leadership of Mustafa Kemal.

From June 1920, the Allies, through British insistence, had assigned to the Greeks the task of protecting the Allied position in Turkey, 'liberating' the country from the Kemalists, and enforcing peace terms upon the Turks. However, the tide was in Kemal's favour. While he successfully drove away the Italian and French troops form Turkey, a shattering victory over the Greeks transformed the military situation. Mustafa forced the Allies to conclude the Treaty of Lausanne (1923) in which the Turks were allowed to retain Constantinople and Eastern Thrace in Europe and Anatolia in Asia Minor. However, they were severed from the provinces of Palestine, Syria, Mesopotamia, and Arabia, over which they had ruled for centuries. In the words of Lipson— 'Mustafa Kemal wished to build a national state and did not resist the break-up of the old Ottoman Empire'.

Regardless the way was now prepared for the Turkish Revolution which refashioned the political, social, and economic structure of Turkey on lines designed to give the Turkish people a European outlook. Its architect was the saviour of the country and Mustafa Kemal, who subsequently assumed the name of Kemal Ataturk (Chief of the Turks) was that architect.

After his resounding victory over the Greeks with the Treaty of Lausanne, he proceeded to begin the task of creating a modern state out of the ruins of a medieval therocracy. In the meantime, on 29 October 1923 the Grand National Assembly approved a declaration asserting that 'the form of government of the Turkish State is a Republic'. That same day, it elected Mustafa Kemal Pasha the President of the Republic. He was elected to this office four times and during his long stay in power he embarked upon a massive programme of modernization.

Mustafa Kemal devised a new administrative policy which transformed the existing structure. His programme was laid down in the six principles of 'Kemalism', which were represented by six white arrows on a red ground:

1. The republicationism by which Turkey ceased to be a monarchy.
2. Nationalism, the spirit of which was infused in every Turkish citizen.
3. Populism, by which administration was conducted on the basis of people's sovereignty.
4. Etatism, in order to promote the economic development of the country, state control over private enterprise was applied.
5. Secularism, by which the Turkish state dropped its semi-theocratic character and the office of the Caliphate was abolished. The republic had no official religion and assumed a wholly secular complexion.
6. Revolutionism, whereby sweeping changes were carried out as part of the process of transforming Turkey into a 'Westernized' nation. All these principles were successfully implemented during the rule of the Ataturk.

As the Kemalist regime was in possession of virtually dictatorial powers, religious opposition was cowed and disheartened by a series of crushing blows. In abolishing the Caliphate in 1924, Kemal was making his first open assault on the forces of Islamic orthodoxy. In 1925, he introduced a new constitution to accomplish administrative reforms. This provided for the election of members through adult suffrage every four years. The legislature in turn elected the head of the state as the leader of the majority political party which was the People's Party.

Kemal tried to westernize Turkey by regulating the Turks in all spheres of national life. Educational institutions were separated from the state, school education was compulsory for children between seven and sixteen years, religious education was disallowed, and government training centres were set up for training teachers and officials in administration, banking, and commerce.

Next, Kemal radically reorganized the entire legal system of the country by borrowing and adapting various Western systems of law to meet Turkish needs. A far-reaching effect of Western law was the altered condition of life for women, which began to change the whole fabric of Turkish society. Polygamy ceased to be tolerated. Women were emancipated, they abandoned the pardah or veil. The cause of female education was enhanced by the founding new schools and colleges for women. He introduced marriage regulations reducing wedding to a simple civil ceremony and marriage before the age of seventeen for women and eighteen for men was prohibited. Kemal also opened the way for women to become public officials. In 1929, women were allowed to vote in municipal elections and in 1934 the franchise was extended to them for the right to vote in parliamentary elections.

Another far-reaching reform was the compulsory introduction of a new Turkish alphabet written in Latin rather than Arabic letters. The Turks gave up their age old modes of dress and social practices in favour of 'Europeanization'. The wearing of the fez and the turban, which had a religious significance, was forbidden. Another visible manifestation of the process of Westernization was the substitution of Sunday as the weekly day of rest instead of Friday which is the Muslim Juma.

Thus, within a few years a new Turkey was born on the ruins of the old. Especially in the sphere of economy, there was the opening of new ports and extension of communication network to several areas. Improvements in irrigation, agriculture, and industry were initiated through a Five Year Plan which was adopted in 1934. A score of factories were built to produce textiles, paper, sugar, and steel. Coal, petrol, and manufacturing of bronze was also undertaken. The extension of cultivable land and the reduction of wastelands equally led to rapid improvement of Turkey.

The remarkable internal progress of Turkey and the relatively smooth sailing of Kemal's domestic politics were paralleled by success in foreign affairs. Relations with Greece improved rapidly and there was new friendly understanding amongst Turkey, Greece, Bulgaria, Romania, Yugoslavia, and Albania. In July 1923, Turkey was admitted to the League of Nations. Almost immediately after Italy's attack upon Ethiopia, Turkey embarked upon diplomatic action to attempt to change the demilitarized status of the Straits of Bosphorus and Dardanelles. In 1937, she made pact with Iran, Iraq, and Afghanistan to bridge the gap between Asia and Europe, and to maintain friendly relations with her neighbours as both continents.

Thus, the Turkish renaissance must be attributed to a large extent, to the personality and ability of Mustafa Kemal. Mustafa Kemal was undoubtedly the creator of a new Turkey and one of the greatest nation-builders of the twentieth century. He brought a new sense of cohesion to his countrymen who had previously been humiliated by defeat. As Bernard Lewis summed up, it was as a soldier that Ataturk first rose to lead his people—as the brilliant and inspired leader who snatched the 'Sick Man of Europe' from his death bed and infused him with new life.

In 1923, at the moment of his triumph, there were many opportunities which might have tempted a military commander to seek more glory or a nationalist leader to arouse new passions. He renounced them all and Kemal Ataturk, the master of social symbolism, made it clear to his people that for the time being, the age off martial valour in holy war had ended. The time had come for the solid bourgeois virtue of industry, skill, and thrift, which were needed in the hard but urgent task of developing the country and raising the standard of living for her people. At a dark moment in their history, the Kemalist Revolution brought new hope and life to the Turkish people, restored their energies and self-respect and set them firmly on the road to independence. On his death on 10 November 1938, all his welfare measures earned for Kemal, the title of 'Ataturk' or the 'father of the Turkish nation'. The next president, Ismat Ironu, followed the footsteps of Kemal to steer Turkey down the road of further advancement.

HIGHLIGHTS

- Turkish domination was established over the Arabs in the eleventh century but the Arabs were swept up by a spirit of nationalism in the beginning of the twentieth century.
- During the First World War, Arab nationalism centred around the personalities of Faisal and Hussein. The British patronized the rising tide of Arab nationalism in various ways.
- In the post-war period, the Arab nationalist movement entered into a new era. Saudi Arabia, Iraq, Transjordan and other nations launched their struggle for freedom and wrested independence from their various controlling powers.
- Turkey took the side of Germany in the First World War. The German defeat in the War brought misfortune for Turkey and the victors forcibly imposed on Turkey many humiliating peace terms and conditions. The humiliation of Turkey in the hands of the Allied Powers triggered off a nationalist reaction in Turkey under the leadership of Kemal Pasha.
- Kemal Pasha decided to steer Turkey towards modernization. Muhammad VI was deposed and power was captured by Kemal Pasha. Under the able guidance of Kemal Pasha, Turkey emerged as a modern state. Kemal Pasha came to be regarded as 'Ataturk' or the 'Father of the Nation'.

MEMORABLE DATES AND EVENTS

1880	Birth of Mustafa Kemal Pasha
1908	The beginning of the Young Turk Movement
1920	British Mandate in Palestine
1923	Foundation of the Republic in Turkey
	Kemal Pasha became the President
1925	Republican Constitution in Turkey
1928	Turkey declared a Secular State
1934	The beginning of Five Year Plan in Turkey
1938	Death of Kemal Ataturk

MEMORABLE PERSONALITIES

Mustafa Kemal Pasha: Leader of Turkish National Movement who became President of Turkey in 1920.
Colonel Lawrence: The British Colonel who helped the Turks in launching a national movement. He was also known as the 'Lawrence of Arabia'.
Abdul Hammid: Sultan of Turkey
Mohammed V: Sultan of Turkey
Mohammed VI: Sultan of Turkey
King Faisal: Ruler of Iraq
Faisal or Hussein: Leader of the Turks who occupied Damascus, he was in touch with Col. Lawrence.

QUOTABLE QUOTES

- 'Turkey too had taken up arms to defend herself from the Treaty of Sèvres, and had driven the Greeks out of Asia Minor. There were rapid and starting nationalist movements in many parts of the Islamic world, in Egypt and Arabia.'   —KETELBEY
- 'What was abundantly clear was that Turkish power, which had been disintegrating for 150 years past was likely soon to crumble further before the renewed pressure of Russia and Austria . . . the "Eastern Question" became of great international importance in the decade after 1870.'   —DAVID THOMSON
- 'It was as a soldier that Ataturk first rose to lead his people as the brilliant and inspired leader who snatched the "sick man of Europe" from his deathbed and infused him with a new life and vitality.'   —BERNARD LEWIS
- 'Over the greater part of Europe, nationalism was the mainspring of political and economic action. It captured Russian Bolshevism, it was the dominant factor in Japan, the power that awakened China, the anchor of the new Turkey.'   —KETELBEY
- 'The granting of independence of Egypt was so limited by these reservations that it amounted in fact to less than Dominion Status.'   —TOYNBEE
- 'During the War we suffered countless humiliations at the hands of the British who failed and still fail to understand that our national interests are not and can never be the same as theirs.... They molested our women, assaulted our men and committed acts of vandalism in public places.'   —GENERAL NEGUIB

CHAPTER 10

Reform and Revolution in Russia

INTRODUCTION

Russia is the largest country in Europe in terms of area, resources, and population. Her vast land mass, covering about one-sixth of the world's surface, stretching from the Baltic to the Pacific and from the Arctic to the Mediterranean, is perhaps its most striking feature. Much of this land is either too cold or barren to make it suitable for human habitation. Historically, the struggle for existence was severe and stood as a barrier to the development of higher culture or social organization. The Russian population increased rapidly in the nineteenth century. The census of 1815 placed it at 45 million people and by 1914 it was estimated at 170 million people. This vast population consisted of a variety of races, the principal of which was Slavic. The latter belonged to the Indo-European family and was divided into three groups: (1) Northern Slavs (Czechs and Poles), (2) Southern Slavs (Serbs and Croats), and (3) the Russian Slavs. The Russian Slavs were further subdivided into the Great Russians, who inhabited the central plains, and formed the most important section of the empire, the Little Russians also known as Ukrainians who lived in the south and south-west, and the White Russians living in the west. The first two groups professed the Greek Orthodox faith; while the last group, having lived in Lithuania under Polish rule, had imbibed Polish culture and thus the Catholic faith. The outward manifestation of this triple division of the Russian people is the difference of language. The Great Russian dialect, being the speech of the Moscovite centre around which the empire was centred, developed into literary Russian.

The enormous size, population, and resources of Russia made her regarded by all Europe as the most formidable of the great powers. In the eighteenth century, under the leadership of Peter the Great and Catherine II, Russia for the first time established her claim to act as an arbiter in the politics of Western Europe. If Peter the Great was the founder of the greatness of Russia, Catherine made that greatness felt among the nations of Europe. Catherine's attitude to the Ottoman Empire gave birth to the great Eastern Question which later became a major issue in European history.

These advantages however were nullified by several internal weaknesses. Until 1905, Russia was an absolute monarchy without a Parliament or even a constitution. There was no central government except for the Tsar's residence and no laws other than his decrees. Rulers in the nineteenth century were either resolute reactionaries—Nicholas I and Alexander III—or inconsistant liberals—Alexander I and Alexander II. There were only two divisions in the society: the nobility, and the peasantry, the majority of whom were serfs. It is against this background that the history of reforms and revolutions in Russia in the nineteenth century has to be understood.

EMANCIPATION OF SERFS

The political repression in Russia under Tsar Nicholas I and the subsequent defeat in the Crimean War (1854–6) were followed by a period of enlightened rule under Tsar Alexander II. The early administrative measures of Alexander II paved the way for a complete reversal of his father's policies. The reform for which Alexander II will ever be remembered was the Emancipation of the serfs.

The Emanicipation of the serfs was an indispensable starting point for national regeneration in Russia. The serfs had limited personal freedom and were tied to the soil surviving at subsistence level. They were very much oppressed and as a result of this, there occurred numerous peasant insurgencies in the Russian countryside between 1828 and 1854. The question of serfdom was of overwhelming importance in Russia as the serfs comprised 90 per cent of the population. It was essential for the economic welfare of the country that the serfs should be freed, because servile labour was bound to be inefficient and serfdom had long outlived its utility. The Tsar felt that in the circumstances, 'it was better it should be effected from above than below'.

As the proverb ran: 'the serf's body belongs to the Tsar, his soul to God, and his back to his lord'. The emancipation of serfs became a pressing concern due to three main factors:

1. Serfdom was a great menace to the established order even though one might not agree with the view of some Russian historians, that, Russia was really experiencing a revolutionary situation on the eve of the Emancipation.

2. Industrial or capitalist development was impossible in Russia without the abolition of serfdom as industrialization in its initial stage required a large supply of cheap labour, and this supply could not be ensured if millions of Russians were tied to the land.

3. There was also a growing popular feeling in Russia in favour of the abolition of serfdom based on moral grounds. Most of the educated Russians wanted the abolition of this institution.

There were about 50 million serfs in Russia who can be classified into three categories: (1) There were 23 million serfs on the crown domains, (2) Over 3 million in private service, and (3) 23 million working on the estates of the nobility. The state had a right to do as it pleased with its own serfs. Similarly those in domestic service could be easily freed, as no land question was involved. The real difficulty was posed by the serfs of the third category for to merely give them freedom without land would mean creating a huge landless proletariat, which could lead to a social revolution or to law and order problems. Equally, to give to the serfs their existing holdings would ruin the nobility. After an exhaustive enquiry, the edict of Emancipation was issued on 3 March 1861. This liberation edict was based on two main principles: (1) The serfs were declared free and liberated from bondage to their masters. However, if they were simply declared free then they would be compelled to starve or to work on the lands of their lords on subsistence wages. Therefore, (2) it was decided to provide the liberated serfs with adequate means of livelihood. Every serf was granted the cottage in which he lived and the adjoining plot of land so he might cultivate food. To ensure some distribution of land, the holdings were redistributed among the cultivators every few years. For the land transferred to the village community, or *mir,* the landlord received compensation which was initially paid by the state but later was extracted from the liberated serfs in 49 instalments. It has been estimated that roughly half of the arable land in Russia was thus transferred from the lords to the village communities and the remaining half was left to the landlords themselves. On the Tsarist estates however, the process was much simpler. There, the serfs were declared free and masters of their lands without having to pay any compensation.

Consequences

The Emancipation Edict of 1861 was a sweeping measure and had momentous consequences in Russia. Russia gained moral credibility in the eyes of other nations and began to transform to a more definitely modern state. Millions of Russian people were now declared to be free human beings and as all citizens had equal liberty, the way was open for constitutional reforms. The serfs became a body of independent peasant proprietors. Industrious peasants prospered, so emancipation led to an increase in the area of cultivation. It thus enhanced the value of land, so there was a greater yield of taxation. So long as labour had been tied to the soil, it could not be employed in the factory, and so the industrialization of Russia could only begin after Emancipation. There was a great influx of ex-serfs to the nearby towns and thus, the gradual urbanization of Russia in the latter half of the nineteenth century was partly the consequence of the Emancipation of serfs.

Emancipation involved less alteration than might have been expected. The nobility lost their labour force and a part of their lands and so agricultural labour became scarce. The money which the nobility received as indemnity for the loss of their serfs and land, was quickly spent up and so the power of many members of the nobility was thus curbed. To the peasants, it was a change for the worse. David Thomson has observed that, 'The imperial decree of the Emancipation gave the Russian peasants legal freedom without economic freedom'. Personal liberty meant little to the peasantry as living conditions had deteriorated and the amount of land distributed among the former serfs was too small to satisfy their needs. To make matters worse, they had to pay money to the state for the next half a century for the inadequate land.

The peasantry, when they were serf, said to their lords, 'We are yours, but the land is ours'. Now, they were no longer tied to their lords, but the land was still not theirs. The fact was that in 1861, the peasants actually received less land than they had utilized in the pre-Emancipation era, and for that lesser amount, they had to pay more than the land would fetch by sale or rent. Kochan and Abraham (*The Making of Modern Russia*, p. 188) calculate that by 1878, only some 50 per cent of the former serfs had received adequate land endowments. The rest were below subsistence level. The terrible land-hunger, which surfaced could not be satisfied until the Bolshevik Revolution in 1917. Another problem was that the ex-serfs did not receive the land in their own right, but rather, the village community, or *mir,* was made the actual owner of the land. Thus, taken as a whole, the Emancipation did not do much to improve the economic condition of the Russian peasant. One scholar has cogently summed up the scenario in the following words: 'The abolition of serfdom, in spite of its important legal consequences, failed to achieve adequate amelioration in the lot of the Russian peasant'.

Other Reforms of Alexander II

The character of Alexander II's reign was certainly more humane and liberal than that of Nicholas I. The reforms, which he introduced, were like a fresh air that helped to purify the atmosphere. The survivors of the anti-monarchical Decembrist Movement (1825) were allowed to return to Russia. Many other political offenders too, were pardoned. The restrictions imposed upon the Russian universities and the Russian press were removed and the Russian intellectuals were also permitted to travel more freely abroad. The whole country was now flooded with utopian schemes of reform, but the prevailing mood of the Russian people was in no way opposed to monarchy. On the contrary, the great majority of the people looked upon the Tsar as the natural fountainhead from whom the reforms so eagerly anticipated were to flow. Like Peter the Great and Catherine II, Tsar Alexander II also adopted the policy of Westernization and sought to introduce some Western reforms in his country, though in a half-hearted hesitating manner. He encouraged trade and commerce and also sought to industrialize Russia. The beginnings of the construction of railroad in Russia could be traced back to his reign.

The reign of Alexander II was also remarkable for his reforms of the law courts and judicial administration. The Russian judicial organization was both corrupt and inefficient. For example, trials were held behind closed doors and without advocates. In November 1864, Alexander II issued a decree to reform the existing judicial system in Russia. The main principles of English and French jurisprudence were now introduced to Russia, namely the separation of the executive from the judiciary, trial in open courts and with the help of advocates, and also trial by jury in criminal cases. Justices of the Peace, a class of judicial officers appointed by the local assemblies, or *Zemstvos*, heard petty disputes while the more important ones were tried by regular tribunals. After the judicial organization was completely reformed, the judges came to enjoy security of tenure and all Russian citizens were declared to be equal in the eyes of law. The ecclesiastical courts however, continued to function and so did the special courts for the liberated serfs who lived largely by their customary laws. The reform decree of 1864 also did not abolish the despotic power of the Russian police.

In January 1864, Alexander II issued an edict which introduced some important changes to local government. By this edict, the whole country was divided into a number of provinces and each of the provinces into a number of districts. In each district was set up a local council called the *Zemstvo* which comprised of the representatives of the landlords, the middle class, and the peasants, although the domination of the landlords was unavoidable. The district *Zemstvo* then elected a representative for provincial *Zemstvo* but these *Zemstvos* were not political or legislative bodies because the Tsar had no intention of sharing his power with the representatives of the people. They did however discharge important administrative functions. The *Zemstvo* assembly met once a year to discuss the annual budget and also the basic policies. The *Zemstvos* in some ways imparted important political training to the people but their utility was however limited by the veto power of the provincial governors, the decrees of the central government, and the lack of funds available. In 1870, Town Councils (*Dumas*) were set up in a similar way and here the system of franchise ensured the preponderance of the wealthier classes.

In 1874, an important group of reforms sought to reorganize the military. They introduced a number of changes in military service the most notable of which was that the obligation of rendering military service to the state was extended from the lower classes to all Russian citizens, and the period of compulsory service in the army was reduced from 25 to 6 years. Alexander II was much more enthusiastic about the dissemination of learning. He encouraged Russians to go abroad for higher studies and through the *Zemstvos* he sought to implement educational reforms by founding a large number of primary and secondary schools.

The reformatory zeal of Alexander II was half-hearted. It failed to satisfy the majority of the Russian people. The Tsar did not accept the criticisms of these reforms lightly and gradually stiffened his attitude towards the people. The plan to modernize the education system was given up, women's education was discouraged, and even the judicial reforms of 1864 were kept in abeyance. This vacillation between liberalism and reaction drove the Russians into the hands of the extremists. The people were now convinced that reforms must hereafter, come not from above but from below.

GROWTH OF EXTREMIST MOVEMENTS IN RUSSIA

The failure of the reforms undertaken by Alexander II convinced the Russian people that the Tsar would act only under the pressure of increasing agitation. Many lost their faith in benevolent autocracy and became convinced that reforms must come from below. It was from this frustration of the educated classes that the Nihilist movement slowly grew up in Russia. The word 'Nihilism' means lack of faith in the existing tradition and values of life. The Nihilists were extreme rationalists who tested every human institution by reason and would not accept any principle on mere faith, however high that principle might stand in the eyes of contemporaries. Since very few existing Russian institutions could meet their rigid test they denounced them all. Government, religion, marriage, ethics—nothing escaped their criticism. Science alone to them was a subject worth studying. It would be wrong to think that the Nihilists were purely negative in their attitude to life. They had a positive programme of action and positive ideas about reorganizing the society as Turgenev has shown in his famous novel *Fathers and Sons*.

The Nihilist movement developed in Russia in three distinct stages. In the first stage, during the 1860s Nihilism was confined to political and philosophical speculations. Pisarev, one of the early Nihilists, began to publish his daring theories from 1861 onwards. In the 1870s these Nihilistic ideas mixed up with the ideas of romanticism, came to be preached by hundreds of Russian youths among the peasants in the countryside. The reactionaries called the revolutionary democrats Nihilists. The Nihilists called themselves *Narodniks* which literally means 'men of the people' and was the activity of its first student supporters, who went out from the universities, clad as peasants to try to convert villagers to socialism. The peasants however, often looked upon them with suspicion and did not easily accept their ideas. Sometimes the peasants even handed them over to the local police. The government took alarm and imprisoned hundreds of these *Narodniks* and even sent many of them to exile. As a result, the Nihilist movement was driven underground and in the 1880s, during its last phase, a tendency towards individual terrorism developed. Attempts were made on the lives of many high placed Russian officials with bombs, pistols, and knives. These attempts came to a climax in 1881 when Tsar Alexander II himself was assassinated by a terrorist belonging to a secret organization called the Peoples' Will.

However, the tide began to turn, the Nihilists soon lost their contact with the Russian masses, and the new Tsar Alexander III inaugurated new era of despotism. The failure of the various movements convinced many Russians that if they wanted to bring about a transformation of their society, they must shun the path of individual terrorism and find a new theory and practice of social reconstruction which would involve the masses. Future history of Russia showed that this new theory was to be Marxian Socialism.

TSAR ALEXANDER III (1884–94)

Bernard Pares has observed that the bomb which took the life of Tsar Alexander II also marked the end of the faint beginnings of constitutional rule in Russia. Alexander III had no faith in the parliamentary institutions of Western Europe, which in his opinion, were unsuitable for Russia. Autocracy, orthodoxy, and Slav nationalism were the three main principles in which he believed and he was determined to translate these principles into action. Under Alexander III's guidance, a course of repression was adopted towards all those elements which failed to conform to the creed of 'One Tsar, one Church, one Russia', and which were alien to his three main principles—orthodoxy, autocracy, and Slav nationalism. He issued a statement which indicated plainly what his future course would be: 'The voice of God', he declared, and 'of Government . . . with faith in the strength and truth of the autocratic power'. However Alexander III could not brush aside the forces of discontent from Russia in the long run for such discontent had only shifted underground for the time being.

Economic development of Russia, particularly industrialization, gained a new momentum in the reign of Alexander III. He encouraged the development of railways, mining, and financial institutions in Russia. To quicken the pace of industrial progress he also sought foreign collaboration and foreign loans whenever necessary.

THE REVOLUTION OF 1905

In the late eighteenth century, Tsarist Russia became a stronghold for the forces of autocracy, despotism, and corruption. The reign of Alexander III saw a severe course of repression towards all those elements which were alien to the principles of orthodoxy, autocracy, and nationalism. Revolutionaries were exiled, the press and the universities were muzzled, a policy of Russification was adopted towards the non-Russian subjects, i.e. Poles, Finns, Jews, and Germans, and religions other than the Greek Orthodox Church were persecuted.

Nicholas II (1894–1917) who succeeded Alexander III was inclined to mysticism and also subject to malign influences such as those of his queen, the Empress Alexandra, and the Siberian monk named Rasputin. He came to the throne at the age of 26 after the death of his father Alexander III. Like Louis XVI of France, Nicholas II had some good personal qualities: he was simple, modest, and devoted to his family. He was not however fit to sit on the Russian throne at this hour of crisis. For nearly 18 years, from 1894 to 1905, he continued his father's repressive policies with scarcely any variation except towards greater severity. Both the reactionary officials—Plehve and Pobedonostsev—remained in power. Plehve, the head of the secret police, was promoted to the rank of the Minister of the Interior with almost dictatorial powers. The police were authorized to arrest any person they suspected and to inflict any punishment they liked. University teachers and students were constantly watched by the police and the censorship of the press became more vigorous than before. Arbitrary arrests of all kinds increased year on year and in course of a single year, nearly one-fifth of the students of the University of Moscow were sent to Siberia and other prison houses in the empire. The policy of 'Russification' was also pursued at the same time with great vigour.

The Industrial Revolution which had begun in Russia in the reign of Alexander III, was in full swing by the reign of Nicholas II. The industrialization of Russia in the long run weakened the autocratic regime. It revolutionized the traditional social fabric and gave birth to two important classes—a middle class and a numerous working class—both of which provided a fertile soil for the seeds of revolution. The industrial workers were naturally attracted to the more radical creed of socialism. As C. Hill has pointed out in his *Lenin and the Russian Revolution*, 'the middle class development in Russia was far from complete . . . power was monopolized in this country by the aristocracy and bureaucracy. . . .' Liberalism, the political philosophy of the rising middle class, which had long been prevented from entering into Russia, now spread all over the country. It found manifestation in the formation of organizations like the Union of Liberators (1903), and the Constitutional Democratic Party (1905). The Constitutional Democratic Party included within its fold, different types of constitutionalists including the constitutional monarchists and the republicans.

The discontent of the peasants and workers was much more widespread and deeply rooted than the middle class. This discontent sought expression through different channels. While Russia was being rapidly industrialized, no attempt was made to change the old social institutions and values. At a time when in other European countries the labour movement was acknowledged, the Russian workers were not allowed to form trade unions or any other organizations. Consequently, their discontent found expression through revolutionary channels: secret radical groups sprang up and working class agitation under the influence of Marxism came to the surface. In the 1860s, Bakunin had translated the *Communist Manifesto* into Russian and in 1872, there appeared a Russian translation of the first part of *Das Capital*. Both Marx and Engels were in regular contact with the Russian exiles. In 1883, a group called 'Emancipation of Labour' was formed under the leadership of Georgi Plekhanov. It gave its main attention to the working class and was prepared to cooperate even with the middle class. In 1879, the socialist groups united under the Social Democratic Workers Party. Initially, this Party did not have much influence and in 1903 it split into two groups—Bolsheviks and Mensheviks—over the question of methods and tactics. Nevertheless, they worked together till 1912.

The discontent of Russia's massive agrarian population found expression through a mass organization called the Socialist Revolutionary Party. Their programme, it has been said, 'disclosed an effort to link up populism with Marxism and Henry George'. Its slogan was 'the whole land to the whole people' thus it appealed to the peasants and to their appetite for land.

By 1904, there were therefore already four main sources of active opposition to the autocratic regime: (1) the discontented subject nationalities repressed by the policy of Russification, (2) the land-hungry peasants, (3) the bourgeois liberals, and (4) the class conscious industrial proletariat. Added to this was the humiliating defeat of Russia in the Russo-Japanese War (1905). It served as the immediate stimulant for the rising of 1905.

Troubles started in Russia from the beginning of the twentieth century. Student strikes and demonstrations became more frequent from 1898 onwards. Sporadic peasant disturbances kept rural society in a state of tension and the Socialist Revolutionaries resumed the terrorist tactics of the Nihilist leaders resorting to the massacre of the high officials of the Tsarist Government. In July 1904, Plehve was assassinated by a Socialist Revolutionary.

The final spark came on 22 January 1905, when the police opened fire on a procession of about 1,50,000 striking workers who under Father Gapon's leadership, were peacefully marching towards the Winter Palace in the St. Petersburg to present a petition to the Tsar. The shootings were a political error of colossal dimensions and at the end of the so-called 'Bloody Sunday', there were perhaps a thousand dead and many more thousands wounded earning the Tsar the nickname of 'Bloody Nicholas'. In February 1905, the Tsar's uncle Grand Duke Sergius, who had by his rough conduct alienated almost every section of the public in Moscow, was murdered by a Socialist Revolutionary. Meanwhile, a series of peasant uprisings in the countryside continued to threaten the landlords. In June 1905, there was a mutiny on the Russian battleship *Potemkin* and a strike by flue workers in the port off Odessa. All these events culminated in the general strike of October 1905. This strike was a spontaneous rising which was not controlled by any central organization. Everywhere the people demanded a constituent assembly elected by universal male suffrage.

Failure of the Revolution

The attempt to overthrow the Tsarist government by paralysing the social and economic life of the country however, ended in a failure, perhaps because it was premature. The government savagely put down the movement, killing nearly 15,000 people and arresting about 70,000 over the course of six months. However, the movement was not completely unsuccessful because it compelled Nicholas II to revise his policy to some extent. The Tsar issued two imperial decrees in October and November 1905, which included a guarantee of civil liberty, male suffrage (though on a class basis) for the Duma elections, and a promise that no law could be passed without the approval of the Duma. Furthermore, Nicholas also dismissed some of his reactionary officials. These two decrees of October and November virtually transformed the empire of the Romanovs into a constitutional monarchy, though for a short while. The concessions offered by the Tsar failed to satisfy the revolutionary leaders and the general strike continued through November 1905. Gradually however, the revolutionary forces began to lose their strength and in 1906 the revolution petered out.

Several explanations for the failure of the revolution of 1905 have been offered:

1. Nicholas II enjoyed the support of a vast military machine which rallied to his side. Most faithful of all were the Cossacks, who formed a special 'rough rider' contingent in the Russian army. Moreover, the end of the Russo-Japanese War also enabled the Tsar to mobilize his forces against the revolutionaries.

2. As Russia was a vast country with poor means of communication, it was difficult for the revolutionaries to organize their forces effectively. There was no central revolutionary organization to direct the movement and so in effect, it was a series of sporadic uprisings without effective leadership.

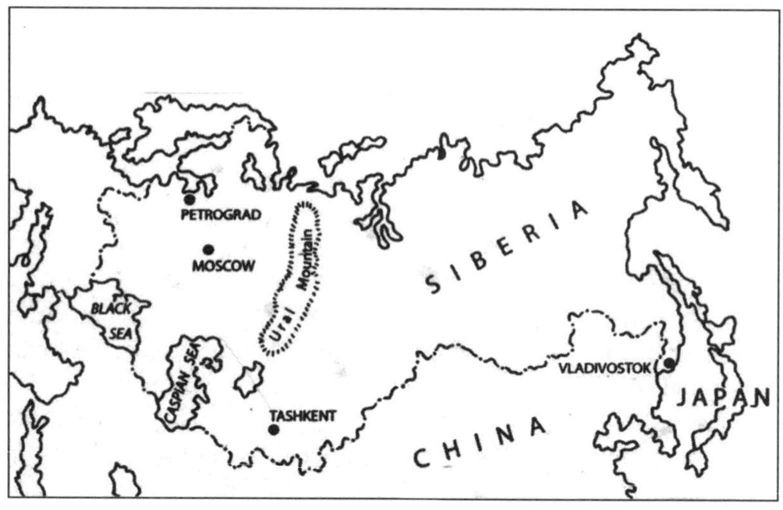

MAP 10.1: Russian Empire (1914)

3. Foreigners generally hailed the uprising against Tsarism with enthusiasm, but not so foreign governments. Both republican France and imperial Germany extended help to the tottering autocracy, the former with money and the latter by arresting the fleeing rebels.

4. There developed internal conflicts among the revolutionaries. The Bolsheviks quarrelled with the Mensheviks and both of them were opposed to the Socialist Revolutionaries.

The middle classes hated the autocracy, but they hated still more the possibility of losing their property, hence many of them rallied to the side of the Tsar when the revolution was only half accomplished. Naturally, the radical groups lost their faith in the middle class liberals, the latter again were divided into a number of factions like the Kadets, the Octobrists, and so on.

The significance of the Revolution of 1905 was somewhat similar to those of the Revolution of 1848 in Western Europe. By far the greatest outcome of the Revolution was the moral downfall of the autocracy. A positive gain was an elected parliament which gave a taste of constitutional rule even if only a faint degree. There are moments in history when mass struggle is essential for the further training of the masses. In this sense, though the Russian Revolution of 1905 was a failure, it was the first great step in the political education of the Russian masses who, in 1917, were to wipe out the Tsarist regime under the leadership of V.I. Lenin.

THE RUSSIAN REVOLUTIONS OF 1917

The Bolshevik Revolution or the Russian Revolution of 1917 brought about far-reaching changes and created a new consciousness among the people of the world. In Russia, there were two revolutions: (1) the political revolution (March 1917) which sealed the fate of Tsarist autocracy, and (2) the socio-economic revolution (November 1917) which brought the Bolsheviks into power and established the first communist state in the world.

The roots of the Russian Revolution were firmly embedded in the social, economic, and political structure of Russia. It was an expression of popular discontent against continuous economic hardship and political repression of the government as has been discussed earlier.

Despite the events of 1905, the period between 1907 and 1912 witnessed some economic prosperity in Russia. However, the Russian government during this period returned to its pre-revolutionary character and power was held by the existing ruling classes. Stolypin, who enjoyed the full confidence of the Tsar, encouraged the rich peasants, or *kulaks,* to squeeze the poorer peasants off the soil. Considerable holdings belonging to the state and to the imperial family were put up for sale to these *kulak* peasant proprietors. The rise of the *kulaks,* who constituted only a small minority of the peasantry, inflicted a new kind of hardships on the poorer peasants. The bulk of the peasantry was now reduced to the status of ordinary day-labourers or landless wage earners. In short, there was great tension and restlessness in Russian agrarian society on the eve of the Bolshevik Revolution.

The industrial labour force too, was one of the classes which was adversely affected. The plight of Russia's 25,00,000 industrial workers was deplorable. Russia was then going through the earliest phase of her industrial revolution and the rise of the factory system brought along many associated hardships for the working class.

The number of strikes continued to rise between 1905 and 1914 and the increasing working class agitation in Russia mirrored the growing discontent of Russian society more widely.

The situation was very fluid in Russia and the stage was well-set for a revolutionary movement. The gulf between the rich and the poor was widening, there was a small middle class which was very feeble and there was a lack of education among the majority of Russians. The Tsarist regime did not take much initiative to spread education and the percentage of illiteracy among the Russians was one of the highest in Europe. The Bolsheviks took an active role to reform the society and bring political consciousness among the people.

During the period from 1907 to 1912, the Russian Government carried out land reforms, passed law regarding workmen's insurance, and extended primary education under the control of the church. The period from 1907 to 1912 was also, generally speaking, a period of economic prosperity for Russia, but, the Russian government during this period again got back its pre-revolutionary character and power was captured by the existing ruling classes. Pyotr Stolypin, who enjoyed the full confidence of the Tsar till his assassination in September 1911, encouraged the rich Russian peasants and *kulaks* to squeeze out the poorer peasants from the soil. Considerable holdings, belonging to the state and to the imperial family, were put up for sale to these *kulaks* or big peasant proprietors because Stolypin believed that a prosperous peasantry would be the chief support of the Tsarist regime. At the same time Stolypin persecuted the revolutionaries, imprisoned or banished political suspects, oppressed the Jewish people living in the Russian empire and sponsored new legislations against the Poles.

It was not until the First World War that the Russian people got another opportunity to challenge the autocratic Tsarist regime. At first the war triggered a great outburst of patriotic feelings in Russia and served as a unifying force in politics. However, as the news of Russian defeats came in quick succession, the angered public began to blame the incompetence and corruption of the Tsarist regime. Nearly 5,000 Russians were either injured or killed in this war and there was great destruction of property. The common people, particularly in the towns, faced great difficulties in obtaining food and fuel, inflation became rampant, and the government remained largely indifferent to the peoples' sufferings.

Popular disaffection began to spread more widely during the winter of 1916–17, particularly on account of the chronic food shortages. In December 1916, Rasputin, who was regarded as an evil advisor of the Tsar, was assassinated. The subject nationalities became restless, the middle class began to grumble, and there were riots by peasants in the countryside and strikes by industrial workers in the towns. Simultaneously, just as the philosophers prepared the French mentally for the French Revolution, the Russian writers and philosophers too, played a significant role in the Russian Revolution. Writers and thinkers like Turgenev, Gorkey, Tolstoy, Bakunin, and Karl Marx, infused new ideas into the minds of the Russians and such ideas helped to generate a deep hatred for the Tsarist regime among the common people.

The March Revolution (1917)

The March Revolution was neither premediated nor carefully organized, and was the result of an almost spontaneous popular reaction against military defeat and economic crisis (particularly shortage of food). The cry of 'Bread!' was followed by cries of 'Down with the war' and 'Down with the autocracy!'

On 8 March 1917, the industrial workers of Petrograd (modern day St. Petersburg), went on a strike demanding higher wages. They were joined by the students on the following day and on the third day the strike became universal. Even the police forces were overpowered in some parts of the city. The Revolution was finally precipitated by the Tsar's decree of 11 March 1917, which asked the striking workers to go back to work. The workers refused to obey the decree and won over to their side some of the soldiers whom the Tsar had sent to suppress them. The ministers of the Tsar fled.

The crowd seized the armoury in St. Petersburg, distributed the weapons among the common people, and set fire to the police station. Shortly after this, striking workers and many of the soldiers formed a Soviet or revolutionary council. Tsar Nicholas II was forced by the army to abdicate and the monarchy was abolished in favour of the Provisional Government led by Prince Georgy Lvov. Although the workers launched the revolution, they surrendered power to the middle class. The Petrograd Soviet together with the Duma decided to set up the Provisional Government. The Provisional Government released thousands of political prisoners and allowed the return of the political exiles to Russia. It proclaimed freedom of association, freedom of press, and freedom of religion. It declared that a national constituent assembly would shortly be elected on the basis of universal male suffrage to draw up the future constitution of Russia.

So, the March Revolution placed political power in the hands of the liberal elements among the bourgeoisie. The provisional government was weak and it failed to solve the problems which had topped the centuries-old structure of Tsarist autocracy. However, it placed all the races and nationalities within the ambit of the Russian Empire on a level of equality. Attempts were made to prosecute the war with renewed vigour.

The October Revolution (1917)

The war-weary soldiers and the peasantry did not want war, and Bolsheviks were persistent in their advocacy for peace. Second, the provisional government could not solve the problem of distribution of land among the peasants. Third, the provisional government failed to satisfy the industrial proletariat. Thus Russian society contained all the explosive elements needed for a social upheaval: war-weary soldiers, clamorous peasants, and a dissatisfied proletariat. These chaotic elements were united and forged into a mighty political instrument by the Bolsheviks. The Mensheviks and the Socialist Revolutionaries gave conditional support to the war efforts but the Bolsheviks wanted Russia's defeat and peace as a presage to a world revolution.

In July 1917, Prince Lvov was replaced by a socialist revolutionary Alexander Kerensky at the head of the provisional government. But, the partial reforms had failed to satisfy the Bolsheviks. When the February Revolution broke out, the leader of the Bolsheviks, Lenin was in Switzerland. He arrived in Russia in April 1917. He was followed by Trotsky. They did not want a parliamentary republic nor a bourgeois democracy but rather they wanted a 'Soviet of workers', soldiers, and labourers. In Russia, Soviets had been in existence since 1905, and the Soviet system played an especially important role under the Provisional Government. Lenin utilized it for the purpose of establishing on the ruins of Tsarist autocracy, the 'dictatorship of the proletariat'. The Bolsheviks also demanded termination of the war at any cost, so that radical changes might be carried out within Russia. The Bolshevik influence began to spread rapidly in Russia. In September 1917, the Moscow and St. Petersburg Soviets were captured by the Bolsheviks. Increasing economic difficulties weakened the Provisional Government. In November 1917, the Provisional Government under Kerensky was thrown out and its leader fled abroad. The Bolsheviks captured political power under the leadership of Lenin. This was the famous Bolshevik Revolution of October 1917 which ushered in a new age in Russian and world history.

For the first three years of its existence, the Soviet regime had to fight for its life. The easy victory achieved by the Bolsheviks in wresting state power from the hands of their adversaries was followed by a struggle which involved the nation in a civil and interpersonal war. The dispossessed classes did not passively accept the verdict of the October Revolution and with the support of the Allied powers, they organized armed resistance under General Denikin in the South and Admiral Kolchak in Siberia. There were savage reprisals and atrocities, but the new Soviet government was ultimately able to consolidate its authority.

In foreign policy, the first important step taken by the new government was to withdraw from the war and accept the terms dictated by Germany through the Treaty of Brest-Litovsk on 3 March 1918. At home, the large estates was confiscated and the peasantry were finally won over. A 'workers and peasants State' was established. Though Lenin died in 1924. Under Stalin's leadership the socio-economic revolution made further progress.

Significance

The Bolshevik Revolution of 1917 opened up a fresh chapter in human civilization. The importance of this Revolution is no less than the French Revolution of 1789. The impact of the French Revolution was confined to Europe, but, the influence of the Bolshevik Revolution was global. It encouraged the downtrodden and suffering people of the world to combine and fight for freedom.

The Russian Revolution of 1917 brought about far-reaching social, economic and political changes in Russia. It led to the birth of the USSR or the Union of the Soviet Socialist Republic. For the first time in the history of the world, a socialist state was created. Production and distribution were hereafter controlled by the state. Private ownership of the means of production and private profit making were no more allowed. Land was taken away from the landlords and redistributed among the peasants. In time, the Bolshevik Revolution came to exert a far-reaching global impact. Germany, Italy, England, France, Eastern Europe, Asia, and Latin America were influenced indirectly by the Bolshevik Revolution although the degree of influence varied from place to place. The affairs of the Soviet Union were keenly observed by the rest of the world as it was the first implementation of the philosophy preached by Karl Marx. The Bolshevik Revolution made possible the dream of the dictatorship of the proletariat a reality. The writings and speeches of Marx and Lenin were translated into various languages of the world. Under the forceful impact of Marxian-Leninism, communist parties were founded in different parts of the world. Through the Comitern, the Russian Revolution helped to strengthen the anti-colonial nationalist movements in different countries of Asia. For example, the Indian nationalist struggle derived great stimulus from the Bolshevik message. This great upheaval left a permanent imprint on the future course of world history. In a long term sense, it indirectly contributed to the growth of Fascism in Europe and the beginning of the Cold War between Russia and the United States in the post-Second World War period.

CIVIL WAR IN RUSSIA (1918–21)

The post-revolutionary period, the new Soviet Government became occupied with the job of reconstruction. The Bolsheviks, led by Lenin and Trotsky, embarked on a project of national consolidation. It proved to be a difficult task for as yet, they were only a minority of the Russian population. They faced challenges from both within and without Russia. It was imperative to form a government in keeping with communistic principles but there was a counter-revolutionary attempt to wipe out the Bolshevik regime in Russia. This counter-revolutionary group received support from various foreign countries like the United States, England, France, Japan, Italy, etc. Under the circumstances, the task of consolidation became difficult for the Bolsheviks.

The first essential requirement to secure the new regime was external peace, which was necessary to enable the Bolsheviks to concentrate their full strength and energy on the pressing problems at home. Lenin opened negotiations with the Central Powers and concluded a separate peace with Germany and her allies by the Treaty of Brest-Litovsk. This treaty was humiliating for Russia. But, for Lenin and the Bolsheviks no sacrifice was too great to secure the triumph of the ongoing social revolution. Lenin had to follow a ruthless policy of repression to ensure the safety of the socialist government in Russia. The landlords, businessmen, and others made a broad united front against the Bolsheviks led by Lenin. The sacrifice of individual liberty and political democracy at the altar of the dictatorship of proletariat was disliked by them. But, the Bolsheviks adopted a ruthless method against their opponents. They set up a tribunal called the Cheka which supervised thousands of executions. As in the days of French Revolution, opposition, whether within the country or without, increased the violence of the terror.

The post-war economic recession and depression was alarming

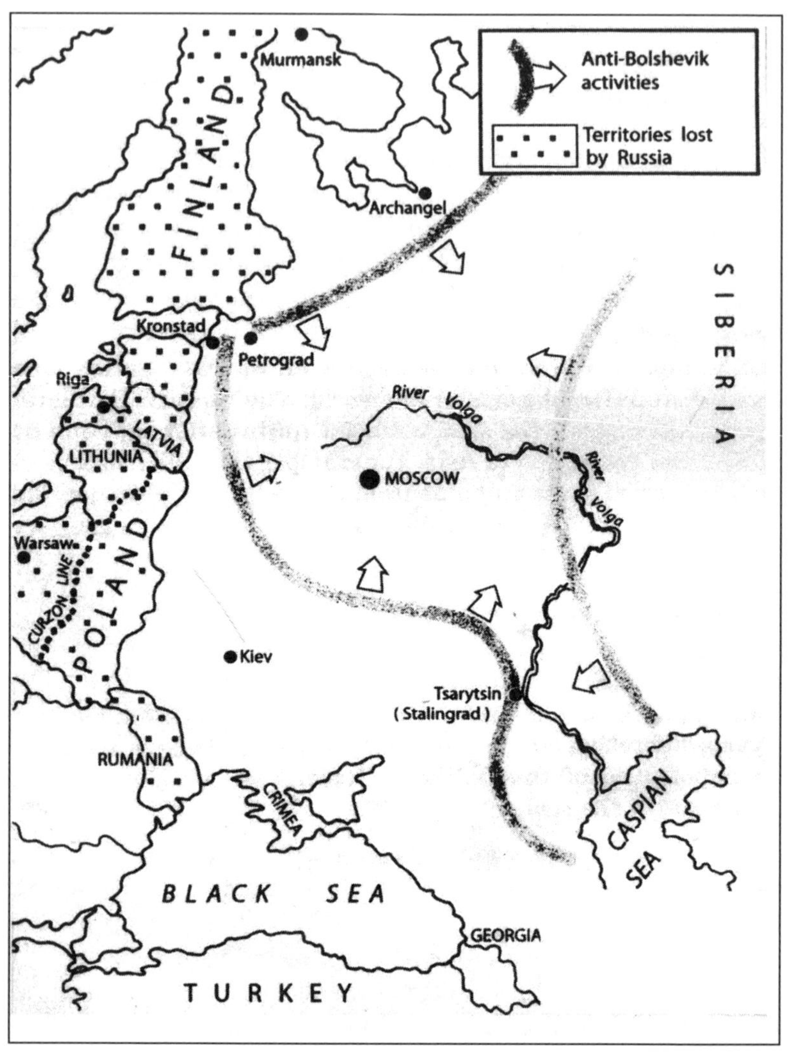

MAP 10.2: Civil War in Russia 1918

and the Western powers feared that the example of Russia might incite revolt among the working classes within their territory. This fear was intensified by the Bolshevik propaganda for a 'world revolution'. The foreign powers were further alienated by Lenin's rejection of foreign debts contracted during the Tsarist regime. The Western powers now felt it necessary to offer help to the opposition in Russia. Their object was twofold: (1) to prevent Germany from exploiting the disturbed situation in Russia to her own advantage, and (2) to overthrow the Bolshevik government by supporting the various attempts at counter-revolution. England, France, and Czechoslovakia therefore sent expeditionary forces to Russia whilst maintaining their operations elsewhere during the Second World War. This invasion came at a time when the country was engaged in a civil war between the Red Army (Bolsheviks) and the White Army (counter-revolutionary forces). For sometime, it seemed as though the Bolshevik government would collapse in the face of foreign intervention and internal disorder. The Bolsheviks however, pulled through all the struggles and several causes contributed to their victory:

1. The counter-revolutionaries were not united. The Royalists were against the Republicans and the military leaders did not like the politicians.
2. The new government enjoyed the full support of the peasants who feared the return of the old landlords which would mean the loss of their newly acquired land.
3. The Allied intervention was inadequate and half-hearted as the Allied army was not able to undertake the extensive military operations which were necessary to subjugate a huge country like Russia. Hence, they withdrew their forces in 1919.
4. The Red Army proved to be a much more organized fighting force under Trotsky. The counter-revolutionary forces were beaten everywhere and Poland was forced to come to terms.

LENIN AND HIS NEW ECONOMIC POLICY (NEP)

The Bolsheviks had made important changes in the social and economic structure of Russia. Their programme of socialism and state ownership of capital was very ambitious and it put communism to a very severe test. The peasants were happy to get rid of their landlords but they wanted the confiscated lands for themselves rather than for the state. They were reluctant to hand over the surplus produce to the government. This was why they decided to reduce production. This resulted in food shortage. To make matters worse Russia was hit by a drought in 1921. A terrible famine occurred which took away 5 million lives. The industrial scenario was equally bad. Industries were nationalized and thrown under the management of workers, but few of them were trained in management. As a consequence, production declined sharply and prices of goods rapidly increased. Shortages of food and diminishing industrial output caused acute distress across the country. All these developments made the socialist government very unpopular. The socialists now realized that their enthusiasm for socialism had carried them too far. It was now high time for Lenin, the supreme leader of the new government, to handle the situation with caution.

Lenin (1870–1924), family name Ulyanov born at Simbirsk on the middle Volga, was the son of a school inspector. When he was sixteen his elder brother was hanged for complicity in a plot to assassinate the Tsar. Lenin graduated in law as an external student at St. Petersburg University while living under restrictions in Samara, a thousand miles away. He studied Marx, contacted political exiles, was arrested, and spent three years in Siberia. He left Russia in 1900 and settled in Germany, later living for a time in Brussels, Paris, and London. Through his pamphlets, with their penetrating analysis of post-Marxian socialism, and through his newspaper, *Iskra* (the Spark), Lenin became recognized as the leader of the militant wing of the Russian Social Democrats, a group known as the Bolsheviks from 1903.

Lenin returned to Russia in November 1905, and for three months organized the resistance of the workers in St. Petersburg, but he was exiled for this in 1906. While in England as an exile, Lenin attended a session of the Russian Socialist Democratic Party. He put forward the proposal for the political party of the proletariat. The majority accepted the proposal. Hereafter, the majority group of the party came to be known as the Bolsheviks and the minority group as the Mensheviks. In 1914, he settled in Switzerland. After the February Revolution of 1917, Lenin returned to Petrograd, passing through Germany in a sealed train provided by the German General Staff, who counted on Lenin and his followers spreading disaffection among the Russian soldiery. Lenin remained in Petrograd from 16 April to 18 July 1917, when an abortive Bolshevik *coup d'état* forced him to flee to Finland. He returned in October and, from his headquarters in the Smolny Institute, led the rising that captured the government offices (6 November). Lenin became head of the new government, the Council of Peoples Commissars.

Lenin was quick to understand the seriousness of the economic crisis of 1921. He felt that a change of policy was needed. He proclaimed a New Economic Policy (NEP) for the Soviet Union. The policy was a turning away from Marxian Socialism and involved a compromise between socialism and capitalism. The chief features of the policy may be briefly summed up as follows:

1. The peasants were required to pay a fixed tax, at first in kind and after 1924, in cash. The requisition of food stuffs from the peasants was dropped.
2. The peasants were allowed to sell their surplus in the open market.
3. Private enterprise on a small scale was to be allowed.
4. To secure liquid capital, concessions were allowed to foreign capitalists, but the state retained the option of purchasing the products of such concerns.
5. Private retail trading was allowed on a small scale.

The NEP was a crucial departure from the Marxian path though it was not a full scale restoration of capitalism and Lenin and his followers considered it to only be a temporary arrangement. The new policy helped to revitalize the economy. The NEP thus helped to avoid a great catastrophe and thereby saved the Bolshevik government.

Lenin did not live long enough to see the full working of the NEP. He died in 1924, but his contribution to the making of a new Russia was immense. He had a driving force, a very strong will, and a fanatical faith in communism. He saved the revolution by reversing his policy. He will be remembered forever, in the history of communism, as a hero.

STALIN (1879–1953)

The death of Lenin paved the way for the rise of Joseph Stalin. Stalin, the son of a cobbler, was born in Georgia. He was educated in a seminary, from which he was expelled for holding revolutionary views in 1899. He was twice exiled to Siberia, but escaped each time. In 1902–3 he was in Paris, in 1906 at the Stockholm Conference of Russian Socialist Democrat exiles, in 1907 at the London Conference. When the Bolshevik Central Committee was established in 1912, he was recognized as its expert on racial minorities and in 1913 in Vienna, he completed his study entitled *Marxism and the Nationalities Problem*. He became editor of the *Pravda* newspaper in 1917, assisted Lenin in Petrograd during the October Revolution, and was made Commissar for Nationalities in the Government that Lenin established, holding the post until 1922 when he became Secretary of the Communist Party. In the civil war, he helped to organize the defence of Petrograd against the 'Whites' of General Yudenich, and distinguished himself in defending Tsaritsyn (renamed Stalingrad in his honour) against General Denikin.

On the death of Lenin two prominent communist leaders, Stalin and Leo Trotsky, contested for the leadership of the party. Lenin expressed the desire to see Stalin as his successor but Stalin was a realist in politics.

Everyone in Russia was of the impression that Trotsky would automatically succeed Lenin. He was the Commissar of War and in organizing the Red Army, he played the most important role. After Lenin's death a bitter rivalry between Stalin and Trotsky started. This rivalry was both ideological as well as personal. Trotsky believed in the concept of 'world revolution', for he held that the success of socialism in Russia depended upon the conversion of the whole world to communism. Stalin however, wanted to concentrate on national revival, i.e. upon the economic advancement of the country, rather than upon attempts to dislodge capitalism from the whole world. Stalin worked astutely to dash out Trotsky and his supporters from the Communist Party. Trotsky had to leave Russia to save his life. He was eventually assassinated in Mexico in 1940. Stalin now emerged the new leader of the Soviet Union.

Stalin wanted to set up a planned economy in Russia. For the economic regeneration of the country he introduced the Five Year Plan in 1928. The Plan mainly focused on nationalism, increase in production, and rapid industrialization. Stalin's objective was to attempt economic self sufficiency and elimination of capitalism in the long run. The First Five-Year Plan (1928–32) concentrated on increased productivity which was a success. During this phase huge factories, new blast furnaces, etc., were constructed in Russia. Technical schools and industrial training centres were created. Expert opinion was sought from abroad. The Second Five-Year Plan (1933–8) pushed the country's development project further. The Second Plan period saw a great deal of industrial progress. The Soviet Union turned into one of the leading industrialized countries of the world during the Third Plan Period (1938–43).

Removal of illiteracy was an important element of the Five Year Plans and the progress in this direction was considerable in Russia under Stalin. There is no doubt that under the stimuli of the Five Year Plan programme Soviet Russia made great economic progress. The condition of the Russian people improved considerably during that time.

Stalin realized that peace with foreign state was necessary to ensure the success of his Five Year Plans. Without the help of foreign capital and foreign technical knowledge, Russian industrialization would not have been possible. This was why he rejected the Comintern plan of an instant world revolution. He firmly held that for the safety and security of Russian communism, peace was necessary. But, Stalin did not like the conciliatory policy of France and Britain towards Germany. Later he reversed his policy and signed a pact of neutrality with Hitler on the eve of the Second World War.

Stalin's contribution to the rise of Soviet Union was remarkable. However, after the collapse of the Soviet Union in 1991, the role of Stalin has become a subject of great controversy. With the opening up of the Soviet archives, scholars have started to scrutinize Stalin's contribution in a new light. Today, the Soviet Union is gone, instead of the USSR, there are now fourteen independent states one of which is the pre-revolution Russia.

HIGHLIGHTS

- The Revolution of 1905 failed to overthrow the autocratic regime of the Tsar in Russia, but it was not a failure in the long term sense; it was a dress rehearsal for the Bolshevik Revolution of 1917.
- The [March] Revolution (1917) brought about the downfall of monarchy in Russia. Russia then became a bourgeois republic under the Provisional Government.
- The Provisional Government had many limitations. In October 1917 the Bolsheviks captured power in Russia under the leadership of Lenin. The Bolsheviks were successful due to a number of reasons.
- The Bolshevik Government under Lenin had to struggle hard for survival. The new regime was threatened from both within Russia and without. Civil War broke out in Russia at that time but the Bolsheviks dealt with the crisis with a strong and efficient hand.
- To save Russia from the economic crisis Lenin formulated his New Economic Policy (NEP). The NEP showed Lenin's political vision and statesmanship.
- After Lenin's death Stalin consolidated the socialist regime in Russia but at great cost.

MEMORABLE DATES AND EVENTS

1861	Emancipation of Serfs
1864	Political reforms and the creation of *Zemstvo*
1898	Foundation of the Social Democratic Party
1905	9 January—Bloody Sunday
	October—October Manifesto
1912	Publication of *Pravda*

1917	March—The March Revolution
	End of the Tsarist regime
	November—The Bolshevik or the November Revolution
1921	The New Economic Policy of Lenin
1924	January—The birth of USSR
	Death of Lenin
1928	The beginning of Five Year Plan
1953	Death of Stalin

MEMORABLE PERSONALITIES

Nicholas I: Tsar of Russia
Alexander II: Tsar of Russia who emancipated the serfs in 1861
Alexander III: Tsar of Russia
Nicholas II: Tsar of Russia at the time of the Revolution of 1905 and 1917
Rasputin: The Siberian monk who influenced Tsar Nicholas II
Karl Marx: The philosopher who influenced Lenin and Bolsheviks
Lenin: The leader of the Bolsheviks and the founder of the USSR
Trotsky: Associate of Lenin, leader of the Bolshevik Revolution
Stalin: Succeeded Lenin as leader of the Bolsheviks

QUOTABLE QUOTES

- 'This momentous event [the Emancipation of Serfs] was a landmark in the modern history of Russia, not so much because it betokened the acceptance of Western ideas of individual freedom and rights, but rather because it inaugurated a social and economic revolution and opened the door to a more massive material Westernization of Russian life.' —DAVID THOMSON

- 'In reality the position of the peasants was not radically improved; and it continued to remain very unsatisfactory. The terms of their emancipation, so far from awakening their enthusiasm provoked profound discontent.' —LIPSON

- 'An alarming decline in production, together with peasant outbreaks and a revolt of the sailors in the Soviet fleet, forced Lenin in 1921 to adopt the New Economic Policy.' —LIPSON

- '...the New Economic Policy...was neither socialism, nor capitalism, but a temporary mixture of both.' —HAYES AND MOON

- 'This was the spark that set alight the flame of revolution. In all social groups, in all parts of the country, revolt flared up. By the end of January nearly half million workmen were on strike . . . In many parts of the country a state of anarchy prevailed that all the Tsar's court martialing and repression could not abolish.'   —L. KOCHAN
- 'The movement spread like a fire. It was revolution of hunger, misery and fatigue, dashed with feelings of wild resentment as men called to mind the recent ruin of Russian armies, the long tale of military disasters . . . the strong suspicion that the Tsarina under the influence of the profligate Rasputin had been playing into German hands and finally the reactionary and oppressive methods of Protopopoff, the last and least intelligent of the Tsar's advisers.'   —H.A.L. FISHER

The Far East

OPENING OF CHINA—THE CANTON TRADE SYSTEM

Western penetration into Asia stands as one of the most important features of the economic history of the late eighteenth century. With the rapid development of capitalism in Europe in the eighteenth century, the Western capitalists felt it imperative to search for new colonies in order to gain raw materials and a market for selling their finished products—as Karl Marx suggested, 'The special task of bourgeois society is the establishment of the world market, at any rate, in its main outlines and of a production upon their basis'. The merchants of Portugal, Russia, America, etc., attempted to trade with East Asia, but Britain's colonial victories, her established position in India, and her leading role in the Industrial Revolution all served to stimulate her trade with East Asia. In fact, from 1750 to 1834, China's relations with Western Europe were essentially her relations with the British East India Company. Trade preceded flag and political power came in the wake of commercial expansion.

The Canton trade (as the China trade was known at that time), is an episode in the history of commercial relations between China and the West. In the sixteenth and seventeenth centuries, the Portuguese and later the British adventurers and merchants gradually opened the China trade. The Portuguese built up the first commercial outpost in Macao near Canton. Side by side with other European powers, Russia also joined, not by sea but by land, and she signed two trade treaties with China, one in 1689 and the other in 1727. Faced with European commercial challenges, China was uncertain how to respond. It is true that China was used to traders, but she was still essentially a central land power with an ancient civilization and heritage to draw on. Outsiders were treated as barbarians and she retained a sense of cultural superiority. Contrary to the conditions in India, where there grew up trading centres like Malabar and Surat, China was not interested in maritime trade. This was because China's economy was, as a whole, a natural economy combining individual farming with household handicrafts. The Chinese had no particular need of, nor did they have the money to buy, the manufactured goods of foreign capitalism. So when Chien Lung wrote to King George III that his Empire possessed 'all things in prolific abundance' and desired nothing from outside, he was voicing a Chinese tradition which looked upon the exchange of commodities with foreign countries as unnecessary and against the Chinese tradition.

The special position enjoyed by Britain was not a reflection of British satisfaction with the commercial system that prevailed at Canton. On the contrary, the British, like all other foreign traders in China, regarded the system as irksome, for China imposed severe restrictions and humiliating condition on foreign trade.

The British capitalists regarded the limited sale of their goods (cotton, opium, etc.) as the result of the closed door policy pursued by the Ching government. All import export business was done with special government permission by the *hong* merchants, backed by the Chinese comprador classes. Anxious to force its way into China, Britain sent three trade missions, headed by Catheart (1787), Macartney (1792–94), and Amherst (1816), but all failed. The presents sent by King George III to the Chinese Emperor were accepted, not as presents but as tributes.

The tribute system, which preceded the treaty system, was an expression of the cultural superiority of the Chinese. It was an application to foreign affairs of the Confucian doctrine by which the Chinese rulers gained an ethical sanction for the exercise of political authority. The concept was that it was only natural for foreign 'barbarians' to appreciate China's cultural superiority and to seek the benefits of Chinese civilization. The emperor, who held the 'Mandate of Heaven' to rule all mankind, would be respected by men from faraway countries. As such, imperial benevolence should be reciprocated by humble submission on the part of the foreigners which should be expressed in the form of rituals, gifts, and tribute. This was the attitude of the Chinese government to foreign trade and traders.

The Canton trade in its peak period (1760–1840) was carried on under a working compromise between the Chinese system of tributory trade and European mercantilism. Women were not allowed to be brought into the factories. Foreigners could not employ Chinese servants, nor could they use any form of transport, except walking. They had to sit down (i.e. *kowtow)* before the Chinese emperor and had to leave their families in Macao to emphasize the temporary nature of the trade. The American traders were in the second position behind the British. The Chinese set up a monopoly organization through which foreign trade in Canton had to be carried out. In 1702, the Manchus appointed an Emperor's Merchant, which was replaced later on by the *Cohong.* The *Cohong* was to act as the sole medium of communication between the government and foreign traders.

Such were the conditions under which the British capitalists traded in China. The conditions were humiliating to Britain, who took pride in her position as the dominant power in the world. Historians may argue that the humiliating state of affair, imposed by the Chinese caused the military intervention of Britain, but such a judgement would be erroneous. The fact is that in the 1820s and 1830s, with the further development of capitalism, the British capitalists became even more anxious to force open the China trade to their goods. They felt that if the Chinese markets were opened, the British goods sold there would surpass all that sold in the rest of the world. The British government used the unfavourable state of affairs as the pretext for military aggression. The Opium Wars that ensued placed China on the brink of being carved up into a series of European colonies in the scramble for territory and trade.

THE OPIUM WARS

The picture of China in the nineteenth century is one of a country that lagged far behind Western countries in historical development. The political decline, military importance, and

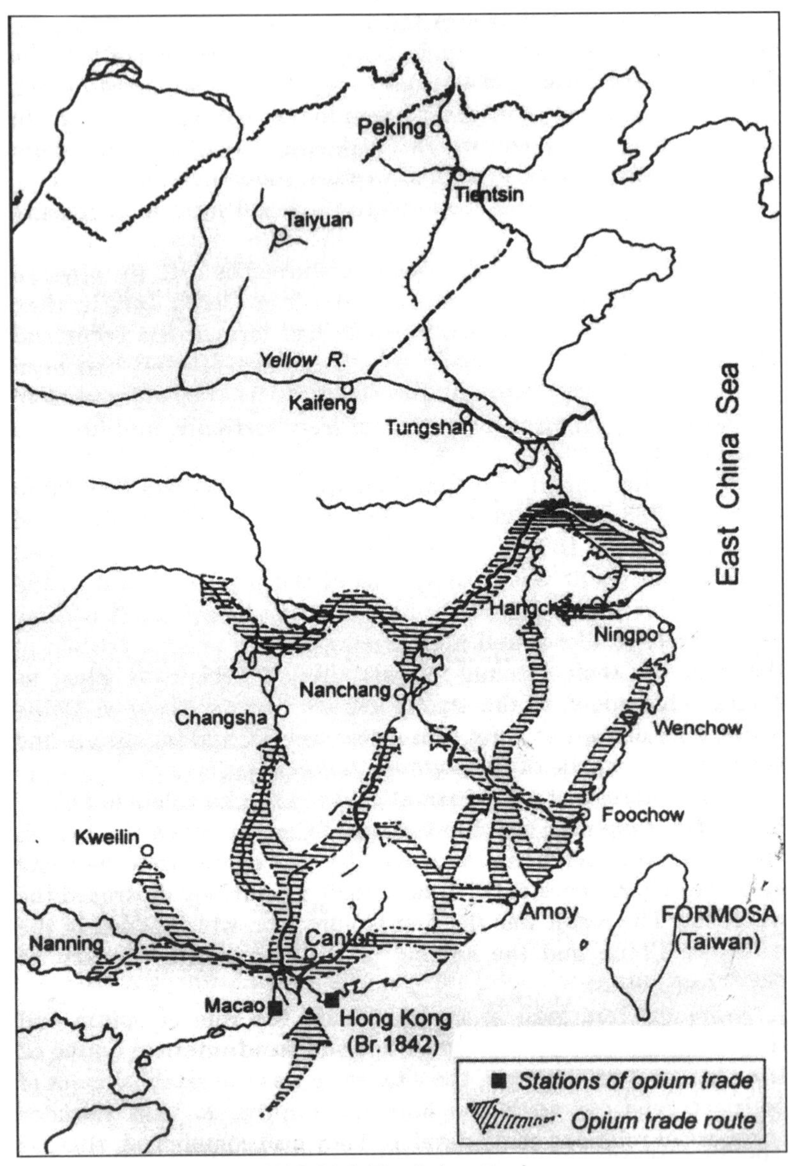

MAP 11.1: The Opium Trade

financial insolvency of the Ching dynasty was obvious. The Chinese state was a typically feudal state where social wealth was being increasingly concentrated in the hands of a minority of nobles, officials, landlords, and rich merchants. Peasants and artisans suffered exploitation through continually rising taxes and the resulting class contradictions led to peasant revolts in different parts of China.

Moreover, with the rapid development of capitalism, Britain became the world's leading capitalist power. The first crisis of overproduction that took place in Britain in 1825, necessitated the quest for new and bigger markets. This is because, according to Lenin, 'the capitalist system cannot exist and develop without extending its sphere of domination, without colonizing new countries and without drawing ancient non-capitalist countries into the whirlpool of world economy'. The Opium War (1839–42) was a part, and at the same time an inevitable outcome of the process of colonization. It was the first of a series of aggressive wars launched by the capitalist powers to turn China into a colony or semi-colony.

During the middle of the eighteenth century the British East India Company became the leader in the lucrative China trade. However, as China was dominated by a natural and largely agrarian economy, the British merchants could sell very little in China. For most of what they bought, they had to pay in solid silver and so the British company looked for other ways to pay for Chinese goods. Thus they hit upon opium.

After the first shipment of Indian opium to China in 1781, the trade grew by leaps and bounds. Soon, China's exports of tea, silk, and other goods were not enough to pay for the imported opium, and silver began to flow out of the country. In the words of Fairbank, 'In China the opium trade remains a classic symbol of western commercial imperialism, foreign greed and violence, demoralizing and exploiting an inoffensive people'.

In 1800, Emperor Ching, seriously disturbed by both the physical and economic effects of opium, banned it from China. By then however, too many people had formed the habit and too many merchants and officials had been corrupted by the profits from their partnership in the traffic: smuggling and bribery virtually nullified the official ban.

The annual import of opium grew from 2,000 chests in 1800 to 40,000 in 1838. Meanwhile, the outflow of silver from China increased to a torrent. In 1832–5 alone, 20 million ounces were shipped abroad. The result was a sharp rise in the price of metal in the country as it became more sought after. The burden fell on the peasants since grain prices became lower, while landlords and tax collectors took a greater portion of the crop, so that their income in silver would remain as great as before. This added to the strains on the feudal society of China which were already so great that a new cycle of peasant revolts had begun in the middle of the eighteenth century.

In the interests of self-preservation, the Manchu rulers in Peking felt that they had to act. Commissioner Lin-tse-hsu of Canton forced the British and American merchants to surrender the opium they had and to hand over 20,000 chests. On June 1839, he publicly destroyed the whole lot. The result was the First Opium War, which ended in the defeat of China and the signing of the humiliating Treaty of Nanking in 1842.

Some scholars tend to underestimate the role of opium and consider it as the occasion, but not the fundamental cause of the Opium War. To them the vital issue was the establishment of political relations with the Manchu Empire, so that more sound commercial relations could develop. They also complained that as a consequence of the credit nature of the trade, considerable sums were owed to the British traders which the Chinese authorities refused to accept. There were also the legal and social restraints on foreigners at Canton. The British historians argue that due to all these factors, the British were bound to choose application of force rather than abandon China trade or submit to existing conditions.

On the eve of the war, China was a feudal state and Britain a capitalist one. Chinese society was more or less a static society based upon self-sufficient natural economy. The British society, on the other hand, was a dynamic society based upon the mastery of capital. So, the war was a struggle between two types of economies—between feudalism and capitalism. In this sense we can safely echo K.S. Latourette's observation that the Opium War issued from the conflict between two opposing civilizations.

The war was however much more than this. Opium was an issue which was created by the British and turned into a conflict by Britain. The arrival of Western colonizers in China was a part of their global strategy, it was in keeping with the nature of expanding capitalism. Fresh from their gains in India, the British turned to China and used opium as an instrument with which to extract rich dividends. By this argument, when faced with the resistance of the Chinese people, the British waged a predatory war. In this sense, opium was the cause and not the occasion of the war. But an intensive study will reveal that opium or no opium, Britain, on one pretext or another, would have started the Anglo-Chinese War. And in this sense, opium is the occasion and British colonization the root cause of the war. Although arguably the causes of all the Anglo-Chinese wars can be explained by Western colonization, each particular war has unique aspects. In the First Anglo-Chinese War, however, the principal aspect was opium.

The Course of the War (1839–42)

In 1839, the Chinese officials in Canton confiscated a quantity of opium which belonged to the British merchants. The British government held that Chinese courts had no jurisdiction over British subjects and therefore could not authorize the seizure of their property. The Chinese authorities did not appreciate the British standpoint and opened fire on the British warship. They also prohibited all trade with Britain. The British retaliated by bombarding Canton and occupying Hong Kong. The fighting came to an end by the Treaty of Nanking. Compensation was duly paid for the confiscated opium.

SCRAMBLE FOR CONCESSION:
'CUTTING OF THE CHINESE MELON'

At the end of the nineteenth century world capitalism entered the stage of imperialism. The rapid growth of industries in the West

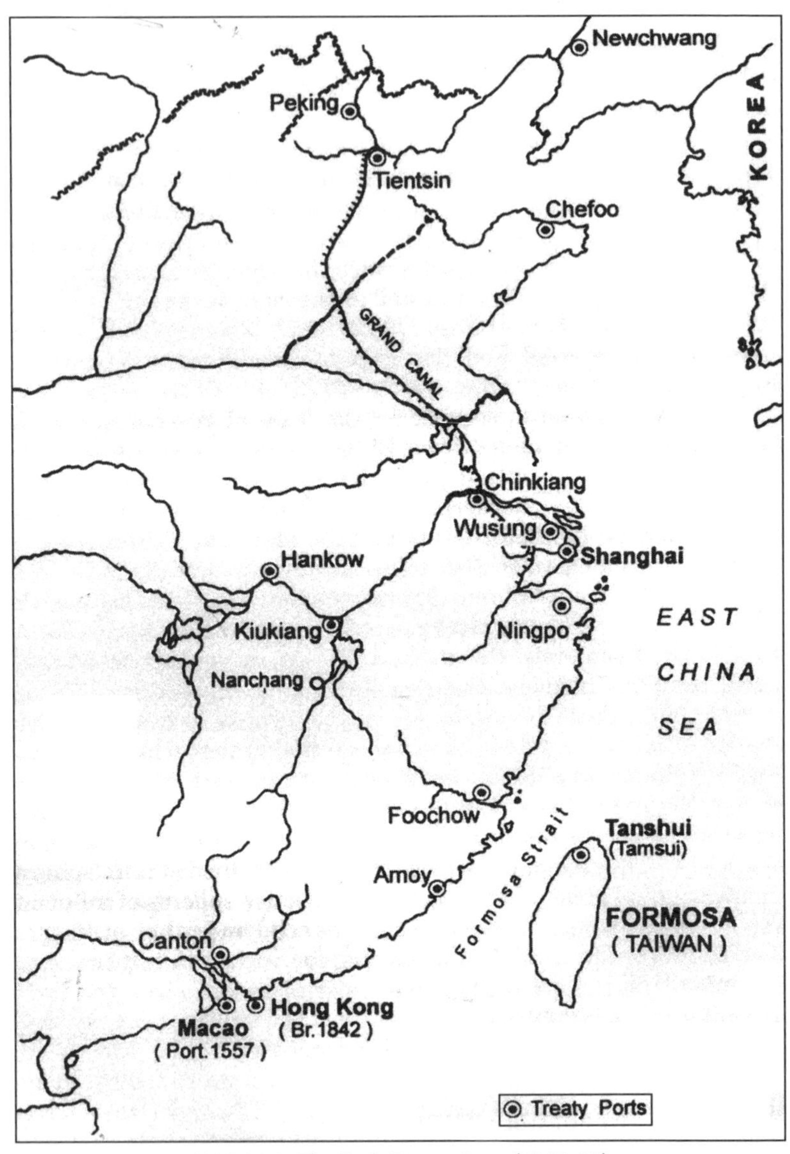

MAP 11.2: The Early Treaty Ports (1842–74)

stimulated their appetite for new markets, new sources of raw materials, and new fields for capital investment. Trying to establish a foothold in the Far East was very important as far as trade and commerce were concerned. Meanwhile, the defeat of China in the Sino-Japanese War of 1894 had exposed the weakness of China and the Western powers now started open imperialist aggression in China. They began to demand that certain parts of the country became leaseholds, and opened factories and mines, constructed railways, and set up banks, etc.

By the Treaty of Shimonoseki (1895), China agreed to hand over the Liaotung Peninsula together with Port Arthur to Japan. Russia had also coveted Port Arthur and did not like this move. Therefore under Russia's leadership, a triple intervention by Russia, France, and Germany took place forcing Japan to retrace her steps. The Russians offered loans to China and thereby became heroes in the eyes of the Chinese. The so-called 'battle of concessions' however, was initially inaugurated by France in 1895. A fresh delimitation of the boundaries between French occupied Tonkin and China was effected in favour of France. France was also granted options on mines in the southern provinces of China and the right to extend the railways from French Indochina northward.

Russia was not lagging far behind. Taking advantage of her new position as protectress of the integrity of China, she persuaded China to grant Russia the right to build the Chinese Eastern Railway across Manchuria. Russia was also permitted to establish in China the Russo-Chinese Bank and she received some mining privileges. China entered into a fifteen years defensive alliance with Russia which gave her the right in case of war to utilize Port Arthur and Kiao-chou as naval bases.

Germany was also in search of a suitable pretext to squeeze China. The murder of two German priests in Shantung Province in November 1897 provided the Germans with the opportunity they were looking for. Shortly thereafter, capitalizing on this incident, Germany demanded and obtained as compensation from China a 99 year lease of the harbour of Kiao-chou with the surrounding territory as well as full jurisdiction within the leased territory. She also secured large commercial and financial privileges, including first refusal on any undertaking in the province of Shantung in which foreign assistance was needed. The other powers became jealous of this new German gain and demanded compensation which triggered off a scramble for concession,

By two agreements in 1898, the Russians were granted lease of Port Arthur and Daizen for 25 years, the right to extend the Chinese Eastern Railway southward and mining rights in Manchuria. France too, pressed for fresh privileges and obtained a 99 year lease of Kwang Chouan. China agreed to a non-alienation agreement covering the Chinese provinces bordering Tonkin, conceded France the right to extend the Indochinese Railway into Yunan, as well as the right to designate French advisers to the Chinese Post Office. As a compensation for these, Japan received a declaration of non-alienation regarding Fukien. This led England to request the lease of Wei-Hai-Wei for 25 years. She also demanded from China:

1. A declaration that she would not alienate to any power the provinces bordering on Yangtze River,
2. a promise that an English Inspector General of the Maritime Customs would hold office so long as British trade supremacy was maintained in China, and
3. an extension of the lease of the territory on the mainland opposite of Hong Kong. Even Italy, the weakest European power, demanded a naval base in Chekiang this China refused to grant.

So quickly these developments came and so little resistance had the Imperial Government been able to make, that the end of the Chinese Empire seemed imminent. By the non-alienation declaration of 1898, the whole of China was divided into 'spheres of influence' of great powers. In their respective spheres, the different powers enjoyed special financial and other privileges. The railways and mining concessions, for which an international scramble began, carried economic imperialism deep into the heart of China.

The imperialists forced China to open 82 of her coastal and inland ports to their trade and marked off areas in 16 cities as 'concessions'. Their investments in China mounted to 2,000 million silver dollars, more than 10 times those held by China's national capitalists.

Through unequal treaties, loans, and indemnities, they also seized control of China's customs and inland taxes. Thus, they established domination over China's financial and economic lifelines to the point that China's political sovereignty was menaced. Sun Yat Sen lamented that 'China is not the colony of one nation but of all and we are not the slaves of one country but of all'.

The strong rivalry among the powers gave rise to three developments which eventually saved China: (1) The Open Door, (2) The Boxer Uprising, and (3) The Anglo-Japanese Alliance (1902). Owing to the Spanish-American War, the USA could not actively participate in the scramble for concessions. After the war however, the new economic and political situation inspired America to take interest in China. As the richest provinces had already been occupied, America sought to find an alternative method to safeguard her interest in China. The Americans enunciated the doctrine of the 'Open Door'. It was the logical outcome of the most favoured nation clause in the treaties signed between China and the Western powers. At this juncture, alarmed by the growing Russian influence in the Far East, Britain approached the United States for some form of joint action. The American Secretary of State, John Hay expressed his desire to prevent European spheres of influence from developing into exclusive colonial possessions. In September 1899, Hay sent notes to his ambassadors in England, France, Germany, Russia, and Japan for transmission to the respective governments. The Hay Note highlighted three important points:

1. No power should interfere with any Treaty port or any vested interest therein,
2. the Chinese government should be allowed to collect all necessary duties, and

3.	no power should discriminate against other countries within its sphere of influence as regards harbour dues and railroads. Hay thus urged all the powers to guarantee an open Chinese market and a uniform tariff towards the merchants of all nations. All the powers except Russia, agreed to this in principle.

The acceptance of this 'Open Door' policy checked, at least temporarily, any movement towards the partition of China. It was however inadequate to stop further encroachment on China's integrity in an age of aggressive imperialism. If China was saved from dismemberment, it was not so much because of this policy, as because of the mutual rivalry between the Western powers.

CHINESE REACTION TO IMPERIALISM

After the First Opium War (1839–40), China's feudal society began to change into a semi-feudal and colonial society. Between 1840 and the 1860 the invasion of foreign capitalism and the growth of a commodity economy in China created rifts between the landed classes and the peasantry. It sparked off a chain of reactions at various levels. Subjected to aggression and oppression, the growing frustration of the Chinese people found manifestation in the growing number of peasant revolts and reform movements of various types. These included for example, the Taiping Revolt of 1850, the reform movement of 1898, named the Yi Ho Tuan Movement, and the Boxer Rebellion of 1899.

Taiping Revolt (1851–64)

The scale of peasant uprisings and peasant wars in Chinese history has no parallel anywhere else. The Taiping Revolution effected the whole of central China as well as large parts of the north and south, altogether an area with more than 100 million inhabitants.

The Taiping Revolution reveals in essence, the traditional character of Chinese peasant revolts. Like the great revolution at the end of the Mongol period, it united social, religious, and

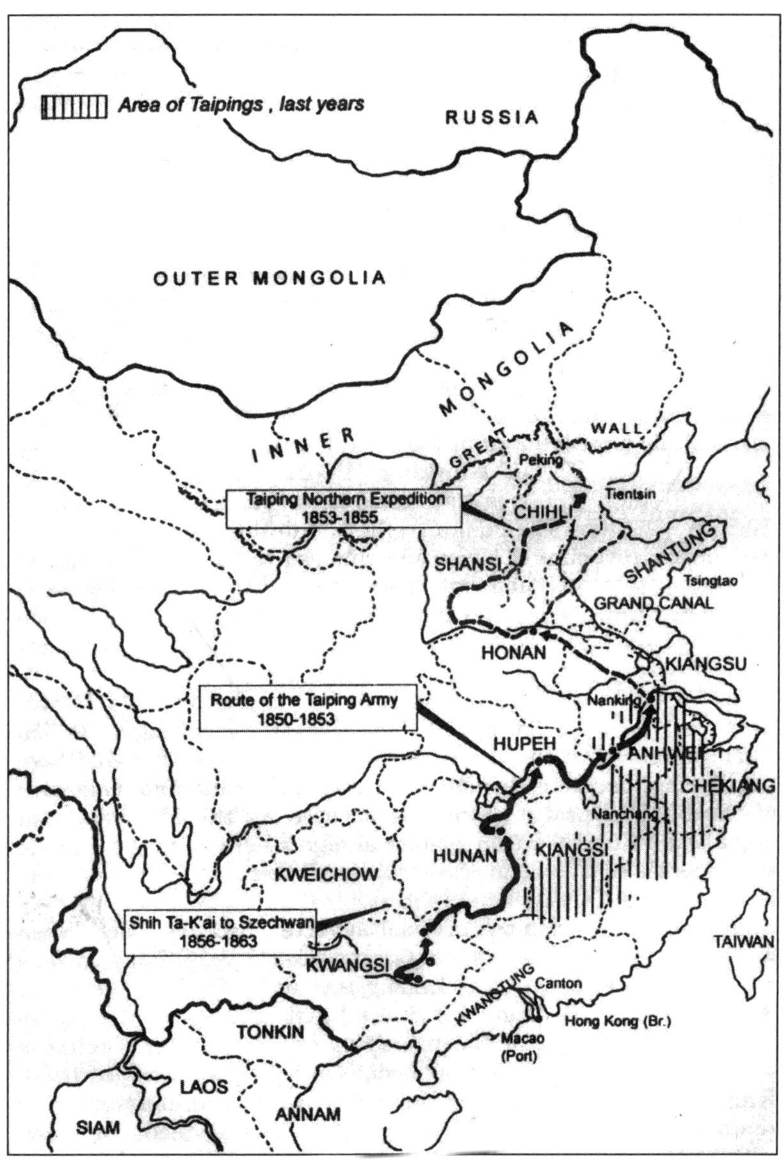

MAP 11.3: The March of the Taipings and the Taiping Areas

nationalist elements. Along with this, however, there occurred for the first time elements which originate in Western influences. This in itself is sufficient justification for regarding the Taiping Revolution as a precursor to the revolutionary movements of the twentieth century. Finally, in its suppression the attitude of foreign powers—especially England and France—played a significant role.

At the end of the eighteenth century, the Ching dynasty began to decline and signs of decadence at the court and in the central government led to mismanagement in the provinces. There was extensive corruption and greed among officials: for example, the sale of official positions fetched a large personal profit while taxes were arbitrarily doubled by the local officials and landlords who also acted as tax collectors. Thus economic failure followed hard on the heels of political decline.

On top of these abuses, which also caused popular uprisings at other times, the middle of the nineteenth century saw the addition of a special factor, namely the population explosion. Within a century, from 1751 to 1851, the total population of China had risen from approximately 180 million to over 430 million. The area of cultivated land, however, had not increased and there was no industry to absorb the surplus population or territory to which it might migrate. The only alternative therefore, was further division and more intensive cultivation of land that was already being used; poverty and the lowering of living standards were the inevitable consequences for the great majority.

It was no coincidence that this powerful peasant outburst occurred in the period of the Opium Wars and the opening of China by the Western powers. The age-old contradiction between the peasants and the feudal holders of power, land, and learning were deepened and brought to a climax by a combination of exceptional circumstances while the political and social crisis was exacerbated by the First Opium War and the Treaty of Nanking (1842).

The Manchu dynasty was discredited by its readiness to give in to Western demands. The opium traffic had drained China of a large part of her revenues of silver and changed, to the disadvantage of the peasants, the exchange rate between silver and copper. Moreover, the opening of other ports in the East deprived Canton of much of its previous commerce, with the result that thousands of boatmen and porters were thrown out of their work.

It had a strong colouring of what Jean Chesneaux calls 'proto-nationalism'. Woolfgang Franke compares the Taiping revolution with the revolts at the end of the Mongol rule, and says that here too, the nationalist element played an important role. Followers of the Ming dynasty, which was deposed by the Manchus, had organized a literary battle against foreign rulers at the end of the seventeenth century and writings of this sort influenced the leaders of the Taiping revolution.

Both these agrarian and national characteristic become evident when we analyse the revolutionary measures taken by the Taipings. The principles advanced by the Taiping revolutionaries and the measures carried through, denoted a direct break with ancient Chinese tradition. Many of the principles of the Taiping revolution served as an inspiration and model for Sun Yat Sen and the Kuomintang as well as for the 4 May Movement and the communists in the twentieth century.

The Christian idea of the equality of all men, combined with certain ancient and Utopian Chinese conceptions explain some of the particularly revolutionary points of the social programme:

1. Private property was abolished and property was held in common. In 1853, the Taipings set up their capital at Nanking and promulgated their 'land system of the Celestial Dynasty'.
2. Men and women were to be regarded as equals which was a revolutionary act of unprecedented significance.
3. Opium was strictly prohibited and the ban was enforced in practice.

Moreover, the revolutionaries destroyed images, statues, and temples of Buddhism and Taoism as well as Confucian ancestor-tablets. As a result of the Christian influence, the Taipings regarded all nations as having equal rights and did not regard the Chinese, for instance, as the chosen people. They adopted a semi-solar calender in place of the old lunar calendar, and they envisaged modern reforms, such as the construction of a network of railways, a postal service, hospitals, and banks. Thus, the Taipings under the leadership of Hung Hsing Chuan created a complete politico-religious system, which combined obedience to the will of God with the political and military defence of the rebel state.

Symbolically, the Taipings cut off their queues, which had been imposed upon the Chinese population by the Ching Emperors as a sign of humiliation, and allowed their hair to grow. This nationalist element explains the recruitment by the Taipings of a number of educated and relatively wealthy people who had no particular reason to support the social struggle of the peasantry, but whose anti-Manchu patriotism made them sympathetic to the rebel cause.

This brings us to the reasons for the successes and failures of the revolution. An analysis of the strong and weak points of the belligerent parties will help to explain the point. The Taiping revolutionaries had a clear and unified religio-political-social ideal, in which they had been trained and for which they fought. Second, the insurgents were militarily well-organized whereas the government troops were suspicious of one another and made no effort to cooperate. Third, the revolutionary army had excellent discipline, whereas, government troops were undisciplined, and they ravaged, plundered, and raped. Fourth, the Taiping leaders were able strategists whose military technique was particularly admired and imitated later by the Chinese communists.

Yet, with all these positive aspects the Taiping revolution failed. Like many other peasant rebels in history, the Taipings were subject to the contradictions inherent in a rebel order. If the revolt could have transformed itself into a stable social structure without becoming a prisoner of the exigencies of such a structure, it could have been a success. There is no doubt that the Taipings conducted a real 'peoples' war'. However, once established in Nanking, the Taipings created the apparatus of a government which soon became a privileged class. To make this governmental machinery work involved increasing demands upon the peasantry, who ceased to be the driving force of a movement and instead became the subjects of a government. Second, the anti-traditional character of the Taiping leaders gave way to many traditional vices. Third, with many of the earlier Taiping leaders fallen in battle, there were no capable men able to step into their shoes. Fourth, the Taipings also failed to join with other movements of a similar nature. Fifth, the educated class in China was still strictly conservative and was opposed to revolutionary ideas. In many respects, the ideas of the Taipings were ahead of their time, but incompetent leadership did not help to make them popular among the Chinese people. In the final years, the full weight of foreign intervention was also thrown against the rising. However, the most important cause of the failure of the Taipings was similar to those which had led to the miscarriage of the First Indian War of Independence in 1857. Despite their peasant ideal of an egalitarian utopia, their reforms were actually of such a character as to pave the way for capitalism although the development of production and of social forces in China were not yet ripe for the change.

Reform Movements

Due to the selling off of much of China by the Manchu government before the Revolution of 1911, there were grave encroachments on China's territorial and cultural integriy. There was a sharpening contradiction between the imperialist aggressors and the Chinese nation. Feudal power combined with the aggressive strength of foreign capitalists to make a strong reactionary force. The growing frustration of the Chinese people found manifestation in the growing number of reform movements of various types. Coming into contact with the West, the Chinese middle class intellectuals realized that the only way to save China would be to carry out reforms along Western lines. One such movement was the Young China Movement. Kang Yu Wei, the great Chinese patriot and intellectual, was the central figure of this movement. He was known as the 'Modern Sage'. On 2 May 1895, he presented a petition signed by 1,300 Chinese intellectuals, to the Chinese emperor Kwang Tsu. The petition included a comprehensive plan to reform Chinese society and economy. The Chinese intellectuals openly supported the proposals and study circles were set up to popularize the demand for reform.

In June 1898, Kwang Tsu announced a reform programme. He appointed Kang Yu Wei and his associates as imperial officials. The reform programme continued for about one hundred days between 11 June 1898 and 21 September 1898 hence it was known as the Hundred Days Reform. The reform measures undertaken by the Emperor, in collaboration with the Chinese intellectuals, brought under its purview all aspects of Chinese society, economy, and administration. It revamped the army, reorganized the Chinese education system, introduced some amount of freedom of expression, and touched upon agriculture, mining, and industry. Although Emperor Kwang Tsu and Kang Yu Wei vigorously pushed the reform movement, it was boycotted by most of the high officials in the central and provincial administrations. These groups were not in favour of any modernization of China but sided with the forces of reaction. They dared to challenge Emperor's orders in the knowledge that the real power of state was not at that time in his hands but in those of the Empress Dowager, who was ill-disposed towards the reforms. Orders were quickly issued to arrest Kwang and the reformers. Five leaders of the movement were sentenced to death, Kang Yu Wei and Liang Chi-Chao fled to Japan, and the conservative Emperor reversed most of the reforms.

Among the principal causes of the failure of the reform were the inexperience of the reformers and their ill-considered strategy, the reluctance of the Empress to give up power, and the powerful conservative opposition. The most enduring contribution of the Hundred Days Reform was the educational changes it brought. The new educational system which flowered during this movement continued to disseminate modern ideas and produced a new generation of Chinese people who were to play an important role in future. It paved the way for the growth of a modern and scientific attitude in China. The movement encouraged anti-foreignism and fostered the Boxer Movement, which incurred the eight-power occupation of Peking in 1900. The anti-Chinese policy to punish the reformers thereby widened the cleavage between the Manchus and the Chinese. It also became clear that peaceful change was not possible, and that only a revolution from below could perhaps effect it. Sun Yat Sen was left with this prospect if he wanted to change the face of China.

The Boxer Rebellion

The Boxer Rebellion which swept over China 35 years after the Taiping Rebellion, is regarded by scholars as the first nationalist uprising in Chinese history. It was a mass uprising of the Chinese people which threatened the foreigners who were trying to dominate Chinese civilization. Half a century of foreign humiliation had wounded the national pride of the Chinese. The presence of foreign consulates, aggressive Christian missionaries, and self-seeking traders constantly reminded them of China's misfortune. All these generated a burning desire for revenge which then erupted in the form of a massive anti-foreign movement. Capitalizing on the mass discontent, which had resulted from the hardships inflicted by foreign domination, a number of secret societies sprouted up in different parts of China. The Chinese secret society called the Yi Ho Tuan or the 'Righteous and Harmonious Fists' came to be known by foreigners as 'Boxers' as the members of this group practiced various kinds of physical exercises including boxing. The Boxer movement raised the slogan, 'Save China, drive out the foreigners'. Anti-foreignism was the primary characteristic of the movement. Shantung became the powerhouse of the Boxer movement. Apart from anti-foreignism, there were of course larger social, economic, political, and religious factors which contributed to this uprising.

The chief causes of the Boxer Uprising may be briefly summed up as follows:

1. The grave foreign encroachments on China's territorial and cultural integrity became a matter of concern to the Chinese people. Imperialist aggression and the attempt of the foreigners to inferiorize Chinese culture wounded the self-respect of the Chinese. The people took it as an insult to their nation and the sense of injustice generated a burning desire for revenge.

2. The Christian missionaries were given permission to enter China. The Treaty of Tientsin (1858) and the Treaty of Peking (1860) helped the missionaries to tighten up their grip over China. The missionaries were permitted to purchase property and settle down in China. Their missionary zeal to convert the Chinese to Christianity led to the birth of an indigenous group of Chinese Christians which posed a threat to the internal harmony of the Chinese society. The entire process bred a sharp antipathy among the Chinese people towards the Christian missionaries and the converted Chinese people. The encroachment on religion became a major issue which in turn led to the growth of anti-foreignism. Protected by the flag and the treaties, the missionaries moved about freely in China, although they had great difficulty winning converts.

3. As the foreign powers sought to make space for themselves by establishing 'spheres of influence' in China, those areas were lost to the Chinese, and the Chinese people in those areas were left at the mercy of foreigners. The imperialists had forced China to open 82 of her coastal and inland ports to their trade and marked off areas in 16 cities as 'concessions'.

4. The influx of foreign imports after the Opium War created a depressant effect on the native economy. Foreign cotton cloth sold for only one-third of the price of the Chinese cloth, driving native weavers and textile manufacturers into bankruptcy. Chinese handicraft industries went down in the face of foreign competition, throwing many workers into unemployment.

5. The foreign device of the railway wrecked havoc on the traditional communication system, which could not compete with railways, and so thousands of people became unemployed. Thus, European penetration into China inflicted a new kind of hardship on the Chinese people which they had never experienced before.

6. The economic hardships of the Chinese people were multiplied due to a series of natural calamities, particularly flooding. The Yellow River which shifted its course from Hunan to Shantung

in 1852, and flooded frequently after 1882, broke loose again in 1898. It washed out hundreds of villages and made millions of people homeless.

The Boxer movement was initially anti-Manchu, anti-foreign, and anti-Christian in spirit, but gradually, it dropped its anti-Manchu attitude under the influence of the Chinese Empress Tzu Hsi who came to an understanding with the rebels. She wanted to try to drive out the foreigners with the help of the Boxer insurgents and so the rebels sided with the Manchus.

The Boxer movement first broke out in Shantung. The rebels resorted to indiscriminate killing of foreigners, Christian priests, and Chinese Christians. Foreign establishments like churches, residential houses owned by the foreigners, and consulates became the targets of their attacks. The rebels captured Tientsin and also Peking, the Chinese capital where the Chinese army made common cause with the rebels. The foreign consulates received no help from the Chinese government in their crisis. Eventually, the combined forces of eight foreign powers reached Peking in August 1900 and crushed the insurgents. The Empress and her associates had to flee from Peking. The crisis came to an end with the Boxer Protocol signed between the Chinese government and eleven foreign powers on 7 September 1900. The Chinese government was forced to pay compensation to the foreign powers, and the European powers used the situation to their own advantage by extorting additional commercial privileges in China. For example, the Chinese government had to agree to allow the foreigners to maintain their own military establishments on the Chinese soil.

The Boxer Uprising failed because there was no proper coordination or constructive planning among the rebels. There was no political ideology to sustain the movement and basically, the movement was the product of a deep xenophobia which assumed fanatic proportions. The rebels expected the active support of Tzu Hzi, but her involvement was only minimal for the Empress could not directly assist the rebels due to the strong opposition of a section of the Chinese bureaucracy. The movement did not spread all over China, but remained confined to the north-eastern region. Finally, the failure of the uprising could be also attributed to the superior weapons used by the Europeans against the traditional technology of warfare followed by the Chinese.

Historians disagree as to the revolutionary motivation of the Boxers. Some scholars think that the primary motive was to drive the foreigners out from China. Jean Chesneaux however, sees the movement as a nationalist reaction. The movement was actually very complex in nature and it was a combination of various motives which brought about the uprising. These various ingredients included peasant discontent, patriotic feeling, fanaticism against the foreigners, and feudal narrowness. All said, it has to be acknowledged that this uprising marked the beginning of a new chapter in Chinese history. Despite its limitations, the Boxer uprising was to exert a profound influence on the future course of Chinese history. The movement was an unmistakable symptom of China's growing unrest, of her resentment of foreign intrusion and exploitation, and of her will to resist. Indeed, it paved the way for the emergence of Sun Yat Sen and the foundation of the Chinese Republic.

SUN YAT SEN AND THE REVOLUTION OF 1911

Sun Yat Sen, the 'father' of the Chinese Revolution, was born in 1866 in Hsiang Shan near Canton of peasant parentage. Socially, as well as geographically, Sun Yat Sen's origin was opportune to become a revolutionary. Born just two years after the fall of the Taiping Kingdom, Sun Yat Sen often heard the stories of the revolution and secretly aspired to be the second Hung Hsing Chuan. He went to Honolulu and studied an English curriculum in a Church of England boarding school. He also studied in Queen's College, Hong Kong where he was baptised and became a Christian. In 1884–5, the French seized Indochina from the Chinese and Sun Yat Sen felt the humiliation of defeat. It was at this time that he began to develop his own nationalist ideology and come into contact with the Triad Society, a secret society of China.

After graduating in 1892 as a doctor, he began to practice in Macao, but he was forced to leave Macao for lack of a diploma from Portugal. Having being concerned over the fate of China since her defeat against France in 1885, Sun Yat Sen submitted a reformist petition to the chief Westernizer of the day Li Hung Chang, but got no reply. This petition reflected the reformist political agenda which he was then nurturing. Thwarted as a doctor, disregarded by those in power, he turned to a new calling—neither merchant, peasant, scholar, nor medical practitioner, but a revolutionary, ready to work with and for all classes.

Sun Yat Sen started his revolutionary career in earnest by organizing the Hsing Chung Hui (Revive China Society) in Honolulu in 1894. In 1895, using Hong Kong as his base, he attempted to seize the government of Canton. Unfortunately, the plot was discovered and Sun Yat Sen had to flee for his life, with a price on his head. Instead, he embarked upon his dynamic career which would take him around the world preaching revolution. In 1896, he went to London where he was recognized in the Chinese legation, 'kidnapped', and held for twelve days. His old teacher James Cantile was also mobilize British opinion and got him released. This London episode showed the powerful image of a revolutionary fighting for reform, freedom, and democracy. He did not leave England immediately but spent the next two years studying economics, politics, and making contacts with Chinese revolutionary organizations in Europe. His social and political philosophy was therefore shaped mostly by Western education and experience. In 1897, he developed the idea of a social revolution to complement his earlier ideas of a nationalist and democratic revolution. Herein lies the basis of his famous Three Principles of the People—nationalism, democracy and socialism. The Three Principles subsequently became the revolutionary philosophy of Sun Yat Sen and his followers. The first Principle—nationalism—called for not only the overthrow of the alien Manchu rule but also the removal of the imperialist yoke. The Principle of democracy aimed at achieving four rights for the people—initiative, referendum, election, and recall—and five powers for the government—executive, legislative, judicial, control, and examination. Finally, socialism was to meet the new problems of industrial growth and thus check the enrichment of speculators and monopolists.

Thus, by 1900 Sun Yat Sen was well known in China and abroad. He began to evolve a revolutionary philosophy but still lacked concrete success. He stressed the need for creating a broad front of all the revolutionary groups. This was finally achieved in 1905 with Japanese encouragement. At a meeting in Tokyo in August 1905, the Tung Menh Hui (United League) was founded with Sun Yat Sen as its chief executive.

Sun Yat Sen put forward his three stage programme:

1. there would be military rule for three years in the areas liberated by the revolutionary forces followed by local self-government beginning district by district,
2. there would be six years under a provisional constitution which later came to be known as the period of tutelage,
3. eventually there would be constitutional government with an elected president and parliament.

The stage was set in China for the type of democratic revolution Sun Yat Sen was looking for. The causes of the revolution of 1911 may be briefly summed up as follows:

1. The grave encroachments on China's territorial and cultural integrity became a matter of concern to the Chinese people. The wholesale imperialist aggression and the attempt of the foreigners to inferiorize the Chinese culture wounded the self-respect of the Chinese. The people took it as an insult to their nation and the sense of injustice generated a burning desire for revenge.
2. There were grave encroachments on China's territorial integrity. As the foreign powers sought to make space for themselves by establishing 'spheres of influence' in China, those areas were lost to the Chinese and the Chinese people in those areas were left at the mercy of foreigners. The imperialists had forced China to open 82 of her coastal and inland ports to

their trade and marked off areas in 16 cities as 'concessions'.

3. The influx of foreign imports after the Opium War created a depressant effect on the native economy. Foreign cotton cloth sold for only one-third of the price of the Chinese cloth, driving native weavers and textile manufacturers into banckruptcy. Chinese handicraft industries went down in the face of foreign competition throwing many workers into unemployment. Again, the foreign devise of the railway worked havoc on the traditional communication system which lost out in competition with railways and thousands of people were thrown out of employment.

4. European penetration into China inflicted a new kind of misery on the Chinese people while they had never experienced before. The imperialists continued to expand their aggression against China and exploited the Chinese people. The Manchus made common cause with the foreigners. The failure of the reform movement of 1898 had convinced the Chinese that the complete overthrow of the Manchu dynasty would be possible only by a bloody revolution. Dr Sun Yat Sen took the lead in promoting this approach,

5. The economic hardship of the Chinese people was multiplied by a series food shortage and made the people determined to fight back.

6. The able leadership of Sun Yat Sen, helped to bring about the anti-feudal revolution of 1911.

By 1911, Sun Yat Sen had organized ten revolutionary outbreaks but all were unsuccessful. Finally, the Wuchung Revolution in October 1911 proved to be fruitful. Sun Yat Sen was elected as the president but he offered to resign in favour of Yuan Shi Kai, the military general. After the revolution, the republic was formally set up but Yuan Shi Kai used the republic to cloak the counter-revolutionary character of his bourgeois dictatorship. Finally, he made himself emperor in 1915. The revolution of 1911 started by Sun Yat Sen had both its successess and failures. This revolution triggered off a spirit of nationalism which was to bring far-reaching changes in future. Sun Yat Sen was not a Marxist, his was a democratic revolution. However, his reading of Marxist literature and later contacts with Russian communists made him more conscious of the potential danger of Western economic imperialism. His bitterness was all the more as the West had turned a deaf ear to his repeated requests for Western assistance for his Canton government. The West had already launched its long career of backing those horses in Asia who would not oppose their economic exploitation of the region. It was not surprising therefore, that the West should support the unscrupulous warlords of the North over a genuine patriot like Sun. The West thus drove Sun Yat Sen into the waiting hands of Russia but although he accepted the Marxist theory of Western economic imperialism, he rejected Marxism.

Sun Yat Sen was by no means a brilliant theoretician or a competent organizer. Nevertheless, he was a great visionary, a man with many connections and a magnetic personality. He has been called 'the father of Chinese revolution' and he paved the way for Mao Tse Tung, who was to lead the peoples' revolution of 1949 and establish the People's Republic of China.

THE MAY FOURTH MOVEMENT AND
THE RISE OF THE COMMUNISTS

The Revolution of 1911 failed to bring peace and unity to China. Instead, the early republican years were chaotic and characterized by moral degradation, monarchist movements, warlordism, and intensified foreign imperialism. The western-educated middle class Chinese intellectuals now stood for a radical change. They called for a critical evaluation of China's cultural heritage in the light of modern western standards. This intellectual revolution taking place somewhere between 1917 and 1923 hailed a new cultural movement which had sometimes been described as a 'Chinese Renaissance'.

A most significant event of this formative period was the student demonstration in Peking on 4 May 1919, which quickly evoked a nation wide response. It is called the May Fourth Incident and the whole period is known as the May Fourth Movement. In the narrowest sense, it refers to the students demonstration on 4 May and in its broadest sense, it was a cultural movement which had started long before and lasted several years after it.

This age of intellectual revolution could not have come to the surface without certain significant developments both at home and abroad. New hopes had arisen for the liberation of the nation as China's revolutionary intellectuals saw the collapse of the imperialist powers like Russia, Germany, Austria, etc. The Shantung resolution at the Paris Peace Conference stirred up Chinese nationalism. These external developments made the Chinese intellectuals determined to revive their strife-ridden motherland.

Contributing to the rise of new nationalism, was the rapid emergence of a politically conscious merchant class and a labour force which numbered between two and three million by 1919. Other internal developments like the growth of treaty ports, the Western association, modern education, the fall of the Manchus, and the rise of the republic too, contributed to the new intellectual ferment. Social change was evident not only in the rise of the new capitalist and labour classes, but also in the new status for youth and women. The Chinese students who had studied abroad were particularly aware of China's plight and were eager to introduce reforms.

Socialism had appealed to the educated Chinese students. European theories of anarchism, especially the Anarcho-Communism of Kropotkin, also found a wide response among Chinese intellectuals bent upon destroying the traditional order. In fact, Chinese anarchism could be defined as a combination of the most radical theories of contemporary West and repudiation of Confucianism. In this way, the May Fourth Movement was just as revolutionary as the Taiping revolution and just as opposed to Confucian orthodoxy. Peking National University became the centre of this intellectual revolution with the arrival of the revolutionary intellectual, Tsai Yuan Pei. Until then, the university was looked upon by the students as a mere stepping stone to an administrative career. After the coming of Tsai Yuan Pei an attempt was made to defend academic freedom. Tsai Yuan Pei appointed another revolutionary intellectual, Chen Tu Hsiu, as the Dean of Letters. Chen attributed China's decay to Confucianism and in the radical monthly journal (*New Youth*) he called upon Chinese youth, 'to be independent not servile, progressive not conservative, dynamic not passive, cosmopolitan not isolationist, scientific not imaginative'.

Chen's principle ally at Pieta was a younger man named—Hu Shi, who was another revolutionary intellectual. Hu Shi proposed that all Chinese writers henceforth should use the spoken language (pai hua) instead of the literary language (wen-yen). This was the essence of the Liberty Revolution. The switch over from wen-yen to pan hua was much like the switch over from Latin to the national vernaculars in Europe. Hu Shi also urged that literature be releated more directly to the life of the people. Li Ta Chao, who was soon to be become China's first Marxist, was the librarian at Peita and Mao Tse Tung, who was to lead the people's revolution in 1949, worked as the assistant librarian. By 1919, the University of Peking had become the meeting ground of these revolutionary youths.

In 1919, the victors of the First World War met in Paris and it was decided that Japan should take over all the privileges previously enjoyed by Germany in Shantung. The students of Beijing organized demonstrations against it on 4 May 1919, and 30 students were arrested. In protest the students went on strike. Soon, the movement spread to Shanghai and Canton. Thousands of students were beaten up or arrested by the police. The workers and merchants of Beijing, Canton, and Shanghai also joined the movement which was initially launched by the intellectuals. The movement soon assumed a national and patriotic character.

This patriotic movement, in a broad sense, was a part of the New Cultural Movement, which had already begun against feudalism and the perceived failures of traditional Chinese culture for the promotion of science and democracy. It profoundly transformed the lives and ideas of people and rejected Confucianism as responsible for the prevailing despotism in both family and the state. The positive features of the movement were the ideas of democracy, science, and reason. Born of a nation's will to live, this revolutionary cultural movement could count among its legitimate heirs both the Kuomintang, the party of the nationalists, and the Chinese communists.

Appraisals of the significance and character of the movement varied according to different view points. Liberals proclaimed it as a movement of emancipation from traditional thought. The conservatives appreciated its nationalist content but criticized its lack of respect for traditionalism. The Marxists hailed it as an anti-imperialist and anti-feudal bourgeois democratic revolution. Mao Tse Tung said that the May Fourth Movement came into being at the call of the 'World Revolution' and Lenin. It was not simply a triumph of marxism over nationalism, but the absorption of the latter by the former. Writers like Chien Mu and Immanuel Hsu suggest that the May Fourth Movement succeeded primarily in destroying Chinese traditionalism, rather than creating new systems of thought. Out of this movement emerged China's Mew Nationalism of the 1920s (as Schwartz holds), which was to be marked by the rise of party dictatorship, the growth of Marxism-Leninism, and the struggle against imperialism.

RISE AND GROWTH OF THE COMMUNIST MOVEMENT IN CHINA

After the Revolution of 1911, two rival regimes were established in China. General Yuan Shi Kai was appointed Prime Minister by a national assembly in Peking, while Sun Yat Sen was elected President by a Revolutionary Assembly in Nanking. In February 1912 the child Emperor Puyi was induced to abdicate and in order to unite the country, Sun Yat Sen agreed to hand over authority to Yuan Shi Kai, who became provisional President of the Chinese Republic. Yuan Shi Kai however, sought to strengthen his personal authority, and so he had himself proclaimed Emperor in December 1915. His death in the following June allowed the restoration of the Nanking Constitution, but the rivalry of ambitious warlords prevented the national government. Sun Yat Sen formed the Kuomintang or the Nationalist Party to create a broad front against the warlords.

After the Bolshevik Revolution in Russia, Marxism-Leninism made considerable headway among the Chinese youth. Quite a number of communist groups sprouted up in China and intellectual activity in China at that time was mostly dominated by Marxism-Leninism, though the nationalist and liberal groups remained outside its fold. The Chinese Commmunist Party was founded by two Peking University Professors Chen Tu Hsiu and Li Ta Chao in July 1921. The divided state of China in the 1920s, made it a profitable area for Communist expansion. Chen Tu Hsiu received considerable support from the Russians. For a time however, the Russians were also assisting the Kuomintang, to whom they sent military advisers.

As long as Sun Yat Sen was alive, the communists were allowed to become members of the Kuomintang. In 1925, Chiang Kaishek became the leader of Kuomintang after the death of Sun Yat Sen. He recaptured Peking with the help of Chinese communists. Thereafter, the relationship between the Chinese communists and Kuomintang became bitter due to various reasons.

The original Chinese Communist Party was virtually destroyed but a new communist group emerged in China in 1930 under Mao Tse Tung, a guerilla leader from the Kiangsi region. Mao became extremely popular among the Chinese peasantry and Kiangsi became the powerhouse of the communist movement led by Mao Tse Tung. In 1931, the communists under Mao established a Chinese Soviet Republic in Kiangsi province but after three years of military operations against Mao by the forces of General Chiang Kaishek, the communist position became untenable. The communists moved from Kiangsi and undertook a march of some 8,000 miles heading north-west for a year through difficult mountainous country to Yenan on the Yellow River. This is known as the 'Long March'.

In the Shensi Province, Mao established an independent communist regime with its capital at Sian. Chiang Kaishek deployed his troops to combat and crush the communists, but Mao and his men at this time were willing to strike an alliance with the Kuomintang to defend China against Japanese aggression. Chiang Kaishek arrived in Sian and he was kidnapped by one of his army commanders. He was detained for fifteen days and thereafter, agreed to work with the communists against the Japanese threat. Russia played an important role in this episode known in history as the Sian Incident. Mao had already inflicted several reverses on the Japanese in the course of 1938. China campaign became engulfed in the Second World War after the Japanese attack on Pearl Harbour in December 1941. The Chinese inflicted a serious defeat on the Japanese in Kiangsi. The Japanese eventually signed an act of capitulation to Chiang Kaishek in Nanking on 9 September 1945.

Japan surrendered in 1945 and the Second World War came to an end. The end of the war also put an end to the communist-Kuomintang alliance and the communist forces began to capture different parts of China. Civil War broke out in China and Chiang Kaishek and his followers fled to Taiwan. On 1 October 1949 Mao Tse Tung founded the Peoples Republic of China in Peking becoming the first Chairman of the Chinese Republic. The emergence of communist China is a significant landmark of the twentieth century and marked the beginning of a new era in the history of China. Under Mao the transition to socialism in China began.

THE OPENING OF JAPAN—PERRY'S ARRIVAL

The years from 1853, when Commodore Perry of the USA sailed into the Bay of Yedo, to the end of the Sino-Japanese War, witnessed what is usually called the transformation of Japan. Her achievements were made possible because the events and changes of the years following her opening effected a gradual transition from the old order to the new. In this process of transition the Meiji Restoration of 1868 was a great landmark. Having established their hegemony over China, the European powers turned their attention to Japan. On 8 July 1853, Commodore Perry arrived at Yedo and submitted a charter of demands and a letter from the President of the United States to the Japanese Emperor. Four factors had combined to stimulate American interest in Japan which were: (1) the development of trade with China through Canton, (2) the growth of the American whaling industry in the Pacific, (3) the opening of California, symbolized by the Gold Rush (1849), and (4) the progress of steam navigation. Thus, ostensibly the purpose of Perry's expedition was to obtain future Japanese assistance to American seamen, but this was minor motivation behind Perry's visit to Japan. There was an expectation that a useful trade could be carried out between Japan, a closed country and America. The coming of Perry proved to be crucial for the future course of Japanese history for it led to the opening up of Japan.

Japan, at the time of Perry's visit, was in a turbulent state. Theoretically, the emperor was both the temporal and spiritual head, but in reality, since the twelfth century he had 'reigned without governing'. The actual power was in the hands of the Tokugawa Shogunate—a feudal chief. As a result of seclusion for more than 200 years, there had been internal peace and the Shogun had relaxed his grip on the country to the point that the dissatisfied clans had consolidated their power. Thus, when Perry arrived power of the Shogunate had been gradually declining. When Perry returned to Japan with ships in the following year, he opened negotiations with the shogun to gain concessions for America. Finally, on 31 March 1854, the Treaty of Kanagawa was signed between the America and Japan, which opened the ports of Hakodate and Shimoda to American ships. The Treaty of Kanagawa was the first step, and advantage was taken of the success of his mission by other powers like England, Russia, and Holland, who made similar treaties with Japan. In July 1858, another American commander named Harris, signed another treaty called the Treaty of Amity and Commerce or the Harris Treaty with the Japanese which granted the right of extra-territoriality to the Americans.

The Meiji Restoration

When the question of foreign interaction could not be evaded, the Shogun submitted it to the advice of a council of the feudal chiefs. All but a small minority declared themselves in favour of maintaining the traditional policy. However, with a larger knowledge of the actual conditions, both internal and external, the Shogun and his council at Yedo were forced to side with the minority, and the decision was made to comply with the demands of the foreigners. The opening of the country exposed the weakness of the dual system of government. When troublesome questions arose, the foreigners hesitated to recognize the plea of the Shogun and wanted to refer the matter to the Emperor in Kyoto.

The very fact that for the first time in generations matters of importance were referred to the Emperor, indicated a recognition of weakness within the Shogunate. Gradually the centre of political power shifted from Yedo back to the ancient capital of Kyoto. If the Shogun had made a decision without consulting the Emperor, or if he had left the matter for the Emperor to decide then the Shogunate might have been saved. However, the Shogun, doubting his ability to control the country, turned to the Emperor on the question of foreign relations. Unfortunately for the Shogun, the western clan leaders like Satsuma and Choshu, who had long been jealous of the Tokugawa Shogunate, had great deal of influence in the imperial capital. Under their influence, during the early period of the foreign interaction, the Emperor insisted upon maintaining political seclusion. There was division even within the Tokugawa clan over the question of the advisability of departing from the political seclusion and some continued to promise the Emperor that the foreigners would be driven out as soon as possible.

There was widespread opposition to the concessions granted by the Shogun to the foreigners. As a result of the influx of cheaper foreign goods into Japan, thousands of Japanese workers were thrown out of employment. The economic discontent of the people intensified the popular apathy to the foreigners. The opposition was symbolized by the slogan 'Revere the Emperor, expel the barbarians'. Several incidents of violence including murder of foreigners and attack on foreign establishments took place. In 1866, a broad anti-shogun alliance, comprising various clans and the Osaka merchant community, was formed. It is also probable that the Emperor himself was associated with this alliance. Shortly after this union, in 1866, the young Shogun died and was succeeded with some reluctance by his guardian Keiki. In the following year, Emperor Komai died and was succeeded by his young son Meiji.

The accession of a new Emperor provided a good opportunity to the different clans to attempt to make their aims materialize. In 1867, a memo was sent by the Western clans to the new Shogun requesting that actual power be restored to the Emperor. It was an expression of patriotism and nationalism on the part of western clan leaders. The new shogun responded to the memo by abdicating his position. The centre of power now shifted from Yedo to Kyoto, the ancient capital in what became known as the Meiji Restoration. The period between 1886 and 1912 is known as the 'Meiji Era' and during this time, Japan saw a process of modernization under the guidance of Emperor Meiji. The democratic reforms including the new constitution of 1889 transformed Japan into a modern nation. The Meiji Restoration had not aimed at the establishment of a personal rule by the Emperor by driving out the Shogun, but rather, it was to replace the Tokugawa as 'advisers' to the Emperor. There followed a civil war between the Western clans and the Tokugawa but the new regime overcame all opposition by 1869.

There are two main schools of opinion on the causes of the fall of the Shogunate and the Restoration of 1868. The first school holds that the Tokugawa system of government might have continued unchanged had it not been for the economic opening of Japan by the USA and other countries. The second view focuses on the fact that the whole regime had been under direct attack from many angles inside Japan long before Perry's arrival. The growth of a merchant class in Japan had already eroded the foundation of Japanese feudal society and so Western penetration merely provided the final impetus towards a collapse that was seemingly inevitable. Richard Storry however, thinks that the most important factor behind the Restoration of 1868 was the opening of Japan. Among the feudal classes the sense of shock induced by the advent of foreigners was catastrophic. It is possible that the Shogunate could have survived if it had resisted the demands made by the foreigners.

Modernization of Japan

The Meiji Restoration, the opening of Japanese trade and the fall of the Shogunate triggered off a chain of reactions within Japan. The years from 1853 when Commodore Perry of USA arrived in Japan, to the end of the Sino-Japanese War in 1894, witnessed a thorough transformation and modernization of the socio-economic and political fabric of Japan. Once Japan was set on a course of modernization, certain underlying conditions made possible her rapid progress. The startling difference between Japan's response and that of China lies precisely in the domestic conditions of the two countries before their opening. The tradition of Dutch learning, for example, gave Japan a head start with Western science and modernization that most Western countries lacked.

One important factor guiding the modernization of Japan was the peculiar status of the imperial institution. The process of modernization centred round the personality of the Emperor. Whereas the Chinese had to rationalize modernization by accepting strange foreign ideologies, the Japanese could justify it as a strengthening of a native institution understood by all. This was an important feature of the Japanese response to the mid-nineteenth century crisis.

Pro-imperial sentiment and a spirit of confident nationalism came to the surface when the clan leaders voluntarily abolished feudalism, which would otherwise have been a challenging task. While surrendering their fiefs, the lords made a public demonstration and declared: 'There is no soil in the Empire that does not belong to the Emperor . . . we therefore reverently offer up all our feudal possessions . . .'. In this manner the age-old system of feudalism came to an end in Japan. The Samurai class also voluntarily gave up their special privileges. Feudalism in Japan was formally abolished by an official order in 1871.

The Japanese took lessons from what was happening simultaneously in China. They realized that a weak Japan would serve as a constant temptation to those powers who had already begun to carve out commercial empires for themselves. The rulers also realized that modernization could never be accomplished without foreign help. The official attitude to the West was stated by the young emperor himself, in what was known as the 'Charter Oath' of 1868: 'Knowledge shall be sought from all over the world and thus shall be strengthened the foundation of the imperial policy'. This attitude paved the way for the dissemination of knowledge across the country. Compulsory education was instituted in 1872 on an ambitious scale for the educational plan called for the establishment of nearly 54,000 elementary schools—roughly one to every 600 individuals. The Japanese quickly became the most literate people in Asia and the University of Tokyo was founded in 1877. However, no provision was made for university education for women until 1902. One of the important features of modernization of Japan was that students were encouraged to travel to Europe and America. Until foreign-trained Japanese teachers were available, foreigners were engaged by the Japanese government as advisers. Christian missionaries were also allowed to open schools and educational institutions in Japan.

Military reorganization was taken up by the Japanese authorities in earnest. Prior to the abolition of feudalism, the Japanese military system was based on the samurai class so in 1873 the army was nationalized and universal military service was introduced. The army was equipped with modern weapons and trained under French and German directions. Steps were also taken, so far as the national finance permitted, to build up a navy.

The end of feudalism resulted in a fusion of all classes of commoners, and the policy of the government was to direct the energies of the previously feudal classes into commercial and industrial undertakings by insisting on their respectability. It fostered the textile industry in several ways: (1) the product of the Japanese loom was presented to the world at several international expositions, and (2) model factories, with modern machinery, were established under government auspices. Within a short span of time, Japanese technology came to be admired by the rest of the world. Richard Storry has aptly commented, '. . . the first two decades of the Emperor Meiji's reigns saw a Japan to all appearances intoxicated with the strong wine of western thought, techniques and customs'.

JAPANESE IMPERIALISM

The Meiji restoration in 1868 was in fact an economic revolution which was triggered off by the entry of Western capitalism into Japan. With the Meiji Restoration, the feudal economy was abolished and a modern capitalist economy emerged in Japan. The government took active interest in industrialization and provided facilities for industrial development. The rapid growth of industry and production inspired Japan to find new sources of raw materials, new markets for her goods, and new fields for capital investment. Like the Western imperialist powers, Japan too, looked for colonies and jumped into the fray of an international competition.

Japan emerged as an imperial power after 1868, more as a product of modernization than of native tradition. By the time Japan had embarked on her imperial career, imperialism was already an accepted theory among the Western powers whom Japan joined in the latter half of the nineteenth century.

Japan had economic and strategic interests in Korea. Korea was a major producer of rice and also provided a good commercial market for Japanese products. However, in Korea, Japanese interests collided with those of China and Russia. China tried to maintain her political hold over Korea while Russia had political and military objectives there. In 1891, when Russia undertook the construction of the Trans-Siberian Railway in Korea, Japan became seriously alarmed. At this point China supported Russia for she wanted to play off Russia against Japan as a counterpoise to the Japanese threat to her territories. Under the circumstances, Japan could no longer remain indifferent to the Korean problem.

The Tonghak rebellion in Korea (1894) served as the immediate pretext of the Sino-Japanese War. The Korean government was unable to cope with the Tonghak rebellion and appealed to China for help. No sooner had the Chinese forces crushed the rebellion than 8,000 Japanese troops landed in Korea. China's refusal to withdraw her troops on the pretext that Japan was unwilling to do the same precipitated the crisis which brought the two sides into an open conflict in August 1894. The Sino-Japanese War, which then broke out ended with the defeat of China in April 1895. By the Treaty of Shimonoseki that followed, China recognized the independence of Korea and handed over to Japan Formosa, the Liatung Penisula, and Port Arthur. She was also forced to pay a huge war indemnity to Japan. Japan's overwhelming victory upset the power balance within China as well as on the international scene. The defeat of China exposed her weaknesses and there began a scramble for concessions among the big powers. Japan also took part in it and asked China for an agreement not to alienate Fukien Province to any other power.

The Three Power Intervention (Russia, Germany, and France) in 1895, which prevented Japan from enjoying the gains of the victory of the Sino-Japanese War made her hostile towards them. Moreover, Japan was concerned by Russian penetration into Manchuria and Korea for it stood as a stumbling block on her road to supremacy. England too, disapproved the Russian designs in Asia as it might run counter to her own interest in the British Indian Empire. The common interests of Japan and England brought about the Anglo-Japanese Alliance (1902). This alliance provided that Britain would help Japan in the eventuality that France helped Russia, and thus this alliance would 'hold the ring' keeping France and Germany away from a Russian war against Japan. Apart from Korea, Japan's interest in Manchuria also collided with that of Russia. Russia was trying to control Manchuria by pretending to be a protector of Chinese interests in that country. Japan took note of the rapid increase of Russian influence in Manchuria and Korea, but at first, sought to settle the issue on the principle of reciprocity. She offered negotiations to recognize Russian interests in Manchuria in return for Russia's reciprocal recognition of Japanese interests in Korea. However, Russia was not prepared to reconsider her original position. Finding no other way out, Japan declared war against Russia in February 1904.

The Russo-Japanese War ended with the victory of Japan over Russia. The Treaty of Portsmouth (1905), which was signed between the two powers, was mediated by Theodore Roosevelt, the US President. Russia was forced to recognize Japan's paramount political, military, and economic interests in Korea. The victory of Japan over Russia shattered the myth of Western invincibility and paved the way for the emergence of Japan as one of the leading powers of the world. Japan's rise as a world power then brought her into a bitter rivalry with the USA whose capitalistic interests in the Far East were threatened. After 1905 Russia withdrew from Korea. Initially, Japan sought to control Korea through a Korean ruling house. In 1910, Japan finally annexed Korea and brought her into the fold of the Japanese Empire. Moreover, after the Russo-Japanese War, Japan also strengthened her control over Manchuria.

The outbreak of the First World War, gave Japan the opportunity to realize her imperialistic designs in the Far East. Japan took the fullest advantage of the engagement of the European powers in the war and she declared war against Germany in Tsingtao, Chinese neutrality was violated and Tsingtao was occupied. Shantung fell at the feet of Japan and was turned into her 'sphere of influence'. Japan proceeded to bring China completely under her control with the notorious 'Twenty One Demands'. China was forced to accept a modified version of those demands and she virtually became a protectorate of Japan. The 'Twenty One Demands' have been described as the Monroe Doctrine of Asia ('Asia for the Asians'). Thus, Japan emerged as a powerful imperialist nation and became treated as an equal of the Western powers.

The Western powers could not accept Japan's supremacy and her increasing influence over Asia and the Pacific region. The rise of Japanese power ran counter to the commercial interest of the United States. The United States therefore continued to oppose the 'Twenty One Demands' and eventually compelled Japan to sign the Treaty of Washington in 1921. The Treaty of Washington tailored Japanese influence in Manchuria and other areas. In 1931, Japan invaded China and captured Manchuria. China appealed to the League of Nations for justice. The League of Nations marked the Japanese as aggressors and so Japan resigned their membership of the League of Nations in 1933. In 1937, Japan invaded China again. The League of Nations advised the member nations to impose military sanctions on Japan. This was however, never implemented. In 1941, the Japanese joined the Second World War. The Japanese air-strikes on Pearl Harbour, the American naval base, and on several British establishments in Asia were important events of the Second World War. In retaliation the United States dropped atomic bombs on Horoshima and Nagasaki in 1945. Shortly thereafter, Japan surrendered. Japanese imperialism was thus eventually contained by the USA.

HIGHLIGHTS

- China was cut off from the rest of the world. The foreigners were hated by the Chinese.
- China clashed with the British on the issue of Opium Trade. There broke out the Opium Wars. The Chinese were defeated in two consecutive wars. Capitalizing on their victory in the Opium Wars, the English gained certain commercial privileges in China. Gradually, other European powers too gained concessions. China turned into a site of European power politics. There began a scramble for concessions among the Western powers which is known as the 'cutting of the Chinese melon'.
- Western penetration into China evoked a chain of reactions which found manifestations in the Taiping Revolution and the Boxer Uprising. These uprisings resulted from the growing discontent of the Chinese people.
- As a result of Boxer Uprising, there began a political reform movement in China under the leadership of Sun Yat Sen. Sun Yat Sen was a nationalist who steered China towards the Revolution of 1911 in which China became a republic led by Sun Yat Sen.
- The ideas of Marxism-Leninism made considerable headway in China after the Bolshevik Revolution. The May Fourth Movement of 1919 was an expression of the growing Marxist ideas in China.
- Like China, Japan, was also cut off from the rest of the world. The isolation of the Japanese came to an end after the arrival of an American fleet under Perry.
- The coming of the imperialist foreigners was disapproved of by the Japanese. It evoked a spirit of nationalism among the people. The growing spirit of Japanese nationalism found manifestation in the Meiji Restoration.
- In the decades following the Meiji Restoration, Japan gradually turned into an imperialist power, established her hegemony in Korea, and

fought with China and Russia. The next phase of Japanese imperialism began in 1931 with her invasion of Manchuria.

- Japan joined the Second World War on the side of the Axis powers but she was defeated in the war and finally surrendered in 1945.

MEMORABLE DATES AND EVENTS

1839	First Opium War
1842	Treaty of Nanking
1850	Beginning of the Taiping Revolution
1853	Arrival of Perry in Japan
1856	Second Opium War
1858	Treaty of Tientsin
	Treaty of Harris
1868	Meiji Restoration
1894	Foundation of Hsing Chung Hui
1895	Treaty of Shimonoseki
1898	Hundred Days Reform
1899	Boxer Uprising
	Open Door Policy
1901	Boxer Protocol
1911	End of Manchu rule
1912	Foundation of the Republic
	Foundation of Kuomintang
1921	Foundation of the Chinese Communist Party
	Washington Pact
1925	Death of Sun Yat Sen
1934	Long March
1941	Japan joins the Second World War
1949	Mao Tse Tung founded the People's Republic of China

MEMORABLE PERSONALITIES

Hung Hsiu Chuan: Leader of the Taiping Revolution
Kang Yu Wei: Chinese intellectual reformer, leader of the reform movement of 1898, also known as the 'Modern Sage'
Kwang Tsu: The child Emperor of China
Tzu Hsi: The Chinese Empress
Sun Yat Sen: Leader of the Revolution of 1911
Yuan Shi Kai: Leader of the Revolution of 1911

Tsai Yuan Pei: Leader of the May Fourth Movement
Chen Tu Hsiu: Leader of the May Fourth Movement
Li Ta Chao: Chinese Marxist Leader
Chiang Kaishek: Leader of Kuomintang after Sun Yat Sen
Mao Tse Tung: Founder of the Peoples Republic of China and its first Chairman Commodore
Perry: American Naval commander who came to Japan in 1853
Mikado: The Japanese Emperor
Mutsuhito: The minor Emperor of Japan
Shogun: The chief feudal lord of Japan

QUOTABLE QUOTES

- 'Opium . . . was the occasion, and not the cause of the war between the British and the Chinese.' —VINACKE
- 'For the Chinese, the war [Opium War] was primarily a crusade against opium.' —IMMANUEL HSU
- 'It [the May Fourth Movement] was a movement of Chinese Enlightenment, a movement that advanced such eminently reasonable ideals as science and democracy. . . . More important, it was a ground clearing enterprise, it foreshadowed and paved the way for the New Democratic Revolution of Mao just as Voltaire had for 1789.' —L. BIANCO
- 'The Movement [May Fourth] had united all the "new intellectuals" around such vague or general concepts as democracy, science, humanitarianism, liberalism and reason, and even more around a common desire for destruction.' —L. BIANCO
- '. . . the Boxer movement was an unmistakable symptom of China's growing unrest, of her resentment against foreign intrusion and exploitation, and of her will to resist.' —CLYDE AND BEERS
- 'The occasion [arrival of Perry] indeed marked the real end of the long period of virtual isolation from the world; but it was only the beginning of a many-sided invasion by the West that was to have consequences beyond the wildest fears of dreams of any who lived in Yedo on that day.' —RICHARD STORRY
- 'Gradually, during the ten years that followed the American Minister's reception by the shogun in 1857, the centre of political gravity shifted from Yedo to the ancient capital Kyoto.' —RICHARD STORRY
- '. . . the first two decades of the Emperor Meiji's reign saw a Japan to all appearances intoxicated with the strong wine of Western thought, techniques and customs.' —RICHARD STORRY

CHAPTER 12

Fascism in Europe

INTRODUCTION

The post-First World War period saw the emergence of two mutually hostile power blocs in European as well as international politics. The post-war politics, largely moved in two crucial ways: (1) it aimed at maintaining international peace, and (2) it endeavoured to cultivate democracy. This ushered in a large-scale social, economic, and political transformation in Europe in the decades which followed the First World War. The shortage of resources, which stemmed from the economic exhaustion caused by the Great War, was responsible for this transformation to a considerable extent. People of different countries were hit hard by the post-war depression. This economic crisis posed a severe challenge to the democracies of Europe and it became extremely difficult for them to survive. Taking advantage of this crisis of democracy, dictatorial forces unfolded in countries, like Italy, Germany, Austria, Greece, Spain, Portugal, and Poland. In one sense, the rise of authoritarian rule was a response to the failure of democratic institutions. The internal chaos in these countries due to various cultural, racial, and ethnic diversities also fostered the rise of dictatorial powers in these countries. Among the dictatorships which followed the First World War in Europe, the most noteworthy were those founded by Mussolini in Italy, Hitler in Germany, and General Franco in Spain.

FASCIST ITALY UNDER MUSSOLINI (1922)

The introduction of one-party rule and the end of democracy in Italy was not a sudden process. For various reasons, Italy had been passing through a critical phase of social frustration and political vacuum. The expectations of Italy were belied at the post-First World War Versailles Conference. During the War Italy parted with Germany and sided with the Allied Powers. The Versailles Pact of 1919 went back on the terms of the London Treaty of 1915 which promised to allow Italy to retain her supremacy over some territories.

Besides, failure in foreign affairs, Italy fared badly on the economic front in the post-First World War era. Rising inflation was followed by a fall in production and the closure of factories. Labour unrest led to an overall worsening of the situation and thus gave rise to intensified working class unrests. The political situation of Italy, too, had in the meantime turned volatile. Despite the Unification of Italy in the nineteenth century and the introduction of the British form of parliamentary system, democracy did not find a solid foundation.

The situation turned fluid after the First World War. Six ministries were formed between 1919 and 1922, but none could last long for lack of an absolute majority of single party. However, Giolitti, the leader of the moderately liberal party of Italy, was at the helm of most of these ministries. Lack of political stability drove Italy into a state of near civil war. The doctrine of socialism fast started taking roots in the country and in 1920, industrial areas like Milan witnessed widespread labour strikes. This ultimately resulted in increased wages and even sporadic capture of factories by workers. In 1921 the leftist faction of the Socialist Party formed the Communist Party of Italy.

On the other hand, the intensification of the labour movement, along with the spread of socialist ideology, alarmed the rich landlords and capitalists who were interested in finding ways to maintain the status quo through a stable government. The middle class and even the lower middle class felt frustrated and anxious about political stability. One historian, Langsam, has argued that 'Many landlords and property-holders were much affected by the incidents of the reign of radicalism. They were determined that Italy should have a government strong enough to protect private property'. Besides, the army and decommissioned soldiers also felt that in the post-war period, Italy needed a strong government. There were many determined to stem the tide of socialism in Italy.

Unrest in the socio-economic and political spheres in Italy paved the way for the emergence of dictatorship. Benito Mussolini, who became the leader of the Fascist Party, was an admirer of socialism in his early life. He joined the army during the First World War but later gave up the soldier's life and took up journalism as a profession. In 1919 he brought together the decommissioned soldiers and anti-socialist, ultra-nationalist factions and formed the Fascist Party. Taking advantage of the weaknesses of the government, the fascists indulged in violent activities against the communists in different parts of Italy which the government made no move to curb. The socialists adopted a policy of appeasement with regard to the fascists and their violent tactics. In May 1921, the fascists took part in the parliamentary elections in Italy and scored major gains. The Fascist Party was formally formed at the Rome Conference in November 1921.

The most remarkable aspect of Mussolini and his fascist movement was the steady increase in the number of his supporters. Immediately after the meeting held in Milan, offices of the Fascist Party were opened in about 70 cities, and the number of supporters kept on increasing. The fascists captured 35 seats in the Italian Parliament in 1921 fuelling the ambition of Mussolini. From then on, the fascist workers dressed in black shirts while continuing to unleash terror on leftist and democratically minded people in different urban areas.

In the meantime, faced by a grave crisis, the post-war Italian government became dependent on the fascists. Mussolini was invited to join the Cabinet of the Prime Minister although he was not willing to serve merely as a petty cabinet member. Cashing in on the situation, Mussolini led his fascist brigade to 'March on Rome'. Under the circumstances, King Victor Emmanuel III invited Mussolini to form a new government and so on 30 October 1922 Mussolini took over as the Prime Minister of Italy. Weaknesses in the Italian democracy as well as the anti-communist stance of the ruling faction facilitated Mussolini's rise to power.

The Internal Reconstruction

Between 1922 and 1926 Mussolini completed all the arrangements for the setting up of a fascist dictatorship in Italy. First, he inducted politicians of moderate parties and removed the socialists. The electoral law of Italy, as amended in 1924, stated that the party gaining the highest number of votes in the election would have two-thirds of the members in the legislature. Other parties, especially the socialists, were marginalized through terror and various repressive measures. Eventually, in 1926, only the Fascist Party was recognized as a legal political party. From around 1925, Mussolini came to be known as *Duce* or the 'Duke'. The cornerstone of the Fascist Party was the Grand Council, which comprised twenty nominated members, and which was the repository of state authority. The Council would oversee the provincial and local branches of the Fascist Party, which outfit numbered about 10,000.

A crucial element of Mussolini's internal work of reconstruction was the effecting of a long-standing compromise between the Church and Italian government or state. The Lateran agreements signed between Roman Catholic Church and Mussolini in 1929 settled the dispute with a reciprocal arrangement. It was resolved that Italy would recognize the Vatican City under the Pope as a sovereign state and would get in turn the Pope's recognition of Fascist Italy as a state.

Mussolini imposed state control in every sphere of economic activity. The fascist ideology proclaimed the state to be all-powerful and called for the sacrifice of individual interests at the altar of state. So, just as a one-party dictatorship replaced democracy in politics, rigorous control was introduced at the same time in the economic sphere. A corporate state was set up in Italy with this end in view. Mussolini lavished funds on education. This resulted in the spread of education to the lowest segment of society but the prime concern of the education system was to help develop unconditional loyalty to the state. Italian art, literature, and culture were utilized in such a manner that they could offer their full support to Mussolini's government.

Thus, Mussolini, along with his Fascist Party, established a dictatorship in Italy with little participation by the people. The restructuring of the electoral system ensured the entry of a fascist majority into the National Assembly. Freedom of speech, the press, and assembly were totally curbed and opposition to the Fascist Party was treated as treason. In reality, Mussolini's dictatorship in the country depended on military power. There was no room for the ventilation of popular will and democracy was throttled during his regime. Mussolini also had no coherent economic policy and extravagant spending on construction and defence mounted heavy pressure on the economy. The Italian economy did not achieve balanced growth and southern Italy particularly suffered from social and economic backwardness. Lipson has aptly commented in this connection that 'she [Italy] was rushing heading on the road to complete anarchy'.

The Foreign Policy of Fascist Italy— Expansionism in Africa

Italy asserted its militancy by pursuing an imperialist policy. In 1927, Mussolini declared, that 'We must be in a position at a given moment to mobilize five million men and we must be in a position to arm them'. In the post-First World War era, Italy was one of the countries calling for a revision of the Versailles Treaty, as it was determined to repudiate the pact. Therefore, Italy came to be looked upon as a revisionist power. Initially, Mussolini's main objective was to pursue an imperialist policy which would set Britain, France, and Germany against one another and also instigate them against the Bolshevik Russia. Italy's nonchalant attitude towards collective security promised by the League of Nations was reflected in Mussolini's foreign policy.

The dispute between Greece and Italy over Corfu was a case in point. The treaty of 1924 with Yugoslavia gave Italy control of Fiume and Yugoslavia. In 1925 Italy concluded a treaty of friendship which came to be known as the Nettuno Convention. The friendship between the two countries did not last long. Shortly thereafter, Italy sought to bring Albania under her control, thereby threatening the security of Yugoslavia. Yugoslavia had signed a treaty of friendship with France for its own safety. Albania, on the other hand, signed a 22-year defence treaty with Italy. In 1928, the king of Albania made an attempt to free his country from Italian influence. His efforts however proved futile as in April 1939, Italy occupied Albania.

Primarily, the Franco-Italian rivalry in foreign affairs had created the excitement in European politics. Langsam has observed that, 'The most threatening of Italy's foreign relations in the early post-war years were with France'. While Italy opposed the Versailles Treaty, France supported it. Italy had to enter the fray against France to extend its area of influence in North Africa, the Mediterranean, the Danube areas, and the Balkans. Besides, the dispute over colonial possessions between France and Italy caused bitterness between the two.

However, the Franco-Italian relationship improved in 1928 and the Laval-Mussolini Pact of 1935 amicably settled the colonial dispute between France and Italy as well as addressing more pressing European concerns. The Nazi design of the forcible unification of Germany with Austria brought France and Italy closer. French foreign minister Pierre Laval favoured the formation of a broad united front comprising Italy, Britain, and France against the expansionist policy of Germany. At a conference held in Stresa in April 1935, the representatives of Britain, France, and Italy agreed to resist any unilateral violation of the Treaty of Versailles by Germany, and to strengthen collective security under the League of Nations. However, within a short period, the Stresa front showed signs of weakness, for in 1935, Britain signed a secret naval treaty with Germany. This obviously, provoked Italy and France, and so they made the Lava-Mussolini Pact. Thereafter, the relationship between Italy and France deteriorated as the international situation became contested over the Italian invasion of Abyssinia.

The international political situation in 1935 was conducive to Mussolini's long-cherished conquest of Abyssinia. Around this time the friendship of Italy was sought by England and France who had become disturbed by the prospect of a German revival. Therefore, the Anglo-French front accepted Abyssinia as part of the Italian sphere of influence. The empire of the Abyssinian King Haile Selassie extended from Eritrea to Somaliland, which were both African colonies of Italy. The border dispute between Italy and Abyssinia had been continuing since 1934. In 1935 the League of Nations, on an appeal from Abyssinia following the border conflict at Walwal, appointed a Committee of Conciliation for a negotiated settlement. The committee comprised France, Britain, Poland, Spain, and Turkey. Italy however refused to accept any negotiated settlement. She attacked Abyssinia on 3 October 1935. Hitler alone lent support to this Italian policy of open aggression and so the limited punishment which the League of Nations imposed on Italy for its expedition to Abyssinia, helped cement the bond of friendship between Germany and Italy. This was ratified in a treaty of friendship in 1936 which became known as the Rome-Berlin Axis. Italy reaped little benefit from the alliance. She was virtually reduced to a stooge of Germany. The treaty gave Germany specific advantages but it badly impaired the international image of Italy.

RISE OF HITLER AND THE NAZIS TO GERMANY

Shortly after the conclusion of the First World War Germany faced a severe crisis in internal and external affairs. As per the Treaty of Versailles, Germany was to remain subordinate and restricted. Following the defeat of Germany at the hands of the Allied Powers in the First World War people across Germany rose in revolt, in the German navy but later spreading to Munich, Berlin, and other cities. On 9 November 1918 the German Emperor Kaiser William II abdicated the throne and took shelter in Holland.

This helped establish democracy in Germany for a socialist called Frederich Ebert became Chancellor of Germany, and along with the socialists summoned the Constituent Assembly to dicide the future of Germany. But the communists led by Rosa Luxembourg took the initiative of setting up a democratic government on the Soviet model with workers and peasants at the helm. Known as Spartacists in Germany, they opposed convening the Constituent Assembly. However, at a session at Weimar near Berlin, the Assembly framed a democratic constitution which came to be known as the Weimar Republic. Ebert was elected the first French President under the new constitution which also provided for a bicameral legislature in Germany. The upper house was named Reichsrat and the lower house the Reichstag. The Chancellor and his council of ministers would be elected to the Reichstag on the basis of a universal franchise. The great onus of restoring peace in post-First World War Germany devolved upon the Weimar Republic. David Thomson (*Europe Since Napoleon*) is of the opinion that the Weimar Constitution was 'one of the most completely democratic paper constitutions ever written'. Thus, the Weimar Constitution transformed Germany into a republican state, but the Weimar Republic failed to earn loyalty in Germany. Many unjustifiably attributed all the contemporary socio-economic problems to the Weimar Republic hence the republic lacked popularity.

In the meantime, the Weimar Republic had been gripped by the post-war economic problems. The economic depression of the post-war period found manifestation in the weaknesses of state fiscal policy, tardiness in realizing tax from profiteers and industrialists, price rises, fall in exports and the burden of huge compensation. As Germany was reeling from unemployment, starvation, food shortages and economic crisis, France occupied the Ruhr, the hub of German industry. This added to the economic woes of the country. During this period England, Belgium, and the USA had appointed a committee known as Dawes Committee.

The Treaty of Versailles aimed at permanently crippling Germany. The primary objective of the Weimar Republic was to restore the lost glory of Germany in the international arena. During the post-First World War phase, Germany became totally alienated from the outside world. Soviet Russia, too, came to be treated as untouchable in international politics in this era. Obviously, both the states solicited each other's friendship, burying old rivalries. Russian and German representatives met at the international conference in Genoa in 1922 and concluded the Treaty of Rappolo.

Gustav Stresemann became the Chancellor of Germany in 1923. He used the Treaty of Rappolo to serve German interests. His design was to remove the French antipathy to German interests and to ensure England's cooperation in the revival of Germany. It was at his initiative that the Locarno Treaty was signed in 1925 followed by the adoption of the Young Plan in 1929 for the economic development of Germany.

By this time, the global economic crisis had exerted its influence on Germany where the disaster proved ominous for the Weimar Republic. In the wake of the global economic depression Germany experienced food shortages, price hikes, and rising unemployment, therefore bringing internal reconstruction to a halt and hardship to the common people. The Nazi Party under Hitler emerged at this critical juncture in the national history of Germany.

The Nazi Party and its Organization

Adolf Hitler was born in Austria in April 1889. Completing his school education he went to Vienna and unsuccessfully tried to get admitted to the Academy of Fine Arts there. Then he joined the German army and took part in First World War. In 1919 Hitler joined the National Socialist German Workers' Party which later came to be known as the Nazis or the Nazi Party. As a member of the Nazi Party, Hitler began his political career in Munich. Within a short period of time the party, led by Hitler, gained considerable strength. Allan Bullock in his *Hitler: A Study in Tyranny*, has described Hitler as the 'greatest demagogue in History'. Hitler's fiery speeches, the flag with the symbol of the swastika on it, large-scale terror and 'Brown Shirt' worn by the Nazis—all these combined to evoke popular support. Anti-Jewish and anti-communist feeling, lack of faith in parliamentary democracy, opposition to the Versailles Treaty, the dream of building a far-flung German empire, and ultra German nationalism formed the core of the Nazi ideology.

The Nazi ranks were swelled by conservative monarchists, frustrated soldiers, hopeless workers, and troubled businessmen. Then there were anti-Jewish, anti-Catholic, as well as anti-communist people who all looked upon the Nazi as a means of realizing their dreams. In November 1923 Hitler in collusion with General Ludendroff made an abortive bid to overthrow the Weimar Republic. This was known as Ludendroff-Hitler Putsch.

As a consequence Hitler was imprisoned and subsequently wrote his autobiography, *Mein Kampf* or 'My Struggle'. The book presented in detail his political thoughts and programmes of the Nazis. Released from prison within just nine months, Hitler set about building his party with renewed vigour. Stormtroopers were formed to protect party interests as well as to give security to its leaders. Also called the SA, they were required to wear brown shirts and they would be deployed for security at Nazi rallies and entrusted with the job of forcibly disrupting oppositional political meetings. Besides, a specially trained contingent of personal security guards for Hitler called the SS was also created, as well as the Gestapo or secret state Police. Thus, by 1926 Hitler had built up a strong Nazi movement even though it was restricted to north Germany.

The economic crisis in the wake of the Great Depression in Germany in 1929 helped the Nazis to seize power. Between 1919 and 1933 Germany witnessed nineteen ministries assuming power in quick succession. Following Ebert's death in 1925, Von Hindenburg defeated his socialist and communist rivals to become the President of the Republic. The extremist parties saw an increase in their power bases in the election to the Weimar Republic as a consequence of the economic crisis in Germany triggered off by the global depression from 1929. Von Hindenburg was re-elected President in 1932.

Taking over as Chancellor in May 1932 Von Papen engaged himself in a conspiracy to get Nazis installed in power. Under Papen's patronage Nazi influence grew to such an extent that they captured 230 seats in the Reichstag in July 1932 and became the largest party. The Socialists bagged 133 seats and communists 79 seats in this election. The next election in November saw the Nazis lose 34 seats and the communists increase their tally by 11 seats. In the meantime, Germany had been plunged into anarchy, Nazis harassing their opponents through terror tactics. In the context of this political turmoil, Hindenburg, acting on Papen's advice appointed Hitler as Chancellor of Germany on 30 January 1933. Taking charge, Hitler declared an election to the Reichstag to be held in March the same year.

On 27 February 1933, the Reichstag building went up in flames on the eve of the election, thanks to the conspiracy hatched by the reactionaries. The fire was blamed on communists and the communist party was declared to be illegal. Hitler then went about annihilating all other opposition parties. Armed with the Enabling Act he usurped autocratic power to himself for four years, which won popular endorsement in the plebiscite. When Hindenburg died in August 1934, Hitler assumed power both as President and Chancellor and declared himself the Führer.

Herrenvolk or 'Master Race' Theory

Herrenvolk theory had its origin in bitter racial hatred. Hitler spoke of 'lebensraum' or 'living space' for the German nation, i.e. the ruling nation had the right to occupy the space by driving out the people staying there and wiping out the degraded nations. In other words, Hitler applied racial theory in the context of exterminating the Jews. His racial theory aimed at creating a 'new order' in Europe in which he envisaged the use of all Europe for the German nation, enslaving others to the German cause, extinguishing Jews and Slavs, especially the former. According to the Herrenvolk theory, the industries of Russia and Poland needed to be destroyed and their machinery transported to Germany so that the Slavs were deprived of their factories. Above all, Europe had to be freed from the Jews. Hitler translated this theory into reality by getting millions of Jews executed by the firing squad, calling it 'final solution'. The number of Jews killed by 'final solution' was 42,00,000 to 46,00,000. Historian Allan Bullock is of the opinion that Hitler conceived of the plan between 1930 and 1933. For Hitler, destruction of Jews would be the first step towards the imperial rule by 'Herrenvolk' or the 'master race'.

Over one million Jews were massacred prior to the 'final solution' but their systematic killing at the hundreds of concentration camps (across Germany and Europe), the horrors of the gas chambers, medical experiments and slave labour was yet to come. The Holocaust or genocide of Jews under the Nazi regime has been documented and studied in detail. However, exploring the evidence from the death camp sites, German documents, and survivors' stories are beyond the scope of this book.

HITLER'S REJECTION OF THE VERSAILLES TREATY: GERMAN REARMAMENT

Hitler showed the same opportunism in foreign affairs as he did back home to capture power. Allan Bullock argues that, 'Hitler had only one programme; Power, first his own power in Germany and then the expansion of German power in Europe. The rest was window dressing'. To achieve this end Hitler wanted to cultivate friendships with Italy and Japan, neutralize the French and British opposition to Germany, and destroy communist Russia. The thrust of Nazi policy was to rehabilitate Germany first to make it a major power and then to make it the most powerful state by nullifying the terms of the Versailles Treaty. Lest the move to flout the Versailles terms should evoke opposition from the anti-revisionist coalition of states, the Nazis encouraged their Austrian counterpart through active cooperation. In 1934 the Austrian Chancellor, Englebert Dollfuss was killed as a fall-out of an Austrian Nazi conspiracy the results of which, however, were temporarily neutralized mainly by the Franco-Italian hostility to Austro-German unification or Anschluss. Hitler made up for his failure by uniting Germany with Austria following the annexation of the Saar. The Austrian territory became an inalienable part of Germany following a plebiscite in 1935.

Germany then moved towards a full-scale rearmament. Goering disseminated the news through a correspondent of the *Daily Mail* in London that Germany had built up an air-force with a superior strike power to that of Britain. The lack of adverse reaction to the despatch enthused Hitler. At the same time, the campaigns for the unification of those areas with a strong German presence like Danzig, Memel, and Sudetenland into Germany began. Within a year as the Chancellor, Hitler had rapidly increased the strength of his army to 2,40,000 men. In flagrant violation of the rearmament terms of the Versailles treaty, Hitler introduced compulsory enrolment in the army.

Stunned by this development, England, France, and Italy met at a conference at Stresa where Germany was criticized for violation of the Versailles Treaty and support was extended to the League of Nations. The inner conflict among the powers who came together at Stresa helped Hitler's aggressive design further. In June 1935, Britain signed the Anglo-German Naval Pact without the knowledge of France and the League of Nations, thereby approving of the increase in the German naval power. This marked the collapse of the anti-German coalition and emboldened Germany to flout the Versailles terms.

Within a short period Italy attacked Abyssinia. The failure of the League of Nations and the collective security system to respond adequately to Italian expansion added to Hiter's resolve to ignore the Versailles Treaty. Though England and France supported the move in the session of the League of Nations for adopting measures against Italy, the Hoare-Laval pact demonstrated that they were not sincere about collective initiative against fascist aggression. As world attention remained focussed on the Abyssinian war, Hitler remilitarized the Rhineland on 7 March 1936 for the first time since the First World War and in gross violation of the Versailles Treaty. With Britain still recultant to put up resistance to the German offensive, the French Government did not feel inclined to act on its own against Hitler. Thus, began Hitler's transgressions of the territorial terms of the Treaty of Versailles.

Formation of the 'Rome-Berlin-Tokyo Axis': Anti-Comintern Pact

Hitler's immediate concern on assuming power had been to nullify the Versailles Treaty and pursue an expansionist policy. Mussolini, who had never been favourably disposed to this revival of Germany, had actively resisted Hitler's move to take Austria, but the Italian invasion of Abyssinia in October 1935 elicited only Hitler's support and so Mussolini turned to Germany while Hitler used the distraction to deploy the German army into the Rhineland in March 1936. When the Spanish Civil War started in July 1936, Germany and Italy stepped forward to the aid of the fascist General Franco. Ideologically, Germany and Italy developed a kind of kinship for both Hitler and Mussolini favoured revision of the Versailles Treaty, brought about the end of democracy, and actively sponsored the rise of dictatorship in their respective countries. The anti-communist stance of the two countries also brought them closer to each other. The Rome-Berlin Axis was formed on 25 October 1936. The non-Interventionist Committee formed around that time under the leadership of England and France ensured that the warring sides obtained no other external assistance, but despite being members of the committee, Italy and Germany extended help to France. Thus, the Spanish Civil War cemented the Rome-Berlin Axis.

Within a few months of the formation of the Rome-Berlin Axis, Japan and Germany signed the Anti-Comintern Pact which strengthened the former further. The origins of the Anti-Comintern Pact can be traced back to the Japanese invasion of Manchuria in 1931. Japan at that time expected that the League of Nations would not initiate measures against it. Though the League failed to take steps against the aggressor, the League, on the basis of the report of the Lytton Commission in 1932, ultimately censured Japan as the invader and the aggressor. In March 1933, Japan gave up the membership of the League in protest, thereby alienating itself diplomatically even though Japan considered her alienation to be a safe measure for its security. Japan shared no common interests within Germany prior to the rise or Hitler but in 1935 Germany made a trade agreement with Manchukuo. The bilateral trade relations which developed from then matured into a political understanding which ultimately led to the signing of the Anti-Comintern Pact between the two countries. Under the agreement, both the countries consented to oppose Bolshevik Russia. When Italy joined hands with Japan and Germany, there emerged the Axis Powers out of the union of three dictatorial regimes. The Rome-Berlin-Tokyo Axis came into existence following the signing of a treaty between Italy, Germany, and Japan in 1940. The treaty stipulated that in the event of any of the three countries coming under attack by a fourth power, they would stand by one another with economic, political, and military assistance. The agreement was to be valid for ten years.

Policy of Appeasement by England and France:
Russo-German Non-Aggression Pact

The history of international relations in the post-First World War period is one of crisis, due to the militant expansionist policies pursued by the countries under dictators on the one hand, and the collapse of the collective security system on the other. The Western powers followed no deterrent policy against expansionism in the interest of peace and security. Moreover, Britain and France followed a policy of appeasement. The British Prime Minister, Neville Chamberlain, sought to appease Hitler and Mussolini to settle the dispute between Britain and France on the one side, and Germany and Italy on the other. He was eager to appease Nazi Germany, fascist Italy and militant Japan by making selective concessions to them. In a bid to prevent these imperial powers from pressing ahead with their conquering missions, he sliced out favours to Ethiopia, Austria and Czechoslovakia. Chamberlain, however could not foresee that this policy would weaken England and France, and would lead to Nazi and fascist attack on the democratic forces in near future. The first step in Hitler's expansionist foreign policy was the unification of Germany with Austria which he achieved with the Anschluss in March 1938.

During this period Britain adopted a policy of appeasement in regard to Nazi Germany and France appeared to be reluctant to work out a military strategy towards preserving the unity of Austria. Czechoslovakia became the focal point of Hitler's imperialist design in the wake of the capture of Austria. As the German minorities of Czechoslovakia demanded autonomy in Sudetanland, Hitler made a claim on the German-populated areas of Czechoslovakia. England and France did not stand by Czechoslovakia against Germany. Chamberlain, on the contrary, met Hitler at Berchtesgaden on 15 September 1938 to try and maintain peace, but Germany kept on adding to their territorial demands.

Under the circumstances, Mussolini invited the Prime Ministers of France and England to meet Hitler at a four-nation conference in Munich to attempt to avert conflict. By signing the Munich Pact on 30 September 1938, Chamberlain and Daladier conceded the Sutherland to Hitler in what proved later to be a failed attempt at appeasement. In the meantime the German army took control of Memel in Lithuania and Italy seized Albania. Then Hitler staked his claim on Danzig in Poland with a large concentration of German-speaking people. Initially, Hitler offered friendship to the Polish government which was also hostile to the Soviet Union.

England and France decided on 30 March 1939, that Anglo-French power would extend military help to Poland if it ever came under attack. The Allies were hopeful of Russian support but despite the threat of German attack, Poland was not forthcoming in cooperating with the Soviet Union. Britain, on the other hand, was eager to seek the Russian help in view of the emerging reality even though England and France considered both Russia and Germany to be a potential threat. However, the Russo-German Non-Aggression Pact was signed on 23 August 1939. Scared and aggrieved by the policy of appeasement pursued by the democratic forces, Russia made the agreement virtually in self-defence. This foreclosed the possibility of England and France securing the cooperation of Russia.

The German Invasion of Poland:
The Beginning of the Second World War in 1939

The policy of appeasement alone cannot be held to be responsible for expediting the Second World War. Britain stuck to her commitment to safeguard the territorial integrity of Poland. Still, lack of active British resistance to Germany evidently made it easier for Hitler to start the war. The British Prime Minister, Chamberlain had hoped that a softening towards the stance taken by the dictatorial countries would help ensure both Polish independence and German satisfaction. Had Britain and France made a diplomatic agreement with Russia, it is possible that Hitler would not have risked war. However, the war began as Hitler marched his troops into Poland on 1 September 1939. England and France, as protectors of Poland, declared war on Germany on 3 September. Thus, Europe plunged headlong into the worst global confrontation in human history.

THE SPANISH CIVIL WAR (1936–9)

The Spanish Civil War evolved out of a regional crisis but it gradually assumed the dimension of a continental problem. Therefore, this civil war in a way, foreshadowed Second World War. Assumption of power by the democratic government in Spain, Germany and Italy created bitter resentment among the supporters of monarchy like state employees and soldiers. High level military officials took to revolt under the leadership of General Francisco Franco. On 17 July 1936, Franco raised the first banner of revolt in Morocco. The Republican government called for resistance against the counter-revolutionary uprising. The supporters of the Republic were mainly comprised of workers and middle-class people. On the other hand, the feudal class and rural agricultural areas came under the influence of the counter-revolutionaries. Thus, Spain witnessed a clash between the reactionary feudal and militaristic forces on the one hand and the democratic reformist ones on the other. Italy and Germany sided with the counter-revolutionaries from the outset. Some 1,50,000 Italian soldiers joined the war along with the insurgents while the German assistance consisted of tanks, cannons, guns, and other ammunitions of war, as well as 5,000 air force personnel.

The democratic government of Spain failed to procure the necessary arms from foreign governments to suppress the rebellion. With the very outbreak of war the Spanish Prime Minister Gieral turned to his French counterpart Leon Blum for help. Though Blum was ideologically and ethically inclined to extend help, the British Prime Minister Baldwin was not inclined to get embroiled in the Spanish Civil War. Besides, he warned France that interference in Spain would lead to a complex international conflict. In this situation Britain and France adopted a policy of non-intervention in Spain.

The Spanish Civil War threatened to grip the whole of Europe hence 27 European states including the major ones decided upon the policy of non-intervention in Spain in order to confine the rebellion within the territory of the affected country. The terms of the policy forbade the countries involved to extend help to either of the warring sides. Italy and Germany however provided Franco

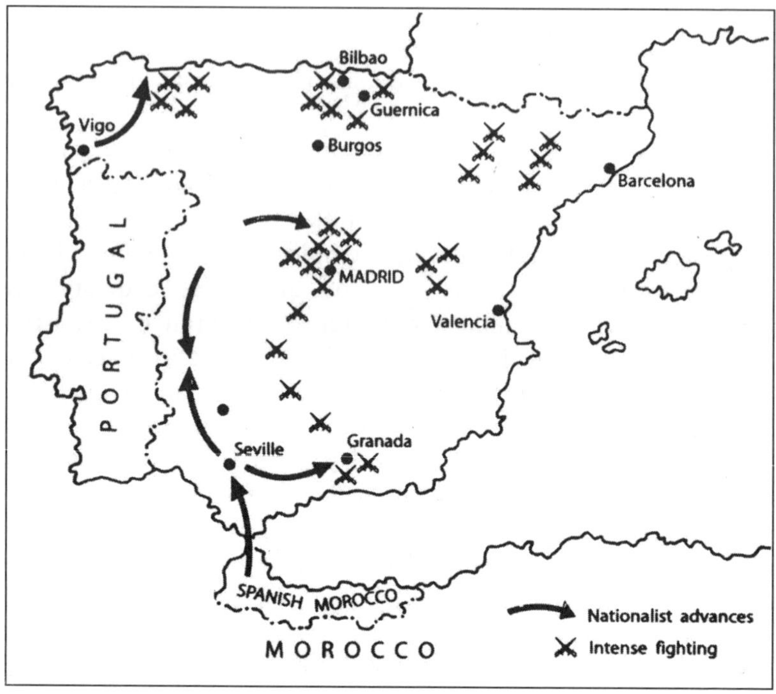

MAP 12.1: Spanish Civil War

with all kinds of help while Britain and France blocked all aid to the democratic government of Spain. As General Franco and the nationalists posed a danger to Madrid, Valencia, and Catalonia, the Spanish capital was shifted from Valencia to Barcelona. In January 1937, the Spanish President Azaña fled to Paris and the official army of Barcelona surrendered unconditionally. Thousands of Spaniards and soldiers loyal to the Spanish government took shelter in France. In the emerging situation the Spanish government gave up resistance to General Franco and the nationalists under his command. The commander-in-chief of the Spanish army, General Miaza appealed for peace. As a result, communists revolted in Madrid, and rampant killing and anarchy continued for a week. This made Miaza leave Madrid and General Franco entered the city unopposed with his forces in March 1939. In the meantime, Britain and France had recognized the nationalist government of

Franco in February 1939. Thus dictorial rule came into force in Spain putting an end to the revolutionary unrest in the country.

HIGHLIGHTS

- In the post-First World War period, Europe saw the rise of fascism in different countries. The European countries which experienced the rise of fascism were Italy, Germany, and Spain.
- The Treaty of Versailles came as a profound shock to Italy. Apart from this, the post-war economic depression in Italy paved the way for the rise of facism which in Italy was led by Mussolini.
- In Germany too, the economic conditions of the post-war period triggered off political insecurity. This facilitated the rise of the Nazis under the leadership of Hitler. All the opposition parties in Germany were suppressed by the aggressive politics of the Nazi Party led by their supreme leader Hitler, who was regarded as 'Führer'.
- The sole objective of Hitler's foreign policy was to establish the superiority of the Aryan race in the world. He pursued this policy, violating the terms and conditions of the Treaty of Versailles. The aggressive foreign policy of Germany planted fear in the minds of other European nations and led to the Second World War.
- A dictatorship was established in Spain under the leadership of General Franco. Behind the rise of General Franco the policy of England and France was responsible to a considerable extent.

MEMORABLE DATES AND EVENTS

1883	Birth of Mussolini
1889	Birth of Hitler
1919	The Foundation of the Fascist Party
1922	Mussolini became the Prime Minister of Italy
1925	The Publication of *Mein Kampf* (Autobiography of Hitler)
1926	Mussolini became the Dictator of Italy
1934	Hitler became the Dictator of Germany
1937	Rome-Berlin-Tokyo Axis
1938	Dictatorship in Spain under Franco
	Russo-German Non-aggression Pact
	November—Germany attacked Poland
	3 November—The beginning of the Second World War

MEMORABLE PERSONALITIES

Benitto Mussolini: Fascist Dictator of Italy
Gustav Stresemann: Chancellor of Germany
Adolf Hitler: Nazi Dictator of Germany
Neville Chamberlain: The British Prime Minister
General Francisco Franco: Nationalist Leader of Spain
Joseph Goebbels: One of the Leaders of the Nazi Party
Victor Emmanual III: The King of Italy
Laval: The French Foreign Minister

QUOTABLE QUOTES

- 'Their [the Nazi] programme was a strange mixture of racial intolerance, socialist policies and Communist politics.'   —SCHAPIRO
- 'She [Italy] was rushing heading long [down] the road to complete anarchy.'   —LIPSON
- 'The war is here and it is a war of the people. The war of today will be the revolution of tomorrow.'   —MUSSOLINI
- 'France is the eternal and mortal enemy of the German nation.'   —HITLER
- 'The most threatening of Italy's foreign relations in the early post-war years were with France.'   —LANGSAM
- 'Mankind has grown great in war; it will decay in eternal peace.'   —HITLER
- 'The Washington Conference was hailed, not without reason, as an outstanding success. It had, to all appearances, restored the pre-war balance in the Pacific.'   —E.H. CARR
- 'The First World War, the twenty years of uneasy peacekeeping, and the Second World War, seemed in one sense, to be part of a continuous single process—one war rather than two—in which Europe was involved in a self-destructive struggle centred in the unresolved problem of Germany.'   —M. BARBER

CHAPTER 13

Second World War (1939–1945)

INTRODUCTION

Between 1919 and 1939 the major European powers were primarily preoccupied with the rise of Germany. The interwar years came to be known as the 'Twenty Year Truce', and the whole era between 1914 and 1945 as another 'Thirty Years' War'. There were many similarities between the two wars as both began in eastern Europe and both arose from treaty obligations towards smaller powers. Yet, the similarities should not be overemphasized for there were significant differences between the two wars. Hardly had the world forgotten the traumatic memory of the First World War (1914–18) when the horizon was showing the signs of a new war. Although the Second World War started in 1939, just like many other events in history, the causes for its outbreak started to take shape much earlier. In fact, it would not be an exaggeration to say that the seeds of the Second World War were sown just after the end of the First World War.

THE GENESIS OF THE SECOND WORLD WAR

It was the Treaty of Versailles (1919), which the Germans resented most. Historian E.H. Carr has commented that '. . . in the Treaty of Versailles the element of dictation was more apparent than in any previous peace treaty of modern times'. By this treaty Germany was compelled by the victor nations to accept bitter humiliation and injustice. Through the war guilt clause, the German army was reduced drastically. The economic clauses were also severe for Germany for she lost 15 per cent of her arable land and 12 per cent of her industrial areas. Added to this was the reparation payment and the deprivation of her colonies. The French occupation of the Ruhr Valley deeply injured the German national sentiment. In the 1920s Germany was going through an economic crisis due to hyperinflation and currency devaluation. This crisis was further aggravated due to the worldwide great depression of the 1930s following the Wall Street crash of 1929. Economic crisis gave birth to social crisis. The maximum advantage of this situation was taken by Hitler and the Nazi Party. By denouncing the Treaty of Versailles, they strengthened their position and could then start a period of ultra-nationalism: mentally the Germans were against the treaty and Hitler only utilized the situation.

The League of Nations was established with the ambitious aim of maintaining peace and stability, but in reality, things took an opposite shape. The League could not establish itself as an international centre of command for the big powers were never ready to cooperate with each other on various issues. Each power tried to use the League to serve its own ends. For example, Britain tried to use the League to corner Bolshevism, France regarded

Adolf Hitler waves a Nazi Flag

Adolf Hitler listens to radio broadcast of Parliamentary election results

the League as an instrument to secure the Versailles Treaty, and Germany regarded the League as an assembly of the victorious nations. The final blow to the prestige of the League came when the League failed on the question of aggressions in Manchuria and Abyssinia. Gradually, all states big and small lost their confidence in the League.

As the member states had no confidence in the League of Nations, the disarmament initiatives ultimately failed. Germany was disarmed by the Treaty of Versailles, but the other powers were not ready for disarmament. The disarmament conferences called by the League resulted in a stalemate where France and other European nations refused to disarm by putting forward the argument of national security. When Hitler came to power in Germany, he started the process of armament. In 1935, conscription was allowed in Germany, and Japan and Italy too started armament. The arms-race of the Axis powers thus started the competition for more and more armament.

Finally, it must be remembered that imperialism and imperialist ambition was also a cause of the outbreak of Second World War.

By the Treaty of Versailles the Allied Powers defended their imperialist interests but hit hard the imperialist interests of Germany and Italy. The bulk of the backward, underdeveloped regions of the world were under the control of Britain, France, the USA, Belgium, etc. Being deprived of colonies, Germany and Italy were facing a dearth of raw materials and markets. Out of the 125 essential raw materials and minerals, Britain enjoyed adequate supply of 18, whereas Germany was compelled to remain content only with 4. Italy had no coal and Japan had no oil. The economic situation of the Axis powers worsened after the Great Depression of the 1930s. Under these circumstances, it became necessary for the Axis powers to pursue a course of aggression to secure the question of raw materials and markets.

A series of acts of aggression by Germany served as the immediate cause of the war. German invasions of Austria, Czechoslovakia, and Poland made the war seen inevitable. These attacks and Hitler's Non-Aggression Pact with Russia served as the spark to bring about the conflagration. The attempt of the allies to pacify the Germans by the Munich Pact failed. The war started in September 1939 and ended in 1945.

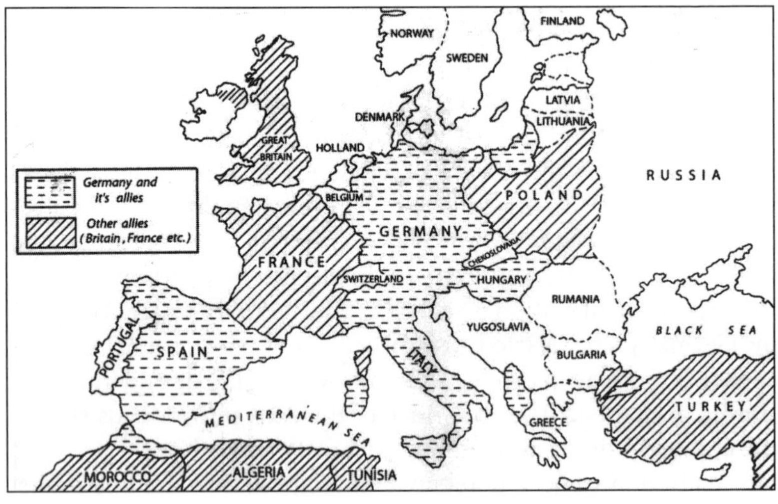

MAP 13.1: Europe—1939

THE COURSE OF THE WAR

The Second World War was a new type of war. The First World War was fought largely by conventional army and with guns. In the First World War fighting meant long weeks of battle and then advancement or retreat of few kilometres. The Second World War was qualitatively different from all wars which preceded it. It was a war of rapid movement, a mobile war with armoured cars, tanks, aircrafts, etc. Then, fighting meant advancement or retreat of 50 or 100 km. in a day. In the Second World War for the first time civilians also had to directly face the force of war due to air raids and bombings on towns.

The German army attacked Poland at 4.40 a.m. on 1 September 1939. This opening move started the Second World War. The defeat of Poland was only a matter of time. The Luftwaffe (German air force) bombed the Polish airfields, bases, training centres, and disrupted the entire railway network of Poland. In the face of highly mechanized, armoured German attack, the Polish resistance went down and Britain and France could do nothing to save Poland. On 17 September, Russians invaded Poland from the east. As a result, Poland was divided between Germany and Russia. Since Russia was concerned with the safety of Leningrad, she attacked Finland in November 1939. Russia thought that a German conquest of Finland would endanger her security. The Russo-Finnish War ended in March 1940 with a peace treaty between Russia and Finland through which Russia received a naval base in Finland. During this period Russia also annexed and established military bases in the Baltic states of Latvia, Lithuania, and Estonia.

No major event occurred in the West for the next five months although there were a few naval encounters between Britain and Germany. During this time, the French and the Germans reinforced their respective lines of defence—the Maginot and Siegfried lines. This period of five months is known as the 'Phoney War' for no major offensives were launched. However, on 9 April 1940 the German army launched an offensive on Denmark and Norway, thus ending the period of 'Phoney War'.

Denmark surrendered quickly and Norway was defeated with the active support of Norwegian Nazis and their leader Vidkun Quisling. Control of Norway was an important consideration for Germany as Sweden was a major supplier of iron ore to Germany and Swedish supply used to come through Norway. The conquest of Norway secured an uninterrupted supply of iron ore for Germany which directly helped the German arms manufacturing industry.

On 10 May 1940, the German army launched a simultaneous attack on Holland, Belgium, Luxembourg, and ultimately France. Cities, bases, and communication systems were bombed, and a vast stretch of frontier was crossed by the German army. Nearly a thousand people were killed by the bombing of Rotterdam. Holland surrendered within four days while Luxembourg surrendered within just a few hours. Although Belgium tried to withstand German advances, they also surrendered after 17 days on 28 May. Only Dunkirk remained in Allied hands where a large number of Allied troops took shelter. On 26 May started the evacuation of 3,50,000 troops from Dunkirk which ended on 4 June. The troops had to leave behind all their heavy equipments

French Assault

German Flame Thrower Group

German Assault

German Machine Gun Group

and weaponry at Dunkirk and so Dunkirk was a serious blow for the Allies.

Now the Germans moved southwards and concentrated their attack on France. Paris was captured on 14 June and France surrendered on 22 June 1940. At Hitler's insistence, a ceasefire was signed at Compiegne in the same railway carriage in which the Germans were compelled to sign the Versailles Peace Treaty in 1918. The Germans annexed northern France and the Atlantic coast. The remaining territory of France was allowed to be ruled under Henri Petain's government. This was a puppet government which collaborated with the Nazis and which came to be known as the Vichy Government. On the other hand, under the leadership of General Charles de Gaulle, the Free France movement was established in England to fight against Nazi Germany. Whilst this attack was taking place in France on 10 June, Italy also declared war on France and Britain.

After having conquered continental Europe, Hitler now decided to launch a direct attack on England. To conquer England it was necessary to try to gain control of the English Channel, which cold only be achieved by destroying the Royal Air Force (RAF) and the Royal Navy. The plan for the attack of England was given the code name of 'Operation Sea Lion'. The German offensive started in the month of August 1940 when German bombers bombed British ships, convoys, seaports, harbours, airfields, aircraft, and factories. The idea was to destroy the morale of the RAF and its installations and to clear the route to London.

The Luftwaffe also started to raid Britain's cities, particularly London, and heavy bombing continued. But the Britishers gave a very stiff resistance to the Germans. There were battles between the RAF and the Luftwaffe in the skies above southern England as well as RAF raids on Germany. This aerial conflict between Britain and Germany is known as the Battle of Britain. Due to the stiff British resistance both civilian and military, German air raids on London decreased and by 17 September 1940, Operation Sea Lion was indefinitely postponed.

By this time the war had also spread to Eastern Europe and Africa. The Tripartite Pact was signed between Germany, Italy, and Japan on 27 September 1940 by which they pledged to give full support to each other. In October 1940 Italy invaded Greece but although they met resistance backed by the British, the German's ultimately triumphed and occupied Crete. From November of 1940 to March 1941 Germany conquered Hungary, Rumania, Slovakia, and Bulgaria. In April, Yogoslavia was subjugated and then partitioned between Germany and her allies. During this time in Africa, Italy invaded British Somaliland and Sudan, and started to advance towards Egypt, although by the end of 1940 Britain had recovered most of her colonies in Africa after fierce fighting. In Libya, fighting continued between the British and German-Italian combined forces. As has been mentioned earlier, General de Gaulle of France organized Free France movement at that time. In the Middle East, and particularly in Syria, De Gaulle's Free France movement and British forces successfully resisted the Axis attacks during this period.

Involvement of the USSR in the War

To Hitler, communism was the greatest enemy. Hitler had always maintained that the real war of the Nazis will be against the Russians. Apart from this political-ideological factor there were also economic reasons for which Hitler attacked the Soviet Union. Hitler believed that conquest of Russia would enable Nazi Germany to control a vast amount of natural resources. From a military point of view Hitler was worried that the Russians would attack Germany if the German forces remain engaged in Western Europe. Hitler also calculated that if Germany attacked Russia from the West then Japan would start attacking Russia from the East. However, Nazi hatred towards communism and the question of Lebensraum were still the leading factors behind the attack. The German invasion of the Soviet Union started on 22 June 1941. It was a huge operation supported by 3,550 tanks and 5,000 aircrafts and was code-named Operation Barbarossa. Germany occupied Riga, Kiev, Smolensk, and Odessa. However, they could not capture Leningrad and Moscow. The Russians started their counter-attack during the December when the temperature fell below −40 °C. Severe cold halted the German advance and the Russians drove them back from Moscow. The biggest blow to Germany was given by Russia in the Battle of Stalingrad in July 1942. It was a battle waged in the city, in buildings and on the streets. The Russians fought hard and ultimately German Field Marshal Van Paulus surrendered on 24 January 1943. The Battle of Stalingrad reduced the city to rubble but Russian victory changed the whole course of the Second World War. To Germany, it was a moral and political defeat and are with a high military cost.

The German invasion of Russia brought England, the US, and Russia closer. This cooperation and unity of the UK, the US, and the USSR later largely contributed to the final defeat and surrender of Germany. The anti-fascist coalition of these countries came to be known as the 'Grand Alliance'.

Involvement of Japan and US

Before 1941, the US maintained neutrality in the Second World War. The US Government followed a uniform policy towards Britain and France. Before 1941 Britain bought arms from the US by direct cash payment. From 1941 however, Britain's position worsened and so in that year, the US Congress passed a law by which the President was given the power to lend or lease arms to those countries whose defence was considered vital to the defence of the US. As a result, Britain started to receive a huge supply of arms from the US and the lend-lease system was later extended to Soviet Union also. In August 1941 the US, Britain, and the USSR declared the Atlantic Charter. Apart from declaring democratic principles the Atlantic Charter gave a call for the final destruction of the Nazi Germany.

At this time, the US was against Nazi aggression but at the same time remained aloof from the war. Japanese imperialism was however, taking shape at that time. Japan had already occupied Vietnam. Now, Japan's desire was to control the Pacific. Already the relationship between the US and Japan had deteriorated when the US demanded Japanese withdrawal from Indochina and China. On 7 December 1941, the Japanese Air Force bombed on the US naval base at Pearl Harbour in Hawaii. The Pearl Harbour bombing took the US completely by surprise and is the process some 350 aircrafts, 5 battleships, and more than 3,000 men were destroyed and killed.

On 8 December, the US declared war on Japan. On 11 December, Germany and Italy declared war on the US and the US reciprocated. So, from mid-1941 when Soviet Union got involved in the war, and in the last month of that year when the US also became involved, the war took the form of a global or world war.

Defeat of Italy and Mussolini's Fall

Allied forces invaded Sicily on 9 July 1943 beginning the final assault on Italy. There was already internal dissenssion in Italy and repeated defeats broke the morale of the Italian soldiers who frequently surrendered themselves to the Allied forces. The internal political crisis of Italy resulted in the arrest of Mussolini on 26 July 1943. On 3 September, the Allied forces invaded southern Italy and due to the initiative of Victor Emmanuel, Italy surrendered. However, the Germans invaded northern Italy on 10 September and occupied Rome. Later Mussolini was rescued by Hitler and he established a government in northern Italy under German protection. In southern Italy a new government was formed which declared war against Germany and civil war ensued. Mussolini was later captured in 1945 and was shot by the Italians.

Allied Invasion of Europe on
D-Day (6 June 1944)

While facing the Nazi onslaught in eastern Europe, Russia called for the opening up of a second front. Russia's opinion was that if the Allies started attacking the Nazi army from the West then the concentration of German forces or Russia would be reduced and diverted. For strategic reasons, the US and the UK declined to open the second front before 1944. On 6 June 1944 however, Allied troops landed on the beaches of Normandy, on the north coast of France. This event is known as D-Day and took months of preparations and innovative intelligence work to effect successfully. The Allied armies liberated France and Belgium by September 1944. In the Adennes region of Belgium there took place heavy fighting between the Russian and the German forces. This battle came to be known as the Battle of the Bulge. Ultimately, due to massive Russian attack on the eastern front the Germans started to retreat.

Hitler Commits Suicide—
Germany Surrenders

After the surrender of Italy in 1943, the civil war in Italy continued. The anti-fascist movement inside Italy grew stronger by the day and the anti-fascists started an uprising in the fascist-occupied northern Italy on 23 April 1945. Allied forces freed Rome in 1944 and with the execution of Mussolini in 1945. Italy became free from fascist rule. Germany was attacked by the Allies from the West and Soviet Union from the East and by March 1945, Allied forces occupied a large amount of territory in West Germany. On 25 April, Soviet forces reached Berlin. Realizing the imminence of defeat Hitler committed suicide on 30 April 1945. On 7 May,

Germany unconditionally surrendered to representatives of the US, the UK, France, and the USSR.

Japan's Surrender

The war continued in the Asia-Pacific region for nearly another four months. The only Axis force of this region was Japan who was waging war in China, Manchuria, Korea, and South-East Asia. To force Japanese surrender on 6 August 1945, the US dropped an atomic bomb on Hiroshima and on 9 August, another bomb was dropped on Nagasaki. The result was devastating for Japan. On 8 August, the Soviet Union also declared war against Japan and these combined pressures ultimately forced Japan to retreat. Chinese communists defeated them in China, the Soviet Union in Manchuria, and the British army in South-East Asia. On 2 September 1945, Japan also surrendered and with this the Second World War officially came to an end.

HIGHLIGHTS

- The Second World War began in 1939. This war broke out due to a number of causes including the weaknesses of the Treaty of Versailles, the rise of the Nazis, intense colonial rivalry among the European Powers, and the failure of the League of Nations.
- Although the War began over the issue of Poland, gradually the war spread to other parts of the world.
- The Nazis conquered France by England continued to try to contain Germany.
- The big powers of the world like Russia, Japan, and America joined the war on different grounds. The Japanese bombing of Pearl Harbour added a new dimension to the war.
- Over time, the Axis powers faced a number of losses and were eventually defeated. Mussolini was killed and Hitler committed suicide. France was recaptured by the Allied forces and thus both Germany and Italy were defeated.
- With the Japanese surrender to the allies on 2 September 1945 (after nuclear bombs were dropped on Hiroshima and Nagasaki) the Second World War came to an end.

MEMORABLE DATES AND EVENTS

1939	Russo-German non-aggression pact
	German invasion of Poland
	3 September—the Second World War began
1940	13 June—Fall of Paris
1941	German invasion of Russia
	August—Atlantic Charter
	December—Bombing of Pearl Harbour by the Japanese
1943	September—Surrender of Italy
1945	April—Hitler committed suicide
	August—Bombing of Hiroshima and Nagasaki
	2 September—Japan surrendered

MEMORABLE PERSONALITIES

Chamberlain: Chamberlain was the Prime Minister of Great Britain up to 1940

Winston Churchill: Churchill became the Prime Minister of England in 1940

Franklin D. Roosevelt: Roosevelt was the President of the United States during the Second World War

Adolf Hitler: The Fascist ruler of Germany and the leader of the Nazis

Joseph Stalin: Stalin was the Head of the Russian during the Second World War

Daladier: Daladier was the Prime Minister of France until 1940. He resigned from his position in March 1940.

Zhukov: One of the most notable army officers of Russia

Eric Rommel: Nazi army officer under whom the German army launched successful operations in Africa

Admiral Yamamoto: The Japanese army bombed the Pearl Harbour under the leadership of Admiral Yamamoto

Hideki Tojo: General Hideki Tojo came to power in Japan in 1941

QUOTABLE QUOTES

- 'It [the Nazi invasion of Russia] was the biggest invasion the world had ever seen.'
  —PHILIP SUAVAIM
- 'Pearl Harbour united the American people more fully than ever before in history.'
  —M.M. PARKES

- 'The military alliances which were forged in 1941 and 1942, in the face of the triumphant common enemy, were therefore clouded from the start by memories of recent 'treacheries' on both sides. The unhesitating support offered to Stalin by Churchill in June 1941 did something to dispel these deep seated animosities.'

  —DAVID THOMSON

- 'The most far-reaching consequence of the Pacific War for the Western European nations was the colonial revolution which was precipitated, though not created, by Japanese conquests. The coloured peoples of the overseas colonial territories of Britain, France, and the Netherlands were stirred as never before to revolt against the domination of the white man.'   —DAVID THOMSON

CHAPTER 14

The World after the Second World War

INTRODUCTION

The political and social fabric of the world underwent remarkable changes after the end of the Second World War. There emerged the new phenomenon of the Cold War which resulted in the division of the world into two rival camps. In the face of huge anti-colonial movements, the era of direct colonial rule ended. In this period the Socialist forces too, started to establish themselves as a power in different parts of the world. In order to understand the Cold War and the division of the world into two rival camps, we shall have to survey the various conferences and agreements which took place in different parts of the world during the last phase of the war.

PRE-YALTA CONFERENCES

We have already discussed the Atlantic Charter through which the Allies pledged for the total destruction of Nazism. The anti-fascist coalition took a more concrete shape on 1 January 1942, when the representatives of 26 countries announced the declaration of the United Nations. In January 1943, Churchill and Roosevelt met at Casablanca in Morocco. In this meeting the US emphatically put forward the demand of unconditional surrender of the fascists. This became the political standpoint of all the Allied nations.

The Moscow Conference was held from 19 to 30 October 1943. This Conference was attended by the foreign ministers of the US, the UK and the USSR. In this meeting, the decision was taken to discuss the terms of surrender for the fascist states and their allies. The Moscow Conference also issued a four-nation declaration to establish an international organization for maintaining international peace. In December 1943, the US, the UK, and

China signed the Cairo Declaration. The Cairo Declaration called for the unconditional surrender of Japan.

The most important meeting of the Allies took place at Teheran between 28 November and 2 December 1943. The Teheran Conference was attended by Churchill, Stalin, and Roosevelt. At the Teheran Conference, the US agreed to join the war effort and the Soviet Union to join the war against Japan. The future of Poland was also discussed in this meeting. A communist majority Polish national council was established with Soviet support which agreed with the decisions of the Teheran Conference. However, the London-based Polish government in exile disagreed with the Teheran decisions. The Dumbarton Oaks Conference which was attended by the US, the UK and the USSR to discuss plans for the UN, was held in the August-September of 1944.

THE YALTA AGREEMENT, FEBRUARY 1945

The Yalta Conference was held in Russia from 4 to 11 February 1945. This Conference was attended by the three Allied leaders, Churchill, Stalin, and Roosevelt and was held at a time when Germany's defeat seemed imminent: the leaders gathered to map out a plan for the future. Many important decisions were taken in this Conference.

The three states present at the Conference declared that their aim would be to secure the unconditional surrender of Germany. The meeting declared that the aim of the Allies was to destroy German militarism and nazism and to ensure that Germany would never again be able to disturb the peace of the world. The Allies decided that Germany would be divided into four zones. These zones would be under the control of Russia, the US, Britain, and France. A decision was also reached to divide Berlin into four corresponding zones.

As has already been mentioned, when the Russian army entered Poland, they established a Socialist government in Lublin. At the Yalta Conference it was agreed that some of the non-communist members of the London-based Polish government would be allowed to join the Lublin-based Polish provisional government.

A decision was also reached regarding the frontiers of Poland. As Russia agreed to include members of the London-based Polish government in the Lublin government, in return, she was allowed to keep that part of eastern Poland which she had annexed in 1939.

The Yalta Conference is also famous for the decisions made about the establishment of the United Nations. The members agreed about the future structure of the Security Council. The date of 25 April 1945 was fixed for a meeting at San Francisco to discuss the details of the charter of the UN.

Finally, the Soviet Union agreed to join the war against Japan after the surrender of Germany. In return, Russia wanted the whole of Sakhalin Island. No agreement was reached regarding the Russian demand that Poland should receive all the German territory east of the rivers Oder and Neisse. In order to assist the countries of Europe to establish post-war democratic institutions, the Allies also formulated a 'Declaration on Liberated Europe'.

THE POTSDAM CONFERENCE, JULY 1945

Between 17 July and 2 August 1945, the Potsdam Conference was held in Germany. This conference was attended by the three leading Allied powers. The new US President Truman attended this conference as the US representative and from 28 July, Churchill was replaced by the new British Labour Prime Minister, Clement Atlee.

The central focus of the Potsdam Conference was the future of Germany. The declaration of the conference proclaimed that, 'German militarism and nazism will be extirpated, and the Allies will take in agreement together, now and in the future, the other measures necessary to assure that Germany never again will threaten her neighbours or the peace of the world'. The Allies reached an agreement on the destruction of the military power of Germany, the control of German arms manufacturing industry, and the division of Germany into four occupation zones. Germany had to pay reparations in order to repair the damages caused by her during the war. It was agreed that the major portion of this reparation would go to Russia, who would take non-perishable goods from their own zone. Also, the leaders agreed that the Nazi Party would be disbanded and its leaders tried as war criminals.

The main controversy among the Allies occurred regarding Poland. Britain and the US were displeased with Russia since Russian troops had occupied Germany east of the Oder-Neisse line. This area was run by a pro-communist Polish government which expelled nearly 5 million Germans from the area. However, agreement was reached about the western border of Poland.

In this meeting, the US President Truman informed Churchill about the true nature of the atomic bomb while not revealing the information to Stalin. Russia agreed to declare war against Japan on 8 August 1945, but just four days after the conference, on 6 August, America dropped an atomic bomb on the Japanese town of Hiroshima and then another one on Nagasaki on 9 August forcing the conclusion of the war in the Pacific. Nevertheless, Russia declared war on Japan on 8 August and thus according to the Yalta agreement, was able to annex South Sakhalin.

Germany remained a source of tension between the Allies forever at the Potsdam Conference, the Allies could not reach a conclusion regarding the future of Germany. For example, they could not decide when the four zones of Germany would be allowed to join together to form a state. From this time onwards, started the period of cooling-off in foreign relations.

ECONOMIC REHABILITATION AND THE COLD WAR

The Second World War resulted in enormous destruction of both material and human resources. Russia, France, Germany, and Italy were heavily damaged.

France lost almost 50 per cent of her total wealth in terms of damage to factories, railways, mines, housing, and other assests. A large part of western Russia, southern Italy, and nearly the whole of Germany were completely devastated. The Allied powers felt an immediate necessity to attend to the problem of the economic rehabilitation of Europe. The programme of economic rehabilitation was initiated through the United Nations Relief and

Rehabilitation Administration, or UNRRA. Up until 1947, this organization provided vital economic aid for the reconstruction of industry and agriculture in all the countries devastated by the Second World War. On 12 March 1947, US President Truman gave a speech which came to be known as the Truman Doctrine. In June 1947, the Marshall Plan was also developed. Although these were both ostensibly aid programmes, the US ambition behind these policies was to stop the expansion of communism in Europe and later on in other parts of the world under the patronage of Socialist Russia. The Truman Doctrine has been taken to mark the beginning of the Cold War at which point the world became divided into two rival camps hostile to each other.

The US and the USSR emerged as the two most powerful nations of the world after the Second World War. The US faced comparatively little loss during the war and gained significantly by supplying the Allies with the required war materials. Moreover, the US had in its possession the atomic bomb. On the other hand, although Russia suffered huge losses in the war, she recovered quickly. She had in her possession the biggest army of the world. The main basis of the contradiction between the two powers was that the US was suspicious about the Soviet Union's aims, while the Soviet Union was suspicious about US policies. This mutual distrust gradually gave way to such tension in world politics that it influenced the whole world. This tension between the powers, which, although did not lead to any actual war, resulted in low intensity conflicts and undeclared wars. This war was called the Cold War and it was characterized by continued hostility, and efforts to weaken or undermine the enemy by every means other then direct military conflict.

Although many historians sought to trace the origin of the Cold War in 1947 when the Bolshevik revolution took place, the phenomenon surfaced in earnest only after the Second World War. In 1946, Churchill, the former Prime Minister of Great Britain gave a speech at the University of Fulton, Missourie, in the US in which he stated that, 'from the Stettin in the Baltic to Trieste in the Adriatic an iron curtain has descended across the continent.' This notion of an 'Iron Curtain' referred to the Soviet Union European countries and has since become the pervasive image of the Soviet Union during the Cold War. Already the Western Allies under the leadership of the US had had differences with the USSR on the question of Germany and Poland and they became increasingly alarmed by the spread of communism in Eastern Europe. In Poland, in the elections of 1946, the Communist Party won nearly 90 per cent seats while in Czechoslovakia, a communist-dominated government came to power in 1948. Similar developments took place in Bulgaria, Romania, Hungary, Yugoslavia, and Albania. Thus, seven countries in Europe came to have governments under communist leadership.

Germany became another source of contention between the Soviet Union and the Western Allies. Although initially Germany was divided into four occupation zones, she later became divided into just two zones. The three zones under the US, Britain, and France became one, forming West Germany and the Soviet zone became East Germany. They each had a separate currency and in East Germany, landholdings were confiscated and redistributed among the peasants while many industries were nationalized. In West Germany, with considerable US aid, rapid development took place along capitalist lines. The German communists, who had been banished by the fascist regimes and their allies during the war, were encouraged in East Germany. In West Germany, various political parties hostile to communism were encouraged. In this way, by 1947 Germany became divided and later two independent states were formed.

In Greece the communists united to attempt to oust the fascist occupants. Subsequently, the communists became engaged in a civil war against the monarchical military regime in Greece. There were 10,000 British troops in Greece who were trying to restore the rule of the monarchy by driving out the communists but in 1947, due to the increasing burden of supporting the Greek Government in civil war, Britain decided to withdraw. It was at this juncture that the US decided to intervene in the Greek civil war in order to prevent a communist seizure of political power there.

When the US government decided to intervene in the civil war in Greece, the Truman Doctrine was taken as a justification of the intervention and thus, according to most, the era of Cold War began.

THE TRUMAN DOCTRINE, MARCH 1947

The communist guerillas in Greece received help from Albania, Bulgaria, and Yugoslavia during the civil war and thus were growing. In Turkey too, the communists were gaining strength. In the case of Greece, the British appealed to the US for aid while the Turkish government appealed to the US for assistance against the communists. The US President Truman addressed a Joint Session of the US Congress on 12 March 1947 with a speech that later came to be known as the Truman Doctrine. The US President told the Congress that, 'the very existence of the Greek state is today threatened by the terrorist activities of several thousand armed men led by the communists who defy the Government's authority. . . Greece must have assistance if it is to become a self-supporting and self-respecting democracy. . . I believe that it must be the policy of the United States to support free peoples who are resisting attempted subjugation by armed minorities or by outside pressures'. As a result, Greece began to receive huge amount of arms and other supplies and Turkey received aid amounting to 60 million dollars.

In essence, the Truman Doctrine was a statement of belief which later assumed the form of a policy. The policy of the US Government was to intervene militarily and economically in the civil wars against the communists. Due to US aid, the communists in Greece were defeated by 1949. The same thing happened in the case of Turkey. The Truman Doctrine initiated the phase of the US policy of containment of communism across the world.

THE MARSHALL PLAN, JUNE 1947

The Marshall Plan was an economic extension of the Truman Doctrine. The American Secretary of State George Marshall planned the European recovery programme or ERP and in his speech at the Harvard University on 5 June 1947, declared that:

The truth of the matter is that Europe's requirements for the next three or four years of foreign food and other essential products—principally from America—are so much greater than her present ability to pay, that she must have substantial additional help or face economic, social and physical deterioration of a very grave character. It is logical that the United States should do whatever it is able to do to assist in the return of normal economic health in the world without which there can be no political stability and no assured peace.

At that time the communist parties were gaining strength in France and Italy. Moreover, the influence of the communists were spreading in other parts of Europe. The US administration thought that with economic aid, Western Europe would become prosperous and this would prevent the communists from gaining strength. The US Government gave $522 million to France, Italy, and Austria. This amount was increased to $577 million in March 1948. In the next four years (from 1947) a sum of over $13,000 million entered Europe in the form of Marshall Aid. The Soviet Union felt that Marshall Aid was fundamentally aimed at countering the spread of communism. Asia's foreign minister termed the Marshall Plan 'dollar imperialism' for Russia saw it as a tool through which the US was trying to gain control over western Europe. Marshall aid was rejected by Russia and the other European socialist states which further worsened relations between Russia and the US. The Soviet Union also criticized the Marshall Plan because it undermined the importance of the United Nations.

SPREAD OF NATIONALISM AND UNREST IN THE SUBJECT COUNTRIES

One of the most important outcomes of the Second World War was the end of direct colonial rule in different parts of the world, and particularly in Asia. Due to the rising tide of anti-colonial movements, British, Dutch, French, and Portuguese colonial rule ended in many countries. During the 1940s anti-colonial political ideology was spreading fast in colonies like India, Burma, Sri Lanka, Indonesia, and Indochina. As a result of these movements most of the former colonies achieved independence by 1950.

The Second World War had put tremendous pressures on the exchequers of the former colonial powers. Due to US aid, Britain became able to merge her financial necessities created during the war. However, immediately after the war, Britain accumulated an overseas debt of £3,000 million. France was nearly bankrupt and most of the powers were in the same situation.

At that time, public opinion in Europe was also not in favour of colonial empires. Socialist states and the communists were against colonial rule but equally, again USA was against the reimposition of colonial rule in the former colonies. Simultaneously, anti-colonial movements were spreading fast in the colonies. One example of this would be the Quit India Movement (1942) in India. These movements compelled the already overstretched colonial powers to look for compromise.

During the war, most of the British, Dutch, and French colonies in Asia were occupied by Japan. These were the colonies of Malaya, Burma, French, Indochina, and the Dutch East Indies. When the Japanese realized that they were facing defeat, they started to encourage the nationalist movements in these colonies to destabilize their enemies. They encouraged the nationalists in Indonesia, Indochina, and India and even supplied weapons to the Indonesian nationalists.

The spread of nationalism and the growing financial and administrative inability of the former colonial powers to rule the colonies directly ultimately resulted in the birth of independent states. India became independent in 1947, Burma in 1948, Indonesia in 1949 and Sri Lanka in 1948. The republic of Vietnam was formed in 1946.

Triumph of Socialistic Forces and their Consolidation in Europe and South-East Asia

The end of the Second World War also witnessed the development and growth of socialistic forces in different parts of the world.

The biggest development took place in Europe and Asia. The Soviet Union was already the biggest socialist state but apart from Soviet Union, socialist governments were established in Poland, Hungary, Romania, Bulgaria, and Albania. In Yugoslavia an elected Socialist government under Marshall Tito came to power in 1945. In Czechoslovakia too, a socialist government was established in 1948. The spread of the Socialist ideology, was also not only confined to eastern Europe for socialism started to gain ground in western Europe too. In the western European countries, where parliamentary democracy prevailed, communist and various socialist parties started to appear. They started to receive considerable mass support and were able to create a mass base. When Japan surrendered in 1945, she was compelled to leave China. Already the Chinese communists were waging a bitter struggle for the seizure of the political power and with Japanese withdrawal, the Chinese communists entered into a prolonged battle with the Kuomintang forces led by Chiang Kaishek. After a protracted civil war with the Kuomintang, the Chinese communists won the battle under the leadership of Mao Tse Tung and the Peoples' Republic of China was founded in 1949.

The nationalist movement of Vietnam took off under the leadership of the Communists. The Viet Minh under Ho Chi Minh established the republic of Vietnam in 1946. However, according to the Potsdam agreement, after the surrender of the Japanese, France wanted to restore Indochina as her colony. The Viet Minh were not ready to surrender their independence to France and in North Vietnam, they established themselves firmly. The Vietnamese communists were receiving help from China but America started to help France and so in south Vietnam, the war continued until May 1954 when the French-held fortress of Dien Bien Phu surrendered to the Viet Minh forces. Under the Geneva Convention of 1954, Vietnam was the partitioned and so north Vietnam remained under communist control. They eventually captured South Vietnam in 1975.

Cambodia had declared her independence in 1945, but this did not translate into reality until 1954. Prince Norodom Sihanouk was the head of the state but he was ousted by Lon Nol's government.

The communist guerillas were already strong in Cambodia and so the Cambodian communists, or the Khmer Rouge, started a civil war against Lon Nol's government. They ultimately won the war in 1975 under the leadership of Pol Pot. Thus, a socialist state was established in Cambodia.

Apart from these important revolutionary movements, communist parties started to gain strength in Sri Lanka, India, Indonesia, Malaysia, Burma, etc., and various popular movements were launched.

HIGHLIGHTS

- During the Second World War, the Allied Powers sat in a number of conferences. The most important of these conferences were the Yalta Conference and the Potsdam Conference. These conferences discussed the various issues relating to the war and the post-war situation.
- For the economic regeneration of the war ravaged Europe, the Allied powers adopted a number of measures. Out of these measures mention may be made of UNRRA, the Truman Doctrine, and the Marshall Plan.
- The post-Second World War era saw the intensification of anti-imperialist nationalist movements in different parts of the world, particularly in Asia and Africa.
- The post-war period saw the rapid progress of communism across the world. The ideologies of Marxism and Leninism made headway particularly in Eastern Europe, China, and Vietnam.

MEMORABLE DATES AND EVENTS

1943	The Foundation of UNRRA
1945	February—Yalta Conference
	July-August—Potsdam Conference
1947	March—The Truman Doctrine
	June—Marshall Plan
	August–India attains independence, the birth of Pakistan
1948	Burma attains independence

MEMORABLE PERSONALTIES

Churchill: Prime Minister of Great Britain
Stalin: Head of the Soviet Union
Roosevelt: The President of the United States
Marshall: The Secretary of State of the US
Truman: The President of the United States
Ho Chi Minh: The communist leader of Vietnam
Hitler: Chancellor of Germany Führer
Atlee: Prime Minister of Britain

QUOTABLE QUOTES

- 'It was recognized as early as 1941 that the economic rehabilitation of Europe after years of German occupation and exploitation would be both difficult and urgent.'   —DAVID THOMSON
- '. . .without it [UNRRA] the material distress of post-war Europe would have been very much worse than it was.'   —DAVID THOMSON
- 'It was the biggest piece of first-aid work in history, and it was a triumph of international co-operation.'   —DAVID THOMSON
- 'When the Marshall Plan programme came to an end in June 1952, it had achieved triumphantly what it had set out to do.'   —FRIEDMANN
- 'We shall not realize our objectives, however, unless we are willing to help free peoples to maintain their free institutions and their national integrity against aggressive movements that seek to impose upon them totalitarian regimes imposed on free peoples, by direct or indirect aggression, undermine the foundations of international peace and hence the security of the United States.   —TRUMAN
- 'The Truman Doctrine was the major opening gun in what journalists called the 'Cold War'—a war waged by means other than shooting. It also inaugurated in a spectacular way the new policy of "containment" or the attempt to stem soviet advances in Vital spots.'   —T.A. BAILEY
- 'The Truman Doctrine was of incalculable significance. It enabled America to seize the offensive in the Cold War to "Contain" Communism.'   —T.A. BAILEY
- 'Advocates of the Marshall Plan, though appealing to simple humanitarianism, stressed the bread and butter argument that a prosperous Europe was essential for America's own prosperity.'
                                —T.A. BAILEY

CHAPTER 15

The United Nations

THE QUEST FOR PEACE

The Second World War brought with it unprecedented destruction, devastation, and loss of human life. Though the world had witnessed large-scale big wars previously, as the Second World War saw the utilization of scientific and technological development, and the deployment of weapons of mass destruction, the magnitude of the devastation was qualitatively different. Approximately 40 million people were killed and 21 million people were left homeless. The world again had to strive for peace in order to stop destruction just as the League of Nation had tried and failed to achieve at the end of the First World War. During the Second World War, it became all the more critical to develop mechanism to preserve to peace and to avoid war. It was the result of this necessity for peace which resulted in the formation of the United Nations. The formation of the United Nations was an evolutionary process which started during the Second World War and matured just after the end of the war. The United Nations would go on prove itself much more successful in maintaining international peace and stability than its predecessor, the League of Nations.

THE EVOLUTION OF THE UN

The roots of the United Nations can be traced back to August 1941 when the Atlantic Charter was issued. The Atlantic Charter was signed by US President Roosevelt and British Prime Minister Churchill on a battleship in the Atlantic Ocean and it declared a few common principles for the future world. For example, it declared that without the freely expressed wishes of the people, there should be no territorial changes and that no country would be able to resort to the policy of aggression. The two signatories stated that they should respect the right of every people to choose and form their own government. They also declared that Nazi tyranny should be ended and that after the defeat of fascist Italy and Nazi Germany, every state would be able to enjoy freedom. They also upheld the policy of disarmament and declared that sea routes would no longer be the monopoly of any single country and that the economic conditions of the labourers of the signatory states would be improved.

On 1 January 1942, the declaration for the formation of the United Nations was issued. Along with the US, the UK, the USSR, and China, the declaration was signed by the representatives of 26 nations. They all pledged that they would cooperate with each other in order to defeat their common enemy. The signatory states also agreed not to hold separate talks or sign peace treaties with the Axis powers.

The Dumbarton Oaks Conference was held on 7 October 1944. The Conference was attended by the US, the UK, the USSR, and China and there, the four powers examined a plan proposed by the US government which was later on circulated to all the UN member states. The plan proposed the creation of a Security Council and further, that the member states of the UN should place their armed forces at the disposal of the Security Council. The United Nations Charter was signed by 51 states (who were known as the original members of the UN) at the San Francisco Conference which was held in 25 April 1945. The Charter was adopted on 25 June 1945 and it declared the aims and objectives of the UN.

THE PURPOSE OF THE UN: ITS ORGANIZATION

Article 1 of the United Nations Charter declared that the aims of the UN were:

1. to maintain peace and security, and to that end, to take effective collective measures for the prevention and removal of threats to world peace, and for the suppression of acts of

aggression or other breaches of the peace, and to bring about by peaceful means, and in conformity with the principles of justice and international law, adjustment or settlement of international disputes or situations which might lead to a breach of the peace;

2. to develop friendly relations among nations on the basis of respect for the principles of equal right and self-determination of peoples, and to take other appropriate measures to strengthen the concept of universal peace;

3. to achieve international cooperation in solving international problems of an economic, social, cultural, or humanitarian character and in promoting and encouraging respect for human rights and for fundamental freedom for all without discrimination as to race, sex, language, or religion; and

4. to create a centre for harmonizing the actions of nations in the attainment of common ends.

The UN Charter also defined the structure of the United Nations. The principal organs of the UN were to be: (i) the General Assembly, (ii) the Security Council, (iii) the Economic and Social Council, (iv) the Trusteeship Council, (v) the International Court of Justice, and (vi) the Secretariat. The Charter also mentioned the need for commissions and specialized agencies like UNESCO and WHO.

The General Assembly

The General Assembly is an important organ of the United Nations in which all the activities of the UN are discussed. Although every member state can send up to five representatives to the General Assembly, no member state can cast more than one vote. This principle encapsulates the nation of the equal rights of every member state. The General Assembly begins its sessions in the month of September every year. In addition to the regular sessions, special sessions can be held according to requirement. The Assembly can discuss any matter written in the Charter of the UN and can forward its recommendations on matters of international importance to the Security Council. It elects the non-permanent members of the Security Council, members of the Economic and Social Council, and the Trusteeship Council. The business of the Assembly is carried out by six committees.

The Security Council

The members of the Security Council are divided into two categories: the permanent members, and the non-permanent members. Until 1966, the Security Council was composed of 5 permanent and 6 non-permanent members, but from 1966 onwards, the number of non-permanent members has been increased to 10 thereby raising the total number of members to 15. The 5 permanent members are the UK, the USA, Russia, France, and China. The non-permanent members are elected for a term of two years by the General Assembly. The Security Council is the most important wing of the UN for its principal duty is to safeguard international peace and security. It holds its sessions fortnightly but the meetings can be held at shorter intervals according to requirements. The permanent members of the Security Council also have the right of veto to reject a majority opinion if necessary.

The Economic and Social Council

The Economic and Social Council consists of 54 members who are elected by the General Assembly for a period of three years. The Council itself then elects one president and one vice-president. This Council observes the economic and social conditions, human rights situation, and health conditions of the member nations and puts forward necessary recommendations to the General Assembly. The purpose of the Council is to assure economic and social welfare and to make people conscious about human rights. The specialized agencies under this council are United Nations Educational, Scientific and Cultural Organization (UNESCO), International Monetary Fund (IMF), International Labour Organization (ILO), etc.

The Trusteeship Council

The Trusteeship Council is vested with the duty of looking after the affairs of underdeveloped countries and its early function was to prevent colonial expansion in the former colonies. The Council elects its chairman and each member of the Council is entitled to one vote.

The International Court of Justice

The judicial body of the UN is the International Court of Justice. The court consists of judges who are elected by the members of the Security Council and General Assembly in two separate votes. The judges enjoy diplomatic privileges. The duty of the Court is to settle international disputes but no member state of the UN comes under its jurisdiction. In that sense this court has no compulsory jurisdiction.

The Secretariat

Under the Secretary-General, it is the Secretariat which conducts the business of the UN. The Secretary-General is the highest authority of the Secretariat and is appointed by the General Assembly on the recommendations of the Security Council for a five-year term.

The first Secretary-General of the UNO was Trygve Li. The Secretary-General has to submit an annual report to the General Assembly regarding the activities of the UN and he is able to draw the attention of the Security Council to any situation he considers serious.

EVALUATION OF THE UN

The United Nations was established with the ambition of maintaining international peace and security. The successful functioning of the UN depends on the mutual understanding and cooperation of the member states. However, since the members of

UN do not all have equal rights, and as the permanent members of the Security Council enjoy special privileges, the principle of equality has not been implemented in practice. Although nearly 57 years after its establishment, the UN has gained a very prominent position in world society, there are still many problems which the UN could not solve. The UN can function much better if the big powers do not intervene in various issues to protect their vested interests.

The UN was created in light of the experience of the League of Nations but it was undoubtedly an improvement on the constitution of the League. The UN Charter is a much longer and a more explicit document than the League Covenant, its membership is more representative, and its functions are more extensive. The League had no armed forces at its disposal, but, UN is provided with a Military Staff Committee to consider the use of armed forces by the Security Council for the maintenance of global peace and security. However, in spite of detailed provisions on paper for the maintenance of global peace, there are major procedural lapses which stand in the way of making them effective. The right of veto which has been granted to each of the 'Big Five' has proved to be the greatest hurdle in the functioning of the Security Council. To take a major decision in international matters, all the Big Five powers have to be unanimous in the Security Council.

Among the global disputes which the UN has failed to solve is the Palestine problem. The struggle between the Arabs and the Jews constitutes a very disturbing factor in the Near East. The UN has appointed a special committee in 1947 which recommended the partition of Palestine into Jewish and Arab areas. Thereafter, the General Assembly deployed a commission to take charge of Palestine after the British had withdrawn. The problem intensified when the Jews declared the establishment of the independent state of Israel. The Arab League declared war against Israel. To reach a peaceful settlement the General Assembly authorized the Big Five to mediate but the UN however, could not offer an enduring solution to the Palestine problem, which still remains one of the sore issues in international diplomacy.

Kashmir is another example of ongoing tension and it still remains a bone of contention between India and Pakistan. Both the Kashmir and Palestine problems acquired new dimensions after the end of the Cold War and in the context of recent changes in the global scenario after the destruction of the World Trade Center in New York on 11 September 2001.

We have now stepped into the twenty-first century and a new world order. With the Cold War over and the Soviet Union gone, the face of global diplomacy has undergone a metamorphosis. After the end of the Cold War and the rise of a (unipolar) world order, we are experiencing the unfolding of a chain of reactions including the rise of nascent national, ethnic, and communitarian aspirations everywhere. To make matters worse, the developing world and the comparatively newer nations seem to be fragile in the face of increasing multiculturalism, and ethnic and religious fundamentalism. The worst manifestation of this threat could be traced in the terrorist attacks on the World Trade Center in New York and the Pentagon in Washington, DC on 11 September 2001. The UN now seems to be interested in combating the 'problem of global terrorism' multilaterally, but here too, problems remain. With the US as the lone superpower, there is the danger that the UN might be forced to respond to US interests alone. The end of the 1980s saw not only the political decay of the Soviet Union but also the intensification of Islamic activism in Asia and Africa. Fawaz A. Gerges in his recent book (*America and Political Islam*) argues that given the US tendency for crusades—the US-Soviet rivalry as a struggle between good and evil—it is tempting to identify another global ideological menace to fill the 'threat vacuum' created by the demise of communism. Terrorism today is looked upon as a threat not only to the US but to the entire free world. In the world after 11 September, a more positive role of the UN is called for. The 11 September 2001 attack has created a situation in which the supposed clash of civilization (Huntington, *The Clash of Civilisations and the Remaking of the World Order*) looked like a reality. It is now left for the UN to resolve this worst threat to humanity.

HIGHLIGHTS

- The origins of the United Nations can be traced back to the various conferences which were held during the Second World War. In this connection mention may be made of the Atlantic Charter and the Dumbarton Oaks Conference. The UN was a reflection of the on-going quest for peace which came in the wake of the great war.
- The Charter of the United Nations explicitly mentions two vital objectives of the organization: (a) The quest for international peace, and (b) all round welfare of the people of the world.
- The UN functions through six crucial organs: (a) the General Assembly, (b) the Security Council, (c) the Economic and Social Council, (d) the Trusteeship Council, (e) the International Court of Justice, and (f) the Secretariat.
- The organization and structure of the UN was different from the League of Nations. The UN is an improved version of the League of Nations.
- The UN has failed to solve many global problems. In the post-Cold War era much has been expected from the UN. It is still hoped that the UN will come forward to resolve many of the outstanding conflicts of the world.

MEMORABLE DATES AND EVENTS

1941   9 August—The Atlantic Charter
1942   January—The UN Declaration
1943   30 October—The Moscow Declaration
        1 December—Teheran Declaration
1945   25 April–26 June—The San Francisco Conference
1950   Indonesia attains Independence

MEMORABLE PERSONALITIES

Churchill: Prime Minister of Great Britain
Franklin D. Roosevelt: The President of the US
Eden: Foreign Secretary of Britain
Molotov: Foreign Commisar of Russia
Stalin: Head of the Soviet Union

QUOTABLE QUOTES

- 'We have learned that we must live as men, and not as ostriches, nor as dogs in the manner, we have learned to be citizens of the world, members of the human community.'　—FRANKLIN D. ROOSEVELT
- 'The United Nations Charter was noteworthy for the unprecedentedly large voice that it gave to the small powers. Throughout the conference they had demanded more influence, had fought big power domination, and had proposed numerous amendments. Perhaps most important of all, in the light of subsequent crises, they were permitted to turn the General Assembly into a kind of town meeting of the world.'

　—THOMAS A. BAILEY
- 'Whatever the weaknesses of the United Nations Charter, the delegates had blueprinted the machinery for the boldest experiment in international organization yet adopted by man.'

　—THOMAS A. BAILEY
- 'The receding of the Soviet threat prompted American officials to reassess the new dangers confronting US interests and allies. Given the US tendency for crusades the US-Soviet rivalry as a struggle between good and evil it is tempting to identify another global ideological menace to fill the "threat vacuum" created by the demise of Communism.'　—FAWAZ GERGES
- 'On both sides the interaction between island and the West is seen as a clash of civilizations.'　—SAMUEL HUNTINGTON

Bibliography

General works covering parts or the complete period discussed in this volume are listed below.

Anderson, M.S., *The Ascendancy of Europe, 1815–1914*, 2nd edn, London, New York: Longman, 1988.

Blanning, T., ed., *The Oxford Illustrated History of Modern Europe*, Oxford: Oxford University Press, 1996.

Bracher, K.D., *The Age of Ideologies: A History of Political Thought in The Twentieth Century*, New York: St. Martin's Press, 1985.

Cook, C., and J. Stevenson, *The Longman Handbook of Modern European History 1763-1991*, London: Longman, 1992.

Gildea, Robert, *Barricades and Borders: Europe 1800–1914*, Oxford: Oxford University Press, 2003; first published 1987.

Hobsbawm, Eric, *The Age of Revolution, 1789–1848*, London: Weidenfeld and Nicolson, 1962.

———, *The Age of Capital, 1848–1875*, London: Weidenfeld and Nicolson, 1975.

———, *The Age of Empire, 1875–1914*, London: Weidenfeld and Nicolson, 1987.

———, *The Age of Extremes: The Short Twentieth Century, 1914–1991*, London: Weidenfeld and Nicolson, 1994.

Jackson, J., ed., *Europe, 1900–1945*, Oxford: Oxford University Press, 2002.

Joll, J., *Europe since 1870*, Middlesex: Penguin Books, 1990.

Kennedy, Paul, *The Rise and Fall of the Great Powers: Economic Change and Military Conflict from 1500 to 2000*, London: Fontana, 1989.

Laqueur, W., *Europe in Our Time: A History 1945–1992*, New York: Penguin Books, 1992.

Mazower, M., *Dark Continent: Europe's Twentieth Century*, New York: Knopf, 1998.

Overy, R.J., *The Times Atlas of the Twentieth Century*, London: Times Books, 1996.

Paxton, R., *Europe in Twentieth Century*, San Diego, California: Harcourt Brace Jovanovich, 1985.

Pugh, M., ed., *A Companion to Modern European History 1871–1945*, London: Blackwell, 1997.

Roberts, J.M., *Europe 1880-1945*, London: Longman, 1989.

Vinen, R., *A History in Fragments: Europe in the Twentieth-Century*, London: Little Brown, 2000.

CHAPTER 1: THE EURO-AMERICAN WORLD IN THE LAST QUARTER OF THE EIGHTEENTH CENTURY

Result of the Seven Years War (1756–63)

Anderson, Fred, *Crucible of War: The Seven Years' War and the Fate of Empire in British North America, 1754–1766*, New York: Knopf, 2001. (For an authoritative recent account of the Seven Years War with special emphasis on British North America.)

Cardwell, M. John, *Arts and Arms: Literature, Politics and Patriotism during the Seven Years War*, Manchester: Manchester University Press, 2004. (For a comprehensive exploration of British public opinion during the Seven Years War; Cardwell uses over a thousand works of political commentary; ballads, newspapers, political pamphlets, plays and some fiction, most of them contemporary, to examine the representations of the Seven Years War in political literature, analysing the interrelationship between politics and culture in Britain between 1756 and 1963.)

Hofstra, Warren R., *Cultures in Conflict: the Seven Years War in North America*, Lanham, Md.: Rowman & Littlefield, 2007. (For broad pattern of events framing the causes of the conflict, the intellectual dynamics of its conduct and impact on subsequent events, most notably on the American War of Independence.)

Parkman, Francis, ed. J.H. McCallum, *Seven Years War*, New York: Harper and Row, 1968. (For a traditional narrative account of the war by one of America's earliest distinguished historians.)

Riley, James C., *The Seven Years War and the Old Regime in France: The Economic and Financial Toll*, Princeton, New Jersey: Princeton University Press, 1986. (For a recent enquiry into the nature of economic and financial impact of the war on France.)

Schumann, Matt and Schweizer, Karl W., *The Seven Years War: A Transatlantic History*, London: Routledge, 2007. (For an overview of the diplomatic, military and maritime history of the causes and conduct of the Seven Years War and its American manifestations, the French and Indian War (1753–63); includes biographical details and critical reappraisals of some of the major figures of the period.)

Szabo, Franz A.J., *The Seven Years War in Europe 1756–1763*, Harlow, England; New York: Pearson/Longman, 2008. (This is a scholarly reinterpretation of Austria's gains from the continental war. This particular work, based on a new reading of primary sources and fresh research in the Austrian State Archives, argues that Prussia did not win, but only survived the Seven Years War. This was despite and not because of the actions and decisions of its King Frederick 'The Great'.)

Rise and Fall of Enlightened Absolutism

Andrews, Stuart, *Enlightened Despotism*, New York: Barnes and Noble, 1968.

Crieger, Leonard, *An Essay on the Theory of Enlightened Despotism*, Chicago: University of Chicago Press, 1975.

Galiardo, John G., *Enlightened Despotism*, New York: Crowell, 1967.

Frederick II (1740–86)

The earliest and perhaps also the most ambitious work on Frederick the Great is Thomas Carlyle's multivolume biography of the Prussian monarch, on which he commenced work since 1852 and which were published between 1858 and 1865. The meticulous volumes emphasize the military genius of Frederick, portraying him as a master strategist who pulled the Prussian army from the jaws of defeat repeatedly with his tactical brilliance. The original publication comprised six volumes. All of them are now available online for general readers and scholars alike, courtesy Project Gutenberg and various collaborating universities. The following link hosted by the Computer Science Department of Carnegie Mellon University has all of them collected together: http://www.cs.cmu. edu/~spok/metabook/fgreat.html

Barker, Thomas Mack, *Frederick the Great and the Making of Prussia*, New York: Holt, Rinehart and Winston, 1971.

Hubatsch, Walther, *Frederick the Great of Prussia: Absolutism and Administration*, London: Thames and Hudson, 1975.

Macdonogh, Giles, *Frederick the Great: A Life in Deed and Letters*, St. Martin's Griffin, 2001. (A new biography that portrays Frederick not only as a feared conqueror, but also a patron of the arts and a progressive lawmaker who transformed Berlin into one of Europe's great capital cities.)

Mitford, Nancy, *Frederick the Great*, Penguin, 1995. (An instructive and readable biography, blending political and military history with amusing personal details about monarchical eccentricities.)

Tuttle, Hubert, *History of Prussia under Frederick the Great*, New York: AMS Press, 1971.

Joseph II (1765–90)

Beales, D.E.D., *Joseph II*, Cambridge: Cambridge University Press, 1987. (A critical and comprehensive biography by one of the world's foremost historians on the reign of Joseph II.)

——, *Enlightenment and Reform in Eighteenth Century Europe*, London: I.B. Tauris; New York: Palgrave Macmillan, 2005. (A comprehensive series of essays by a senior Cambridge historian on a range of themes related to enlightenment, with special emphasis on his pioneering research on Joseph II of Austria.)

——, *Joseph II: Against the World, 1780–1790*, Cambridge and New York: Cambridge University Press, 2009. (The most authoritative recent study of the final years of Joseph's reign by one of the world's foremost experts on the subject.)

Bernard, Paul P., *The Limits of Enlightenment: Joseph II and the Law*, Urbana: University of Illinois Press, 1979.

Blanning, T.C.W., *Joseph II and Enlightened Despotism*, London: Longman, 1979.

Padover, Saul Kussiel, *Joesph II of Austria: The Revolutionary Emperor*, London: Eyre and Spottiswoode, 1967.

Catherine II (1762–96)

Alexander, John T., *Catherine the Great: Life and Legend*, New York: Oxford University Press, 1989.

De Madariaga, Isabel, *Russia at the Age of Catherine the Great*, New Haven, Connecticut: Yale University Press, 1981. (A comprehensive study of the Russian Queen and her times by one of the foremost scholars on the subject; this work has since been followed up by a smaller biography in 2001.)

Dixon, Simon, *Catherine the Great*, Harlow, England: Longman; New York, 2001. (A highly readable summary of Catherine's life and times by an academic historian, making use of some recently published Russian material.)

Rounding, Virginia, *Catherine the Great: Love, Sex and Power*, Hutchinson, 2006. (Examining Catherine's own correspondence and contemporary accounts by courtiers, ambassadors, and foreign visitors, Virginia Rounding probes the character of this powerful and fascinating eighteenth-century figure.)

The Industrial Revolution

Factors Leading to the Industrial Revolution

Allen, Robert C., *The British Industrial Revolution in Global Perspective*, Cambridge: Cambridge University Press, 2009 (Analysing why the Industrial Revolution took place in eighteenth-century Britain and not elsewhere in Europe or Asia, Robert Allen argues in this persuasive new work that the British Industrial Revolution was a successful response to the global economy of the seventeenth and eighteenth centuries. In Britain, wages were high and capital and energy cheap in comparison to other countries in Europe and Asia. The breakthrough technologies of the Industrial Revolution therefore were uniquely profitable to invent and use in Britain.)

Cipolla, C.M., *Fontana Economic History of Europe*, vol. III (Industrial Revolution), London: Fontana Press, 1973. (Yet another handy introduction to all the major issues related to the Industrial Revolution.)

Crouzet, Francoise, *Capital Formation in the Industrial Revolution*, London: Methuen, 1972.

Deane, Phyllis, *The First Industrial Revolution*, Cambridge: Cambridge University Press, 1965; repr. 1979.

Hartwell, R.M., *The Causes of the Industrial Revolution in England*, London: Methuen, 1967. (A collection of significant essays that deal with the specifics of the British experience.)

Hobsbawm, Eric, *The Age of Revolution, 1789–1848*, London: Weidenfeld and Nicolson, 1962. (Contains some brief but very insightful introductory chapters on the early history of the Industrial Revolution.)

Hudson, Pat, *The Industrial Revolution in Britain, 1760–1830*, New York: Oxford University Press, 1992. (Easily among the best of recent comprehensive surveys of the Industrial Revolution, it qualifies the recent revisionist thought that fundamental change in economic, social and political life at the time of the Industrial Revolution was minimal or non-existent. Elements given short shrift in many current interpretations are rehabilitated. This demanding and challenging work will enrich our perceptions of both the Industrial Revolution controversy and eighteenth- and nineteenth-century social, economic and industrial history.)

Pawson, Eric, *The Early Industrial Revolution: Britain in Eighteenth Century*, New York: Barnes and Noble, 1979.

Consequences of the Industrial Revolution

Burnette, Joyce, *Gender, Work and Wages in Industrial Revolution Britain*, Cambridge: Cambridge University Press; New York, 2008. (Contains the latest scholarly position on the impact of the Industrial Revolution on women.)

Clapp, Brian William, *An Environmental History of Britain since the Industrial Revolution*, London and New York: Longman, 1994. (An early contribution to the study of environmental history of England, beginning with the impact of the Industrial Revolution; a most detailed and wide-ranging survey.)

Crafts, N.F.R., *British Economic Growth during the Industrial Revolution*, Oxford: Clarendon Press, 1985. (A leading recent study challenging traditional views of a rapidly growing British economy between 1700 and 1850, arguing that British economic growth was, in fact, relatively slow during much of the so-called industrial 'revolution'. Processing latest research, Crafts explores how the new growth estimates hold important lessons for our understanding of productivity, living standards, structural change, and international trade in eighteenth- and nineteenth-century Britain.)

Hobsbawm, Eric, *Industry and Empire: From 1750 to the Present Day*, Pelican, 1968. (The legendary historian explores the origin and development of the Industrial Revolution over 250 years and its influence on social and political institutions. This is a classic account of Britain's rise as the first industrial power, its decline from domination, its special relation with the rest of the world, and the effects of this trajectory on the lives of its ordinary citizens. New editions of the work contain an illuminating new conclusion.)

Evans, Eric J., *The Forging of the Modern State: The Early Industrial Britain 1783–1870*, Pearson Longman, 2001. (A comprehensive survey of the period in which Britain was transformed into the world's first industrial power. In this period, Britain witnessed revolutionary changes, a transformation, however, achieved without political revolution. The combination of revolution and transition is a major theme of the book, which ranges across the embryonic empire, the Church, education, health, finance and rural and urban life.)

Landes, David, *The Unbound Prometheus*, Cambridge: Cambridge University Press, 1969. (Written over fourteen long years of research and teaching, by one of the major figures behind the development of economic history in post-War Europe, this is easily one of the most profound introductory studies on the Industrial Revolution, absorbing and building on past scholarship and replete with insights of great interest to students, teachers and researchers alike.)

Mokyr, Joel, *The Enlightened Economy: An Economic History of Britain 1700–1859*, New Haven and London: Yale University Press, 2009. (A magisterial new work on the origin and impact of the Industrial Revolution, it promises to replace Landes on the aspects of history, and Floud and Johnson on the economics as the best new introduction to the Industrial Revolution. As the title suggests, Mokyr places great emphasis on ideas and institutions as distinct from material explanations that have predominated studies on the Industrial Revolution so far.)

Rosen, William, *The Most Powerful Idea in the World: A Story of Steam, Industry and Invention*, New York: Random House, 2010. (This new book on intellectual history tells the story of the men responsible for the Industrial Revolution and the machine that drove it, the steam engine. Singling out the point that by the eighteenth century the idea that people had the right to own and profit from their ideas was firmly entrenched in British society, Rosen explores a period of frantic innovation revolving around the promise of steam power. Alongside, we enter the minds of such inventors as

Thomas Newcomen and James Watt, scientists including Robert Boyle and Joseph Black, and philosophers John Locke and Adam Smith.)

The War of American Independence (1776)

There is little need to separate the studies on the War of American Independence, except conduct a broad analytical distinction between works that address themes related to the war as a whole and those that address particular themes and aspects. Specialized works dealing with three particular aspects of the revolution are mentioned along with a select list of comprehensive works that study the overall phenomenon.

For an Overall Understanding

Alden, John Richard, *A History of the American Revolution*, New York: Knopf, 1969.

Bailyn, Bernard, *The Ideological Origins of the American Revolution*, Cambridge: Belknap Press of Harvard University Press, 1967.

Bonwick, Colin, *The American Revolution*, Charlottesville: University Press of Virginia, 1991.

Dull, Jonathan R., *A Diplomatic History of the American Revolution*, New Haven: Yale University Press, 1985.

Greene, Jack P., ed., *The American Revolution: Its Character and Limits*, New York University Press, New York, 1978.

Jensen, Merrill, *The Founding of a Nation: A History of the American Revolution, 1763–1776*, New York: Oxford University Press, 1968.

Maier, Pauline, *From Resistance to Revolution: Colonial Radicals and the Development of American Opposition to Britain, 1765–1777*, New York: Knopf, 1972.

McCullough, David G., *1776*, New York: Simon & Schuster, 2005.

Middlekauff, Robert, *The Glorious Cause: The American Revolution, 1763–1789*, revd edn, New York: Oxford University Press, 2005.

Morgan, Edmund Sears, *The Birth of the Republic, 1763–89*, 3rd edn, Chicago: University of Chicago Press, 1992.

Raphael, Ray, *A People's History of the American Revolution: How Common People Shaped the Fight for Independence*, New York: New Press, 2001.

Wood, Gordon S., *The Radicalism of the American Revolution*, New York: Knopf, 1992.

Resistance

Ammerman, David, *In the Common Cause: American Response to the Coercive Acts of 1774*, Charlottesville: University Press of Virginia, 1974.

Brown, Richard D., *Revolutionary Politics in Massachusetts: The Boston Committee of Correspondence and the Towns, 1772–1774*, Cambridge, Massachusetts: Harvard University Press, 1970.

Jellison, Richard M., ed., *Society, Freedom, and Conscience: The American Revolution in Virginia*, Massachusetts, and New York: Norton, 1976.

Juster, Susan, *Disorderly Women: Sexual Politics and Evangelicalism in Revolutionary New England*, Ithaca, N.Y.: Cornell University Press, 1994.

Labaree, Benjamin Woods, *The Boston Tea Party*, New York: Oxford University Press, 1964.

Marston, Jerrilyn Greene, *King and Congress: The Transfer of Political Legitimacy, 1774–1776*, Princeton: Princeton University Press, 1987.

Olson, Lester C., *Emblems of American Community in the Revolutionary Era: A Study in Rhetorical Iconology*, Washington, DC: Smithsonian Institution Press, 1991.

War Years and Diplomacy

Bowler, R. Arthur, *Logistics and the Failure of the British Army in America, 1775–1783*, Princeton: Princeton University Press, 1975.

Dull, Jonathan R., *A Diplomatic History of the American Revolution*, New Haven: Yale University Press, 1985.

———, *The French Navy and American Independence: A Study of Arms and Diplomacy, 1774–1787*, Princeton: Princeton University Press, 1975.

Higginbotham, Don, *War and Society in Revolutionary America: The Wider Dimensions of Conflict*, Columbia: University of South Carolina Press, 1988.

Scott, H.M., *British Foreign Policy in the Age of the American Revolution*, Oxford: Clarendon Press, 1990.

Shy, John, *A People Numerous and Armed: Reflections on the Military Struggle for American Independence*, New York: Oxford University Press, 1976.

Loyalists

Brown, Wallace, *The King's Friends: The Composition and Motives of the American Loyalist Claimants*, Providence: Brown University Press, 1965.

Calhoon, Robert McCluer, *The Loyalists in Revolutionary America, 1760–1781*, New York: Harcourt Brace Jovanovich, 1973.

Lambert, Robert Stanebury, *South Carolina Loyalists in the American Revolution*, Columbia: University of South Carolina Press, 1987.

McCaughey, Elizabeth P., *From Loyalist to Founding Father: The Political Odyssey of William Samuel Johnson*, New York: Columbia University Press, 1980.

CHAPTER 2: THE FRENCH REVOLUTION (1789–1815)

The reading list here is selective, featuring only the acknowledged classics and the recent research. It begins with general works surveying the entire period, moving on to monographs dealing with individual themes. The literature is so vast and diverse that some arguable classics may be left out although attempt has been made to include as many as possible.

General Surveys Covering the Entire Period

Cobban, Alfred, *A History of Modern France*, 3 vols., Pelican, 1985–6.

Connelly, Owen, ed., *Historical Dictionary of Napoleonic France 1799–1815*, Greenwood Press, 1985.

———, *The French Revolution and Napoleonic Era*, 2nd edn, Holt, Rinehart & Winston, 1991.

Furet, François and Mona Ozouf, eds., *A Critical Dictionary of the French Revolution*, English edn, Harvard University Press, 1989.

General Works: Revolutionary Decade or Parts Thereof

Doyle, William, *The Oxford History of the French Revolution*, Oxford University Press, 1989.

Forrest, Alan, *The French Revolution*, Historical Association Studies, Blackwell, 1995.

Goodwin, A.W., *The French Revolution*, Hutchinson, 1985.

Hampson, Norman, *A Social History of the French Revolution*, Routledge, 1986.

Lefebvre, Georges, *The Coming of the French Revolution*, English edn, Princeton University Press, 1979.

———, *The French Revolution*, 2 vols., London: Routledge, 1962–4.

Roberts, J.M., *The French Revolution*, Oxford University Press, 1986.

Soboul, Albert, *A Short History of the French Revolution, 1789–1799*, English edn, University of California Press, 1977.

Sydenham, M.J., *The French Revolution*, Methuen, 1969.

General Works: Napoleon

Bergeron, Louis, *France under Napoleon*, English edn, Princeton University Press, 1981.

Ellis, Geoffrey, *Napoleon*, Longman, 'Profiles in Power', 1997.

———, *The Napoleonic Empire*, Macmillan, 'Studies in European History', 1991.

Geyl, Pieter, *Napoleon: For and Against*, Cape, 1949; Penguin, 1986. (A survey of French historiography on Napoleon during the nineteenth and early twentieth centuries.)

Lefebvre, Georges, *Napoleon*, English edn, 2 vols., Routledge, 1969.

Lyons, Martyn, *Napoleon Bonaparte and the Legacy of the French Revolution*, Macmillan, 1994.

Tulard, Jean, *Napoleon: The Myth of the Saviour*, English edn, Weidenfeld, 1985.

Old Regime and Revolution

Furet, François, *Interpreting the French Revolution*, English edn, Cambridge University Press, 1981.

Tackett, Timothy, *Becoming a Revolutionary: The Deputies of the French National Assembly and the Emergence of a Revolutionary Culture (1789–1790)*, Princeton University Press, 1996.

Nobility, Clergy, Peasantry, Artisans

Higonnet, Patrice, *Class, Ideology, and the Rights of Nobles during the French Revolution*, Oxford University Press, 1981.

Jones, P.M., *The Peasantry in the French Revolution*, Cambridge University Press, 1988.

Lefebvre, Georges, *The Great Fear of 1789: Rural Panic in Revolutionary France*, English edn, NLB, 1973.

McManners, J.M., *The French Revolution and the Church*, Leicester University Press, 1969.

Rudé, George, *The Crowd in the French Revolution*, Oxford University Press, 1959.

Soboul, Albert, *The Parisian Sans-Culottes and the French Revolution, 1793–4*, Oxford University Press, 1964.

The Terror

Gough, Hugh, *The Terror in the French Revolution*, Macmillan, 'Studies in European History', 1998.

Lucas, Colin, *The Structure of the Terror: The Example of Javogues and the Loire*, Oxford University Press, 1973.

Thermidorian Reaction, Revolutionary Wars, Counter Revolution

Bertaud, Jean-Paul, *The Army of the French Revolution: From Citizen-Soldiers to Instrument of Power*, English edn, Princeton University Press, 1988.

Blanning, T.C.W., *The French Revolutionary Wars, 1787–1802*, Arnold, 1996.

Furet, François and Mona Ozouf, eds., *The Transformation of Political Culture 1789–1848*, vol. 3 of *The French Revolution and the Creation of Modern Political Culture*, Pergamon Press, 1989.

Lefebvre, Georges, *The Thermidorians*, English edn, Routledge, 1965.

Press, Culture and Symbolism

Kennedy, Emmet, *A Cultural History of the French Revolution*, Yale University Press, 1989.

Ozouf, Mona, *Festivals and the French Revolution*, English edn, Harvard University Press, 1988.

Popkin, Jeremy D., *Revolutionary News: The Press in France, 1789–1799*, Duke University Press, 1990.

Women

Godineau, Dominique, *The Women of Paris and their French Revolution*, English edn, University of California Press, 1998.

Napoleonic Period

Bergeron, Louis, *France under Napoleon*, English edn, Princeton University Press, 1981.

Ellis, Geoffrey, *Napoleon's Continental Blockade: The Case of Alsace*, Oxford University Press, 1981.

Esdaile, Charles J., *The Wars of Napoleon*, Longman, 1995.

Gates, David, *The Napoleonic Wars, 1803–1815*, Arnold, 1997.

Hales, E.E.Y., *Napoleon and the Pope: The Story of Napoleon and Pius VII*, Eyre & Spottiswoode, 1962.

MacIntyre, Duncan, *Napoleon: the Legend and the Reality*, Blackie, 1976.

Woolf, Stuart, *Napoleon's Integration of Europe*, Routledge, 1991.

CHAPTER 3: REVOLUTION AND REACTION IN EUROPE (1815–1848)

The Congress of Vienna (1815)

Barkar, Bernard, *The Congress of Vienna*, London: Longman, 1973.

Chapman, Tim, *The Congress of Vienna: Origins, Processes and Results*, London and New York, Routledge, 1998.

Jarrett, M., *Congress of Vienna and the Congress System*, London: Longman, 1998.

Kraehe, Enno E., *The Congress of Vienna 1814–1815*, New Jersey: Princeton University Press, 1983.

Metternich System

Billinger, Robert D., Jr., *Metternich and the German Question: State's Rights and Federal Duties 1820–1834*, London and New Jersey: Associated University Presses, 1991.

De Souvigny, Guillaume de Bertier, *Metternich and His Times*, Darton, London: Longman and Todd, 1962.

May, Arthur James, *The Age of Metternich*, New York: Holt, Rinehart and Winston, 1963.

Sked, Alan, *Europe's Balance of Power 1815–1845*, New York: Barnes and Noble, 1979.

———, *Metternich and Austria: An Evaluation*, Basingstoke: Palgrave Macmillan, 2008.

Revolutions in the Spanish American Colonies

Lynch, John, *The Spanish American Revolutions 1808–1826*, London: Weidenfeld and Nicolson, 1973.

The Greek War of Independence

Brewer, David, *The Greek War of Independence: The Struggle for Freedom From Ottoman Oppression and the Birth of Modern Greek Nation*, New York: Overlook Press, 2001.

Clogg, Richard, ed., *The Struggle for Independence: Essays to Mark the 150th Anniversary of the Greek War of Independence*, Connecticut: Archon Books, 1973.

Dakin, Douglas, *The Greek Struggle for Independence: 1821–1833*, Berkeley: University of California Press, 1973.

———, *British and American Philhellenes*, Thessaloniki: Institute of Balkan Studies, 1955.

The July Revolution of 1830 and its Impact

The works listed below cover both significance and the controversy over the inevitability of the Revolution of 1830.

Jardin, Andre and Andre Jean Tudesq, *Restoration and Reaction 1815–1848*, New York: Cambridge University Press, 1983.

Kroen, Sheryl, *Politics and Theatre: The Crisis of Legitimacy in Restoration France 1815–1830, History Ebook Project*, Berkeley: University of California Press, 2000.

Merriman, John M., *1830 in France, New Viewpoints*, New York, 1975.

Pilbeam, Pamela M., *The 1830 Revolution in France*, London: Macmillan, 1991.

Pinkney, David H., *The French Revolution of 1830*, New Jersey: Princeton University Press, 1972.

February Revolution (1848) in France and its Impact

Collingham, H.A.C., and R.S. Alexander, *The July Monarchy: A Political History of France 1830–1848*, New York: Longman, 1988.

Dowe, Dietar et al., eds., *Europe in 1848: Revolution and Reform*, Oxford: Bergham Books, 2001.

Fortescue, William, *France and 1848: The End of Monarchy*, London and New York: Routledge, 2005.

Harsin, Jill, *Barricades: The War of Streets in Revolutionary Paris*, New York: Palgrave, 2002.

Korner, Axel, *1848: A European Revolution? International Ideas and National Memories of 1848*, New York: St. Martin's Press, 2000.

Price, Roger, *The Revolutions of 1848*, New Jersey: Humanities Press International, 1989.

Sperber, Jonathan, *The European Revolutions, 1848–1851*, Cambridge and New York: Cambridge University Press, 1994.

Stearns, Peter, *The Revolution of 1848*, London: Weidenfeld and Nicolson, 1974.

Traugott, Mark, *Armies of the Poor: Determinants of the Working Class Participation in the Parisian Insurrection of June 1848*, New Jersey: Princeton University Press, 1985.

Zeldin, Theodore, *France 1848–1945/1: Ambition, Love and Politics*, Oxford: Clarendon Press, 1973.

———, *France 1848–1945/2: Intellect, Taste and Anxiety*, Oxford: Clarendon Press, 1973. (Between them, these books form the justly famous 'An Emotional History of France' series.)

Second Empire in France: Louis Napoleon

Hemmings, F.W.J., *Culture and Society in France 1848–1898: Dissidents and Philistines*, London: Batsford, 1971.

McMillan, James F., *Napoleon III*, London: Longman, 1991.

Pinkney, David H., *Napoleon III and the Rebuilding of Paris*, New Jersey: Princeton University Press, 1972.

Price, Roger, *The French Second Empire: An Anatomy of Political Power*, New York: Cambridge University Press, 2001.

Truesdell, M., *Spectacular Politics: Louis-Napoleon Bonaparte and the Fête Impériale*, New York: Oxford University Press, 1997.

CHAPTER 4: SECOND PHASE OF THE INDUSTRIAL REVOLUTION

Introduction and Switchover to the Second Phase
of Industrialization and Results

Cipolla, C.M., *Fontana Economic History of Europe*, vol. IV (The Emergence of Industrial Societies), London: Fontana Press, 1973.

(A very useful introduction to the story of industrialization in the continent.)

Garshenkron, Alexander, *Economic Backwardness in Historical Perspective*, Cambridge, Massachusetts: Belknapp Press of Harvard University Press, 1962. (A landmark early study on the industrialization in the continent; contains a detailed blend of theoretical and empirical perspectives by one of the leading experts of industrialization in Eastern Europe.)

Hobsbawm, Eric, *The Age of Capital 1848–1875*, London: Weidenfeld and Nicolson, 1975. (Still remains the best beginner's guide to an overall understanding of the period, nearly forty years after its first publication.)

Kindleberger, Charles P., *A Financial History of Western Europe*, London: Allen and Unwin, 1984.

Pollard, Sidney, *Peaceful Conquest: The Industrialization of Europe 1760–1970*, Oxford: Oxford University Press, 1981. (Has remained for the last 30 years one of the most comprehensive single book surveys of the industrialization of Europe by one of the Britain's leading historians of industrialization.)

———, *Typology of Industrialization Processes in the Nineteenth Century*, London: Routledge, 2001.

Rostow, W.W., *The Stages of Economic Growth: A Non Communist Manisfesto*, Cambridge: Cambridge University Press, 1960.

———, ed., *The Economics of the Take-Off into Sustained Growth: Proceedings of a Conference held by the International Economic Association*, London: Macmillan, 1971.

Stearns, P.N., *The Industrial Revolution in World History*, Boulder, Colorado: Westview Press, 1993.

Sylla, R., and G. Tonniolo, *Patterns of European Industrialization in the Nineteenth Century*, London: Routledge, 2003, first published 1991. (Contains condensed case studies of industrialization in different countries in the continent by leading economic historians, focusing on specific roles of institutions like the state and banks; with a comprehensive introduction by the editors summarizing latest research directions.)

Trebilcock, C., *Industrialization of the Continental Powers 1780–1914*, Longman, 1981. (Presents a broad survey of the process of European industrialization from the late eighteenth century to the First World War, a closely argued comparative economic study of how different great powers experienced this process.)

Industrialization in the Continent: Case Studies

France

Dunham, Arthur Louis, *The Industrial Revolution in France 1815–1848*, Exposition Press, 1955.

Fohlen, Calude, *The Industrial Revolution in France 1700–1914*, London: Collins, 1970.

Kemp, Tom, *Economic Forces in French History*, London: Dennis Dobson, 1971.

Kindleberger, Charles, *Economic Growth in France and Britain, 1851–1950*, Cambridge, Mass.: Harvard University Press, 1964.

Germany

Birke, Adolf M., and Lothar Ketenacker, *The Race for Modernization: England and Germany since Industrial Revolution*, Munchen: K.G. Saur, 1988.

Borchardt, Knut, *The Industrial Revolution in Germany 1700–1914*, London: Fontana, 1972.

Henderson, W.O., *The Industrial Revolution on the Continent: Germany, France, Russia 1800–1914*, London: Frank Cass, 1967.

Mommsen, Wolfgang J., *Britain and Germany 1800–1914: Two Development Paths to Industrial Society*, London, 1986.

Veblen, Thornstein, *Imperial Germany and the Industrial Revolution*, New York: Viking Press, 1939.

Russia

Black, Cyril et al., eds., *The Modernization in Japan and Russia: A Comparative Study*, vols. I and II, New York: Free Press, 1975.

Blackwell, William L., *The Industrialization of Russia: A Historical Perspective*, New York: T.Y. Crowell, 1994 (1970).

Falcus, Malcom E., *The Industrialization of Russia 1700–1914*, London: Macmillan, 1972.

McCaffray, Susan Purves, *Politics of Industrialization in Tsarist Russia: The Association of Southern Coal and Steel Producers 1874–1914*, Northern Illinois University Press, 1996.

Working Class Movements, Socialism and Marxian Socialism

Berger, Stefan, and Angel Smith, eds., *Nationalism, Labour and Ethnicity, 1870–1939*, Manchester and New York: Manchester University Press, 1999.

———, *Social Democracy and the Working Class in the Nineteenth and Twentieth Century Germany*, New York: Longman, 2000.

Evans, R., ed., *The German Working Class, 1888–1933: The Politics of Everyday Life, in Britain, the USA and Australia from the 1880s to 1914*, Croom Helm, London; Barnes and Noble, 1982; London: Merlin, 2003.

Geary, Dick, *European Labour Protest: 1848–1939*, London: Methuen, 1981.

———, ed., *Labour and Socialist Movements in Europe before 1914*, Oxford and Rhode Island: Berg Publishers Inc., 1989.

Guttsman, W.L., *The German Social Democratic Party, 1875–1933: From Ghetto to Government*, Boston and London: Allen and Unwin, 1981.

Johnson, R.E., *Peasant and Proletarian: The Working Class in Moscow in the Late Nineteenth Century*, New Brunswick, New Jersey: Rutgers University Press, 1979.

Joll, James, *The Second International, 1889–1914*, New York: Harper and Row, 1966.

Katznelson, Ira, and A. Zolberg, eds., *Working-Class Formation: Nineteenth-Century Patterns in Western Europe and the United States*, Princeton, New Jersey: Princeton University Press, 1986.

Lichtheim, George, *A Short History of Socialism*, London: Weidenfeld and Nicolson, 1970.

Lindemann, Albert, *A History of European Socialism*, New Haven: Yale University Press, 1983.

Magraw, Roger, *A History of the French Working Class*, Oxford: Oxford University Press, 1992 (vol. 1: *The Age of the Artisan Revolution 1815–1871* and vol. 2: *Workers and the Bourgeois Republic*).

McDaniel, T., *Autocracy, Capitalism and Revolution in Russia*, Berkeley: University of California Press 1988.

Neville, Kirk, *Comrades and Cousins: Globalization, Workers and Labour Movements in Britain, the USA and Australia from the 1880s to 1914*, London: Merlin, 2003.

Pilbeam, P.M., *French Socialists before Marx: Workers, Women and the Social Question in France*, Montreal: McGill-Queen's University Press, 2000.

Sewell, William Hamilton, *Work and Revolution in France: The Language of Labour from the Old Regime to 1848*, Cambridge: Cambridge University Press, 1980.

Thompson, E.P., *The Making of the English Working Class*, Harmondsworth: Penguin, 1968.

Tilly, Louise, *Politics and Class in Milan, 1881–1901*, New York: Oxford University Press, 1992.

Tilly, Louise, and Joan Wallach Scott, *Women, Work and Family*, New York: Holt, Rinehart and Winston, 1978.

Wilentz, Sean, *Chants Democratic: New York City and the Rise of the American Working Class 1780–1850*, London and New York: Oxford University Press, 2004. (Twentieth Anniversary Edn; first published 1984.)

Woodcock, George, *Anarchism*, Harmondsworth: Penguin Books, 1963.

CHAPTER 5: THE RISING TIDE OF NATIONALISM

General Reading on Nationalism

Anderson, Benedict, *Imagined Communities: Reflections on the Origin and Spread of Nationalism*, London and New York: Verso, 1991.

Breuilly, John, *Nationalism and the State*, Manchester: Manchester University Press, 2nd edn, 1993. (This edition contains substantial revision and an added chapter, a marked improvement on the classic 1982 work.)

Gellner, Ernest, *Nations and Nationalism*, Ithaca: Cornell University Press, 1983.

Hastings, Adrian, *The Construction of Nationhood: Ethnicity, Religion and Nationalism*, Cambridge: Cambridge University Press, 1997.

Hobsbawm, Eric, *Nations and Nationalism since 1780: Programme, Myth, Reality*, Cambridge: Cambridge University Press, 1990.

Hobsbawm, Eric, and Terence Ranger, eds., *The Invention of Tradition*, Cambridge: Cambridge University Press, 1983.

Hutchinson, John, and Anthony D. Smith, eds., *Nationalism*, Oxford: Oxford University Press, 1994.

Nairn, Tom, *The Modern Janus: Nationalism in The Modern World*, Random House, 1990.

Smith, Anthony D., *Theories of Nationalism*, London: Holmes and Meier, 1983.

Teich, Mikulas, and Roy Porter, eds., *The National Question in Europe in Historical Context*, Cambridge University Press, 1993.

Weber, Eugen, *Peasants into Frenchmen: The Modernization of Rural France, 1870–1914*, London: Chatto and Windus, 1977.

Zimmer, Oliver, *Nationalism in Europe, 1890–1940*, New York: Palgrave Macmillan, 2003.

Unification of Italy

Beales, D.E.D., *The Risorgimento and the Unification of Italy*, 2nd edn, London: Allen and Unwin, 1981.

Davis, J.A., *Merchants, Monopolists and Contractors: A Study of Economic Activity and Society in Bourbon Naples*, New York: Arno Press Inc., 1981.

———, *Conflict and Control: Law and Order in Nineteenth Century Italy*, London: Macmillan Press, 1988.

Dickie, J., 'The notion of Italy', in *The Cambridge Companion to Modern Italian Culture*, Z.G. Baranski and R.J. West, eds., Cambridge: Cambridge University Press, 1991.

King, Bolton, *A History of Italian Unity, being a Political History of Italy from 1814–1871*, New York: Russell and Russell, 1967. (A classic late nineteenth century narrative work that underwent several editions.)

Riall, Lucy, *The Italian Risorgimento: State, Society and National Unification*, London: Routledge, 1994.

———, *Garibaldi: Invention of a Hero*, London: Yale University Press, 2007.

Woolf, S.J., ed., *The Italian Risorgimento*, London: Longmans, 1969.

———, *A History of Italy 1700–1860: The Social Constraints of Political Change*, London: Methuen, 1979.

Unification of Germany

Applegate, C., *A Nation of Provincials: The German Idea of 'Heimat'*, Berkeley: University of California Press, 1990.

Berger, Stefan, *The Search for Normality: National Identity and Historical Consciousness in Germany since 1800*, New York: Berghahn Books, 1997.

Blackbourn, D., and R.J. Evans, eds., *The German Bourgeoisie: Essays on the Social History of the German Middle Class from the Late Eighteenth to the Early Twentieth Century*, London: Routledge, 1991.

Blackbourn, David, *The Long Nineteenth Century: A History of Germany 1780–1918*, New York: Oxford University Press, 1998.

Breuilly, J., *The Formation of the First German Nation-State, 1800–1871*, Basingstoke: Palgrave Macmillan, 1996.

Cramer, Kevin, *The Thirty Years War and German Memory in the Nineteenth Century*, Lincoln: University of Nebraska Press, 2007.

Green, A., *Fatherlands: State-Building and Nationhood in Nineteenth-Century Germany*, Cambridge: Cambridge University Press, 2001.

Howard, M., *The Franco-Prussian War: The German Invasion of France, 1870–71*, London: Macmillan, 1961.

Iggers, G.G., *The German Conception of History: The National Tradition of Historical Thought From Herder to the Present*, Middletown, Connecticut: Wesleyan University Press, 1983.

James, H., *A German Identity: 1770 to the Present Day*, London: Weidenfeld and Nicolson, 1989.

Meinecke, Freidrich, *Historicism: The Rise of a New Historical Outlook*, tr. J.E. Anderson, London: Routledge, 1972.

Mosse, G.L., *The Nationalization of the Masses: Political Symbolism and Mass Movements in Germany from the Napoleonic Wars through the Third Reich*, New York: H. Fertig, 1975.

Nipperdey, T., *Germany from Napoleon to Bismarck*, Dublin: Gill and Macmillan, 1996.

Schulze, H., *The Course of German Nationalism: From Frederick the Great to Bismarck 1763-1867*, Cambridge: Cambridge University Press, 1994.

Sheehan, J.J., *German History 1770–1866*, Oxford: Clarendon Press, 1989.

Speirs, Ronald, and John Breuilly, eds., *Germany's Two Unifications: Anticipations, Experiences, Responses*, Basingstoke and New York: Palgrave, 2005.

Sperber, J., ed., *Germany, 1800–1870*, Oxford: Oxford University Press, 2004.

Vick, Brian E., *Defining Germany: The 1848 Frankfurt Parliamentarians and National Identity*, Cambridge, Massachusetts: Harvard University Press, 2002.

Wawro, G., *The Austro-Prussian War*, Cambridge: Cambridge University Press, 1996.

Wehler, Hans-Ulrich, *The German Empire 1871–1918*, Warwickshire: Leamington Spa, 1985.

CHAPTER 6: THE AMERICAN CIVIL WAR (1861–1865)

Blackett, R.J.M., *Divided Hearts: Britain and the American Civil War*, Baton Rouge: Louisiana State University Press, 2001.

Case, Lynn, and Warren Spencer, *The United States and France: Civil War Diplomacy*, Philadelphia: University of Pennsylvania Press, 1970.

Crook, D.P., *The North, the South, and the Powers, 1861–1865*, New York: Wiley, 1974.

Donald, D.H., ed., *Why the North Won the Civil War*, New York: Collier Books, 1962.

Ellison, Mary, *Support for Secession: Lancashire and the American Civil War*, Chicago: University of Chicago Press, 1972.

Hubbard, Charles, *The Burden of Confederate Diplomacy*, Knoxville: University of Tennessee Press, 1998.

Neely, Mark E., *Lincoln and the Triumph of the Nation: Constitutional Conflict in the American Civil War*, Chapel Hill: University of North Carolina Press, 2011.

Owsley, Frank, *King Cotton Diplomacy*, Chicago: University of Chicago Press, 1959.

Parish, Peter J., *American Civil War*, New York: Holmes and Meier, 1975.

Rozwenc, Edwin C., *The Causes of the American Civil War*, Boston: Heath, 1961.

Smith, Alan I.P., *The American Civil War*, Basingstoke: Palgrave Macmillan, 2007.

Varon, Elizabeth R., *Disunion: The Coming of the American Civil War, 1789–1859*, University of North Carolina Press, 2008.

CHAPTER 7: THE EASTERN QUESTION

Once again, most of the works listed below deal with more than one section. The list begins with general works dealing with all aspects of the Eastern Question as it evolved over the medium- and long-term, followed by works focused on specific aspects of the problem.

Anderson, M.S., *The Eastern Question: 1774–1923: A Study in International Relations*, London: Macmillan, 1966.

Argyll, George Douglas Campbell, *The Eastern Question: From the Treaty of Paris to the Treaty of Berlin and to the Second Afghan War*, vol. 1, Elibron Classics Series, London, 2005 (first published in 1879).

Bitis, Alexander, *Russia and the Eastern Question: Army Government, Society*, Oxford: Oxford University Press, 2006.

Bostridge, Mark, *Florence Nightingale: The Making of an Icon*, New York: Farrar, Straus and Giroux, 2008.

Dimirci, Sevtap, *British Public Opinion Towards the Ottoman Empire During the Two Crises: Bosnia Herzigovina (1908–09) and the Balkan Wars (1912–13)*, Istanbul: Isis Press, 2006.

Gooch, Brison Dowling, *The Origins of the Crimean War*, Massachusetts: Heath, 1972.

Hall, Richard C., *The Balkan Wars of 1912–13: Prelude to the First World War*, London: Routledge, 2000.

Helmreich, E.C., *The Diplomacy of the Balkan War*, repr., New York: Russell and Russell, 1969.

Macfie, A.L., *The Eastern Question: 1774–1923*, London and New York: Longman, 1996.

Marriott, J.A.R., *The Eastern Question: A Historical Study of European Diplomacy*, Oxford: Clarendon Press, 1940.

Royle, Trevor, *Crimea: The Great Crimean War 1854–1856*, New York: St. Martin's Press, 2000.

Sweetman, John, *The Crimean War*, Oxford: Osprey, 2001.

CHAPTER 8: FIRST WORLD WAR (1914–1918)

The list includes only the most comprehensive and recent research only, though this might miss out on some classic studies. The subject is so vast, diverse and well trodden that even a select bibliography runs the risk of losing the woods for the trees. The books have been thematically divided.

For General Understanding

Ferguson, N., *The Pity of War*, London: Allen Lane, 1998.

Ferro, M., *The Great War 1914–1918*, London: M. Joseph, 1983.

Gilbert, M., ed., *The First World War*, London: Weidenfeld and Nicolson, 1994.

Hardach, G., *The First World War*, Berkeley and Los Angeles: University of California Press, 1977.

Horne, J., ed., *State Society and Mobilisation during the First World War*, Cambridge: Cambridge University Press, 1997.

Robbins, K., *The First World War*, Oxford: Oxford University Press, 1984.

Rouzeau, S. Audoin, and A. Becker, *1914–1918: Understanding the Great War*, London: Profile Books, 2002.

Stone, N., *World War One: A Short History*, London: Allen Lane, 2007.

Strachan, H., ed., *Oxford Illustrated History of the First World War*, Oxford: Oxford University Press, 1998.

Taylor, A.J.P., *Illustrated History of the First World War*, New York: Putman, 1963.

Winter, J., and A. Prost, *The Great War in History: Debates and Controversies, 1914 to the Present*, Cambridge: Cambridge University Press, 2005.

Triple Alliance/Entente

Schmitt, Bernadotte E., *Triple Alliance and Triple Entente 1902–1914*, New York: Holt and Company, 1934.

Whitesman, Patricia A., *Dangerous Alliances: Proponents of Peace, Weapons of War*, California: Stanford University Press, 2004.

Moroccan Crisis (1905–6)

Anderson, Eugene M., *The First Moroccan Crisis 1904–1906*, Archon Books, 1966; first published 1830.

Bosnia Crisis (1908)

Abizaid, John Philip, *Great Power Diplomacy and the Bosnian Crisis*, US Military Academy, 1973.

Agadir Crisis (1911)

Barlow, Ina Christina, *The Agadir Crisis*, Connecticut: Archon, Hamden, 1971.

Balkan Wars

Hall, Richard C., *The Balkan Wars of 1912–13: Prelude to the First World War*, London: Routledge, 2000.

Course of the War

Strachan, H., ed., *Oxford Illustrated History of the First World War*, Oxford: OUP, 1998.

German Responsibility for the War

Chickering, R., *Imperial Germany and the Great War 1914–1918*, Cambridge: Cambridge University Press, 1998.
Herwig, H., *The First World War, Germany and Austria-Hungary 1914–1918*, London: Arnold, 1997.

Versailles Treaty (1919)

Carr, E.H., *Britain: A Study of Foreign Policy from the Versailles Treaty to the Outbreak of War*, London: Longmans, 1939.
Sharp, A., *The Versailles Settlement: Peacemaking in Paris, 1919*, London: Macmillan, 1991.
Sharp, Alan, and Conan Fischer, eds., *After the Versailles Treaty: Enforcement, Compliance, Contested Identities*, London: Routledge, 2008.

League of Nations

Henig, Ruth, *The League of Nations: Makers of the Modern World, The Peace Conferences of 1919–1923 and their Aftermath*, London: Haus Publishing, 2010.
Northedge, F.S., *The League of Nations: Its Life and Times 1920–46*, Leicester: Leicester University Press, 1986.

CHAPTER 9: ARAB NATIONALISM

Choueiri, Youssef M., *Arab Nationalism*, Oxford: Blackwell, 2000.
Dawisha, A.I., *Arab Nationalism in the Twentieth Century: From Triumph to Despair*, New Jersey: Princeton University Press, 2004.

Khalidi, Rashid et al., eds., *The Origins of Arab Nationalism*, New York: Columbia University Press, 1991.

Orga, Irfan, *Phoenix Ascendant: The Rise of Modern Turkey*, London: R. Hale, 1958.

Shaw, Stanford J., and Ezra Kural Shaw, *Reform, Revolution and Republic: The Rise of Modern Turkey 1808–1975*, Cambridge: Cambridge University Press, 1977; repr. 2002.

Tibi, Bassam, Marion Farouk Sluglett, Peter Sluglett, *Arab Nationalism: A Critical Enquiry*, New York: St. Martin's Press, 1981.

CHAPTER 10: REFORM AND REVOLUTION IN RUSSIA

Reforms in the Nineteenth Century

Eklof, Ben, John Bushnell and Larissa Zakharova, eds., *Russia's Great Reforms, 1855–1881*, Bloomington: Indiana University Press, 1994.

Field, Daniel, *The End of Serfdom: Nobility & Bureaucracy in Russia, 1855–1861*, Harvard University Press, 1976.

Gatrell, Peter, *The Tsarist Economy 1850–1917*, New York: St Martin's Press, 1986.

Hartley, Janet M., *Alexander I*, London and New York: Longman, 1994.

Hoch, Steven L., *Serfdom and Social Control in Russia: Petrovsko, a Village in Tambov*, University of Chicago Press, 1986.

Revolution of 1905

Mckean, Robert B., *Between the Revolutions: Russia 1905 to 1917*, Shaftesbury: Historical Association, 1988.

Reichman, Henry, *Railwaymen and Revolution: Russia 1905*, Berkeley: University of California Press, 1987.

Russian Revolution, Civil War, Lenin and Stalin

Abraham, R., *Alexander Kerensky, the First Love of the Revolution*, New York: Columbia University Press, 1987.

Acton, E., *Rethinking the Russian Revolution*, London: E. Arnold, 1990.

Acton, E., V. Cherniaev, and W. Rosenberg, *Critical Companion to the Russian Revolution, 1914–1921*, London: Edward Arnold, 1997.

Anweiler, O., *The Soviets: The Russian Workers, Peasants and Soldiers' Councils, 1905–1921*, New York: Pantheon Books, 1974.

Brovkin, V.N., *The Mensheviks after October: Socialist Opposition and the Rise of the Bolshevik Dictatorship*, Ithaca: Cornell University Press, 1987.

Carr, E.H., *The Bolshevik Revolution, 1917–1923*, 3 vols., London, 1951–3.

Figes, Orlando, *A People's Tragedy: The Russian Revolution, 1891–1924*, London: Jonathon Cape, 1997.

Fischer, L., *The Life of Lenin*, New York: Harper and Row, 1964.

Fitzpatrick, S., *The Russian Revolution*, Oxford: Oxford University Press, 1982.

Geyer, D., *The Russian Revolution*, Berg, 1987.

Gill, G., *Peasants and Government in the Russian Revolution*, London: Macmillan, 1979.

Harding, N., *Leninism*, Basingstoke: Macmillan, 1996.

Hasegawa, T., *The February Revolution: Petrograd 1917*, Seattle: University of Washington Press, 1981.

Kaiser, D.H., ed., *The Workers' Revolution in Russia, 1917: The View from Below*, Cambridge: Cambridge University Press, 1987.

Kochan, L., *Russia in Revolution, 1890–1918*, London: Granada, 1966.

Koenker, Diane et al., eds., *Party, State and Society In The Russian Civil War: Explorations in Social History*, Bloomington: Indiana University Press, 1989.

Kotkin, Stephen, *Magnetic Mountain: Stalinism as a Civilization*, Berkeley: University of California Press, 1995.

Mccauley, Martin, ed., *Khrushchev and Khrushchevism*, Basingstoke: Macmillan, 1987.

Polan, A., *Lenin and the End of Politics*, Berkeley: University of California Press, 1984.

Reed, John, *Ten Days that Shook The World*, Middlesex, 2007 (first published 1919).

Viola, Lynne, *Peasant Rebels under Stalin: Collectivization and the Culture of Peasant Resistance*, New York: Oxford University Press, 1996.

Volkogonov, Dimitri, *Stalin: Triumph and Tragedy*, London: Weidenfeld and Nicolson, 1991.

Ward, Chris, ed., *The Stalinist Dictatorship*, London: Arnold, 1998.

Werth, Alexander, *Russia at War, 1941–1945*, New York: Dutton, 1964.

Williams, R.C., *The Other Bolsheviks: Lenin and his Critics 1904–1914*, Bloomington: Indiana University Press, 1986.

Zubkova, Elena, *Russia After the War: Hopes, Illusions, and Disappointments, 1945–1957*, London: M.E. Sharpe, 1998.

CHAPTER 11: THE FAR EAST

The books on Chinese history and Japanese history are listed after one another. The sections have not been separately addressed, as titles of books more or less make their specialities more or less clear.

China

Bickers, Robert, *Britain in China: Culture, Community and Colonialism, 1843–1943*, Manchester: Manchester University Press, 1999.

Billingsley, Phil, *Bandits in Republican China*, Stanford: Stanford University Press, 1988.

Buck, Pearl S., *My Several Worlds*, New York: John Day Company, 1954.

Chen, J., *Mao and the Chinese Revolution*, Oxford: Oxford University Press, 1965.

Coble, Parks M., *Facing Japan: Chinese Politics and Japanese Imperialism*, Cambridge, Massachusetts: Harvard University Press, 1991.

Duara, Prasenjit, *Culture, Power and the State: Rural North China, 1900–1942*, Stanford: Stanford University Press, 1988.

Eastman, Lloyd, *Seeds of Destruction: Nationalist China in War and Revolution, 1937–1949*, Stanford: Stanford University Press, 1984.

Hsu, Immanuel, *The Rise of Modern China*, Oxford and New York: Oxford University Press, 1975, 1990, 2000.

Inglis, Brian, *The Opium War*, London: Holder and Stoughton, 1976.

Johnson, Chalmers, *Peasant Nationalism and Communist Power*, Stanford: Stanford University Press, 1962.

Pepper, Suzanne, *Civil War in China, the Political Struggle, 1945–1949*, Berkeley: University of California Press, 1978.

Polachek, James, *The Inner Opium War*, Cambridge, Massachusetts: Harvard University Press, 1992.

Snow, Edgar, *Red Star over China*, London: Victor Gollancz, 1937.

Wakeman, Frederic, 'The Canton Trade and the Opium War', in *Cambridge History of China*, John K. Fairbank, ed., vol. 10, Cambridge: Cambridge University Press, 1978.

Japan

Botsman, Daniel, *Punishment and Power in the Making of Modern Japan*, Princeton, New Jersey: Princeton University Press, 2004.

Caprio, Mark, *Japanese Assimilation Policies in Colonial Korea, 1910–1945*, Seattle: University of Washington Press, 2009.

Fogel, Joshua, *The Cultural Dimension of Sino-Japanese Relations: Essays on the Nineteenth and Twentieth Centuries*, London: M.E. Sharpe, 1995.

Garon, Sheldon, *Molding Japanese Minds: The State in Everyday Life*, New Jersey: Princeton University Press, 1997.

Harootunian, Harry, *Toward Restoration: The Growth of Political Consciousness in Tokugawa Japan*, Berkeley: University of California Press, 1970.

Koschmann, J. Victor, *The Mito Ideology: Discourse, Reform and Insurrection in Late Tokugawa Japan, 1790–1864*, Berkeley: University of California Press, 1987.

Low, Morris, ed., *Building a Modern Japan: Science, Technology, and Medicine in the Meiji Era and Beyond*, New York: Palgrave Macmillan, 2005.

Michio, Nagai, and Miguel Urrutia, eds., *Meiji Ishin: Restoration and Revolution*, Tokyo: United Nations University, 1985.

Walthall, Anne, *Peasant Uprisings in Japan*, Chicago: University of Chicago Press, 1991.

Wilson, George, *Patriots and Redeemers in Japan: Motives in the Meiji Restoration*, Chicago: University of Chicago Press, 1992.

CHAPTER 12: FASCISM IN EUROPE

The books are mentioned with reference to particular countries, apart from general introductions and surveys on Fascism and Nazism. Most of these works cover the entire ranges of issues mentioned in the subsection, therefore, issue centric listing has been avoided. That apart the works have been listed as closely as possible in relation to the subsections mentioned in the content page, more or less in the order in which they appear.

Italy

Blamires, C.P., ed., *The Encyclopedia of World Fascism*, 2 vols., New York: ABC-Clio, 2006; very useful as a starting point on virtually any aspect of fascism.

Bosworth, R.J.B., *The Italian Dictatorship: Problems and Perspectives in the Interpretation of Mussolini and Fascism*, London: Arnold, 1999.

——, *Mussolini*, London: Arnold, 2002; the best recent biography of the Duce.

Payne, Stanley, *A History of Fascism: 1914–1945*, Madison: University of Wisconsin Press, 1995.

Pollard, J.F., *The Fascist Experience in Italy*, London: Routledge, 1998.

Germany

Burleigh, M., and W. Wippermann, *The Racial State: Germany 1933–1945*, Cambridge: Cambridge University Press, 1991.

Evans, R.J., *The Coming of the Third Reich*, London: Allen Lane, 2003.

——, *The Third Reich in Power*, New York: Penguin, 2005.

Frei, N., *National Socialist Rule in Germany: The Führer State 1933–1945*, Oxford: Blackwell, 1993.

Fritzsche, P., *Germans into Nazis*, Harvard: Harvard University Press, 1998.

James, H., *The German Slump: Politics and Economics 1924–1936*, Oxford: Oxford University Press, 1986.

Kersaw, Ian, *Hitler*, 2 vols., London: Penguin, 1999 and 2000.

Panayi, P., ed., *Weimar and Nazi Germany: Continuities and Discontinuities*, London: Longman, 2001.

Shirer, W.L., *Berlin Diary: The Journal of a Foreign Correspondent 1934–41*, New York: Alfred Knopf, 1941.

Shirer, William, *Rise and Fall of the Third Reich*, first published 1960 and has been the most popular book on Nazi Germany ever since.

Turner, H. Ashby, *German Big Business and the Rise of Hitler*, New York: Oxford University Press, 1985.

Welch, D., *The Third Reich: Politics and Propaganda*, London and New York: Routledge, 1993.

War and Diplomacy: Appeasement

Ross, G., *The Great Powers and the Decline of the European States System, 1914–1945*, London: Longman, 1983.

Kennedy, P.M., ed., *The Realities Behind Diplomacy: Background Influence on British External Policy, 1865–1980*, London: Allen and Unwin in association with Fontana Books, 1981.

Ovendale, R., *Appeasement and the English Speaking World*, Cardiff: University of Wales Press, 1975.

Parker, R.A.C., *Chamberlain and Appeasement: British Policy and the Coming of the Second World War*, London: Macmillan, 1993.

Spanish Civil War

Blinkhorn, M., *Democracy and Civil War in Spain 1931–1939*, London: Routledge, 1988.

Graham, H., *The Spanish Civil War: A Very Short Introduction*, Oxford: Oxford University Press, 2005.

Orwell, George, *Homage to Catalonia*, 1938.

Preston, P., *A Concise History of the Spanish Civil War*, London: Fontana, 1996.

Salvado, F. Romero, *The Spanish Civil War: Origins, Course and Outcomes*, Basingstoke: Palgrave Macmillan, 2005.

CHAPTER 13: SECOND WORLD WAR (1939–1945)

In this chapter too, books have not been listed in strict correspondence with the chapter sections. Most of the works listed here deal with the Second World War as a whole, with special reference to its particular aspects as specified in their titles and subtitles. It would not be difficult for the careful reader to identify specialized studies for a more comprehensive understanding.

Origin

Bell, P.M.H., *The Origins of the Second World War in Europe*, 2nd edn, London: Longman, 1997.

Boyce, R., and J. Maiolo, *The Origins of World War II: The Debate Continues*, London: Palgrave Macmillan, 2002.

Chickering, R., S. Förster and B. Greiner, eds., *A World at Total War: Global Conflict and the Politics of Destruction, 1937–1945*, Cambridge: Cambridge University Press, 2005.

Finney, P., ed., *The Origins of the Second World War*, London: Edward Arnold, 1997.

Martel, G., ed., *The Origins of the Second World War Reconsidered: The A.J.P. Taylor Debate after Twenty-Five Years*, London: Allen and Unwin, 1986.

Murray, W., *The Change in the European Balance of Power, 1938–1939: The Path to Ruin*, Princeton: Princeton University Press, 1984.

Taylor, A.J.P., *The Origins of the Second World War*, 2nd edn, London: Penguin Books, 1964.

Weinberg, G.L., *A World at Arms: A Global History of World War II*, Cambridge: Cambridge University Press, 1994.

Course, Economy and Strategic Issues

Calvocoressi, P. and G. Wint, *Total War: Causes and Course of the Second World War*, London: Penguin, 1989.

Gruhl, Werner, *Imperial Japan's World War Two 1931–45*, New Brunswick, New Jersey: Transaction Publishers, 2010.

Mawdsley, E., *Thunder in the East: The Nazi-Soviet War 1941–1945*, London: Hodder Arnold, 2005.

Milward, A.S., *War, Economy and Society, 1939–1945*, Berkeley: University of California Press, 1979.

Overy, R., *Why the Allies Won*, London: Jonathon Cape, 1995.

Overy, R.J., *The Air War, 1939–1945*, London: Europa Publications Ltd., 1980.

CHAPTER 14: THE WORLD AFTER THE SECOND WORLD WAR

The following titles have not been listed according to section but they correspond to the themes included in this chapter.

Calvocoressi, P., *World Politics since 1945*, 6th edn, London and New York: Longman, 1991.

Dunbabin, J.P.D., *International Relations since 1945*, 2 vols, London, Longman, 1994.

———, vol. 1: *The Cold War: The Great Powers and their Allies*, Harlow, UK; New York: Pearson, 2008.

——— vol. 2: *The Post-Imperial Age: the Great Powers and the Wider World*, London: Longman, 1994.

Beschloss, M., *The Crisis Years: Kennedy and Khrushchev*, New York: Harper Collins, 1991.

Brown, J.F., *Eastern Europe and Communist Rule*, Durham: Duke University Press, 1988.

Cotton, J. and I. Neary, eds., *The Korean War in History*, Manchester: Manchester University Press, 1989.

Crampton, R.J., *Eastern Europe in the Twentieth Century*, London: Routledge, 1994.

de, Senarclens, P., *From Yalta to the Iron Curtain: The Great Powers and the Origins of the Cold War*, London: Berg, 1995.

Deighton, A., ed., *Britain and the First Cold War*, New York: St. Martin's Press, 1990.

Duiker, W.J., *The Communist Road to Power in Vietnam*, 2nd edn, Boulder, Colorado: Westview, 1996.

Gaddis, J.L., *Strategies of Containment*, New York: Oxford University Press, 1982.

Hogan, M., *The Marshall Plan*, Cambridge: Cambridge University Press, 1987.

Keylor, W.R., *The Twentieth Century World: An International History*, New York: Oxford University Press, 1984.

Kim Khanh, Huynh, *Vietnamese Communism 1925–45*, Ithaca, New York: Cornell University Press, 1982.

Kiraly, B., and P. Jonas, *The Hungarian Revolution of 1956 in Retrospect*, New York and Boulder, Colorado: Columbia University Press and East European Monographs, 1978.

Kramer, M., *From Dominance to Hegemony to Collapse: Soviet Policy in Eastern Europe, 1945–1991*, Oxford: Oxford University Press, (forthcoming).

Leffler, M.P., *A Preponderance of Power: National Security, the Truman Administration and the Cold War*, Stanford: Stanford University Press, 1992.

Mastny, V., *The Cold War and Soviet Insecurity: The Stalin Years*, New York: Oxford University Press, 1996.

Nathan, J.A., ed., *The Cuban Missile Crisis Revisited*, New York: St. Martin's Press, 1992.

Post, K., *Revolution, Socialism and Nationalism in Viet Nam*, Aldershot: Dartmouth, 1989.

Raack, R.C., *Stalin's Drive to the West. 1938–1945: The Origins of the Cold War*, Stanford: Stanford University Press, 1995.

Reynolds, D., ed., *The Origins of the Cold War in Europe: International Perspectives*, New Haven: Yale University Press, 1994.

Swain, G., and N. Swain, *Eastern Europe since 1945*, New York: Palgrave Macmillan, 1993.

Woodside, A., *Community and Revolution in Vietnam*, Boston: Houghton Mifflin, 1976.

Young, J.W., *Cold War Europe, 1945–89: A Political History*, London, Edward Arnold, 1991.

CHAPTER 15: THE UNITED NATIONS

The most important resource for this chapter is the United Nations website and those of its various agencies. Please go to www.un.org and from there to the websites of individual agencies. Information about these institutions is available here, including the very latest updates about the role and activities of these agencies. The list of books below is mainly concerned with the general history of the UN over the last 60 years.

Bennett, A.L., *Historical Dictionary of the United Nations*, London: Scarecrow Press, 1995.

Chowdhury, A., *UN Blues: 50 Years of the United Nations*, London: The Guardian, 1995.

Davies, W.R., *The Challenge of Internationalism: Forty Years of the United Nations (1945–1985)*, Welsh: Welsh Centre for International Affairs, 1985.

Eichelberger, C.M., *UN: the First Twenty Years*, 1st edn, New York: Harper & Row, 1965.

Luard, E., *A History of the United Nations*, 2 vols., London: Macmillan, 1982, 1989.

Osmanczyk, E.J., *The Encyclopedia of the United Nations and International Agreements*, 2nd edn, New York: Taylor and Francis, 1990.

Yoder, A., *The Evolution of the United Nations System*, 2nd edn, Washington DC: Taylor and Francis, 1993.

Index